Understanding God's World Series

Understanding God's World Series

Understanding
NORTH AMERICAN
HISTORY

—A Christian Perspective—

Grade 8

Teacher's Manual

Rod and Staff Publishers, Inc.
P.O. Box 3, Hwy. 172
Crockett, Kentucky 41413-0003
Telephone: (606) 522-4348

ACKNOWLEDGMENTS

We are indebted first of all to God who created the world and who upholds all things by the Word of His power. We are grateful that He has enabled the many who worked on this project. Kenneth Auker wrote the basic text; Marvin Eicher and Bennie Hostetler served as editors. We are also grateful to Mary Jane Auker for permission to use the photograph on the front cover, and to Corel for the use of the earth-from-space photograph on page 1 and on the back cover.

—The Publishers

Copyright, 2005
by
Rod and Staff Publishers, Inc.

Printed in U.S.A.

ISBN 0-7399-0655-0

Catalog no. 19891

2   3   4   5   6   —   16   15   14   13   12   11   10   09   08   07

TABLE OF CONTENTS

UNIT SEVEN: MODERN TIMES, 1920–2000

INTRODUCTION FOR THE TEACHER
Teaching American History From a Christian Perspective

In a history course, the Christian teacher needs to maintain a Biblical perspective so that his students can develop a Biblical world-view. The teacher also wants to familiarize his students with a common core of knowledge about people and events of the past. However, this study must always be governed by Bible principles. For example, the Christian recognizes that God rules in the affairs of men and that God's people are in the world but not of the world. From a study of history, we can learn how Christians of bygone years faced the challenges of their times and how we can face similar challenges in our day.

This course is an endeavor to approach American history from such a Bible perspective. The text does not only present the affairs of earthly people and nations, but it also gives recognition to the overruling hand of God and discusses how the affairs of nations affected the people of God. Along the way, Biblical applications are made with appropriate Scripture verses.

The events selected for coverage are those that have had the greatest impact on American history—those recognized by most historians as part of a common core of knowledge about America. The text seeks to discuss these events in a factual manner, without a patriotic emphasis and with little interpretation. Though wars and military actions are covered, deliberate effort has been made not to overemphasize those things or glorify military heroes. In regard to cultural affairs, some of the larger trends are explained (such as progressivism), while aspects such as women's rights and entertainment receive only passing mention. The primary emphasis is on the mainstream events rather than on minor points of interest.

American history is a fascinating study. This course gives the main facts, but the teacher must make the story live. By your own interest, study, and input, you can spark the interest of your students. Approach this subject enthusiastically but also prayerfully.

Organization of the Text

The text is divided into seven units. The first unit covers the geography of North America, and the other units each cover a segment of United States or Canadian history. Each unit includes several chapters (except Unit 1) that are divided into three sections each. Each chapter and subdivision begins with an introduction to its contents. This gives students an idea of what they will study, and it also raises questions for them to answer as they read. Sections are further subdivided, with a centered heading identifying each subdivision. Main points under each heading are in bold italics. An example follows.

Maryland

Lord Baltimore's Settlement. A number of colonies were founded by ***proprietors*** (pruh PRY ih turz) rather than companies. Proprietors were individuals, usually rich nobles, who received land and a charter from the king.

Within the text, vocabulary words appear in a type style like that for ***proprietors*** in the sample above; these words can be found in the glossary at the back of the book. Each chapter subdivision is followed by a set of questions entitled *Focus for Thought*. At the end of each chapter, a section called ***Historical Highlights*** (***Geographical Highlights*** for Chapter 1) provides a review of the chapter. A separate test booklet contains tests to follow every one or two chapters.

Plan ahead to determine the amount of material to be covered each marking period so that you can complete the book by the year's end. If you cannot cover the whole book, you may consider omitting Chapter 3 (on the Indians). You may also consider omitting Chapter 18 (on Canadian history) if you teach school in the United States. Chapter tests are designed to allow for these omissions.

The text is generally chronological; however, it is thematic in areas such as economic or cultural matters. A chronological approach allows for a simple, common-sense study of history in the order that events took place. This gives students a frame of reference from which to understand previous and subsequent history, and important relationships such as cause and effect.

Using the Exercises

The course is designed to provide an ample amount of work for the students. Assign enough to meet your goals for the chapter; some of the more subjective questions could be given to faster students. A typical assignment could include reading a chapter section and doing the *Focus for Thought* questions after it. These questions address the main points in the text as given in *Chapter Objectives* in the teacher's manual.

The first sections of *Historical Highlights* have matching exercises to review the vocabulary words and other significant names and terms. These are important, for the most significant ones appear on the test and are not always addressed in *Focus for Thought*.

Some parts of *Historical Highlights* go beyond the facts and check the students' comprehension. ***Deeper Discussion*** is intended to develop a broader understanding of the events in focus, or of related Biblical principles. *Deeper Discussion* questions are optional. You may want to pick out some of these questions that you find most enlightening, and assign only those. The rest could be used as a basis for class discussion rather than homework.

The part entitled **Chronology and Geography** addresses the *when* and *where* aspects of history to build a frame of reference for students. This section includes such work as making time lines and doing map work relating to the material covered in the chapter.

Some exercises ask the student to work with an outline map. The outline maps to use are found in the back of the pupil's book in the "Map Section." Tracing of maps is educational, but if you prefer to photocopy the outline maps, you may do so without special permission from the publisher. Enlarging the maps would be helpful for exercises requiring many details.

Provide each student with a notebook for the map exercises. Teach students to follow the "Guidelines for Neat Maps" that are given at the beginning of the Map Section. (Guidelines for Neat Maps apply to hand-drawn maps. They do not apply to maps produced by publishers, who can distinguish map features by using different styles and sizes of type.) If they do a good job with these exercises, their notebooks will be attractive keepsakes.

You may want to assign parts of *Chronology and Geography* with the individual sets of *Focus for Thought* exercises to avoid having all the time line or map work at one time.

A section called **So Far This Year** comes at intervals throughout the book. It has objective exercises that give cumulative review of the main facts to be remembered. **The final test for the year is based on the *So Far This Year* reviews.**

Several approaches could be used in class. History is a good subject in which to lecture, especially if the teacher has done a good bit of study. With this approach, you might begin by checking the exercises assigned in the previous lesson; and then you could lecture, staying close to the outline in the book, while the students take notes. Another approach is to develop the main points further in class, using *Focus for Thought* or *Deeper Discussion* questions as a springboard. This approach will be especially profitable if your students are interested in history and can contribute freely.

Tests, which follow every one or two chapters, are available. They test the points covered by *Focus for Thought* and the factual sections of *Historical Highlights*. The tests contain several types of exercises, including some essay questions. These do take longer to answer and score, but they should be given because they often summarize important points in the chapter.

Using the Teacher's Manual

The teacher's manual begins with **Chapter Objectives,** which show the main points that the teacher should cover and that the students should know after they have studied the chapter. Next is **To the Teacher,** which gives direction to the teacher for approaching the chapter as well as further explanation not given in the student's text. The third section, *Christian Perspectives,* gives a Bible viewpoint on concepts or events in the chapter, along with appropriate Bible verses.

Further Study (in the teacher's manual) is a guide for further research on the era covered in the chapter. Items in this section can be used as the basis for assignments such as oral or written reports. Reports like this can be linked to English assignments for composition as well. These things help students (and teachers) to dig a little deeper and get more interested in what they are studying, besides giving practice in speaking and writing. If the reports are given in class, all the students can benefit from the research of a few.

The teacher's manual includes a quiz on each chapter, which may be given as an oral or a written exercise. (If you wish to photocopy the quizzes, you may do so without special permission from the publisher.) Use these quizzes to check students' grasp of the material, as class starters, or as review; and give some of your own if practical. A quiz should be short, with five to ten questions on main facts or ideas. If students know they will get frequent quizzes unannounced, it will help to keep them alert.

The *Answer Key* includes both the students' exercises and the answers to them. The material from the pupil's book is italicized, and the answers appear in boldface. The page numbers that are given refer to where the exercises are found in the pupil's text.

Many teachers want their students to answer questions in complete sentences (especially essay-type questions). *The Answer Key* does not always give answers in complete sentences because a model answer would be just one of several possibilities. The items or main ideas are given that should be included in the student's answer. The teacher may judge if the sentence is complete.

Allow *Deeper Discussion* answers to reflect various opinions or approaches. These exercises can be expected to call forth more discussion and differing viewpoints than most others. The important thing is that students have thought through their answers and can substantiate them with sound logic.

"If any of you lack wisdom, let him ask of God, that giveth to all men liberally" (James 1:5). May God bless you as you endeavor to teach North American history.

UNIT 1: NORTH AMERICAN GEOGRAPHY

1 Geography of the United States and Canada

1. HISTORY AND GEOGRAPHY

   History

   Geography

2. UNITED STATES GEOGRAPHY

   Location and Size

   Geographic Regions

3. CANADIAN GEOGRAPHY

   Location and Size

   Geographic Regions

Alabama · Alaska · Arizona · Arkansas · California · Colorado · Connecticut ·
Delaware · Florida · Georgia · Hawaii · Idaho · Illinois · Indiana · Iowa · Kansas ·
Kentucky · Louisiana · Maine · Maryland · Massachusetts · Michigan · Minnesota ·
Mississippi · Missouri · Montana · Nebraska · Nevada · New Hampshire ·
New Jersey · New Mexico · New York · North Carolina · North Dakota · Ohio ·
Oklahoma · Oregon · Pennsylvania · Rhode Island · South Carolina · South Dakota ·
Tennessee · Texas · Utah · Vermont · Virginia · Washington · West Virginia ·
Wisconsin · Wyoming

United States

Canada

Alberta · British Columbia · Manitoba · New Brunswick · Newfoundland and Labrador ·
Northwest Territories · Nova Scotia · Nunavut · Ontario · Prince Edward Island · Quebec ·
Saskatchewan · Yukon Territory

Unit 1: North American Geography

Chapter 1 (pages 10–35)

GEOGRAPHY OF THE UNITED STATES AND CANADA

Chapter Objectives

- To introduce students to both history and geography.
- To show how geography and history are related, and how a knowledge of geography can provide a basis for understanding history.
- To understand the size and location of the United States and Canada.
- To survey the geographic regions of the United States and Canada.
- To introduce the major geographic features, bodies of water, climates, cities, and economic activities of the various regions.

To the Teacher

"Introduction for the Student" gives an overview of the layout of the pupil's text, corresponding to "Introduction for the Teacher" in this teacher's manual. Go over this section with the students so that they understand how to use the textbook. Also help them to gain an overall view of the contents of the text. Try to stimulate their interest in studying history, especially American history. It will help if you can give interesting stories or other facts related to the history they are studying.

The main emphasis of this chapter is geography, not political divisions or economic activities, though those things are addressed. Stay close to this focus on geography. This chapter also contains an abundance of geographic facts, so beware of getting bogged down with too many details. Keep it interesting with the use of maps and pictures. Use an encyclopedia as a source for pictures, or have students bring in pictures or picture books of different areas. If you have traveled to some of the places, your personal experience will communicate more than a brief chapter can. Maintain an overview approach, trying to present a broad picture that will give students a frame of reference as they study American history. That is the primary aim of this chapter.

Note on chapter test: Chapter 1 has its own test. The next test is for Chapters 2 and 3.

Christian Perspectives

- God has created the earth and its features to reveal His wisdom and power (Psalm 104:24; Isaiah 40:12–14).
- God has given the natural resources, fertile soil, and other natural advantages that nations enjoy (Deuteronomy 8:7–9).

- God wants man to use natural resources to subdue the earth for man's benefit and God's glory (Genesis 1:28–30).
- Though nations may be large and cover great areas, they are as nothing to an infinite God (Isaiah 40:15–17).

Further Study

This chapter is intended to be an overview of United States and Canadian geography. Many generalizations must be made in such a broad picture. Since many more details can be learned about the geography of your local region, you could use this as a topic for further study in this chapter. In which of the larger regions does your area fit? What are the special geographic, climatic, and economic details of your particular area?

Large color photographs of the different regions can help students to understand and appreciate their varied topography and climate. An encyclopedia will have articles on specific features. A good geography text will also help to give a better understanding of the material in this chapter. Another resource is a world atlas, which has detailed maps of the United States, Canada, and the individual states and provinces. The *World Almanac* also gives facts about individual nations, states, and provinces. Such a study should provide a basic familiarity with the places of major importance in United States and Canadian history.

Teacher: Following is a quiz on Chapter 1. You may give chapter quizzes orally or copy them to be done on paper. (If you wish to photocopy the quizzes, you may do so without special permission from the publisher.)

Chapter 1 Quiz

Write the correct word or phrase for each blank.

1. A climate with four distinct seasons is a _____ climate.

_____

2. The broad, flat region along the east coast of the United States is the _____.

_____

3. Two main features of the Appalachian region are the _____ and the _____.

_____

4. Two main features of the Pacific Coast region in the United States are the _____ and the _____.

_____

5. The river that drains about 40 percent of the United States is the _____ River.

_____

6. A rocky region in Canada that curves like a horseshoe around Hudson Bay is the _____.

_____

7. The heartland of Canada in Ontario and Quebec is a region called the _____.

_____

8. A very cold climate in northern Canada is the _____ climate.

_____

Quiz Answers

1. **humid continental**
2. **Atlantic Coastal Plain**
3. **(Any two.) Piedmont, Appalachian Mountains, Allegheny and Cumberland Plateaus**
4. **(Any two.) Pacific ranges, Coast Ranges, Pacific valleys**
5. **Mississippi**
6. **Canadian Shield**
7. **Great Lakes-St. Lawrence Lowlands**
8. **arctic *or* subarctic**

Answer Key

Focus for Thought (page 13)

1. a. *What is history?*
   the story of people in the past and their activities
   b. *What questions does history answer?*
   "What happened?" "When did it happen?" "Where did it happen?" "Who did it?" "Why did it happen?" "What were the later effects of this incident?"
2. a. *What is geography?*
   a study of the earth, especially of the features of the earth's surface
   b. *What questions does geography answer?*
   "Where is a place located?" "What is that place like?" "What happened there?" "Why did it happen there rather than somewhere else?"
3. *Summarize how history and geography are related.*
   The things that happened (history) took place somewhere (geography). Understanding what happened involves understanding where it happened. The geography of a place provides the setting for its history, and it even affects its history.

Focus for Thought (page 23)

4. *How has the development of the United States been affected*
   a. *by its large size?*
   Because land was abundant, almost everyone could own property. This contributed to a spirit of liberty and equality.
   b. *by its natural resources?*
   The people could produce plenty of food and could use things like lumber, copper, and iron ore to make many useful products.
5. *Copy and complete this chart of the seven geographic regions of the United States. You may want to turn an unlined page sideways and make each block about 1½ inches wide and 1 inch high. The first row is filled in for you. (One or two blocks may remain empty.)*
   (Teacher: Consider that this chart will take the students longer to complete because it requires them to use their own judgment. Answers in parentheses are optional.)

Region	Geographic Features	Bodies of Water	Climate	Major Cities	Economic Activities
Atlantic Coastal Plain	low, flat, rolling narrow in north; wider in south	Atlantic Ocean Gulf of Mexico Chesapeake Bay Susquehanna River Mississippi River	temperate in north humid subtropical in south	Boston New York Houston	farming industry
Appalachian Region	Piedmont Appalachian Mountains Allegheny Plateau Cumberland Plateau	Ohio River Tennessee River Hudson River Susquehanna River Potomac River	humid continental	Philadelphia Baltimore Richmond Pittsburgh	industry along Fall Line coal mining
Central Plains	level plains some higher areas	Mississippi River Great Lakes	hot summers cold winters	Chicago St. Louis	wheat growing cattle ranching industry
Rocky Mountain Region	Rocky Mountains Continental Divide Great Basin	Missouri River Snake River Great Salt Lake	dry	Denver Salt Lake City	(cattle)
Pacific Coast	Pacific ranges Pacific valleys Coast Ranges	Pacific Ocean Columbia River San Francisco Bay	west coast marine Mediterranean	Seattle Portland San Francisco Los Angeles	vegetables oranges olives grapes (industry)
Alaska	coastal plain Alaska Range Mt. McKinley Alaska Peninsula	Arctic Ocean Yukon River Pacific Ocean	cold	Anchorage Juneau	minerals
Hawaii	eight islands volcanoes	Pacific Ocean	pleasant rainy some places	Honolulu	sugar cane pineapples (tourism)

Focus for Thought (pages 29, 30)

6. a. *What geographic regions of Canada are parts of similar regions in the United States?*

the Appalachian region, the Interior Plains, and the Cordillera region

b. *What regions does Canada have that the United States does not have?*
the Great Lakes-St. Lawrence Lowlands, and the Canadian Shield and Arctic Islands

7. *How has the climate of Canada affected the settlement of the nation?*
Because of the cold winters and short summers, farming is impossible in much of northern Canada. Most of the people live within 200 miles (322 km) of the United States border, and much of Canada is sparsely populated.

8. *Copy and complete this chart of the five geographic regions of Canada. Follow the same pattern as for the chart of United States regions that you made in number 5.*

Region	*Geographic Features*	*Bodies of Water*	*Climate*	*Major Cities*	*Economic Activities*
Appalachian Region	**Appalachian Mountains (Gaspé Peninsula)**	**St. Lawrence River (Atlantic Ocean)**	**humid continental cold**	**(Halifax)**	**dairying potatoes, fruit fishing**
Great Lakes-St. Lawrence Lowlands	**low-lying land along St. Lawrence River Ontario Peninsula level, rolling**	**St. Lawrence River Lake Ontario Lake Erie Lake Huron Niagara Falls**	**humid continental**	**Toronto Montreal**	**farming shipping industry hydroelectric power commercial life**
Canadian Shield, Arctic Islands	**low, marshy, rocky lakes snow and ice on islands**	**Hudson Bay**	**cold**		**mining lumbering furs**
Interior Plains	**level land**	**Mackenzie River Lake Winnipeg Great Slave Lake Great Bear Lake**	**dry in west cold in north**	**Winnipeg Edmonton Calgary**	**wheat, other grains oil and gas**
Cordillera Region	**Rockies Coast Ranges plateau fiords St. Elias Mountains**	**Fraser River Yukon River Columbia River Pacific Ocean**	**(cold) mild, rainy on west coast**	**Vancouver**	**lumbering fishing aluminum hydroelectric power**

GEOGRAPHICAL HIGHLIGHTS (pages 30–34)

A. Matching: Terms 1

i   1. *Pertaining to the country, as opposed to the city.*

e   2. *Land formed by soil deposited at the mouth of some rivers.*

f   3. *Broad bay at the mouth of a river.*

j   4. *Low-lying region where rivers rise and fall with ocean tides.*

g   5. *Place at the edge of the Piedmont plateau, where waterfalls occur in rivers descending to the Coastal Plain.*

k   6. *Pertaining to the city, as opposed to the country.*

b   7. *Kind of trees that bear cones and usually have needles instead of broad leaves.*

h   8. *Flowing of water into inland lakes having no outlets to the ocean.*

a   9. *Low, bowl-shaped area surrounded by higher land; also, the area drained by a river system.*

d   10. *Kind of trees that lose their leaves for part of the year.*

c   11. *High ridge that separates water flowing into the Pacific Ocean from water flowing into the Gulf of Mexico.*

a. *basin*
b. *coniferous softwood*
c. *Continental Divide*
d. *deciduous hardwood*
e. *delta*
f. *estuary*
g. *Fall Line*
h. *internal drainage*
i. *rural*
j. *tidewater*
k. *urban*

B. Matching: Terms 2

g   1. *Subsoil that stays permanently frozen.*

i   2. *Surface features of a region.*

a   3. *In contact; adjoining.*

f   4. *Level land lying some distance inland from the ocean.*

b   5. *Crack or break in the crust of the earth, where earthquakes occur.*

e   6. *Account of happenings in the past.*

c   7. *Long, narrow bay extending inland in a steep-sided valley.*

j   8. *River flowing into a larger river.*

d   9. *Study of the earth, especially its surface features.*

h   10. *Large, elevated area of the same general height.*

a. *contiguous*
b. *fault*
c. *fiord*
d. *geography*
e. *history*
f. *interior plain*
g. *permafrost*
h. *plateau*
i. *topography*
j. *tributary*

C. Matching: Bodies of Water

a. *Arctic Ocean*
b. *Atlantic Ocean*
c. *Chesapeake Bay*
d. *Columbia River*
e. *Fraser River*
f. *Great Bear Lake*
g. *Great Lakes*
h. *Great Salt Lake*

i. *Great Slave Lake*
j. *Gulf of Mexico*
k. *Hudson Bay*
l. *Hudson River*
m. *Lake Winnipeg*
n. *Mackenzie River*
o. *Mississippi River*
p. *Missouri River*

q. *Niagara River*
r. *Ohio River*
s. *Pacific Ocean*
t. *Potomac River*
u. *Snake River*
v. *St. Lawrence River*
w. *Susquehanna River*
x. *Yukon River*

l, t, w   1. *United States rivers flowing east into the Atlantic Ocean (three answers).*
a   2. *Ocean to the north of North America.*
n   3. *Longest river in Canada.*
v   4. *Important river for shipping between the Great Lakes and the Atlantic.*
h   5. *Body of water in the Great Basin.*
f, i   6. *Lakes that are part of the Mackenzie River system (two answers).*
o   7. *River system draining about 40 percent of the United States.*
d, u   8. *River and its tributary draining the northwestern United States (two answers).*
s   9. *Ocean to the west of North America.*
g   10. *Lake Superior, Lake Michigan, Lake Huron, Lake Erie, Lake Ontario.*
q   11. *River flowing over a great waterfall between Lakes Erie and Ontario.*
e   12. *River of British Columbia that flows into the Pacific Ocean.*
j   13. *Body of water south of the United States.*
k   14. *Bay surrounded by the Canadian Shield.*
b   15. *Ocean to the east of North America.*
x   16. *River that drains central Alaska and flows into the Pacific Ocean.*
p   17. *Major tributary of the Mississippi that begins in the Rockies.*
r   18. *River that flows west out of the Appalachian Mountains.*
c   19. *Long, wide mouth of the Susquehanna River.*
m   20. *Canadian lake that drains into the Hudson Bay.*

D. Matching: Geographic Features

a. *Allegheny and Cumberland Plateaus*
b. *Appalachian Mountains*
c. *Coast Ranges*
d. *Great Basin*
e. *Central Plains*
f. *Mt. Logan*
g. *Mt. McKinley*

h. *Mt. Robson*
i. *Mt. Whitney*
j. *Ontario Peninsula*
k. *Pacific ranges*
l. *Pacific valleys*
m. *Piedmont*
n. *Rocky Mountains*

g   1. *Highest mountain in North America.*

n   2. *High western mountains stretching from Canada to New Mexico; part of a chain extending into South America.*

h   3. *Highest mountain in the Canadian Rockies.*

d   4. *Region of internal drainage where the Great Salt Lake is located.*

a   5. *Land stretching west from the Appalachian Mountains.*

e   6. *Vast, treeless, grassy land stretching from the Mississippi to the Rockies.*

m   7. *Region of rolling hills and valleys separating the Atlantic Coastal Plain from the Appalachian Mountains.*

i   8. *Highest mountain in the contiguous United States.*

b   9. *Rounded, forested mountains stretching from Alabama to Maine and extending into Canada.*

j 10. *Land in Canada extending southwest between the Great Lakes.*

f 11. *Highest mountain in Canada.*

l 12. *Valleys with a west-coast marine climate.*

k 13. *Mountains just west of the Great Basin.*

c 14. *Mountains along the western ocean.*

E. Matching: Regions

a. *Alaska*

b. *Appalachian region*

c. *Atlantic Coastal Plain*

d. *Canadian Shield*

e. *Central Plains*

f. *Cordillera region*

g. *Great Lakes-St. Lawrence Lowlands*

h. *Hawaii*

i. *Pacific Coast*

j. *Rocky Mountain region*

d   1. *Rocky region curving like a horseshoe around the Hudson Bay.*

c   2. *Low land bordering the Atlantic Ocean in the east and the Gulf of Mexico in the south.*

h   3. *Volcanic islands in the Pacific.*

i   4. *Mountains and valleys farthest west in the United States.*

f   5. *Canadian region including the Rocky Mountains and the Coast Ranges.*

g   6. *Heartland of Canada where most of the people live.*

e   7. *Broad region of fertile land drained by the Mississippi River system.*

a   8. *Largest state, which contains the highest mountain in North America.*

j   9. *Region including the Rocky Mountains and the Great Basin.*

b 10. *Piedmont, Appalachian Mountains, and Allegheny and Cumberland Plateaus.*

F. Matching: Climates

a. *Arctic*
b. *humid continental*
c. *humid subtropical*
d. *Mediterranean*
e. *subarctic*
f. *west coast marine*

b   1. *Climate with four distinct seasons and a great contrast between summer and winter.*
c   2. *Very warm and moist climate.*
d   3. *Warm, dry climate suitable for raising oranges, grapes, and olives.*
f   4. *Mild, wet climate of the Pacific valleys.*
e   5. *Cold climate in Canada and Alaska where coniferous trees grow.*
a   6. *Very cold climate where no trees grow and deep soil layers are permanently frozen.*

G. Matching: Cities

a. *Anchorage*
b. *Boston*
c. *Calgary*
d. *Chicago*
e. *Denver*
f. *Edmonton*
g. *Honolulu*
h. *Houston*
i. *Juneau*
j. *Los Angeles*
k. *Montreal*
l. *New York*
m. *Pittsburgh*
n. *Portland*
o. *Salt Lake City*
p. *San Francisco*
q. *Seattle*
r. *St. Louis*
s. *Toronto*
t. *Vancouver*
u. *Winnipeg*

e   1. *Major Rocky Mountain city in the United States.*
c, f, u   2. *Three major cities of the Canadian Plains.*
t   3. *Major western port city of Canada.*
m   4. *Major Appalachian city in Pennsylvania.*
b, h, l   5. *Three cities of the Atlantic Coastal Plain.*
d, r   6. *Two great cities of the Central Plains in the United States.*
k, s   7. *Two largest cities of Canada.*
j, p   8. *Two large cities on the Pacific coast of California.*
a, i   9. *Two cities in Alaska.*
n, q   10. *Two major cities in the Pacific valleys.*
g   11. *Main city of Hawaii.*
o   12. *Major city of the Great Basin.*

H. Deeper Discussion

1. *Read Isaiah 40:12–17.*

   a. *What can a study of geography teach us about God?*

It teaches us about the greatness of God. His matchless wisdom and

boundless power are clearly evident; He needed no counsel from anyone else in deciding where to put various features, climates, and resources. God is infinite—to Him the nations are as a drop of a bucket and as nothing and less than nothing.

b. *What should be our response as we observe the works of God in our world?*
We should fear God, worship Him, and give all honor to Him rather than to man and his achievements. Isaiah 40:18–28 indicates that man tends to take pride in the works of his own hands, when really God should receive the glory.

2. *Explain how a knowledge of geography can improve your understanding of history.*
A knowledge of geography helps you follow the events as historical figures traveled from one place to another. It helps you understand why the events took place where they did, and why they turned out as they did.

3. *What two factors encouraged the growth of cities along the Fall Line?*
One factor was the waterpower produced as rivers descended to the coastal plain. This encouraged the building of factories, which attracted workers to the cities. The second factor was the hindrance in shipping. Since boats could not travel upstream beyond the Fall Line, they had to be unloaded in the cities along the Fall Line; and thus the cities became centers of trade and transportation.

4. *How do climate, soil, and topography affect the work that people do, the way they travel, and their general manner of life?*
People tend to live where the climate is moderate and where the soil and topography are suitable for raising food or for providing some other means of supporting themselves. Where the soil is fertile, farming can flourish. Where power, raw materials, and transportation are available, industry develops. Many rugged areas have more minerals, so mining is important there. Transportation is usually easy on a plain but difficult in mountainous regions. Navigable rivers aid transportation; in fact, many roads and railroads run through gaps in mountains or follow a river. Thus the climate, soil, and topography are strong influences in determining people's general manner of life in a certain area.

5. *How have the United States and Canada benefited from their large size and abundant resources?*
The large size of both countries has contributed to a spirit of independence and equality because anyone could own land, not just

certain classes as in Europe. It also contributed to a large population in the United States, though not in Canada because of the cold climate there. The abundant resources enabled both countries to develop flourishing economies, with productive industry and prosperous farming. It has allowed them to become strong, wealthy nations.

I. Chronology and Geography

1. *Trace the outline of Map A in the Map Section, and label it "Geographic Regions of the United States." (You do not need to trace the state borders.)*
   a. *Draw the boundary lines of the five main geographic regions of the contiguous United States. Label the regions.*
   b. *Label the Piedmont, the Great Basin, Mt. Whitney, and Mt. McKinley.*
   c. *Using a blue colored pencil, trace the Hudson, Susquehanna, Potomac, Mississippi, Ohio, Missouri, Columbia, and Snake Rivers. Label them.*
   d. *Label the Atlantic Ocean, Pacific Ocean, Arctic Ocean (on the inset map of Alaska), Chesapeake Bay, Great Lakes, Great Salt Lake, and Gulf of Mexico.*
   e. *Label Boston, New York City, Pittsburgh, Chicago, St. Louis, Houston, Denver, Los Angeles, San Francisco, Seattle, Anchorage, and Honolulu.*
   (Individual work.)
2. *Trace the outline of Map B in the Map Section, and label it "Geographic Regions of Canada." (You do not need to trace the province and territory borders.)*
   a. *Draw the boundary lines of the five main geographic regions of Canada. Label the regions.*
   b. *Label Mt. Logan, Mt. Robson, the Rocky Mountains, and the Coast Ranges.*
   c. *Using a blue colored pencil, trace the St. Lawrence, Mackenzie, Columbia, and Frazer Rivers. Label them.*
   d. *Label the Atlantic Ocean, Pacific Ocean, Arctic Ocean, Hudson Bay, Great Lakes, Lake Winnipeg, Great Slave Lake, and Great Bear Lake.*
   e. *Label Montreal, Toronto, Winnipeg, Calgary, Edmonton, and Vancouver.*
   (Individual work.)
3. *Save your maps in a notebook or folder.*

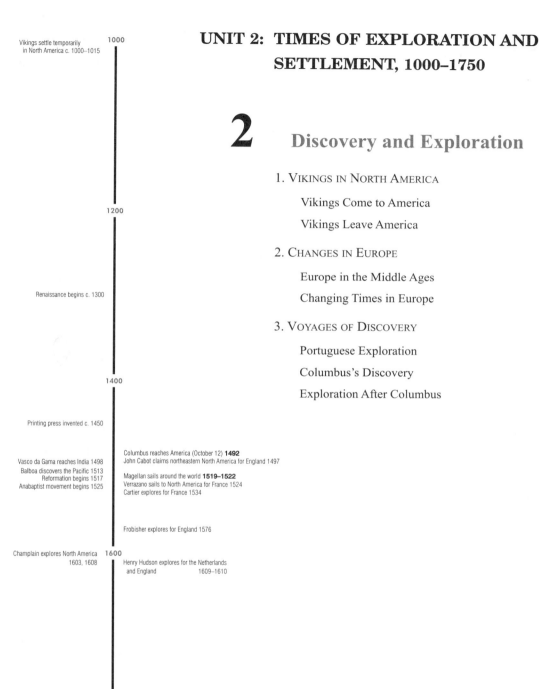

Vikings settle temporarily
in North America c. 1000–1015

1000

1200

Renaissance begins c. 1300

1400

Printing press invented c. 1450

Vasco da Gama reaches India 1498
Balboa discovers the Pacific 1513
Reformation begins 1517
Anabaptist movement begins 1525

Columbus reaches America (October 12) **1492**
John Cabot claims northeastern North America for England 1497

Magellan sails around the world **1519–1522**
Verrazano sails to North America for France 1524
Cartier explores for France 1534

Frobisher explores for England 1576

Champlain explores North America
1603, 1608

1600

Henry Hudson explores for the Netherlands
and England   1609–1610

1800

UNIT 2: TIMES OF EXPLORATION AND SETTLEMENT, 1000–1750

2

Discovery and Exploration

1. VIKINGS IN NORTH AMERICA

   Vikings Come to America

   Vikings Leave America

2. CHANGES IN EUROPE

   Europe in the Middle Ages

   Changing Times in Europe

3. VOYAGES OF DISCOVERY

   Portuguese Exploration

   Columbus's Discovery

   Exploration After Columbus

"The honour of kings is to search out a matter."
Proverbs 25:2

Unit 2: Times of Exploration and Settlement
1000–1750

Chapter 2 (pages 36–55)

DISCOVERY AND EXPLORATION

Chapter Objectives

- To understand that the North American continent was undeveloped and sparsely populated just five hundred years ago.
- To understand that the Vikings reached North America five hundred years before Columbus.
- To be acquainted with some of the changes that ultimately led to the discovery and settlement of the New World.
- To understand why the Reformation took place and what changes it produced.
- To be acquainted with the earliest explorers and how their work led to European claims in North America.

To the Teacher

Christopher Columbus receives the credit for discovering America because of the results of his exploration. He should be understood within the framework of God's sovereignty. It appears that the changes in Europe and the subsequent exploration and settlement of America were the fulfillment of God's plan for history. Though the Reformation occurred after 1492, it provided a significant impetus for people to move to America. These concepts may seem lofty for eighth graders, but they should be able to grasp the basic truth that a number of major changes in Europe led to the discovery of America, and that Columbus's discoveries opened a whole New World for Europeans.

Historians have found some indications that other men may have sailed around the world before Magellan. However, the evidence is not strong enough for this to be accepted as fact.

Note on chapter test: There is a single test for Chapters 2 and 3. If you decide to omit Chapter 3, give the test immediately after completing Chapter 2. The test is set up to allow for this.

Christian Perspectives

- God has given the earth to man (Psalm 115:16).
- God intended that man spread out and subdue the wild, uncultivated parts of the earth (Genesis 1:26, 28; 11:6–9).

- God is able to manage the activities of men in order to work out His own purposes and receive glory to Himself, regardless of any evil intentions on man's part (2 Chronicles 20:6; Job 34:21–30).
- The upheavals of the Reformation resulted because some men sought to obey New Testament doctrine (Matthew 10:34–39). The Anabaptists were the most consistent in this.

Further Study

The topics listed below can be researched by faster students or given as assignments. Written or oral reports could be given on any topic suggested, as well as on others that the teacher assigns. These topics could also be used for stories based on actual happenings. For example, a student could write a story about the day when the lookout on the *Pinta* first sighted land. This section can also serve as a guide to additional background material for teachers to include in the class discussion.

- The Vikings and their exploits.
- The manorial and feudal systems of Europe.
- The Crusades.
- The story of Marco Polo.
- The culture and civilization of the Arabs.
- The culture and civilization of the Chinese.
- The invention of printing.
- The Reformation.
- The school of Prince Henry the Navigator.
- The story of each of the four voyages made by Columbus.
- The story of Ferdinand Magellan.
- The story of Vasco da Gama or another explorer discussed in this chapter.

Chapter 2 Quiz

1. Who met both the Vikings and Columbus when they arrived in North America?

2. When did Leif Ericson explore the North American coast?

3. What were three things that helped to prepare Europe for discovery and exploration of the New World?

4. Who discovered the New World in the 1400s, and on what date did he make his discovery?

5. What effect did the Reformation have on Europe, which caused many people to move to America?

Quiz Answers

1. **Indians (called Skraelings by the Vikings)**
2. **about A.D. 1000**
3. **(Any three.) trade with the Orient; the Crusades; decline of manorialism (or feudalism); rise of nationalism; spirit of adventure; the Renaissance; revival of humanism; advances in scientific thought; improvements in navigation**
4. **Christopher Columbus, on October 12, 1492**
5. **It brought much war and persecution (suffering).**

Answer Key

Focus for Thought (page 40)

1. *Give the date of the Viking settlement in Greenland, and name the man who established it.*

   A.D. 986; Eric the Red

2. *Who led the first group of Vikings to reach North America, and when did they arrive there?*

   Leif Ericson; about A.D. 1000

3. *Why did the settlements in Vinland eventually fail? Give at least two reasons.*

   (Any two.) Vinland was too far from the Viking strongholds in Iceland and Norway. The settlements were also attacked by the native people, whom they called Skraelings. The bitter cold climate may have been too harsh.

4. *Why does Christopher Columbus receive credit for discovering the New World when the Vikings had reached it earlier?*

   The Viking settlements were not permanent, but Columbus's discovery led to a continuing exploration and settlement by Europeans. Viking settlements held little importance to later people. Europe in the eleventh century was not ready to settle America.

Focus for Thought (pages 44, 45)

5. *How did the following developments increase European interest in exploration?*
   a. *trade with the Orient*

   Europeans were introduced to luxuries they had not known before. Their high cost led Europeans to search for new trade routes.

   b. *the Crusades*

   Crusaders developed a liking for the spices, foods, clothing, and other luxuries of the Orient and wanted them to be brought to Europe. This led to a search for better trade routes.

   c. *the rise of nationalism*

   People of different nations competed with each other to establish their own trade routes with the Orient so that their nations would become strong and wealthy.

   d. *the spirit of adventure*

   Marco Polo visited China and wrote a book about his experiences, which aroused interest in Asia. (Columbus himself read Marco Polo's book.)

e. *advances in scientific thought*

New ideas (such as the fact of a spherical earth) moved men to experiment and explore further.

f. *improvements in navigation*

Because of the compass, the astrolabe, better ship designs, and better maps, explorers were able to go on long voyages of exploration.

6. *Why was Gutenberg's printing press such an important invention?*

Large numbers of books became available. Some of these books spread humanistic ideas throughout Europe, but others spread the most important message of all—the Word of God.

7. a. *Give the names of four religious leaders who helped to bring about the Reformation. Place a star beside the one out of which Anabaptism eventually grew.*

John Wycliffe, Martin Luther, John Calvin, Ulrich Zwingli*

b. *What doctrine taught by the Anabaptists seemed threatening to governments in Europe?*

that the church should be entirely separate from the civil government and should be guided only by the Bible

8. *How did the Reformation in Europe cause many people to move to the New World?*

It brought wars and persecution to Europe, from which many people sought relief by moving to the New World.

Focus for Thought (page 50)

9. *Why is Amerigo Vespucci important in American history?*

The name *America* is derived from his name.

10. *How was it decided which lands in the New World belonged to which European nations?*

Possession of a new region was given to the nation that discovered it.

11. *For each of the following nations, name the men who explored the New World and the areas each nation claimed as a result of that exploration. In one case the same explorer's name will be used for two different nations.*

a. *Portugal (not including Amerigo Vespucci)*

Pedro Cabral—Brazil (or South America)

b. *Spain (two men, not including Vespucci or Magellan)*

Christopher Columbus—Hispaniola, Cuba, and other islands of the West Indies; Central and South America. Balboa—Pacific Ocean and all the land touching it.

c. *England (two men, not including Martin Frobisher)*
John Cabot—northeastern North America; Henry Hudson—Hudson Bay

d. *France (three men)*
Giovanni da Verrazano and Jacques Cartier—St. Lawrence River valley; Samuel de Champlain—Canada

e. *Netherlands*
Henry Hudson—Hudson River area

HISTORICAL HIGHLIGHTS (pages 51–53)

A. Matching: People

a. *Amerigo Vespucci*
b. *Christopher Columbus*
c. *Ferdinand and Isabella*
d. *Ferdinand Magellan*
e. *Giovanni da Verrazano*
f. *Henry Hudson*
g. *Jacques Cartier*
h. *John Cabot*
i. *Leif Ericson*
j. *Vasco da Gama*
k. *Vasco de Balboa*
l. *Vikings*

h 1. *Explorer who claimed northeastern North America for England in 1497.*

b 2. *"Admiral of the Ocean Sea" who discovered the New World in 1492.*

a 3. *Man who described the new lands as being a new world rather than part of the Orient.*

i 4. *Viking who explored the northeastern coast of North America around* A.D. *1000.*

d 5. *Captain of five ships, one of which became the first to sail around the world (1519–1522).*

l 6. *Scandinavian people who settled Iceland, Greenland, and Vinland around* A.D. *1000.*

e 7. *Explorer of the North American coast for France in 1524.*

f 8. *Explorer who claimed part of America for the Netherlands in 1609.*

k 9. *Explorer who discovered in 1513 that a great ocean lay west of America.*

g 10. *Explorer of the St. Lawrence River area for France in 1534.*

j 11. *Explorer who reached the Orient by sailing around Africa.*

c 12. *King and queen of Spain when Columbus went on his voyage of discovery.*

B. Matching: Names and Terms

a. *astrolabe*

b. *capitalist*

c. *feudalism*

d. *Line of Demarcation*

e. *manorialism*

f. *middle class*

g. *nationalism*

h. *Orient*

i. *Reformation*

j. *Renaissance*

k. *saga*

l. *San Salvador*

m. *Santa María*

n. *Vinland*

j   1. *Rebirth of learning and culture in Europe.*

m   2. *Ship commanded by Columbus when he discovered the New World.*

d   3. *Boundary drawn by the pope to give Spain rights to the New World.*

h   4. *The East.*

a   5. *Instrument used by medieval sailors to determine the latitude of their ship.*

e   6. *System in which a lord owned the land and serfs farmed it for him.*

n   7. *Temporary Viking settlement in North America, probably in present-day Newfoundland.*

b   8. *Person who invests money in a project in order to make a profit.*

l   9. *Island where Columbus landed in the New World.*

f 10. *People who were neither lords nor serfs.*

k 11. *A story of Viking adventures, first handed down orally and later put into writing.*

i 12. *Great change in the religious system of Europe.*

c 13. *System of loyalty in Europe during the Middle Ages, by which noblemen of lower rank received land from noblemen of higher rank.*

g 14. *Pride in belonging to one's nation; patriotism.*

C. Multiple Choice

Write the letter of the best answer.

1. *The Renaissance*

    a. *led to a revival of Roman Catholic thought.*

    b. *encouraged people to reject all their old ideas.*

    c. brought a renewed interest in art, music, literature, and science.

    d. *brought an age of mental and spiritual darkness.*

2. *Why did the Reformation take place?*

    a. *Materialism moved men to seek the truth.*

    b. *Martin Luther was upset because of errors in the Roman Catholic Church.*

    c. *Certain kings left the Roman Catholic Church and established Protestant churches.*

   d. Various men saw errors in the Roman Catholic Church and determined to correct them.

3. *The Anabaptist movement*

   a. *grew out of Calvin's teaching.*

   b. *emphasized thrift and hard work.*

   c. promoted the idea that the church and state should be separate.

   d. *reformed the Roman Catholic Church from within.*

4. *How did the Reformation affect American history?*

   a. Many people sought relief from troubles in Europe by moving to America.

   b. *It broke the power of the Roman Catholic Church.*

   c. *It resulted in several new Protestant denominations.*

   d. *Calvin, Zwingli, and Luther sent many of their followers to the New World.*

5. *The Italians*

   a. *sought ways to reduce the price of goods from the East.*

   b. *tried to improve the overland trade routes to the East.*

   c. *were the first Europeans to reach the East by sailing around Africa.*

   d. were the first Europeans to control the trade routes to the East.

6. *Christopher Columbus*

   a. *was a capitalist who financed his own voyages.*

   b. was right in thinking that the East could be reached by sailing west, but was wrong in estimating the distance.

   c. *was honored all his life for having discovered the New World.*

   d. *was eager to establish Protestantism in new lands.*

D. Deeper Discussion

1. *Make an application of Job 12:22 in terms of European discovery and exploration. Remember that the Atlantic Ocean was known as the Sea of Darkness at this time.*

   God arranged things so that men crossed the "Sea of Darkness" and discovered a new land. This discovery enlightened the European understanding of the earth and profoundly affected subsequent history.

2. *Would the explorations in the 1400s have taken place without the Renaissance? Explain.*

   Probably not. The increase in scientific knowledge helped men to improve their methods of exploration. Otherwise exploration would have been crude and inconclusive. The experience of the Vikings seems to support this.

3. *Compare the timing of the Reformation and the exploration of the New World. What does this timing suggest?*

It suggests that God was opening a new land where His truth could flourish unhindered by Old World traditions. It also suggests that God had prepared a place of refuge for His persecuted people.

4. *What kind of personality and character did Columbus have?*

Columbus was a determined man and an excellent sailor. He was willing to prove a new idea—reaching the East by sailing west. His extreme devotion to his idea made him obnoxious to many, who regarded him as a tiresome fanatic. In his moments of triumph, he proved to be boastful and egotistical. Columbus spent his last bitter years in trying to regain his lost glory.

5. *Why can it be said that Columbus's discovery of the New World is one of the most important happenings in history?*

With Columbus's discovery, a whole new world was opened to people of Europe and Asia. The new opportunity gave men and nations a chance to start over without many of the restraints of Old World history and custom. There was a great exchange of foods, animals, diseases, and other things. This discovery had a major impact on the later history of the world.

6. *How do the discoveries and explorations of about five hundred years ago affect you today?*

Depending on where you live in North America, the English, Spanish, or French culture around you dates from the original claims of the mother countries. If these countries had claimed different areas, your surrounding culture would be different.

E. Chronology and Geography

These activities are designed as additional material or review. Assign them as best suited to your schedule and your class.

1. *Make a time line of some of the important events that changed Europe, using the list below. First, choose a scale that fits the span of years to be covered. For this time line, use 1 centimeter = 50 years. The illustration at the right shows you how to begin. (Metric units work well because they are based on tens. In later chapters, a more practical scale will be 1 centimeter = 10 years.) Draw a line and mark it off in centimeters. Then label the marks.*

    Write in each event for your time line at the appropriate place. If you write the years directly on the line instead of to

1000

1050

1100

1150

the left, you can place events on both sides of the time line. (See the time line on page 37.) A brace (}) may be used to indicate a span of years.

Printing press invented   *Marco Polo publishes his book*
Reformation begins   *Renaissance*
Trade with the Orient begins   *Crusades*

c. 1000—Trade with the Orient begins
1096–1291—Crusades
1298—Marco Polo publishes his book
1300–1500—Renaissance
c. 1450—Printing press invented
1517—Reformation begins

2. *Match the numbers on the map to the names below.*

   3 a. Cabot
   5 b. *Cartier*
   6 c. *Champlain*
   8 d. *Columbus*
   2 e. *Frobisher*
   4 f. *Hudson (1609)*
   1 g. *Hudson (1610)*
   7 h. *Verrazano*
   9 i. *Vespucci*

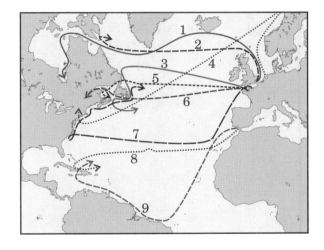

3. *Copy and complete this chart of early explorers in the New World.*

Explorer	Exploration Dates	Sponsoring Country	Areas Explored
Cabot	1497	England	northeastern coast of North America (Newfoundland and Labrador)
Cabral	1500	Portugal	east coast of South America (Brazil)
Balboa	1513	Spain	Panama, Pacific Ocean
Magellan	1519–1522	Spain	circled the earth
Verrazano	1524	France	North American coast from North Carolina to Maine
Cartier	1534	France	St. Lawrence River
Frobisher	1576	England	Frobisher Bay
Champlain	1603, 1608	France	Canada
Hudson	1609 1610	Netherlands England	Hudson River Hudson Bay

SO FAR THIS YEAR (page 54)

These exercises review what you have learned so far this year. Try to do as many as you can without looking back for the answers.

A. Matching: Climates

c   1. *Sunny and mild; good for oranges and olives.*
b   2. *Very warm and moist.*
e   3. *Wet and mild; found in Pacific valleys.*
d   4. *Cold climate in Canada and Alaska.*
a   5. *Climate of four seasons.*

a. *humid continental*
b. *humid subtropical*
c. *Mediterranean*
d. *subarctic*
e. *west coast marine*

B. Matching: Physical Features

a. *Appalachian region*
b. *Atlantic Coastal Plain*
c. *Pacific Coast*
d. *Central Plains*
e. *Rocky Mountain region*

f. *Canadian Shield*
g. *Great Lakes-St. Lawrence Lowlands*
h. *Mississippi River*
i. *Mackenzie River*

h   6. *Drains about 40 percent of the United States.*
f   7. *Rocky region curving like a horseshoe around Hudson Bay.*
c   8. *Made up of the Coast Ranges, the Pacific ranges, and the Pacific valleys.*
e   9. *High, western mountains extending from Canada to New Mexico; region includes Great Basin and plateaus.*
i 10. *Longest river in Canada.*
d 11. *Vast, treeless, grassy land stretching from the Mississippi to the Rockies.*
g 12. *Heartland of Canada in Ontario and Quebec.*
b 13. *Broad, flat region bordering the Gulf of Mexico and the ocean east of the United States.*
a 14. *Made up of the Piedmont, the Appalachian Mountains, and the Allegheny and Cumberland Plateaus.*

C. Matching: Explorers

a. *Amerigo Vespucci*
b. *Christopher Columbus*
c. *Vasco de Balboa*
d. *Ferdinand Magellan*
e. *Giovanni da Verrazano*

f. *Henry Hudson*
g. *Jacques Cartier*
h. *John Cabot*
i. *Leif Ericson*
j. *Vasco da Gama*

h 15. *Explorer of the northeastern coast of North America for England in 1497.*

b 16. *"Admiral of the Ocean Sea" who discovered the New World in 1492.*

c 17. *Explorer who discovered in 1513 that a great ocean lay west of America.*

i 18. *Viking who explored the northeastern coast of North America around* A.D. *1000.*

j 19. *Explorer who reached the Orient by sailing around Africa.*

e 20. *Explorer of the North American coast for France in 1524.*

f 21. *Explorer who claimed part of America for the Netherlands in 1609.*

a 22. *Man who described the new lands as being a new world rather than part of the Orient.*

g 23. *Explorer of the St. Lawrence River area for France in 1534.*

d 24. *Captain of five ships, one of which became the first to sail around the world (1519–1522).*

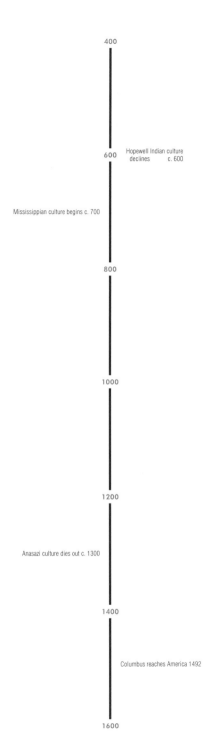

400

600   Hopewell Indian culture
       declines   c. 600

Mississippian culture begins c. 700

800

1000

1200

Anasazi culture dies out c. 1300

1400

Columbus reaches America 1492

1600

3 American Indians

*"In [God's] hand is the soul of every living thing,
and the breath of all mankind."*

Job 12:10

Chapter 3 (pages 56–71)

AMERICAN INDIANS

Chapter Objectives

- To summarize Indian developments in the centuries preceding Columbus.
- To gain an overview of Indian customs and cultures as they existed when Indians encountered the Europeans.
- To lay the groundwork for a fair and accurate understanding of the Indians so that subsequent events can be properly understood—especially the clash between European and Indian cultures.
- To instill respect for people whose ideas and customs are very different from our own, realizing that all men have eternal souls created in the image of God.
- To inspire interest in and further study of the Indians.

To the Teacher

A study of Indian life can be both fascinating and controversial. Avoid extremes when teaching this chapter, and try to present the facts from a Biblical perspective and without bias. We cannot explain why God allowed whites to wrest the land from the Indians, but we know He had a purpose. Be careful to leave an impression of respect for the Indians as human beings created by God, but do not condone their heathen practices.

This chapter is an overview, not a detailed account, to give students a broad perspective of the Indians. If you will be unable to cover the entire book, this is a chapter that could be omitted.

Note on chapter test: There is a single test for Chapters 2 and 3.

Christian Perspectives

- The heathen have erroneous fears, beliefs, and religious practices because they do not know God or His Word (Psalm 2:1). Many try to please the spirits, not realizing that those spirits are nonexistent or evil.
- No matter how wrong their practices, all men must be respected because they have eternal souls created in the image of God (Ezekiel 18:4; Genesis 1:26, 27; Malachi 2:10; Acts 17:25, 26).
- All men have enough light to be aware of God (Romans 1:19, 20; Acts 17:27).
- God expects us to be interested in the spiritual welfare of the heathen and to have compassion on them (Matthew 28:18–20; John 4:1–42; Acts 18:6).

Further Study

This chapter presents an overview of the Indians. Much more can be learned. When studying Indians, be on guard against bias in favor of the Indians or against them. Many authors color their views on the Indians with strong emotion. Remember that many Indian practices, especially their religious practices, were heathen. Also, beware of evolutionary thinking about the Indians' past, such as the idea that the first ones came to America over twenty thousand years ago, after the Ice Age ended. With these cautions, study of the following topics can be enjoyable and profitable.

- Indian civilizations before Columbus, including those of South America.
- Indian culture areas.
- Individual Indian tribes.
- Indian wars.
- Indians today.

Chapter 3 Quiz

1. What term is used for a region where Indian tribes lived similarly?

   _____

2. What name was given to the group of tribes called the Five Nations?

   _____

3. What are two things that Indians contributed to Europeans?

   _____

4. What was one cause of conflict between Indians and Europeans?

   _____

   _____

5. How were some people able to get along well with the Indians?

   _____

   _____

Quiz Answers

1. **culture area**
2. **Iroquois (Iroquois League)**
3. **foods: tomatoes, corn, potatoes, peanuts, pumpkins; inventions: canoe, hammock, snowshoes; words, especially place names; help for surviving in the new land**
4. **Europeans wanted to develop farms and towns, but Indians wanted to keep their land and maintain their own way of life. Europeans wanted Indians to accept Christianity, but many Indians wanted to keep their own religion.**
5. **People who followed God's way of peace (nonresistance) and respect for others were able to get along well with the Indians.**

Answer Key

Focus for Thought (page 60)

1. a. *What is meant by the term culture?*

   Culture is the set of customs and values associated with a certain group of people. (It includes the language, clothing, art and music, and beliefs of a people, as well as their technology and their established ways of doing things.)

   b. *What are some specific things that are part of your culture?*

   (Examples for most students in conservative Mennonite schools.) We speak English. Men wear trousers and shirts; women wear dresses. We sing in four-part harmony as an expression of worship. We believe in God the Father and in His Son Jesus Christ, the Saviour of the world. We live in a technologically modern culture, with permanent dwellings, electricity, and telephones.

2. *What was similar about the Hopewell and Mississippian cultures?*

   Both cultures built huge mounds of earth for ceremonial use and for burials.

3. *What was similar about the two Southwestern farming cultures?*

   They grew the same kinds of crops (corn, squash, beans). They used irrigation and other techniques for farming dry land. (They also lived in pueblos.)

4. *Which group of Southwestern farming cultures*

   a. *especially used irrigation?* **the Hohokam**

   b. *were cliff dwellers?* **the Anasazi**

   c. *made spectacular pottery?* **the Mogollon**

Focus for Thought (page 66)

5. *What is an Indian culture area?*

   It is a region where a number of Indian tribes had basically the same culture. (They had similar foods, languages, customs, and beliefs.)

6. *List the five main Indian culture areas, and give their locations and boundaries in terms of the present-day United States.*

   (1) Northeast: from the Great Lakes south to North Carolina and from the Atlantic Ocean west to the Mississippi River

   (2) Southeast: from North Carolina south to the Gulf of Mexico and from the Atlantic Ocean west to the Mississippi River

   (3) Plains: from Canada to the Gulf of Mexico, and from the Mississippi River to the Rocky Mountains

(4) Southwest: present-day Arizona, New Mexico, and parts of Texas
(5) Far West: California, the Great Basin, and the Columbia Plateau

7. *Copy and complete the following chart. The spaces for Indians in the Northeast are filled in for you. (You may leave a blank space if the text gives no information for that category.)*

	Living Quarters	*Economic Activities*	*Tribal Government*	*Religion*
Northeast	Longhouse villages	farming hunting	Sachems (appointed by women) five-nation confederacy	animism, shamans, supreme being, life after death
Southeast	**houses of poles covered with grass and mud villages of 100 or more houses**	**farming hunting**	**village chief and warrior council**	
Plains	**tepees earth lodges of sod and brush supported by logs**	**hunting buffalo farming**		**powers of nature, sun dance, "Great Spirit"**
Southwest	**pueblos of adobe hogans of logs and mud**	**mainly farming**		**kivas kachinas universal spirit ceremonies to please the spirits**
Far West	**simple log and earth houses, partly underground**	**hunting gathering fishing digging for roots**	**villages with men leaders**	**supernatural spirits animal spirits shamans**

Focus for Thought (page 68)

8. *What were some contributions*
   a. *of the Europeans to the Indians?*
   livestock (sheep and horses); the Bible and Christianity; crops (wheat, sugar cane, bananas); tools (kettles, traps, guns); liquor; diseases; names and words
   b. *of the Indians to the Europeans?*
   teaching on how to hunt and fish, and how to grow new crops (tomatoes, corn, potatoes, peanuts, pumpkins); inventions (canoe, hammock, snowshoes); words (including many place names)

9. *What were two main causes of the conflict that developed between the Europeans and the Indians?*
   One cause of the conflict was the economic difference, because the Indians had no concept of private land ownership as the Europeans did. The Indians also believed that the earth was sacred because of their nature gods, but the Europeans believed in God's command to subdue the earth. Another cause of conflict was religious. The white men saw the Indians as savages to be converted, and they fought the Indians who refused to accept Christian beliefs.

10. *Read Paul's message to the Athenians in Acts 17:22–31.*
    a. *Verse 27 says that God is "not far from every one of us." How was this true for the Indians? (Compare Romans 1:19, 20.)*
    The Indians were well acquainted with God's creation. They knew through the creation that God existed.
    b. *How do verses 29–31 apply to the Indians and their beliefs?*
    The Indians needed to repent and believe in Christ, just as all men do.

HISTORICAL HIGHLIGHTS (pages 68–70)

A. Matching: Culture Areas

Match the culture areas to the descriptions. Letters may be used more than once.

b	1. *Area from North Carolina to the Gulf of Mexico and from the Atlantic Ocean to the Mississippi River.*	a. *Northeast*
c	2. *Area from the Mississippi River to the Rocky Mountains.*	b. *Southeast*
a	3. *Area where Indians lived in longhouses.*	c. *Plains*
b	4. *Area where Indians had houses of poles covered with grass and mud.*	d. *Southwest*
		e. *Far West*

b   5. *Area where Indians grew corn, beans, melons, and pumpkins on good farm-land.*

d   6. *Area in present-day Arizona and New Mexico.*

c   7. *Area where warriors counted coups.*

c   8. *Area where Indians prepared pemmican.*

e   9. *Area where Indians used acorn flour.*

d   10. *Area where Indians herded sheep*

c   11. *Area of sun dance tradition.*

a   12. *Area between the Great Lakes and North Carolina.*

e   13. *Area in California, the Great Basin, and the Columbia Plateau.*

c   14. *Area where Indians used travois.*

B. Matching: Tribes and Groups

Match the tribes or groups to the statements below. Letters may be used more than once.

f   1. *Indians that were divided into clans.*

g   2. *Culture that made large piles of earth for ceremonies and burial.*

h   3. *Tribe that lived in hogans.*

d   4. *Tribe that lived in pueblos.*

b   5. *Tribe that lived on the Central Plains.*

f   6. *Group that adopted some captives and killed others.*

d   7. *Tribe that used kivas.*

i   8. *Indians who lived along riverbanks and fished for salmon.*

e   9. *Eskimos who lived in the Arctic.*

f   10. *Indians governed by sachems.*

a   11. *Indians who made foods from acorn flour or went fishing.*

b   12. *Plains tribe of fierce fighters.*

c   13. *Indians called "diggers" who lived on poor land.*

f   14. *Tribes called the Five Nations.*

d   15. *Tribe that farmed with irrigation.*

a. *California Indians*
b. *Comanche*
c. *Great Basin Indians*
d. *Hopi*
e. *Inuit*
f. *Iroquois*
g. *Mound Builders*
h. *Navajo*
i. *Plateau Indians*

C. Matching: Terms

c 1. *Customs and values associated with a certain group of people.*

i 2. *Indian village of multilevel apartment houses made of stone or adobe.*

e 3. *Underground room used for religious ceremonies.*

j 4. *One of the old men who governed the Iroquois.*

k 5. *Pair of poles drawn by a dog or horse, used by Plains Indians to carry their belongings.*

b 6. *Manmade object, such as a tool or weapon, that is of interest in archaeology.*

d 7. *Region where a number of Indian tribes had basically the same culture.*

g 8. *Fence made of vertical poles.*

a 9. *Bricks made of sun-dried clay.*

f 10. *Dwelling made of poles bent in a U shape and covered with bark.*

h 11. *Dry, crumbled meat mixed with buffalo tallow.*

a. *adobe*
b. *artifact*
c. *culture*
d. *culture area*
e. *kiva*
f. *longhouse*
g. *palisade*
h. *pemmican*
i. *pueblo*
j. *sachem*
k. *travois*

D. Matching: Lifestyles

c, e 1. *Areas where Indians obtained food mainly by hunting (two answers).*

d 2. *Area where Indians obtained food mainly by farming.*

a, b 3. *Areas where Indians obtained food by both hunting and farming (two answers).*

d 4. *Area where Indians lived the most peaceably.*

c, e 5. *Areas where Indians wandered about as nomads (two answers).*

a. *Northeast*
b. *Southeast*
c. *Plains*
d. *Southwest*
e. *Far West*

E. Deeper Discussion

1. *Give a Biblical explanation of Indian origins.*
   Adam is the ancestor of all mankind, so Indians also are descended from Adam. According to Genesis 10:25, 32 and 11:9, God scattered people across the earth after the Flood and after the confusion of tongues at the Tower of Babel. Among these people were the ancestors of the American Indians.

2. *How did different Indian cultures develop?*
   Different Indian cultures developed because of the different climate

and geography of various regions. For example, the Southwest Indians could not farm like the Indians of the Northeast or Southeast, because their region was too dry. Therefore, they developed a system of farming based on irrigation and other techniques for farming dry land. The Plains Indians had access to herds of buffalo, so they depended on them for food and other needs.

3. *Many primitive peoples have practiced animism. What is animism?*

Animism is the belief that animals and other natural objects have a soul or spirit.

4. a. *Why did the Columbian exchange take place?*

The Indians had been isolated from Europe and the rest of the world for many centuries. Consequently, they had foods, inventions, and ways of living that were different from those of the Europeans. Likewise, the Europeans had developed technology and had the Bible, while the Indians did not. When the two different cultures met, the result was an intermingling of ideas, foods, animals, and practices.

b. *What were some results?*

New foods (such as potatoes and corn) were brought from the New World to the Old World. New foods and animals (such as wheat and horses) were brought from the Old World to the New. The greatest migration of people in history began. Thousands of Indians were killed by European diseases. The Europeans took control of the Americas.

5. *In the 1800s, white men almost wiped out the great buffalo herds in the West. Why did this cause severe hardship for the Plains Indians?*

The Plains Indians depended on the buffalo for all the basic necessities of life: food, clothing, and shelter. When most of the buffalo were gone, the Plains Indians had to change their lifestyle or perish.

6. *When the Europeans brought guns and horses to the American plains, the Plains Indians quickly recognized the value of these things. How did guns and horses affect the lifestyle of the Plains Indians?*

Both guns and horses helped the Plains Indians to be more successful in hunting buffalo and fighting their enemies. Horses were also useful in moving their camps from place to place.

The Plains Indians became more nomadic, hunting buffalo and living in tepees all the time. They had more time for warfare.

7. *How were some people able to get along well with the Indians?*

Some people got along well with the Indians by following the New

Testament teachings on kindness and nonresistance. They practiced the Golden Rule, and the Indians respected them for it.
William Penn's dealings with the Indians is a good example of this.
When nonresistant people did suffer from the Indians, it was usually because of circumstances beyond their control.

F. Chronology and Geography

1. *Give the approximate number of* centuries *between each of the following
   things and the arrival of Columbus.*
   a. *The decline of the Hopewell people.* **nine centuries**
   b. *The rise of the Mississippian Mound Builders.* **eight centuries**
   c. *The end of the early southwestern farming societies.* **two centuries**
2. *Trace the outline of Map C in the Map Section, and label it "Indians of North
   America." (You do not need to trace the rivers or the outlines of Greenland
   and Iceland.)*
   a. *Draw boundary lines to show the five main Indian culture areas discussed
      in the second section of this chapter. Also draw boundary lines to show the
      Northwest Coast, the Subarctic, and the Arctic areas. Label these areas
      using all capital letters.*
   b. *Label the following groups or tribes: Iroquois, Huron, Algonquin,
      Delaware, Cherokee, Creek, Seminole, Choctaw, Natchez, Blackfoot,
      Cheyenne, Comanche, Crow, Sioux, Hopi, Zuni, Apache, Navajo, Pomo,
      Shoshone, Paiute, and Nez Perce.*
   (Individual work.)

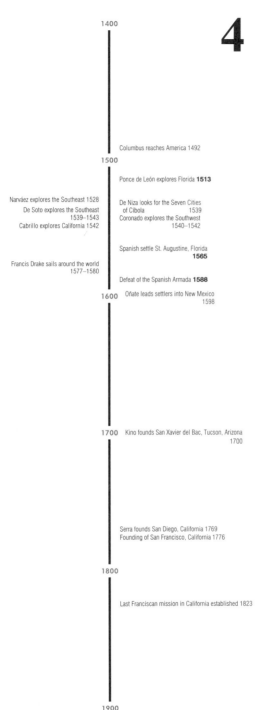

4 Spanish Exploration and Settlement

"He that is greedy of gain troubleth his own house."
Proverbs 15:27

Chapter 4 (pages 72–89)

SPANISH EXPLORATION AND SETTLEMENT

Chapter Objectives

- To learn about Spanish explorations in present-day Anglo-America, particularly in the southwestern region.
- To learn about the Spanish mission system.
- To learn about the Spanish settlements in the Southwest.
- To learn about Spain's decline and England's rise as a world power after 1588.

To the Teacher

Spanish exploration and settlement is important to understanding the development of the United States. Much of what is discussed in this chapter affected the growing United States in the 1800s. Most important is the decline of the Spanish, which allowed England to gain a foothold on the continent—though only in places that the Spanish had not already colonized. Nevertheless, this movement resulted in the colonies that became the United States and eventually displaced the Spanish in Florida and the Southwest.

You may want to discuss absolutism and its effects in relation to the Spanish settlements. In Roman Catholicism, authority is ultimately invested in one man, the pope. A religious bureaucracy manages religious affairs down to the local level. Since Spain was a Roman Catholic nation, it was only natural that New Spain operated on the principle of absolutism. The next chapter deals with French settlements, which also had an absolutist form of government.

In contrast, Protestant England operated more on the principle of individual liberty. The rise of English power allowed English customs and freedoms to be transplanted to the new nation, making it possible for the persecuted peoples of Europe to find a haven in the New World.

Note: An enlarged copy of Map C should be provided for each student if you assign "Historical Highlights," Part G, #2.

Note on chapter test: There is a single test for Chapters 4 and 5.

Christian Perspectives

- The Spanish explorers operated out of selfishness and greed in spite of professing Christianity.
- God did not overlook the mistreatment of the Indians by the Spanish. Neither did He overlook the bitterness and rebellion of the Indians toward their Spanish oppressors. (See Ecclesiastes 12:14).
- The Spanish believed that their cruelty was a necessary part of conquering the heathen. They saw a parallel between their conquest of the Indians and Israel's conquest of the Canaanites. (The Puritans of New England had a similar outlook.)
- God rules in the kingdoms of men, and uses the weather to do His bidding (Psalm 148:8).

Further Study

Following are some topics for further research by the teacher or students.

- The Spanish conquest as compared with the British and French conquests.
- The Spanish missions (which were established on any territory conquered by Spain).
- The settlement of the Spanish Southwest.
- The lives and travels of the Spanish men who explored North America. (The story of Cabeza de Vaca is especially interesting.)
- The Invincible Armada.

Chapter 4 Quiz

Write the correct word or phrase for each sentence.

1. Francisco de Coronado explored the (northwestern, southwestern, southeastern) part of the present-day United States to find the fabled Seven Cities of Cíbola.

   _____

2. The oldest town in the United States is _____, which was founded in the year _____ in the present-day state of _____.

   _____

3. The climate of the southwestern United States is _____ .

   _____

4. Spanish _____ were established to civilize and convert the Indians.

   _____

5. _____ were built to keep order and to protect Spanish missions on the frontier.

   _____

6. New Spain operated on the principle of _____, whereby those in authority held strict control over the missionaries and Indians.

   _____

7. The Pueblos _____ against the Spanish in 1680.

   _____

8. A fleet of ships called the _____ was defeated in 1588, after which Spain declined as a world power.

   _____

Quiz Answers

1. southwestern
2. St. Augustine, 1565, Florida
3. dry (arid)
4. missions
5. Forts (Presidios)
6. absolutism
7. revolted (rebelled)
8. Spanish Armada (Invincible Armada)

Answer Key

Focus for Thought (page 77)

1. *Name the Spanish explorer who discovered Florida, and tell when he discovered it.*
   Ponce de León; 1513
2. a. *What two Spaniards explored southeastern North America while searching for wealth?*
   Pánfilo de Narváez and Hernando de Soto
   b. *What major river did one of them discover?*
   the Mississippi River
3. *Which Spaniard went out in 1540 and explored the southwestern part of what is now the United States?*
   Francisco de Coronado
4. *What man claimed California for Spain?*
   Juan Rodríguez Cabrillo
5. *What were the results of the Spanish explorations in the Southeast and the Southwest?*
   The Spanish explorers failed to find gold, riches, or great empires to conquer. They failed to establish settlements in the regions they explored. But the explorations did establish Spain's claim to the areas explored, they increased geographical knowledge, and they opened the way for later settlers.

Focus for Thought (page 82)

6. a. *What were the goals of the Spanish missions?*
   to protect their borders against foreign nations, to develop the land, and to convert the Indians to Catholicism
   b. *What was the purpose of the presidios?*
   to keep order and to protect the missions
7. *How successful were the Spanish in converting the Indians?*
   The Spanish missions were successful only in part. Many Indians returned to their former religion and lifestyle. Others were never civilized or converted to Catholicism.

8. *Why did the Spanish try to settle New Mexico in the 1590s and again in the early 1600s? Give two reasons.*
They wanted to protect their northern frontier against the English. They wanted to convert the Indians.

9. *Why did the Spanish begin settlements in eastern Texas in the late 1600s and early 1700s?*
to counter the French, who had claimed the Mississippi River valley

10. *What two men brought Spanish settlers to California in the 1700s?*
Eusebio Kino and Junípero Serra

11. a. *In what year was St. Augustine founded? San Francisco?*
1565; 1776
b. *How much time passed between these years?*
211 years

12. *In what part of the present United States were the Spanish missions located?*
from Texas west to California (the southwestern part of the present United States)

Focus for Thought (page 85)

13. *In what two ways did other European nations weaken Spain through trade?*
Other nations traded secretly with the Spanish colonies. English "sea dogs" and other pirates robbed Spanish ships and raided Spanish colonies.

14. a. *For what two things was King Philip trying to punish the English when he sent the Spanish Armada against them?*
He tried to punish the English for robbing the Spanish of New World treasures and for leaving the Roman Catholic Church.
b. *Why was he confident of success?*
He thought God would help the Catholic nation of Spain to defeat the Protestant nation of England.

15. *In what way was the defeat of the Spanish Armada a turning point in history?*
After this defeat, Spain's power declined while England's power increased. The result was that North America was not settled by Catholics from Spain but by Protestants from England.

16. *What effects did the Spanish have on southwestern North America?*
They brought new animals and crops: horses, sheep, cattle, wheat, oranges, olives. Their names and customs survive in the Southwest. The Spanish influenced architecture.

HISTORICAL HIGHLIGHTS (pages 85–88)

A. Matching: People

a. *Cabeza de Vaca*   h. *Juan Rodríguez Cabrillo*
b. *Elizabeth I*   i. *Junípero Serra*
c. *Eusebio Kino*   j. *Marcos de Niza*
d. *Francis Drake*   k. *Pánfilo de Narváez*
e. *Francisco de Coronado*   l. *Philip II*
f. *Hernando de Soto*   m. *Ponce de León*
g. *Juan de Oñate*

m   1. *Man who sought the Fountain of Youth.*
 f   2. *Explorer who discovered the Mississippi River.*
 a   3. *Man who made an overland journey on foot after being shipwrecked on the Narváez expedition.*
 b   4. *Ruler of the country attacked by the Spanish Armada.*
 g   5. *Spaniard who led settlers to Pueblo country and established San Juan.*
 h   6. *Man who explored California and claimed San Diego Bay in 1542.*
 k   7. *Explorer who lost his life at sea after exploring the Southeast.*
 d   8. *Captain who plundered Spanish ships.*
 e   9. *Explorer who sought the Seven Cities of Cíbola in 1540.*
 i 10. *Franciscan friar who founded San Diego, California, in 1769.*
 l 11. *Ruler who sent the Invincible Armada against England.*
 c 12. *Jesuit priest who planted missions in Arizona.*
 j 13. *Friar who told fantastic stories about "golden cities."*

B. Matching: Terms

a. *absolutism*   d. *mission*
b. *civilize*   e. *presidio*
c. *frontier*   f. *sea dog*

b   1. *To bring out of a primitive state by education and discipline.*
 a   2. *System in which one person has complete authority in all matters.*
 e   3. *Fort built to keep order and protect a Spanish mission.*
 d   4. *Spanish outpost established to convert and civilize Indians.*
 f   5. *Pirate supported by the English government in the 1500s.*
 c   6. *Edge of a settled area.*

C. Matching: Dates

b	1. *De Soto's expedition*	a.	*1513*
d	2. *St. Augustine founded*	b.	*1539–1543*
a	3. *Florida discovered*	c.	*1540–1542*
c	4. *Coronado's expedition*	d.	*1565*
g	5. *First mission in California*	e.	*1588*
e	6. *Spanish Armada defeated*	f.	*1680*
f	7. *Pueblo revolt*	g.	*1769*

D. Matching: Places

a. *Arizona*	f. *New Mexico*
b. *California*	g. *New Spain*
c. *Florida*	h. *Santa Fe*
d. *Georgia and the Carolinas*	i. *Seven Cities of Cíbola*
e. *Mississippi River*	j. *St. Augustine*

i   1. *Legendary places that turned out to be Indian pueblos.*

b   2. *Region settled in the 1700s to oppose English and Russian claims.*

d   3. *Region explored by de Soto.*

g   4. *Spanish colony also called Mexico.*

e   5. *Major feature first crossed by white men as de Soto searched for wealth.*

c   6. *Land discovered by Ponce de León in his search for the Fountain of Youth.*

f   7. *Pueblos' land that was settled by Spanish colonists led by Oñate.*

a   8. *Area where Eusebio Kino set up missions.*

j   9. *First town built by Europeans in what is now the United States.*

h   10. *Capital of New Mexico.*

E. Multiple Choice

Write the letter of the best answer.

1. *How did the Spanish deal with the Indians they found?*
   a. They overpowered the uncooperative Indians.
   b. *They respected the Indians' wishes.*
   c. *They settled in uninhabited areas.*
   d. *They bought supplies from the Indians.*

2. *Why were de Soto and Coronado disappointed when they explored the southern part of what is now the United States?*
   a. *The natives were uncivilized, heathen people.*
   b. *The natives were hostile.*

    c. *The explorers failed to find productive soil.*

    d. The explorers failed to find gold and jewels.

3. *How were the Pueblo Indians bondmen in their own land?*

    a. *They were held in large prison compounds.*

    b. *They were not allowed to raise food on their own soil.*

    c. They were forced to serve the religious and civil leaders who occupied their land.

    d. *Their land was the scene of feuding between Spanish leaders.*

4. *Why did the Pueblo Indians revolt in 1680?*

    a. *They did not like to work in fields, vineyards, and gardens.*

    b. They had suffered mistreatment under the Spanish.

    c. *They found the Roman Catholic doctrines offensive.*

    d. *They resented the strange new customs of the Spanish.*

5. *The Spanish destroyed the Huguenot settlement in Florida for all the following reasons* except *that*

    a. *the Huguenots were trespassing on land claimed by Spain.*

    b. *the Huguenots were Protestants.*

    c. the Huguenots had killed Spanish settlers in Florida.

    d. *the Spanish did not want French people living on their land.*

6. *What was the purpose of the Spanish missions among the Indians?*

    a. *to protect and police the Indians*

    b. to civilize and convert the Indians

    c. *to obtain workers for mission projects*

    d. *to protect the settlers who had moved into the area*

7. *Which one of these was* not *associated with a Spanish mission?*

    a. *missionaries*   e. *carpenter and blacksmith skills*

    b. *fort*   **f. gold mines**

    c. *gardens and fields*   g. *Spanish manners and customs*

    d. *livestock raising*

8. *Why was the arrival of horses in the West so important?*

    a. *Longhorn cattle came with them.*

    b. *Buffalo began to disappear.*

    c. *Horses had never been seen in the West before.*

    d. Horses changed the Indians' lifestyle.

9. *What was the outcome after the Spanish Armada was defeated?*

    a. *Spanish power increased and English power decreased.*

    b. Spanish power decreased and English power increased.

    c. *Both Spanish and English power decreased.*

    d. *Both Spanish and English power increased.*

F. Deeper Discussion

1. *How did absolutism affect the way that the Spanish dealt with hostile Indians?*
By the principle of absolutism, the Indians were to be completely submissive to Spain. After they resisted, they had no more rights and the Spanish felt justified in overpowering them.

2. *Why were some Indian groups open to the Spanish culture and religion, but others were not?*
Some Indian groups may not have valued their culture as highly as others did. However, the openness of some groups may simply have been a survival tactic, in view of the Spaniards superior weapons. This is suggested by the fact that the Yuma (and other Indians) later turned against the Spanish and drove them out.

3. *What were some merits of the Spanish mission efforts?*
The Spanish missions helped primitive people to become civilized. The missions did bring some knowledge of Christianity and the Bible to the Indians. They paved the way for settlement and later American development of the region. (The missions also provided some protection from government officials who were cruel and greedy.)

4. *When the defeated Spanish Armada returned to Spain, Philip II said to the commander, "I sent you to fight against men, not with the winds." According to Job 37:12, why did the winds act as they did?*
God directs the wind to accomplish His purposes among men. In this incident, God used the winds to further the defeat of the Spanish Armada. God works His will on the earth, in governments as well as through weather.

5. *Why were the Spanish ultimately unable to maintain the American Southwest as part of their territory?*
The Spanish concentrated on developing Mexico because they thought it a richer land. Only later did they try to defend their northern frontier against foreign nations. Their mission system may have civilized some Indians, but it did not develop and utilize the land. Also, the Spanish were becoming too weak to defend their faraway settlements. As great numbers of American settlers moved into Texas and California, these Spanish lands fell readily into their hands.

G. Chronology and Geography

1. *Make a time line of Spanish activities that affected America, using the information in Part C. Follow the instructions in Chapter 2 for making a time line.*

   1513—Florida discovered
   1539–1543—DeSoto's expedition
   1540–1542—Coronado's expedition
   1565—St. Augustine founded
   1588—Spanish Armada defeated
   1680—Pueblo revolt
   1769—First mission in California

2. *Using an enlarged copy of Map C, label it "Exploration of North America." (You will use your "Exploration of North America" map in Chapters 5, 11, and 18.)*

   a. *Draw green lines to show the explorations of Ponce de León, Narváez, Cabeza de Vaca, de Soto, de Niza, Coronado, and Cabrillo.*

   b. *Label each route with the explorer's name and the date(s) of his exploration.*

   c. *Make a legend to show that green lines represent Spanish explorations, blue lines represent French explorations, brown lines represent American explorations, and red lines represent British explorations.*

   d. *On your map, label the following important Spanish missions: San Antonio, San Xavier del Bac, San Diego, San Francisco, and Los Angeles.*

   (Individual work.)

SO FAR THIS YEAR (page 89)

A. Matching: Indian Tribes

b	1. *Plains tribe of fierce fighters.*	a. *California Indians*
g	2. *Culture that made large heaps of earth for ceremonies and burial.*	b. *Comanche*
h	3. *Southwest Indians who lived in hogans.*	c. *Great Basin Indians*
f	4. *Indians governed by sachems and called the Five Nations.*	d. *Hopi*
d	5. *Tribe that had pueblos with kivas.*	e. *Inuit*
e	6. *Another name for Eskimos.*	f. *Iroquois*
a	7. *Indians who went fishing or made foods from acorn flour.*	g. *Mound Builders*
i	8. *Tribes who lived along riverbanks and fished for salmon.*	h. *Navajo*
c	9. *Indians called "diggers" who lived on poor land.*	i. *Plateau Indians*

B. Completion

Write the correct word or phrase for each description.

humid continental	10. *A climate of four seasons.*
Great Lakes-St. Lawrence Lowlands	11. *The heartland of Canada in Ontario and Quebec.*
John Cabot	12. *Explorer of the northeastern coast of North America for England in 1497.*
Jacques Cartier	13. *Explorer of the St. Lawrence River area for France in 1534.*
1588	14. *Year the Spanish Armada was defeated.*
Ponce de León	15. *Man who sought the Fountain of Youth.*
Hernando de Soto	16. *Explorer who discovered the Mississippi River.*
Francisco de Coronado	17. *Explorer who sought the Seven Cities of Cíbola, 1540–1542.*
mission	18. *Spanish system used to convert and civilize the Indians, and to fortify their frontiers.*

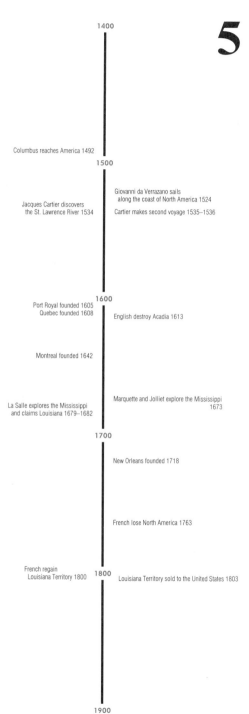

5 New France

Timeline:

1400

Columbus reaches America 1492

1500

Giovanni da Verrazano sails along the coast of North America 1524

Jacques Cartier discovers the St. Lawrence River 1534

Cartier makes second voyage 1535–1536

1600

Port Royal founded 1605
Quebec founded 1608

English destroy Acadia 1613

Montreal founded 1642

La Salle explores the Mississippi and claims Louisiana 1679–1682

Marquette and Jolliet explore the Mississippi 1673

1700

New Orleans founded 1718

French lose North America 1763

French regain Louisiana Territory 1800

1800

Louisiana Territory sold to the United States 1803

1900

"In the multitude of people is the king's honour: but in the want of people is the destruction of the prince."
Proverbs 14:28

Chapter 5 (pages 90–107)

New France

Chapter Objectives
- To understand that France laid claim to the St. Lawrence, Acadia, and Newfoundland areas as a result of the explorations of Verrazano and Cartier.
- To understand the effects of absolutism, the seigneurial system, and the fur trade on New France.
- To understand the contributions of Champlain and La Salle to New France.
- To learn why the French and the Iroquois became enemies.
- To learn about Jesuit missionary efforts among the Indians.
- To compare and contrast New France with the English colonies.

To the Teacher
This chapter lays a foundation for understanding Canadian history. French North America also influenced the United States, especially in the Louisiana Territory. The absolutist French colonial system stands in sharp contrast to the loosely governed English colonies discussed in the next chapter. The French colonies served to benefit France and her king; whereas in the English colonies, individuals were motivated by personal benefits. Also, the economic mainstay of New France was the fur trade, which stunted the development of that colony.

It is important to understand that the French and English would clash in North America, and one or the other would triumph. Use this chapter to lead up to the establishment of English colonies with their freedoms, and to Chapter 8, on the French and Indian War.

Note on chapter test: There is a single test for Chapters 4 and 5. Be sure to cover "Chronology and Geography," number 3, on important dates.

Christian Perspectives
- Man's choices have far-reaching consequences, as did Champlain's decision to support the Huron and Algonquin against the Iroquois (Galatians 6:7).
- Zeal alone is not enough in spreading the Gospel; zeal must be coupled with teaching and living the *whole* Bible truth. The Jesuits had strong zeal, but they taught many false doctrines, such as salvation by baptism. (Compare Matthew 23:15.) Also, the Indians could see that many white men themselves were not living up to Bible standards.
- Wild, unrestrained living results in moral debasement, as illustrated by the coureurs de bois (Romans 1:21–32). Also consider the degrading effects of alcohol on the Indians.

Further Study

Francis Parkman (1823–1893) specialized in the history of this period in a set of volumes called *France and England in North America*. Parkman's work has strongly influenced the history written about this period. The volumes listed below provide a wealth of additional information. Of course, they should be read with discretion.

The Jesuits in North America
Pioneers of France in the New World
The Old Regime in Canada
La Salle and the Discovery of the Great West
Count Frontenac and New France Under Louis XIV

The actual volumes are lengthy and may be difficult to obtain. However, *The Parkman Reader*, edited by Samuel Morison, is a good substitute. In addition, many general histories of Canada have material based on Parkman's work.

Here are several other suggested areas of study.

- The explorers: Cartier, Champlain, Marquette and Jolliet, La Salle.
- The Indian wars.
- The fur trade.
- The later history of Louisiana.

Quiz Answers

1. **c**
2. **b**
3. **b**
4. **a**
5. **d**

6. **c**
7. **b**
8. **d**
9. **a**

Chapter 5 Quiz

1. The first French claim to territory in North America was based on the explorations of
   a. Columbus.
   b. Champlain.
   c. Cartier.
   d. La Salle.

2. Where was Port Royal located?
   a. in Newfoundland
   b. in Acadia
   c. along the St. Lawrence River
   d. in the Mississippi River valley

3. Why were the Iroquois hostile against the French?
   a. The French kidnapped several of their people.
   b. Champlain helped the Huron to fight against the Iroquois.
   c. The Iroquois did not want to be involved in the fur trade.
   d. The French took Iroquois land without paying for it.

4. Why is Champlain known as the "father of New France"?
   a. He founded Quebec and helped to develop New France.
   b. He was the French king when New France was founded.
   c. He was a Jesuit leader in New France.
   d. He was the first to explore the area of New France.

5. The French policy in governing New France is described by the word
   a. democracy.
   b. toleration.
   c. nationalism.
   d. absolutism.

6. The Jesuits were especially noted for their
   a. zeal for Protestantism.
   b. philosophical reasoning.
   c. devotion to Roman Catholicism.
   d. interest in the Iroquois.

7. What did the fur trade do to New France?
   a. It encouraged agriculture.
   b. It lowered moral standards.
   c. It increased government regulation.
   d. It led to the seigneurial system.

8. The French claimed the Mississippi River valley
   a. to oppose the English.
   b. to open a passage to the Orient.
   c. because the Huron and Algonquin lived there.
   d. because La Salle had explored it.

9. Which statement is *not* true of the seigneurial system?
   a. It was part of the fur trade.
   b. It granted land to seigneurs, who subdivided it to habitants.
   c. It grew out of European manorialism.
   d. It placed no great burden on the habitants.

Answer Key

Focus for Thought (pages 96, 97)

1. *Give the meaning of the Indian word from which the name* Canada *is derived.*
   village

2. a. *When did the French establish their first colony in America?*
   in 1541

   b. *Why did the French abandon their early attempts at settlement?*
   One reason was the failure to find gold and other immediate riches. Another was disease (scurvy) and the harsh winters in Canada.

3. *The Port Royal settlement was important for what three reasons?*
   It made a sincere effort to support itself by agriculture. It had a good relationship with the Indians. The Roman Catholic faith was not compulsory (no one was forced to accept any certain religion).

4. a. *The French based their claim to the St. Lawrence region on the work of two explorers. Name these explorers, and give the dates of their explorations.*
   Verrazano—1524; Cartier—1534

   b. *England also claimed the region of Acadia. Give the name of the English explorer and the date of his exploration. (See Chapter 2.)*
   Cabot—1497

   c. *Which of these two nations had the earlier claim to Acadia?*
   England (But according to the pope's Line of Demarcation in 1494, the whole area belonged to Spain.)

5. *Name the founder of Quebec, and give the date of the founding.*
   Samuel de Champlain—1608

6. *Who were the Indian allies*
   a. *of the French?* **the Huron and Algonquin**
   b. *of the English?* **the Iroquois**

7. *In what ways was Samuel de Champlain the "father of New France"?*
   Champlain founded Quebec, the most important settlement in New France. He also did much exploring and mapmaking. He helped establish the fur trade and mission work among the Indians. He made several trips to France and brought new settlers to Canada.

Focus for Thought (page 102)

8. a. *What was the required religion in New France?*
   Roman Catholicism

   b. *What kind of government did the French have?*
   an absolutist government

c. *What was the French system of land ownership?*

the seigneurial system (based on the manorial system of Europe)

d. *What were some weaknesses of the colony at New France?*

(Sample answers.) Most of the people lived in ignorance. People depended on the government instead of providing for themselves. The economy was based on the fur trade rather than on agriculture and industry.

9. *What did the French missionaries hope to accomplish among the Indians?*

They hoped to convert the Indians to the Roman Catholic faith, civilize them, and establish French authority over them.

10. *What were the responsibilities*

a. *of a seigneur?*

A seigneur was to get settlers established on his land to clear it. He was to build a manor house for himself and provide a wine press and buildings such as a mill and a bakery. He was to find a priest for the community.

b. *of an habitant?*

An habitant was to work his own fields, work for the seigneur several days a year, and make annual rent payments of money, grain, and poultry to his seigneur.

11. a. *What was one aspect of the seigneurial system that favored the habitants?*

The habitants were spared the expense of putting up buildings like mills and bakeries. The system placed only light burdens on them.

b. *What was one aspect that did not favor them?*

The habitants were not free to own land themselves, and this diminished their incentive to work hard.

12. a. *What part did the coureurs de bois have in the fur trade?*

They maintained contact with the Indians in the west and helped to bring their furs to the settlements along the St. Lawrence.

b. *What part did liquor have in the fur trade?*

The French used the liquor trade to keep the Indians from trading with the English.

c. *Describe the consequences of departing from God and from God-ordained authority, as the coureurs de bois did. (See Romans 1:28–32.)*

The consequences are a reprobate mind and a life filled with all kinds of sin. The ultimate end of such a course is eternal death.

Focus for Thought (page 105)

13. *What did Marquette and Jolliet discover about the Mississippi River?*

that it was not a passage to Asia, but a river flowing to the Gulf of Mexico

14. *What did La Salle's exploration do for New France?*
    His exploration increased the size of New France so that it stretched from the St. Lawrence River to the mouth of the Mississippi River. (This gave the French access to the sea from both ends of the colony.)
15. *Why did the French build forts in the Mississippi River valley?*
    to use as trading posts, missions, and defense outposts
16. *Describe some present-day effects of the French colonies in America.*
    French is one official language of Canada. Quebec has many French people who are Catholics. The French Canadians follow French customs and laws. Louisiana is divided into parishes instead of counties, and many people in its southern part are Catholic. Many places have French names.
17. *Give several contrasts between New France and the English colonies.*
    New France was large but had few people; the English colonies were smaller but had more people. Land ownership was restricted in New France, but the English settlers were allowed to own property. New France depended heavily on the fur trade, but the English colonies depended more on farming. New France did not have religious or political freedoms as the English colonies did.

HISTORICAL HIGHLIGHTS (pages 105–107)

A. Matching: People

a. *De Monts*
b. *Giovanni da Verrazano*
c. *Jacques Cartier*
d. *Jacques Marquette*
e. *Louis XIV*
f. *Louis Jolliet*
g. *Poutrincourt*
h. *Robert de La Salle*
i. *Samuel de Champlain*

i   1. *"Father of New France."*
d, f 2. *Men who explored the Mississippi to the Arkansas River in 1673 and 1674 (two answers).*
h   3. *Explorer who claimed for France the area drained by the Mississippi.*
c   4. *Early explorer who made three trips to the St. Lawrence region.*
e   5. *French king who ruled by the principle of absolutism.*
b   6. *First explorer sent by France.*
a   7. *Huguenot businessman who headed the Port Royal colony.*
g   8. *Upper-class settler who tried to hold on to the Port Royal colony.*

B. Matching: Groups

g	1. *Strongly dedicated Roman Catholic workers.*		a. *Algonquin*
a, e	2. *Indians who were baptized in large numbers (two tribes).*		b. *coureurs de bois*
f	3. *Indians who sided with the English.*		c. *habitants*
d	4. *French Protestants.*		d. *Huguenots*
h	5. *Noblemen who owned land in New France.*		e. *Huron*
b	6. *"Forest runners" who gathered furs from the Indians and brought them to trading centers.*		f. *Iroquois*
c	7. *Settlers who worked a seigneur's land in New France.*		g. *Jesuits*
			h. *seigneurs*

C. Matching: Places and Terms

k	1. *River along the Quebec and Montreal settlements.*	a. *absolutism*
f	2. *Town where annual fur-trading fair was held.*	b. *Acadia*
h	3. *Town founded by Champlain.*	c. *Canada*
j	4. *Unsatisfactory site for the settlement in Acadia.*	d. *flotilla*
c	5. *Name derived from Indian word for village.*	e. *monopoly*
g	6. *Poutrincourt's beloved settlement, destroyed by the English.*	f. *Montreal*
b	7. *French name for the area around the Bay of Fundy.*	g. *Port Royal*
a	8. *Strict principle by which New France was ruled.*	h. *Quebec*
i	9. *Form of manorialism transplanted to New France.*	i. *seigneurial system*
d	10. *Group of canoes traveling together.*	j. *St. Croix*
e	11. *Exclusive control over the market of a certain product.*	k. *St. Lawrence*

D. Deeper Discussion

1. *The Indians that the French found were primitive and warlike tribes. How do people get into such a condition? Read Romans 3:10–18.*
   People sink lower and lower into barbarism when they are without God or the light of His Word.

2. *How did the French alliance with the Huron and Algonquin against the Iroquois affect the subsequent history of North America?*
   Because of that alliance, the Iroquois allied themselves with the Dutch and English against the French. They competed against the French for the fur trade and kept the French from spreading into eastern North America. The Iroquois helped the English in the French and Indian War, thus helping to retain North America for England.

3. *The French policy of absolutism kept New France from developing into a successful, flourishing colony. Give several factors that hindered its development.*
The people were denied the freedom to manage their own affairs and solve their own problems. They were not allowed to have their own land. They were denied freedom of religion. They were denied the privilege of trading freely with whomever they wanted.

4. a. *To what extent did the Jesuits succeed among the Indians?*
They succeeded in getting many Indians baptized into the Roman Catholic Church, in presenting the Roman Catholic version of the Gospel to them, and in helping some of them to become more civilized.
b. *To what extent did they fail?*
The Jesuits failed in that they did not present a Scriptural message to the Indians.

5. *How did the fur trade*
a. *lower the morals of people in New France?*
The fur trade enticed men to make money without hard work, to cast off restraint and discipline, and to indulge in alcoholic beverages.
b. *affect the Indians?*
The Indians' lifestyle changed as they began using things like guns, kettles, and iron tools. They became dependent on these European goods; and the French in turn became dependent on the Indians for furs, their source of wealth. The Indians were debased through strong drink that the traders gave them for furs.
c. *hinder the development of New France?*
Because the fur trade was so profitable, settlers had little incentive to support themselves by farming or by trade in other products. Also, the fur traders opposed settlement because they wanted to preserve the wild land for their fur-bearing animals. Dependence on the fur trade resulted in a large colony that was sparsely settled and hard to defend.

6. *In what way did La Salle's claim complete a bridge across the North American continent?*
With the addition of La Salle's claim, New France stretched from the mouth of the St. Lawrence in the northeast to the mouth of the Mississippi in the south. Most of that distance could be traveled by boat.

7. *Why did French expansion into the Mississippi River valley lead to conflict?*
In the West, the French came into conflict with the Spanish, who were colonizing Texas. In the East, the English colonies were growing so

rapidly that settlers would soon move westward over the mountains. English settlers from South Carolina were already moving into Louisiana by the time the French colonized it.

E. Chronology and Geography

1. *Match the numbers on the map to the place names below.*

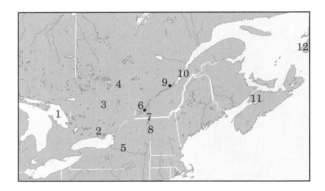

 10 a. *St. Lawrence River*
 7 b. *Richelieu River*
 3 c. *Ottawa River*
 8 d. *Lake Champlain*
 1 e. *Georgian Bay*
 4 f. *Algonquin Indians*
 9 g. *Quebec*
 6 h. *Montreal*
 12 i. *Newfoundland*
 11 j. *Acadia*
 5 k. *Iroquois Indians*
 2 l. *Huron Indians*

2. *On your map entitled "Exploration of North America," draw blue lines to show the explorations of Cartier, Champlain, Marquette and Jolliet, and La Salle. Label the lines.*
   (Individual work.)

3. *Write the dates for the following events.*
   a. *First exploration by Jacques Cartier.* **1534**
   b. *Founding of St. Augustine.* **1565**
   c. *Defeat of the Spanish Armada.* **1588**
   d. *Founding of Quebec.* **1608**
   e. *Exploration of Marquette and Jolliet.* **1673**
   f. *La Salle's claim of Louisiana.* **1682**

English Colonies

1550

Settlers arrive at Roanoke Island 1587

1600

Founding of Jamestown, Virginia **1607**

King James Bible authorized 1611

Pilgrims found Plymouth, Massachusetts **1620**

Dutch purchase Manhattan Island 1626

First Puritans arrive in the area of Massachusetts Bay Colony 1628

Boston in Massachusetts Bay Colony founded 1630

First colonists land in Maryland 1634

Hartford and the Connecticut colony founded 1636

Roger Williams founds Providence, Rhode Island 1636

1650

Charter for Carolina granted to eight proprietors 1663

New York and New Jersey established as English colonies 1664

Founding of Charles Town, South Carolina 1670

New Hampshire separates from Massachusetts Bay Colony 1680

Charter for Pennsylvania granted to William Penn **1681**

Founding of Philadelphia, Pennsylvania 1682

First Mennonites arrive at Germantown **1683**

1700

Founding of Delaware 1704

Carolina officially separates into North and South Carolina 1712

James Oglethorpe founds Savannah, Georgia **1733**

1750

"And they found fat pasture and good, and the land was wide, and quiet, and peaceable."

1 Chronicles 4:40

Chapter 6 (pages 108–135)

ENGLISH COLONIES

Chapter Objectives

- To understand why English colonies were established in America.
- To be acquainted with the story of the lost colony at Roanoke.
- To understand the purposes in founding each of the thirteen English colonies, and what the colonies experienced in their early days.
- To see how complete freedom of conscience became established in the English colonies.

To the Teacher

This chapter is foundational to a proper understanding of later United States history. Many interesting details about the early English colonies are omitted for lack of space. These remain for you, the teacher, to discover and bring to class. However, do emphasize the most important facts, such as the founding of Plymouth as a haven for Pilgrims, to make sure the students understand the overall picture.

The English developed a more stable society in America than did the Spanish or French. One reason was that the English settlers had to work in order to succeed in America, rather than relying on easy wealth from gold or furs. Second, many Englishmen had their own goals in coming, such as a desire for freedom; and this provided the initiative necessary to succeed. (The Spanish and French colonies were founded mostly on government initiatives.) Third, families came to English colonies almost from the beginning, which motivated the colonists to seek a settled lifestyle and think of the new land as their home. Fourth, the English were granted freedoms and a certain measure of self-government, in contrast to the absolutist policies in Spanish and French domains.

Exact dates for this period can be somewhat confusing because in 1752, Great Britain adopted the Gregorian ("New Style") calendar as a replacement for the Julian ("Old Style") calendar. This resulted in dropping ten days so that according to the calendar used by the Pilgrims, they arrived at Plymouth on December 16. This book uses New Style dates for this and associated events.

Founding dates for the colonies are also difficult to pinpoint. Dates given in this chapter are the ones generally considered most important, rather than always being either the charter date or the settlement date. This helps the chapter to harmonize with other sources that students may use, as well as with the fifth grade book of this history series.

A few dates merit specific attention. The founding date of Massachusetts Bay Colony is sometimes given as 1628 and sometimes as 1630. Puritans led by John Endecott first settled there in 1628 under the New England Company. In 1629, the

Massachusetts Bay Company was chartered and John Winthrop was appointed governor of the company. Winthrop led the first wave of the great migration to New England in 1630. He took control from Endecott at Salem, and later that year he founded Boston. Therefore, some sources give 1628 as the beginning of Massachusetts Bay Colony because Puritans settled there, while others give 1630 as the beginning because the Massachusetts Bay Company began settlement in that year. This text uses the 1628 date as the beginning of Puritan settlement.

In Carolina, the charter was granted in 1663, but permanent settlement of what became South Carolina did not begin until 1670 at Charles Town (near modern Charleston). However, the northern part had already been settled by people from Virginia and was called Albemarle; this region received its first English governor in 1664. In 1691, the British government placed Albemarle under the authority of a deputy of the Carolina governor at Charles Town (Charleston), and for the first time that area was called North Carolina. Then in 1712, the two areas were officially separated into two colonies, each with its own government. Finally, the Crown bought the shares of seven of the eight original proprietors in 1729. The southern part of South Carolina was then chartered to James Oglethorpe and others as Georgia in 1732.

New Hampshire was chartered in 1680, when a decree of the king made it a royal province. It had been ruled in 1677 that Massachusetts had illegally usurped the territory comprising New Hampshire.

Note on chapter test: There is a single test for Chapters 6 and 7.

Christian Perspectives

- A number of the English colonies were founded by people who sought religious and economic freedom. The freedoms we enjoy today resulted largely from the efforts of these people.
- Because some Europeans saw a chance to begin new societies in America, they tried to create utopias free from European problems. However, a utopian society, either religious or secular, is impossible for fallen humanity to achieve on earth. Government of some kind, based on the use of force, is necessary to order and regulate any society.
- Peaceable relations between white men and Indians could be maintained when the proper respect for others was present. See Romans 12:10, 18; Philippians 2:3; and 1 Peter 2:17.

Further Study

Following are some topics for further research by the teacher or students.

- The colonial beginnings of your home state, if you live in the eastern United States.
- The immigration of your own ancestors. (Did they arrive during colonial times?)

- The early experiences of groups that promoted nonresistance or pacifism.
- The story of the witchcraft mania in Salem, Massachusetts.
- The Indian wars of the early colonies, including the conflicts at Jamestown and at the Massachusetts Bay Colony.
- The lives of the following persons:

John Smith	Roger Williams
John Winthrop	James Oglethorpe
William Bradford	Peter Stuyvesant
Squanto	William Penn

Chapter 6 Quiz

1. On what island was Sir Walter Raleigh's lost colony?

2. Who was the outstanding leader at Jamestown?

3. Who pioneered freedom of conscience in New England?

4. For what people was Maryland intended to be a haven?

5. What nation controlled New York before the English obtained it?

6. The Carolinas were controlled by a group of _____ at first.

7. What did William Penn call his effort at creating an ideal Quaker colony?

8. Who led the way in the founding of Georgia?

Quiz Answers

1. **Roanoke Island**
2. **John Smith**
3. **Roger Williams**
4. **Roman Catholics**
5. **Netherlands**
6. **proprietors**
7. **"Holy Experiment"**
8. **James Oglethorpe**

Answer Key

Focus for Thought (page 115)

1. *For each country below, give the name of the first permanent settlement founded in North America, when it was founded, and where it was located.*

   a. *England* **Jamestown; in 1607; in Virginia**

   b. *Spain (Chapter 4)* **St. Augustine; in 1565; in Florida**

   c. *France (Chapter 5)* **Quebec; in 1608; in Canada**

2. *Who directed the planting of the colony at Roanoke? (Note that the capital of North Carolina is named in his honor.)*
   Sir Walter Raleigh

3. *Briefly describe what happened to the Roanoke colony.*
   Governor White returned to England for supplies, but he could not return promptly because of the war between England and Spain. When he did return, the settlers had disappeared, leaving only a few clues behind.

4. *Describe three of the problems faced by the Jamestown colonists.*
   (Any three.) Many settlers became sick with malaria transmitted by mosquitoes. They had poor food and water. Many of them were unwilling to support themselves by working. They spent their time looking for gold instead.

5. *Explain how each of the following things contributed to the success of the Virginia colony.*

   a. *tobacco*
   John Rolfe introduced the raising of tobacco, which helped Virginia to become financially successful.

   b. *plots of land*
   Having their own land gave the settlers an incentive to be productive.

   c. *families*
   Families were established, which provided reasons for the settlers to think of Virginia as their home.

   d. *burgesses*
   The colonists were allowed to elect burgesses, which added efficiency to the governing of Virginia.

Focus for Thought (page 124)

6. a. *In what year did the Pilgrims arrive in America?*
   in 1620

   b. *Why did they draw up the Mayflower Compact?*
   They wanted the assurance that the settlers would work together for

the common welfare of the group. (The agreement also served as an authority in the absence of a legal government, since they had settled north of where they were authorized by their charter.)

7. *Explain how the goal of the Puritans in New England was different from the goal of the settlers at Jamestown.*
   The Puritans came to find religious freedom and to be the new Israel of God. The settlers at Jamestown came to make profits, especially by finding gold.

8. *For what is Roger Williams remembered today?*
   He was the first to establish a government that granted liberty of conscience to all citizens.

9. *Name the founder of Connecticut, and give the year of its founding.*
   Thomas Hooker; in 1636

10. *How did New Hampshire become a colony?*
    It first belonged to John Mason and was later taken over by Massachusetts. In 1680, New Hampshire received a charter as a separate colony.

11. *What important freedom was granted by the Act of Toleration?*
    freedom of religion for all professing Christians

12. a. *What was the aim of the proprietors who established the Carolina territory?*
    to establish a manorial system and produce specialty items

    b. *What were two major differences between the northern and southern parts of Carolina?*
    Settlers in northern Carolina produced naval stores and tobacco on a small scale, but those in southern Carolina developed large plantations. Northern Carolina had many Moravians, Quakers, and immigrants from Virginia, but southern Carolina had many French Huguenots and other European immigrants.

Focus for Thought (page 130)

13. *How did New Netherland come under English control?*
    In 1664, the Dutch governor was forced to surrender to the English because his countrymen refused to help him fight a fleet of English warships in the harbor of New Amsterdam.

14. a. *What was William Penn's "Holy Experiment"?*
    a colony settled by virtuous people and governed by godly men acting on Christian principles.

    b. *Is it ever possible to create an ideal society on earth? Explain. (See Genesis 3:16–19 and Romans 3:20–23.)*

This will never be possible. Man has a sinful nature, and the use of force will always be necessary to restrain evildoers.

15. *In what year did the Mennonites first arrive in Pennsylvania, and where did they settle?*

in 1683; at Germantown

16. *In what ways did Penn's "Holy Experiment" fail?*

The Quakers found that they could not govern according to New Testament principles. (Force was required to compel obedience to the laws.) The men appointed to manage the colony refused to follow Penn's constitution and instructions.

17. *What were the two reasons for Georgia's founding?*

It was to be a debtors' colony and a buffer between English South Carolina and Spanish Florida.

18. *Give three ways in which Georgia fell short of its idealistic goals.*

(Any three.) Only a few debtors came to Georgia. Without slavery, Georgia could not compete with nearby slave-holding colonies. Rum and other illegal products were smuggled in, so the prohibition against rum could not be enforced. The colonists did not like the laws made by the trustees.

HISTORICAL HIGHLIGHTS (pages 130–134)

A. Matching: People 1

a. *James Oglethorpe*   f. *Sir Walter Raleigh*
b. *John Winthrop*   g. *Squanto*
c. *King James I*   h. *William Bradford*
d. *Lord Baltimore*   i. *William Penn*
e. *Powhatan*

e   1. *Indian chief in Virginia.*
g   2. *Indian who taught the Pilgrims how to live in the wilderness.*
d   3. *Man who founded Maryland as a haven for Catholics.*
a   4. *Trustee leader in the founding of Georgia.*
f   5. *Founder of the lost colony of Roanoke.*
b   6. *Governor of the Massachusetts Bay Colony.*
i   7. *Quaker who received a land grant as payment for a debt.*
h   8. *Governor of the Plymouth Colony.*
c   9. *Authorized Jamestown settlement and a new version of the Bible.*

B. Matching: People 2

a. *Duke of York*
b. *Henry Hudson*
c. *John Cabot*
d. *John Rolfe*
e. *John Smith*
f. *Lord Berkeley*

g. *Peter Stuyvesant*
h. *Roger Williams*
i. *Sir George Carteret*
j. *Thomas Hooker*
k. *Virginia Dare*

j   1. *Man who established a settlement in the Connecticut River valley.*

a   2. *Nobleman who received the Dutch territory of New Netherland.*

c   3. *First explorer to claim North American land for England.*

g   4. *Dutch governor who surrendered New Netherland to the English.*

k   5. *First English child born in America.*

d   6. *Man who married Pocahontas and introduced a new kind of tobacco.*

f, i   7. *Proprietors who sold their land to Quakers (two answers).*

e   8. *Jamestown leader.*

b   9. *Explorer for whom a river and a bay are named.*

h   10. *Founder of Rhode Island, who insisted on freedom of conscience and fled from the Puritans.*

C. Matching: Terms 1

a. *burgesses*
b. *Huguenots*
c. *London Company*
d. *naval stores*
e. *Pilgrims*
f. *private enterprise*
g. *proprietors*

h. *Puritans*
i. *Quakers*
j. *royal colony*
k. *Separatists*
l. *slaves*
m. *trustees*

m   1. *Persons who care for property entrusted to them.*

e, k   2. *People who withdrew from the Church of England and formed congregations of their own (two answers).*

i   3. *People guided by the "Inner Light."*

j   4. *Colony owned and managed by the king.*

b   5. *French Protestants who settled in South Carolina.*

g   6. *Noblemen who received land from the king and who sometimes expected to rent it to men of lower rank.*

a   7. *Representatives who took part in colonial government.*

c   8. *Group of investors who sponsored Jamestown.*

l 9. *Persons who are considered the property of a master.*

h 10. *People who wanted to purify the Church of England from within.*

d 11. *Pine products such as tar and pitch, used to seal cracks in wooden ships.*

f 12. *System in which individuals have their own property and receive the benefits of their own labor.*

D. Matching: Terms 2

a. *buffer*

b. *charter*

c. *gold*

d. *humanitarian*

e. *pacifism*

f. *tobacco*

g. *Act of Toleration*

h. *Frame of Government*

i. *Fundamental Orders*

j. *"Holy Experiment"*

k. Mayflower

l. *Mayflower Compact*

k 1. *Ship that carried Pilgrims and Strangers to America.*

d 2. *Serving to promote human welfare.*

i 3. *First written constitution for an English colony.*

e 4. *Policy of settling disputes by nonviolent means rather than by fighting.*

c 5. *Item sought earnestly by early explorers and colonists.*

h 6. *William Penn's constitution for Pennsylvania.*

a 7. *Territory between two enemy nations that helps to reduce the likelihood of conflict.*

f 8. *Product that brought economic success to Jamestown.*

g 9. *Maryland law granting religious freedom.*

j 10. *William Penn's attempt to have a colony based on Quaker idealism.*

l 11. *Agreement signed by Pilgrims and Strangers to make "just and equal laws."*

b 12. *Legal document granting the right to settle and govern a certain region.*

E. Matching: Places

a. *Carolina*

b. *Connecticut*

c. *Delaware*

d. *Georgia*

e. *Massachusetts Bay Colony*

f. *New Amsterdam*

g. *New England*

h. *New Netherland*

i. *Northwest Passage*

j. *Philadelphia*

k. *Plymouth*

l. *Providence*

b 1. *Location of Thomas Hooker's settlement.*

k 2. *Name of the Pilgrims' settlement.*

h 3. *Dutch territory in America.*

c   4. *Land first settled by the Swedes and the Dutch.*

f   5. *Town that was renamed New York City.*

i   6. *Shortcut to the Orient sought by Hudson and others.*

e   7. *Name of the Puritans' settlement.*

a   8. *Name derived from the Latin form of Charles.*

g   9. *Region including Plymouth, Massachusetts, Rhode Island, Connecticut, and New Hampshire.*

j   10. *City of Brotherly Love.*

l   11. *Name of Roger Williams' settlement.*

d   12. *Colony established as a haven for debtors.*

F. Place Names

Explain how each of the following received its name.

1. *Jamestown*   **named for King James I**

2. *Maryland*   **named for Queen Henrietta Maria**

3. *New York*   **named for the Duke of York**

4. *New Jersey*   **named for the English island of Jersey (in the English Channel)**

5. *Carolina*   **named for King Charles I (from the Latin form of Charles)**

6. *Pennsylvania*   **named for Admiral Penn (from a Latin form meaning "Penn's Woods")**

7. *Georgia*   **named for King George II**

G. Deeper Discussion

1. *What was involved in starting a colony? Consider such items as obtaining legal rights, transportation, planning, and establishing the actual settlement.*
A man or a group obtained a charter from the king. The planners needed money to buy ships and supplies. They had to attract settlers who wanted to go to America. They had to plan for a government and outline the responsibilities of the settlers. When the settlers arrived in America, they had to clear the land, build a fort and houses, plant fields, and learn to live on the land.

2. *Why was the communal system of Jamestown replaced by a system of private enterprise?*
It was discovered that the private enterprise system worked better. People will put forth more effort when they receive personal benefits for their labors.

3. a. *What did the Pilgrims, Puritans, and Quakers gain by emigrating to America?*

political, economic, and religious freedom

b. *Why were these things important to them?*

In England they had been persecuted for their beliefs, but in America they could practice their beliefs freely. They would also have opportunity for economic improvement.

4. *Explain why systems based on European manorialism did not work in America.*

Since plenty of land was available in America, it was altogether unreasonable for a man to rent or till the land of another man.

5. *Pennsylvania and Georgia were founded with idealistic goals. Why did the idealism fail?*

The goals were not based on reality. The real world often falls short of the ideal. Because of the evil nature, mankind in general cannot live up to lofty ideals.

6. *Why did the Pennsylvania settlers prosper from the beginning while those in Virginia had great difficulties?*

The settlers in Pennsylvania were ready to work hard in order to make new homes in the wilderness. By contrast, the first settlers at Jamestown were gentlemen who had never done hard work and who were seeking easy riches.

7. *What character qualities did the Puritans and Quakers have that made them excellent colonists?*

Both groups were industrious and energetic. They endeavored to live morally upright lives, and they were deeply religious people who respected the Word of God.

H. Chronology and Geography

Note: Concerning dates, see "To the Teacher" on pages 72 and 73. Allow reasonable variation for answers under "Reason for Founding."

1. *The following chart shows the thirteen colonies in the order of their founding* by the English. *Copy and complete the chart, noting these specific directions.*
   a. *Use dates from the chapter time line.*
   b. *Fill in two lines for Massachusetts, as indicated.*
   c. *For New Hampshire and Delaware, write "Separated from ___" in the last column (indicating the colonies that they were separated from).*
   d. *For Carolina, write the dates of the original charter and of the separation of North Carolina and South Carolina under "Year Founded." Fill in the other two columns with just one line for Carolina as a whole.*

Colony	Year Founded	Founder	Reason for Founding
Virginia	**1607**	**London Company**	profit
Massachusetts:			
Plymouth	**1620**	**Pilgrims**	religious freedom
Massachusetts Bay	**1628**	**Puritans**	religious freedom
Maryland	**1634**	**Lord Baltimore**	haven for Catholics
Rhode Island	**1636**	**Roger Williams**	religious freedom
Connecticut	**1636**	**Thomas Hooker**	fertile land, more political freedom
Carolina:		**Eight proprietors**	profit-making manorial system
Chartered	**1663**		
Separated	**1712**		
New York	**1664**	**Duke of York**	taken from Dutch
New Jersey	**1664**	**Berkeley and Carteret**	gift from the Duke of York
New Hampshire	**1680**	**John Mason**	separated from Massachusetts
Pennsylvania	**1681**	**William Penn**	religious freedom for Quakers
Delaware	**1704**	**William Penn**	separated from Pennsylvania
Georgia	**1733**	**James Oglethorpe and 21 trustees**	haven for debtors, buffer with Spanish

2. *Trace Map D in the Map Section, and label it "The Thirteen Colonies."*
   a. *Label the thirteen colonies.*
   b. *Label the following early settlements with their names and founding dates: Jamestown—1607, Plymouth—1620, Fort Orange (Albany)—1624, New Amsterdam (New York)—1626, Boston—1630, St. Marys City—1634, Providence—1636, Hartford—1636, Fort Christina (Wilmington)—1638, Charles Town—1670, Philadelphia—1682, and Savannah—1733. (Parentheses indicate the later name of a place.)*
   c. *Use three different colors to show the New England Colonies, the Middle Colonies, and the Southern Colonies. Include a legend to show what the colors represent.*

   (Individual work.) Check the students' maps for accurate labels. See that they have included a legend. The groups are as follows: New England Colonies—New Hampshire, Massachusetts, Connecticut, Rhode Island; Middle Colonies—New York, Pennsylvania, New Jersey, Delaware; Southern Colonies—Maryland, Virginia, North Carolina, South Carolina, Georgia.

SO FAR THIS YEAR (page 135)

Write the letter of the correct answer.

1. *A wet, mild climate found in the Pacific valleys is a _____ climate.*
   a. *humid continental*　　　　c. *humid subtropical*
   b. *Mediterranean*　　　　**d. west coast marine**

2. *The _____ is a rocky region in Canada that curves like a horseshoe around Hudson Bay.*
   a. *Cordillera region*　　　　c. *Great Lakes-St. Lawrence Lowlands*
   b. Canadian Shield　　　　d. *Appalachian Region*

3. *_____ explored the northeastern coast of North America for England in 1497.*
   a. *Henry Hudson*　　　　**c. John Cabot**
   b. *Giovanni da Verrazano*　　　　d. *Jacques Cartier*

4. *The New World was named after _____.*
   a. Amerigo Vespucci　　　　b. *Christopher Columbus*

5. *_____ claimed part of North America for the Netherlands in 1609.*
   a. *Ferdinand Magellan*　　　　c. *Vasco da Gama*
   b. *Vasco de Balboa*　　　　**d. Henry Hudson**

6. *In the system called _____, a lord owned the land and serfs farmed it for him.*
   a. *feudalism*　　　　**c. manorialism**
   b. *capitalism*　　　　d. *democracy*

7. *The _____ was a form of manorialism transplanted to New France.*
   a. *seigneur*　　　　c. *culture area*
   b. seigneurial system　　　　d. *coureurs de bois*

8. *_____ is called the "father of New France."*
   a. *Jacques Cartier*　　　　c. *Giovanni da Verrazano*
   b. *Robert de La Salle*　　　　**d. Samuel de Champlain**

9. *_____ claimed the area drained by the Mississippi River for France.*
   a. Robert de La Salle　　　　c. *Jacques Marquette*
   b. *Louis Jolliet*　　　　d. *Samuel de Champlain*

10. *The Spanish Armada was defeated in the year _____.*
    a. *1565*　　　　c. *1513*
    b. 1588　　　　d. *1539*

11. *The _____ were the Indian tribes who sided with the French.*
    a. *Iroquois*　　　　**b. Huron and Algonquin**

12. *_____ was the leader at Jamestown who helped the colony to survive.*
    a. John Smith　　　　c. *Roger Williams*
    b. *Thomas Hooker*　　　　d. *Lord Berkeley*

7 Colonial Life in America

Timeline:

1600

Jamestown founded **1607**

Pilgrims found Plymouth, Massachusetts **1620**

Settlers come to New Amsterdam (later New York) 1625

Boston settled 1630

1650 Maryland Act of Toleration issued 1649

Founding of Philadelphia, Pennsylvania 1682
First Mennonites arrive at Germantown **1683**

1700

Great Awakening begins 1725

Founding of Georgia, the last colony **1733**

1750 German *Martyrs Mirror* published at Ephrata Cloister 1748–1749

French and Indian War **1754–1763**

1800

"When thou hast eaten and art full, then thou shalt bless the LORD thy God for the good land which he hath given thee."

Deuteronomy 8:10

Chapter 7 (pages 136–159)

COLONIAL LIFE IN AMERICA

Chapter Objectives

- To give an overview of life in America during the colonial period.
- To learn about colonial education in the various regions.
- To show the economic and religious conditions in the various regions.
- To understand the workings of colonial government.
- To learn about the Great Awakening and its effects.

To the Teacher

This chapter is designed to provide a general understanding of early colonial life. If your class is short of time, you may want to omit this chapter and continue with Chapter 8. However, the third section gives an important perspective on religious trends in America, so that section should receive at least some attention.

Note on chapter test: There is a single test for Chapters 6 and 7.

Christian Perspectives

- Men naturally tend to establish a social order based on classes. In Christ, "there is neither Jew nor Greek, there is neither bond nor free" (Galatians 3:28).
- Man's concept of God affects his concept of himself and his pursuits in life. This is shown in the Enlightenment as men tried to reason things out for themselves.
- God has bestowed authority on the civil government to punish evildoers (Romans 13). Though punishments in colonial America may have been severe, they were within the realm of God's delegated authority. However, Christians should not be involved in law enforcement, since the church is not responsible to avenge evil.
- When the moral standards of the Bible are upheld, society benefits. One way in which this was demonstrated was in the blue laws regulating Sunday activities.
- A revival such as the Great Awakening, which was based largely on emotion, often fails to make a genuine change in a person's heart.

Further Study

- Indentured servants.
- Details of colonial life such as building log cabins, hunting wild animals, attending school or church, going fishing or whaling, and punishing criminals.
- Experiences of colonial Mennonites.
- Triangular trade routes.
- The lives of the following persons:

  Christopher Dock   Benjamin Franklin
  Jonathan Edwards   George Whitefield

Chapter 7 Quiz

1. What was the name of the religious revival in the 1700s?

   _____

2. What term is used for the Age of Reason?

   _____

3. What were three main classes of people in colonial days?

   _____

4. Answer these questions by writing *New England, Middle Colonies,* or *South.*
   a. In which of these regions was education emphasized the most?

      _____

   b. In which region was the township system used for granting land?

      _____

   c. In which region was the headright system used for granting land?

      _____

   d. Which region used the county system for local government?

      _____

   e. Which region used the town meeting for local government?

      _____

   f. Which region included the "breadbasket colonies"?

      _____

5. What were three kinds of colonies according to their government by the British?

   _____

6. Which church was dominant in New England? in the South?

   _____

7. What term describes the colonial system of commerce based on three sea routes?

   _____

Quiz Answers

1. **the Great Awakening**
2. **the Enlightenment**
3. **better class, middling class, meaner sort**
4. a. **New England**   d. **South**
   b. **New England**   e. **New England**
   c. **South**   f. **Middle Colonies**
5. **royal colonies, charter colonies, proprietary colonies**
6. **Congregational; Anglican**
7. **triangular trade**

Answer Key

Focus for Thought (pages 144, 145)

1. *List the three classes of people in colonial society. Then write each of the following after the class in which it would fit: bishop, craftsman, governor, plantation owner, small farmer, unskilled laborer.*
   better class: bishop, governor, plantation owner
   middling class: craftsmen, small farmer
   meaner sort: unskilled laborer

2. *How did the clothing of rich people compare with that of poor people?*
   Rich people followed European fashions and dressed in fine clothes made of expensive fabrics. Poor people wore simple clothes made of homespun wool or linsey-woolsey.

3. *Describe colonial education in New England, in the Middle Colonies, and in the South.*
   In New England, all children were required to attend school. Schools emphasized the basics and were strictly disciplined. In the Middle Colonies, people did not consider education as important as did those of New England. There were some laws for public schools, but they were not always enforced. In the South, education was mostly for the children of wealthy plantation owners. They were often taught at home or in old-field schools, and some went to college.

4. *Why was education emphasized more strongly in New England than in the other regions?*
   The Puritans wanted everyone to be able to read the Bible. Education also served to prepare men for the ministry.

5. *How did the Enlightenment affect colonial America?*
   People began to trust in human reasoning and to accept deism. Various people performed numerous experiments to discover things for themselves.

Focus for Thought (page 150)

6. a. *Because of the township system, how did people tend to settle in New England?*

They tended to live in towns or on small farms.

b. *How did the headright system affect the settlement of the South?*

It allowed rich men to establish great plantations.

7. *What was the difference between an apprentice and a journeyman?*

An apprentice worked without pay to learn a trade. A journeyman had completed his apprenticeship and worked for wages.

8. *In what way were the Middle Colonies the "breadbasket colonies"?*

They produced much grain for export.

9. *Explain how a large industry sometimes developed from a man's effort to supply his family's needs.*

A man became skilled in making a certain product for his household. Gradually he began making the product for other people, and thus a large industry developed.

10. *Give two reasons why shipping and manufacturing became important in New England and the Middle Colonies.*

(Any two.) Farming was not very profitable in New England. There were many natural harbors along the coast. Coal and other raw materials were readily available.

11. *Describe the triangular trade routes of colonial days.*

One kind of merchandise was shipped to one place, another kind was picked up and taken to a second place, and then another cargo was loaded to be carried back home. Examples include the trade in rum, slaves, and molasses, and the trade in lumber or grain, sugar, and manufactured goods.

Focus for Thought (pages 156, 157)

12. a. *What are some rights that the English had because of the Magna Carta and the Bill of Rights of 1689?*

the right to trial by jury, the right to bear arms, and protection against cruel and unusual punishments

b. *What written document did each English colony have, which granted the colonists the same privileges that Englishmen had?*

a charter

c. *What did the colonists consider as the duty of the government in relation to these rights?*

The colonists thought the government was obligated to respect their rights.

d. *What command does the Bible give on this point?*

"Let every soul be subject unto the higher powers."

13. *Name the three kinds of colonies, and tell how each kind was governed.*

The royal colony was governed by the king. The proprietary colony was governed by its proprietor. The charter colony was governed on the basis of its charter.

14. *How would the prompt and severe punishments of colonial times have deterred criminals? (See Ecclesiastes 8:11.)*

When punishments are meted out promptly and effectively, criminals (and others) are afraid to commit the same or similar offenses.

15. *Why did many people's religious devotion cool down in the 1700s?*

Because of the Enlightenment, people were ignoring God and looking to man's ideas for guidance. People became wealthier and lost interest in spiritual things while the churches became more worldly. Churches became cold and formal because the church and state were not separate in some colonies.

16. *Name six effects that the Great Awakening had on colonial America.*

(1) It helped to unite the colonies. (2) It divided several churches, including the Congregationalists and the Presbyterians (and the Mennonites). (3) It favored the common people and the popular churches over the established churches (thus bringing about greater separation of church and state). (4) It led to more outreach work, including missionary endeavors to the Indians and the founding of numerous colleges. (5) It set a pattern for later revival movements. (6) It produced only a limited degree of spiritual improvement.

HISTORICAL HIGHLIGHTS (pages 157–159)

A. Matching: Terms 1

a. *apprentice*

b. *bee*

c. *deism*

d. *headright*

e. *hornbook*

f. *journeyman*

g. *plantation*

h. *quitrent*

i. *township*

j. *better class*

k. *breadbasket colonies*

l. *indentured servant*

m. *meaner sort*

n. *middling class*

o. *naval stores*

p. *old-field school*

q. *pig iron*

r. *triangular trade*

h 1. *Money paid yearly to be free from feudal obligations.*

o 2. *Materials used to seal cracks in wooden ships.*

j 3. *Social group of highest rank.*

m 4. *Unskilled persons who did not own land.*

l 5. *Person working to repay the cost of his voyage to America.*

n 6. *Small farmers and craftsmen.*

q 7. *Crude metal as it first comes from a blast furnace.*

d 8. *System in which each person entering a colony received 50 acres (20 ha).*

a 9. *Boy working without pay under a master for a certain time, in order to learn a craft.*

f 10. *One who worked for wages after completing an apprenticeship.*

e 11. *Flat board used for basic teaching in New England schools.*

b 12. *Social occasion where a group worked together at a certain job.*

k 13. *Middle colonies that exported grain.*

i 14. *Land granted to a group of people in New England.*

g 15. *Huge farm in the South.*

r 16. *System of commerce that involves taking one cargo to a certain place, taking a second cargo from there to another place, and taking a third cargo from there back to the starting point.*

c 17. *False idea that God created the world and then withdrew from it.*

p 18. *Institution located on soil worn out by tobacco growing.*

B. Matching: Terms 2

a. *backcountry*
b. *blue laws*
c. *charter colony*
d. *justice of the peace*
e. *legislature*
f. *lower house*
g. *pillory*

h. *proprietary colony*
i. *royal colony*
j. *salutary neglect*
k. *stocks*
l. *tithing-man*
m. *town meeting*
n. *upper house*

m 1. *New England assembly for discussions and voting.*
l 2. *Person who kept people awake in church.*
c 3. *Colony that operated on the basis of its charter.*
n 4. *Part of legislature representing the better class but having little power.*
f 5. *Part of legislature elected by voters and having greater power.*
j 6. *Lax enforcement of laws, which allowed colonial trade to develop.*
d 7. *Official who was a judge and tax collector.*
a 8. *Hilly region of small farms in the South.*
e 9. *Group of people appointed to make laws.*
h 10. *Colony that was supervised by its upper-class owner.*
g 11. *Device used to fasten the head and hands of lawbreakers.*
b 12. *Regulations on Sunday activities.*
i 13. *Colony owned by the king.*
k 14. *Device used to fasten the hands and feet of lawbreakers.*

C. Matching: Names

j 1. *First colonial law requiring all children to attend school.*
d 2. *Puritan church, dominant in New England.*
h 3. *First college in the United States, in New England.*
c 4. *Second college in the United States, in Virginia.*
g 5. *Religious revival in the 1700s.*
b 6. *Noted schoolteacher in colonial Pennsylvania.*
f, i 7. *Leaders of the Great Awakening (two answers).*
e 8. *Age of Reason.*
a 9. *Church of England, dominant in the South.*

a. *Anglican Church*
b. *Christopher Dock*
c. *College of William and Mary*
d. *Congregational Church*
e. *Enlightenment*
f. *George Whitefield*
g. *Great Awakening*
h. *Harvard College*
i. *Jonathan Edwards*
j. *Ole Deluder Satan Act*

D. Deeper Discussion

1. *Modern conditions are quite different from those in colonial days. Yet the Bible says that "there is no new thing under the sun" (Ecclesiastes 1:9). How can these facts be reconciled?*

   Certain kinds of changes take place when natural and spiritual principles are applied in different ways and different settings. But the principles themselves never change, and human nature never changes. Thus, while physical things change, there is no change in the fundamental things that really matter.

2. a. *Why are class distinctions common among men?*

   People are naturally mindful of their status in relation to others. Those who are born into aristocratic families are considered in a higher class, and so are those with much wealth, power, or land. People without these things are considered in a lower class.

   b. *How should the Christian view class distinctions?*

   To the Christian, all people are equal before God, and all have an equal need of salvation. All Christians are one in Christ; and though there may be differences in wealth or ability, Christians will have no class distinctions if they live the Bible way.

3. *How did the Enlightenment lead to scientific inquiry?*

   Educated people in the Age of Reason believed in deism, the idea that God had created the world and then withdrawn from it. Since they thought God did not reveal things to man, they began trying to find out things for themselves by experimentation and human reasoning; that is, by scientific inquiry.

4. *What is erroneous about deism?*

   Deists believe that God does not sovereignly overrule in the world and does not intervene in the affairs of men. The Bible teaches that God does overrule and that He does intervene in the affairs of His created world. See Psalm 2; Acts 2:23; 4:24–31; 1 Corinthians 2:7, 8.

5. *How did the Bible affect colonial living?*

   It helped people to set a higher standard of right and wrong. The people experienced God's blessings as they followed His principles. The presence of a Bible standard probably helped to reduce crime.

6. *How did the Great Awakening fall short of a true revival?*

   True revival changes a person's heart and leads to godly living. In the Great Awakening, many "conversions" were only emotional experiences that produced no long-lasting change for the better.

E. Chronology and Geography

1. *Find the number of years between each of the following events, using the time line at the beginning of the chapter.*
    a. *The founding of Jamestown, the first successful English colony, and the Mennonites' arrival in Pennsylvania.*
       76 years
    b. *The Mennonites' arrival in Pennsylvania and the founding of Georgia.*
       50 years
    c. *The Mennonites' arrival in Pennsylvania and the beginning of the Great Awakening.*
       42 years
    d. *The Mennonites' arrival in Pennsylvania and the publishing of the* Martyrs Mirror.
       65 or 66 years
    e. *The printing of the* Martyrs Mirror *and the beginning of the French and Indian War.*
       5 or 6 years
2. *Explain how geography contributed to different ways of making a living in colonial America.*
    Because the Atlantic Coastal Plain was wider in the South and the soil was well suited for farming, crops could be raised efficiently on large plantations. The mild climate in the South allowed crops such as tobacco and cotton to be raised. In New England, much of the soil was poor and the climate was harsh, so farms were small. Good harbors there led to the development of fishing, shipping, and trade, as well as the growth of large cities. The Middle Colonies had a combination of farmland and large cities.

8 British North America

1. BRITISH AND FRENCH RIVALRY

    The Basis for Rivalry

    The Colonial Wars

2. THE FRENCH AND INDIAN WAR

    Conflict in the Ohio River Valley

    British Defeats, French Victories

    British Victories, French Defeats

3. NONRESISTANT PEOPLE DURING
    THE COLONIAL PERIOD

    Mennonite Immigration

    The Quakers and the Mennonites

    War Experiences of Nonresistant People

1680

First Mennonites arrive in America **1683**

King William's War begins 1689

Treaty of Ryswick ends King William's War 1697

1700

Queen Anne's War begins 1702   Treaty of Utrecht ends Queen Anne's War 1713

1720

1740

King George's War begins 1744

Treaty of Aix-la-Chapelle ends King George's War 1748
German *Martyrs Mirror* published at Ephrata Cloister 1749

Braddock defeated at Fort Duquesne 1755   Washington defeated at Fort Duquesne; French and Indian War begins **1754**

Jacob Hochstetler massacre 1757
Quebec falls to the British 1759   Fort Louisbourg and Fort Duquesne fall to the British 1758

1760   New France surrendered to the British 1760

Treaty of Paris ends the French and Indian War **1763**

1780

*"Yea, the LORD shall give that which is good; and
our land shall yield her increase."*

Psalm 85:12

Unit 3: Times of Founding, 1650–1790
Chapter 8 (pages 160–181)

BRITISH NORTH AMERICA

Chapter Objectives
- To understand the early conflicts that led to the French and Indian War.
- To see various effects of the wars between France and Great Britain.
- To learn the reasons that Swiss Mennonites emigrated to Pennsylvania, the details of their coming, and the locations of their first settlements.
- To compare and contrast the Mennonites and the Quakers.
- To understand what nonresistant people experienced during the period of the French and Indian War, and how they expressed their nonresistance.

To the Teacher
Wars are history and therefore need to be discussed, but it is important to maintain a Biblical perspective on these events. The purpose of this chapter is to understand the issues surrounding the wars between the French and the British; to comprehend the broader operations in the conflicts without making war seem glorious; to mention details in a general way, thus avoiding sensationalism or an emphasis on brutality; and to understand how the nonresistant people fared during the wars. The discussion of the colonial wars and the French and Indian War provides a context for the discussion of Mennonite and Amish immigration and experiences in colonial America.

Note on chapter test: There is a single test for Chapters 8 and 9.

Christian Perspectives
- The kingdoms of the world are beastlike, engaging in power struggles that lead to fighting (Daniel 7).
- Wars have a bearing on the course of history and must be so recognized. However, warfare must be understood as an ungodly expression of selfishness and hatred (James 4:1). Wars will always exist as long as unregenerate man is on the earth (Matthew 24:6).
- In His sovereignty, God saw fit to establish the British on North American territory formerly occupied by the French (Daniel 4:17).
- Without violating man's will, God is able to move men (like William Pitt) to make decisions that have far-reaching consequences (Proverbs 21:1).
- Those who have wealth need to share it with others (1 Timothy 6:18), as the Dutch Mennonites did. The practice of mutual aid within the brotherhood is taught in 2 Corinthians 8:13–15 and Galatians 6:2, 10.
- According to John 18:36; Romans 13:1–7; 2 Corinthians 6:14–18; and other

Scriptures, the New Testament Christian finds himself at variance with the world and its kingdoms. He will naturally be a citizen of a worldly kingdom, but his higher loyalty is to the eternal kingdom of Jesus Christ. Therefore, people who live by those principles often come into conflict with civil governments and with others who do not understand them (John 15:18–25). The Christian will not take part in the wars of the kingdoms of this world or vote for the leaders of those kingdoms.

- Earthly governments cannot be operated consistently by the principles of Christ's kingdom. They are responsible to "execute wrath upon him that doeth evil," whereas Christ's command to His followers is "that ye resist not evil" (Romans 13:4; Matthew 5:39).

Further Study

- The colonial wars. (*A Half-Century of Conflict* and *Montcalm and Wolfe,* by Francis Parkman, give the history of this time.)
- The French and Indian War, and experiences of nonresistant people in that period.
- The following persons and groups:

  Radisson and Groseilliers   Prince Rupert

  Hudson's Bay Company   the Acadians

Quiz Answers

1. **furs (profits from fur trading)**
2. **Treaty of Utrecht**
3. **Acadians**
4. **France and England both wanted to control North America.**
5. **Quebec**
6. **Treaty of Paris, 1763**
7. **Quakers**
8. **to live in peace as "the quiet in the land" and to enjoy the fruits of their labors**
9. **They took land from the Indians and killed a number of them. They demanded military protection against the Indians.**
10. **They arranged for the publishing of the German *Martyrs Mirror* (and the *Ausbund*).**

Chapter 8 Quiz

1. What were the British seeking when they began taking an active interest in the Hudson Bay region?

   _____

2. What treaty in 1713 granted much French territory to the British and was followed by thirty years of peace?

   _____

3. What people were forced to leave their homes because they refused to promise allegiance to the British king?

   _____

4. What was the basic reason for the French and Indian War?

   _____

5. Name the place where the decisive battle of the French and Indian War was fought.

   _____

6. Give the name and date of the treaty that formally ended the French and Indian War.

   _____

7. Name the peace-loving people who controlled the early Pennsylvania government.

   _____

8. Why did the Swiss Mennonites immigrate to Pennsylvania?

   _____

9. How did the Scotch-Irish make trouble for the peaceful colony of Pennsylvania?

   _____

10. How did the Mennonites reinforce their stand on nonresistance before the French and Indian War?

   _____

Answer Key

Focus for Thought (page 166)

1. *Name and describe three things that caused conflict between the British and the French in North America.*

   (Any three.) (1) Conflicting claims: both nations competed for control of North America (and for world dominance). (2) The fur trade: Both nations wanted to enrich themselves through the highly profitable trade in beaver furs. (3) Alliances with the Indians: The French were allies of the Huron and Algonquin, and the British were allies of the Iroquois. These Indian tribes were at enmity with each other. (4) Religious and political differences: The British were Protestants; the French were Catholics who viewed the British as heretics. The British prided themselves in their liberty and constitutional government; the French followed a policy of absolutism, with power centered in the king.

2. *How did Great Britain develop the fur trade around the Hudson Bay?*

   When the French dealt unfairly with two fur traders who wanted to trade in the Hudson Bay region, the traders turned to the English. Prince Rupert received a charter for the Hudson's Bay Company, which established fur trading posts in the Hudson Bay region.

3. *Write* Great Britain *or* France *to answer each question.*
   a. *Which had more American territory under her control?*   **France**
   b. *Which had more people in America?*   **Great Britain**
   c. *Which one's colonies were better united?*   **France**

4. *What was the general result of the colonial wars from 1689 to 1748, especially the first and last ones?*

   They all involved much fighting and bloodshed, but they did little to solve the problems that caused the wars.

5. *How did the Treaty of Utrecht benefit the British and help them to prosper?*

   The British received Newfoundland, Acadia (Nova Scotia), much of present-day New Brunswick, and the territories taken from the Hudson's Bay Company. During the time of peace that followed, they built up their merchant fleet and traded freely with the colonies. Georgia was established during this time to guard the southern boundary of the colonies. (Not in the text: This gave the British better access to sea routes than before.)

6. *Why were the French Acadians forcibly moved to other locations?*

   They refused to promise allegiance to Great Britain.

Focus for Thought (page 170)

7. *What was the result of General Braddock's defeat at Fort Duquesne?*
The frontier in western Pennsylvania and in Virginia was left unprotected and open to attacks by the Indians.

8. *How did William Pitt transform the British war effort?*
He strengthened the British side by borrowing great sums of money, choosing better generals, and persuading the colonists to volunteer more soldiers.

9. *What troubles were weakening New France at this time?*
The French governor disagreed with the army general over how the war should be conducted. The governor and the treasurer were involved in corruption; they gave stolen presents to their Indian allies to keep them loyal.

10. a. *Give the location and date of the decisive battle in the French and Indian War.*
at Quebec on September 13, 1759

    b. *Give the name and date of the treaty that officially ended the French and Indian War.*
the Treaty of Paris, 1763

11. *What did the British gain as a result of the French and Indian War?*
all the land from the Hudson Bay south to Florida and west to the Mississippi (except New Orleans)

Focus for Thought (page 174)

12. *How were the motives of the Mennonites different from the motives of the Puritans and Quakers for coming to America?*
The Mennonites did not come to establish a utopia as the other groups did. The Mennonites simply wanted to live in peace as "the quiet in the land" and to enjoy the fruits of their labors.

13. *Though most Mennonites and Amish were very poor, few of them had to become indentured servants in America. How did God provide for them?*
The Mennonites in the Netherlands established the Commission for Foreign Needs, which helped many. Individual congregations in Europe and America donated money.

14. *Compare the Mennonites with the Quakers*
    a. *in their beliefs.*
Both believed in freedom of conscience, simplicity in dress and lifestyle, refusal to swear oaths, and refusal to take part in war. Quakers said they were guided by the "Inner Light," whereas the Mennonites accepted the Bible as their guide for life.

b. *in their preferred place of settlement.*

Quakers settled in cities, but Mennonites settled on farms.

c. *in their involvement with government.*

Quakers held government offices, but most Mennonites did not take part in government.

15. *How did it come about that the Quakers lost control of the Pennsylvania Assembly?*

The Quakers refused to provide a military force to protect the Scotch-Irish settlers on the frontier. Finally in 1756, the Quakers lost control of the Assembly even though they were supported by the votes of the Mennonites during an election.

16. *Before the French and Indian War, what two things did the Mennonites do to help maintain their belief in nonresistance?*

They had the *Ausbund* published. They had the *Martyrs Mirror* translated and published in German.

17. *How did nonresistant people put their beliefs to practice during the French and Indian War?*

They suffered rather than killing the Indians. They did not take part in the fighting. They helped refugees fleeing because of frontier raids.

HISTORICAL HIGHLIGHTS (pages 175–179)

A. Matching: People

a. *Dutch Mennonites*

b. *General Braddock*

c. *George Washington*

d. *Jacob Hochstetler*

e. *James Wolfe*

f. *Montcalm*

g. *Peter Miller*

h. *Prince Rupert*

i. *Radisson and Groseilliers*

j. *Scotch-Irish*

k. *William Penn*

l. *William Pitt*

c   1. *American officer who was sent to Fort Duquesne.*

l   2. *Prime minister of Great Britain during the French and Indian War.*

i   3. *French traders who helped to start British fur trading in the Hudson Bay region.*

a   4. *People who helped Mennonites come to America.*

f   5. *French general in the French and Indian War.*

k   6. *Man who founded Pennsylvania.*

h   7. *Nobleman who established British fur trading in the Hudson Bay region.*

e   8. *British general who defeated the French at Quebec.*

d   9. *Amish man who would not kill Indians.*

g   10. *Man in charge of translating and publishing the German* Martyrs Mirror.

j   11. *People who settled in the frontier regions and made trouble with the Indians.*

b   12. *British general defeated at Fort Duquesne.*

B. Matching: Places

a. *Acadia*

b. *British Empire*

c. *Ephrata Cloister*

d. *Fort Duquesne*

e. *Fort Louisbourg*

f. *Germantown*

g. *Hudson Bay*

h. *Northkill*

i. *Ohio River valley*

j. *Palatinate*

k. *Quebec*

l. *Rupert's Land*

i   1. *Area over which conflicting claims led to the French and Indian War.*

d   2. *French fort built where Pittsburgh now stands.*

k   3. *Site of the decisive battle of the French and Indian War.*

a   4. *Area in Nova Scotia from which the British removed French Canadians.*

g   5. *Body of water around which the British developed their fur trade.*

b   6. *All the territory ruled by Great Britain.*

e   7. *French fortress on Cape Breton Island.*

c   8. *Place where the* Martyrs Mirror *was translated and printed.*

l   9. *Another name for the Hudson Bay region.*

j   10. *German region to which the Swiss Anabaptists moved before coming to America.*

f   11. *Town in Pennsylvania where Mennonites first settled.*

h   12. *Amish settlement in Pennsylvania.*

C. Matching: Dates

l   1. *Treaty of Paris.*

g   2. *Beginning of French and Indian War.*

c   3. *Four wars between France and England.*

k   4. *Battle of Quebec.*

h   5. *Braddock's attack on Fort Duquesne; Acadians forced to move.*

e   6. *Treaty of Utrecht ends Queen Anne's War.*

a   7. *Arrival of British expedition in the Hudson Bay.*

f   8. *Treaty of Aix-la-Chapelle ends King George's War.*

j   9. *Hochstetler family massacred; William Pitt becomes prime minister.*

d   10. *Treaty of Ryswick ends King William's War.*

a. *1668*

b. *1683*

c. *1689–1763*

d. *1697*

e. *1713*

f. *1748*

g. *1754*

h. *1755*

i. *1756*

j. *1757*

k. *1759*

l. *1763*

i 11. *Quakers lose control of Pennsylvania Assembly.*

b 12. *First Mennonites arrive in Pennsylvania.*

D. Matching: Names and Terms

a. *Commission for Foreign Needs*   g. Martyrs Mirror
b. *corruption*   h. *Queen Anne's War*
c. *frontier raid*   i. *"quiet in the land"*
d. *Hudson's Bay Company*   j. *Treaty of Paris*
e. *King George's War*   k. *Treaty of Utrecht*
f. *King William's War*   l. *utopia*

d 1. *Company established to develop the fur trade in Rupert's Land.*

j 2. *Agreement in 1763 that officially ended England's conflict with France.*

g 3. *Book published by Pennsylvania Mennonites to encourage nonresistance.*

e 4. *Third colonial war, 1744–1748.*

c 5. *Sudden attack on an English settlement by French and Indians.*

k 6. *Treaty that ended Queen Anne's War.*

b 7. *Misuse of a public office for the sake of illegal gain.*

l 8. *Ideal society desired by the Puritans and Quakers.*

a 9. *Dutch Mennonite organization that aided emigrating Swiss Mennonites.*

f 10. *First colonial war, 1689–1697.*

i 11. *Status desired by Mennonites and Amish in America.*

h 12. *Second colonial war, 1702–1713.*

E. Multiple Choice

Write the letter of the best answer.

1. *How did Great Britain receive the opportunity to establish its influence in Canada?*

   a. Two angered French traders told the British about the opportunities there.

   b. *France failed to develop the fur trade in northern Canada.*

   c. *Henry Hudson had explored the St. Lawrence region for Great Britain.*

   d. *The Indians around Lake Superior preferred to trade with the British.*

2. *Why was beaver fur in such demand?*

   a. *There was an abundance of fur.*

   b. *Women's styles had recently changed.*

   c. *The Indians made most of their clothing from beaver fur.*

   d. Beaver hats were fashionable in Europe.

3. *Which one of the following statements best explains why the Acadians were forced to move?*

a. *Many British colonists began moving into Nova Scotia.*

b. *The Acadians rebelled against the British.*

c. The Acadians were not willing to become British subjects.

d. *The Acadians refused to give up their customs, language, and property.*

4. *What makes the French and Indian War so important in the history of North America?*

a. *The Indians were finally subdued by the British.*

b. *The British were finally subdued by the French.*

c. The French were removed as a power in North America.

d. *All of Canada became Protestant.*

5. *Why was it almost certain that war would break out between the British and the French in North America?*

a. *Both wanted the Indians to support them.*

b. Both were determined to control North America.

c. *The British and the French were traditional enemies.*

d. *The English were Protestant but the French were Catholic.*

6. *What was the strongest factor that determined the outcome of the wars between Britain and France?*

a. *the Indian allies*   c. *the number of people*

b. *the strength of the armies*   **d. God's overruling hand**

7. *How did the French Canadians respond to their new English rulers?*

a. They obeyed English laws but remained French at heart.

b. *They returned to France within a year after the Treaty of Paris was signed.*

c. *They did away with all government corruption.*

d. *They welcomed the English as liberators.*

8. *Why did the British authorities forbid settlers to cross the Appalachian Mountains?*

a. *They wanted to prove their authority over the colonists.*

b. *They were afraid the colonies would stir up more trouble with the French.*

c. They wanted to keep peace with the Indians.

d. *They thought the land west of the Appalachians should belong to the Indians.*

9. *Which of the following was* not *a reason for Quaker immigration to Pennsylvania?*

a. *to have religious freedom*

b. *to have economic opportunity*

c. *to participate in the "Holy Experiment"*

d. to provide a haven for destitute Mennonites

10. *Which religious body was most directly involved in the emigration of the Palatinate Mennonites?*
    a. *French Catholics*
    c. Dutch Mennonites
    b. *English Quakers*
    d. *Scotch-Irish Presbyterians*
11. *Which of the following was* not *a reason for Mennonite immigration?*
    a. to establish an ideal government   c. *for economic opportunity*
    b. *for religious freedom*   d. *to live in peace and quietness*
12. *For what* two *reasons were the Scotch-Irish displeased with the Quaker government?*
    a. *The Quakers sent them to the frontier.*
    b. The Quakers showed equal respect to Indians and white men.
    c. The Quakers refused to protect them by armed force.
    d. *The Quakers refused to let them settle where they wished.*
13. *How were the Quakers able to maintain control of the Pennsylvania Assembly until 1756?*
    a. *by outnumbering the other settlers*
    b. *by the support of Scotch-Irish voters*
    c. *by order of King Charles II*
    d. by the support of German voters, including Mennonites
14. *Which one of the following was* not *an effect of the French and Indian War on the nonresistant people?*
    a. *printing the* Martyrs Mirror
    b. suffering for refusal to help General Braddock
    c. *helping refugees from the frontier*
    d. *massacre by the Indians*

F. Mennonites and Quakers

Write whether each item is associated with the Mennonites (*M*), with the Quakers (*Q*), with both groups (*B*), or with neither group (*N*).

B   1. *persecuted in Europe*
B   2. *freedom of conscience*
M   3. *farmers*
Q   4. *artisans*
B   5. *found economic opportunity*
Q   6. *"Inner Light"*
Q   7. *merchants*
M   8. *"the quiet in the land"*
Q   9. *Philadelphia*
M 10. *German*

M 11. *Lancaster*
Q 12. *held government offices*
M 13. *Skippack-Franconia*
B 14. *nonparticipation in war*
N 15. *Indian fighters*
Q 16. *English*
N 17. *Scotch-Irish*
Q 18. *"Holy Experiment"; attempted utopia*
B 19. *refusal of oaths*
B 20. *simplicity*

G. Deeper Discussion

1. *Is there any connection between the French defeat and the corruption in the French-Canadian government? Explain your answer.*

   Yes. Officials in the French-Canadian government did not agree on important issues, they were dishonest, and they bribed their Indian allies to keep them loyal. Corruption always weakens a nation and makes defeat more likely in time of war.

2. *Compare the reasons for the immigration of the Quakers, Mennonites, and Scotch-Irish by answering the following questions.*

   a. *What did all three groups have in common?*

   All three groups emigrated for religious freedom and economic opportunity.

   b. *What were the major differences?*

   The Quakers wanted to establish a government based on New Testament principles of love and peace. The Mennonites were also a peace-loving people, but they refrained from holding offices in civil government. The Scotch-Irish had no special interest in peace; they were ready to fight and kill in order to get what they wanted.

3. a. *Why did the Mennonites vote in the 1700s?*

   The Mennonites voted to help the Quaker leaders stay in power so that the liberties granted by Penn's charter would not be lost.

   b. *In what way did they succeed by voting?*

   They succeeded in that they helped to keep the Quakers in power until 1756.

   c. *In what way did they fail?*

   They failed in that the Quakers lost control of the Assembly in spite of the Mennonites' votes. Also, they violated the principle of separation of church and state.

4. *Read Matthew 5:38–48 and Romans 12:14–21. From these verses, explain why it is wrong for Christians to take part in warfare.*

   In Matthew, Jesus taught that we must not resist evil by force and that we need to love our enemies. Warfare violates both of these commands. According to the passage in Romans, Christians are not to take vengeance on their enemies, for God will do that. Rather, they should return good for evil.

5. *Read Romans 13:1–7 and 1 Timothy 2:1, 2. Observe that although Christians should not take part in government, they still have certain duties to the government. Name at least two of these duties.*

Christians should obey the government, pay taxes, and pray for their rulers.

H. Chronology and Geography

1. *Trace Map C again, and label it "European Claims in North America About 1755."*
   a. *Use different colors to show British, French, Spanish, and Russian claims at this time. Add a legend to the map.*
   b. *Label the following early settlements: St. Augustine, Santa Fe, San Diego, San Francisco, Quebec, Montreal, New Orleans, Jamestown, Boston, New York City, and Philadelphia.*
   (Individual work.)

2. a. *Why was the location of Fort Duquesne so important to both the British and the French?*
   It was located at the gateway between the Ohio River valley to the west and the British colonies in the east.
   b. *In what way did geography affect this importance?*
   It was geographically important because it stood at the meeting point of the Allegheny and Monongahela Rivers. These rivers gave access to northern Pennsylvania, to Niagara, and to eastern Pennsylvania (via the Susquehanna River); and the Ohio River gave access to the Mississippi.

3. a. *What two major North American waterways did the French control?*
   the St. Lawrence River and the Mississippi River
   b. *How did this give them an advantage over the British?*
   In this way they could control the trade in furs and other resources from the vast territory drained by these rivers.

4. *How did the geography of Quebec help to protect the city against attack?*
   Quebec was situated on a high cliff along the St. Lawrence River, which was the main route to the city. Attackers had to get to the top of the cliff somehow, either by climbing it or by finding a way around it.

So Far This Year (page 180)

A. Matching: Terms

b 1. *Aristocracy; upper-class people.*

e 2. *Person working to repay the cost of coming to America.*

n 3. *Colony governed by the king.*

l 4. *Colony owners hoping to rent land to people of lower rank.*

k 5. *Colony governed by a proprietor.*

i 6. *Small farmers and craftsmen.*

d 7. *Colony operating on the basis of its charter.*

c 8. *Legal document from the king, granting the right to settle a certain region and establish a government there.*

j 9. *People who withdrew from the Church of England and moved to America.*

m 10. *People who wanted to purify the Church of England from within.*

a 11. *Maryland law granting religious freedom.*

h 12. *Unskilled laborers who did not own land.*

g 13. *Agreement signed by Pilgrims and Strangers to make "just and equal laws."*

f 14. *Branch of government that makes laws.*

a. *Act of Toleration*
b. *better class*
c. *charter*
d. *charter colony*
e. *indentured servant*
f. *legislature*
g. *Mayflower Compact*
h. *meaner sort*
i. *middling class*
j. *Pilgrims*
k. *proprietary colony*
l. *proprietors*
m. *Puritans*
n. *royal colony*

B. Names

Give the names of the persons or things described.

John Smith — 15. *Leader of Jamestown who established a policy of "no work, no food."*

Roger Williams — 16. *Founder of Rhode Island, who insisted on freedom of conscience.*

Lord Baltimore — 17. *Founder of Maryland.*

William Penn — 18. *Quaker who received a land grant as payment for a debt.*

James Oglethorpe — 19. *Trustee leader in the founding of Georgia.*

Jonathan Edwards and George Whitefield — 20. *Leaders of the colonial religious revival (two men).*

Great Awakening — 21. *Religious revival in the 1700s.*

Enlightenment 22. *Age of Reason.*

Anglican Church 23. *Church of England; official church in the South.*

Congregational Church 24. *Puritans; official church in New England.*

C. Dates

Give the date of each event.

1681 25. *Pennsylvania received a charter.*

1620 26. *Plymouth was founded.*

1733 27. *Georgia was founded.*

1607 28. *Jamestown was founded.*

9   The American Revolution

1760

French and Indian War ends **1763**

1765

Townshend Acts 1767

1770   Boston Massacre 1770

Tea Act; Boston Tea Party 1773

Coercive Acts; First Continental Congress 1774

Battles of Lexington and Concord,
and Bunker Hill   1775   **1775**   Second Continental Congress; Olive Branch Petition 1775

Common Sense published; Declaration of Independence adopted
     1776

Battles of Germantown and Saratoga 1777

Americans camp at Valley Forge
over winter   1777–1778   France signs an alliance treaty; George Rogers Clark
     conquers the West   1778

1780

British surrender at Yorktown 1781

Treaty of Paris ends Revolutionary War **1783**

1785

*"From whence come wars and fightings among
you? come they not hence, even of your lusts that war
in your members?"*

James 4:1

Chapter 9 (pages 182–201)

THE AMERICAN REVOLUTION

Chapter Objectives

- To learn about the events leading up to the American Revolution.
- To study the general course of the Revolution, with emphasis on the most important events of the war.
- To see what issues faced the nonresistant people before and during the Revolution, and to understand how they dealt with those issues.

To the Teacher

Be sure to present this chapter impartially, not only from the Christian perspective of noninvolvement in political affairs but also from the standpoint of accuracy. It is incorrect and unfair to extol either the Americans or the British, and condemn the other side. Students need to gain an understanding of these troubling times, but they must not develop a spirit of patriotism or an improper admiration for the "heroes" of the American Revolution.

Remind students that Mennonites of that time viewed the American patriots as rebels and the revolutionary governments as illegal. Today we view this in the context of God's sovereignty, so we can see how something good came out of the Revolution. But in those days, many nonresistant people felt that they should obey the government they had promised to obey—the British government.

In teaching the course of the war, aim to teach the fundamental facts of the conflict without covering all the details. Students do not need to become immersed in the horrors of war, but they should have a general idea of its causes and its general progression.

Note on chapter test: There is a single test for Chapters 8 and 9.

Christian Perspectives

- The successful colonial revolution was a result of the overruling hand of God in British and American affairs.
- According to Romans 13:1–7, Christians of colonial times needed to be subject to Great Britain—though of course not to the point of taking up arms. Once the United States was established, those Christians needed to become subject to the new nation. It required God's wisdom and the collective voice of the church to determine when to make this shift.
- Nonresistant Christians do not give special honor to military leaders or glory in their victories.
- War disrupts and demoralizes a people.

Further Study

- The Loyalists versus the patriots.
- The Declaration of Independence.

- Specific battles of the Revolutionary War, such as the ones at Saratoga and Yorktown.
- The experiences of nonresistant people.
- The American Revolution as compared with the French Revolution.

Chapter 9 Quiz

1. Give the slogan repeated by the colonists that summarized their discontent.

_____

2. Why did Parliament pass the Sugar Act, the Stamp Act, and the Townshend Acts?

_____

3. What name was given to those who wanted to be independent from Great Britain?

_____

4. What pamphlet was an effective piece of propaganda in favor of independence?

_____

5. Who was placed in charge of the American army?

_____

6. What nation allied itself with the new United States?

_____

7. What was the main reason for American victory against great odds?

_____

8. What name was given to those who wanted to remain subjects of Great Britain?

_____

Quiz Answers

1. **"Taxation without representation is tyranny."**
2. **to raise revenue from the colonies**
3. **patriots (or Whigs)**
4. ***Common Sense***
5. **George Washington**
6. **France**
7. **the overruling hand of God**
8. **Loyalists (or Tories)**

Answer Key

Focus for Thought (page 188)

1. *Name the law that each description refers to.*

   a. *It stated that lands west of the Appalachians were closed to settlement.*

   the Proclamation of 1763

   b. *It said that the tax on sugar must be strictly enforced.*

   the Sugar Act

   c. *It restricted colonies from issuing paper money and said that all debts must be paid in gold or silver coins.*

   the Currency Act

   d. *It required the colonists to buy stamps for all printed matter, including legal documents.*

   the Stamp Act

   e. *It required the colonists to provide lodging and supplies for British soldiers.*

   the Quartering Act

2. *Why did the colonists especially oppose laws such as the Stamp Act?*

   These laws required the colonists to pay taxes that they had not approved.

3. *What did the colonists do to keep from paying the taxes levied on certain goods?*

   They boycotted those goods (refused to buy them).

4. a. *Who started the events on March 5, 1770, which led to the Boston Massacre?*

   a group of rowdy men and boys from Boston

   b. *Who received the blame for it?*

   the British soldiers

5. *Why were the Committees of Correspondence formed?*

   to spread information about British violations of colonial rights

6. a. *Why were the Coercive Acts passed?*

   to punish Boston for the Boston Tea Party

   b. *What did the colonists call them?*

   Intolerable Acts

Focus for Thought (page 194)

7. a. *At the First Continental Congress, how did some delegates reason that Parliament had no authority over the colonies?*

   They said that since Parliament did not have the right to tax the colonies, it had no authority over them at all.

   b. *What was wrong with their reasoning? (See Romans 13:1, 6, 7.)*

   The Bible says that all people should be subject to the established

civil government. Citizens are to pay tribute (taxes) and give honor to those in authority.

8. *Name the document that officially declared American independence, and give the date when it was adopted.*
the Declaration of Independence; on July 4, 1776

9. *What things made the war discouraging for the Americans in 1776 and 1777?*
The Americans lost New York City and then Philadelphia to the British. They were also defeated at the Battle of Germantown. The American army spent a miserable winter at Valley Forge.

10. *In what two ways was the victory at Saratoga a turning point in the war?*
The victory made it appear that the Americans could actually win the war. It gave hope that the French might help the Americans.

11. *What events led to Cornwallis's surrender?*
Cornwallis's army was trapped when a French fleet blockaded Yorktown and Washington's army attacked by land at the same time. After a fierce battle, Cornwallis surrendered his entire army to Washington.

12. a. *What did the British acknowledge in the Treaty of Paris?*
that the former thirteen colonies were now "free, sovereign, and independent states"
b. *What territory did the United States include at that time?*
all the land south of Canada (except Florida) and east of the Mississippi River

Focus for Thought (page 198)

13. *Name six religious groups opposed to war at the time of the American Revolution.*
Mennonites, Amish, Quakers, Dunkers (also known as German Baptists or Brethren), Schwenkfelders, Moravians

14. *Give two reasons why the nonresistant people did not sympathize with the patriots.*
(Any two.) They cared little about the protests over taxes in far-off Massachusetts. They considered it wrong to revolt against the British government. They were afraid that a patriot government might take away their freedoms. They feared war and wanted to avoid it as much as possible.

15. a. *What three main issues faced the nonresistant people during the Revolution?*
fines, war taxes, and the Oath of Allegiance

b. *How did they respond to these issues?*

Some nonresistant people paid the fines and taxes, but others refused. None of them took the Oath of Allegiance.

16. *How did the nonresistant people practice the Bible principle of showing love to all men?*

They cared for sick and wounded soldiers. They gave food and other aid to soldiers who came to their doors, even though it was risky to do so.

17. *How did the Revolution serve to refine the nonresistant churches?*

It constrained the members of these churches either to be totally committed to their church or to give up their church membership. They withdrew completely from politics and became the "quiet in the land."

HISTORICAL HIGHLIGHTS (pages 198–200)

A. Matching: People

a. *Charles Townshend*

b. *General Cornwallis*

c. *General Gage*

d. *George III*

e. *George Grenville*

f. *George Rogers Clark*

g. *George Washington*

h. *Paul Revere*

i. *Pontiac*

j. *Samuel Adams*

k. *Thomas Jefferson*

l. *Thomas Paine*

b 1. *British officer who surrendered at Yorktown.*

g 2. *Patriot general in command of the entire American army.*

i 3. *Leader of an Indian uprising in the Ohio region.*

d 4. *King of Great Britain.*

k 5. *Writer of the Declaration of Independence.*

j 6. *Patriot leader who helped organize Committees of Correspondence.*

a 7. *British treasurer who proposed laws taxing imports into the colonies.*

f 8. *Patriot leader who gained control of land west of the Appalachians for the United States.*

l 9. *Writer of* Common Sense.

h 10. *Patriot who warned the minutemen that the British were coming.*

e 11. *British prime minister who developed a program to raise revenue in the colonies.*

c 12. *British officer who sent troops from Boston to Concord.*

B. Matching: Terms

a. *boycott*

b. *Loyalists*

c. *mercantilism*

d. *minutemen*

e. *patriots*

f. *propaganda*

g. *repeal*

h. *revenue*

i. *Tories*

j. *Whigs*

k. *writs of assistance*

h   1. *Government income, usually obtained by taxation.*

a   2. *Refusing to buy certain goods as a way to gain what one demands.*

d   3. *Men ready to fight on a minute's notice.*

b, i   4. *Persons who favored remaining subject to Great Britain (two answers).*

e, j   5. *Persons who favored opposition to Great Britain (two answers).*

k   6. *Search warrants allowing officials to search any building for smuggled goods.*

g   7. *To withdraw something, especially a law.*

f   8. *Material publicized to spread certain ideas, usually with a strong, one-sided emphasis.*

c   9. *Idea that colonies should serve for the profit of the mother country.*

C. Matching: Names

a. *Boston Massacre*

b. *Boston Tea Party*

c. Common Sense

d. *Oath of Allegiance*

e. *Parliament*

f. *Pontiac's Conspiracy*

g. *Treaty of Paris*

h. *Committees of Correspondence*

i. *Declaration of Independence*

j. *First Continental Congress*

k. *Olive Branch Petition*

l. *Proclamation of Rebellion*

m. *Second Continental Congress*

n. *Stamp Act Congress*

m   1. *Meeting at which delegates voted to raise an army and declare independence.*

i   2. *Formal statement that the American colonies were an independent nation.*

e   3. *Legislative body in Great Britain.*

j   4. *Meeting in which delegates reasoned that Parliament had no authority over them.*

c   5. *Pamphlet promoting independence from Great Britain.*

a   6. *Incident when British soldiers killed five Bostonians.*

h   7. *Organizations that spread word of British acts that displeased the patriots.*

f   8. *Uprising by a group of Indian tribes in 1763.*

g   9. *Agreement that ended the Revolution in 1783.*

b 10. *Incident when cargo was destroyed to protest tax levied on it.*

n 11. *Meeting held in New York to protest the Stamp Act.*

k 12. *Plea to avert war sent by colonial leaders to King George III.*

l 13. *Declaration from King George III that the colonies were in rebellion.*

d 14. *Promise to support the new patriot government.*

D. Matching: Acts

In this set, the letters may be used more than once.

a. *act(s) mainly for producing revenue*

b. *act(s) mainly intended to assert British authority over the colonies*

c. *act(s) not directly intended for the colonies but affecting them*

a	1. *Sugar Act*	**b**	6. *Coercive Acts (Intolerable Acts)*
a	2. *Stamp Act*	**c**	7. *Quebec Act*
b	3. *Declaratory Act*	**a or b**	8. *Currency Act*
a	4. *Townshend Acts*	**a or b**	9. *Quartering Act*
b	5. *Proclamation of 1763*	**a or b**	10. *Tea Act*

E. Matching: Places

a. *Boston*

b. *Lexington and Concord*

c. *New York City*

d. *Philadelphia*

e. *Saratoga*

f. *Valley Forge*

g. *Yorktown*

e 1. *Turning point of the Revolutionary War.*

b 2. *Place of "shots heard around the world," which started the American Revolution in 1775.*

f 3. *Place where Washington's army camped during the winter of 1777–78.*

g 4. *Location of final British surrender.*

d 5. *Meeting place for First and Second Continental Congresses.*

a 6. *City over which the Battle of Bunker Hill was fought.*

c 7. *Excellent base for military operations, captured by the British in 1776.*

F. Deeper Discussion

1. *Explain the reasoning behind the slogan "Taxation without representation is tyranny."*

The colonists thought the British government was tyrannical because it required them to pay taxes without giving them any voice in levying the taxes.

2. *Suggest a good reason why the tax on tea was retained while the rest of the Townshend Acts were repealed.*
This was a way of showing consideration for the colonists while still asserting British authority over them.

3. *Did England have a right to raise revenue in the colonies for her own benefit? Explain.*
Yes. As the mother country, the British had the right to manage the colonies as they saw fit.

4. *How did Great Britain fail in her management of the rebellious colonies?*
Things would have worked out better if Great Britain had dealt with the Americans as equals rather than as subordinates. Also, if Britain had been ready to listen to the Americans' demands, they might have reached some compromise.

5. a. *Could the colonies have won the war without French aid? Explain.*
Probably not. The British feared France more than they feared the colonists. France also provided ships, soldiers, and supplies to help the Americans. Cornwallis surrendered at Yorktown because of the help that a French force gave to Washington.

b. *Could they have won without the overruling providence of God? Explain.*
Definitely not. American victory in the Revolutionary War was unlikely, yet it happened. It seems that God overruled in America's favor.

6. *Explain why the nonresistant people were misunderstood and resented by the patriots.*
The nonresistant people wanted to be loyal to the British government because God had established it over them. To the patriots, this made the nonresistant people appear to be Loyalists, even though they were not actually trying to help the British.

7. *Read Romans 13:1–7. According to these verses, could Christians have participated in the colonial rebellion? Why or why not?*
No. This Scripture passage plainly teaches that those who resist government power come under God's condemnation. It teaches that citizens are to be subject to the civil government and to pay taxes.

G. Chronology and Geography

1. *Find the dates for the following events; then make a time line of events from 1763 to 1776 that led up to the Revolution. Follow the instructions in Chapter 2 for making a time line.*

Declaration of Independence made public
Townshend Acts passed
Sugar Act and Currency Act passed
Coercive Acts passed
Stamp Act repealed; Declaratory Act passed
Fighting breaks out at Lexington and Concord
Publishing of Common Sense
Boston Massacre; Townshend Acts repealed
Proclamation of 1763
Tea Act passed; Boston Tea Party
Proclamation of Rebellion
Stamp Act passed

The time line should include the following items.
1763—Proclamation of 1763
1764—Sugar Act and Currency Act passed
1765—Stamp Act passed
1766—Stamp Act repealed; Declaratory Act passed
1767—Townshend Acts passed
1770—Boston Massacre; Townshend Acts repealed
1773—Tea Act passed; Boston Tea Party
1774—Coercive Acts passed
1775—Fighting breaks out at Lexington and Concord
1775—Proclamation of Rebellion
1776—Publishing of *Common Sense*
1776—Declaration of Independence made public

2. *Consider General Cornwallis's encampment at Yorktown, Virginia. How did geography contribute to his being trapped there?*

Cornwallis was surrounded by water on three sides. When the French fleet blockaded Yorktown, Cornwallis could escape only by going up the peninsula. But the Americans blocked that route, so Cornwallis was trapped.

10 American Government

1775

Declaration of Independence
adopted   1776

1780

Articles of Confederation ratified **1781**

Treaty of Paris ends Revolutionary War **1783**

1785   Land Ordinance of 1785 instituted

Constitutional Convention held from May to September;
Northwest Ordinance of 1787 instituted   **1787**

Government under Constitution begins **1789**

1790

Bill of Rights added to Constitution **1791**

1795

*"Honour all men. Love the brotherhood.
Fear God. Honour the king."*

1 Peter 2:17

Chapter 10 (pages 202–221)

AMERICAN GOVERNMENT

Chapter Objectives

- To study the history of the United States under the Articles of Confederation.
- To understand how the United States Constitution was written.
- To study the structure of the United States government, and to gain an understanding of the basic principles on which it operates.
- To develop a respect for the Constitution of the United States.
- To develop an appreciation for the blessings that God has provided for His people under the Constitution.

To the Teacher

The history of the Confederation period provides a background from which the movement to the Constitutional government can be understood. Many historians, following John Fiske, view this period as dark and gloomy. Others try to emphasize the good that was accomplished. In fairness, it was a period of both successes and failures. When the weak authority of Confederation government proved inadequate, a stronger Constitutional government was devised to replace it.

Pupils should realize that the United States Constitution has been so successful that other new nations have made it a model for their own constitutions. It has proven effective for over two hundred years. However, the Founding Fathers assumed that public morals would be of high enough quality that a free republic with a limited government would work. As morals degenerate and society deteriorates, government will assume more and more power at the expense of public liberty. Eventually this can lead to tyranny and despotic government.

In our time, even the freedoms prescribed in the Bill of Rights are being twisted to mean things that were never intended. For example, people claim First Amendment protection for corrupt and immoral publications. When people abuse their privileges, they will lose them. May we as Christians act responsibly with the privileges that God has entrusted to us.

The principles of the Constitution are fairly abstract. It would be good to use concrete illustrations and explanations to teach the principles that are presented. For examples, see Parts D and E of "Historical Highlights."

Note on chapter test: Chapter 10 has its own test. Be sure to assign Part G of "Historical Highlights," since students will be tested on those dates.

Christian Perspectives

- Since God provided for the institution of governments among men, their authority comes from God (Romans 13:1–4). Government is necessary to restrain the passions of sinful man, and it must have sufficient power to do so.

However, that power must be limited by law so that rulers do not abuse their own power. This view of government is based on the Biblical understanding of man as a fallen creature.

- The Constitution holds noble ideals and was written under the apparent blessing of God, but that does not necessarily mean that the authors of this document were godly men. By the providential help of God, these men were able to understand human nature and establish a government that worked upon a Judeo-Christian base. To the extent that men honor His Word, God responds with honor for them (1 Samuel 2:30).
- Though they incorporated many Judeo-Christian concepts into the Constitution, the Founding Fathers were deists who were directly influenced by the ideals of the humanistic Enlightenment. Deists believed the false idea that God created the world and then withdrew from it.
- The Bible teaches that though Christians are in the world, they do not belong to the kingdoms of the world. Their citizenship is in heaven even though they now dwell in earthly nations (John 18:36; Philippians 3:20). For that reason they do not vote or hold public office. The best way for Christians to contribute to an earthly nation is to pay taxes, pray for their government leaders, obey the laws, and build homes that make a solid contribution to the community.

Further Study

- The history of the Confederation. (An older book on this subject is *The Critical Period of American History*, by John Fiske.)
- The Constitutional Convention.
- The entire Constitution of the United States, including the Bill of Rights. (Because of its length, individual students could be assigned to read just certain segments of the Constitution or its amendments.)

Chapter 10 Quiz

1. Why does government exist?
   a. to make laws
   c. to create a peaceful society
   b. to protect citizens against invaders
   d. to restrain the evil nature of man

2. In a republic, which of the following control the government?
   a. the police force
   c. the constitution
   b. the king or queen
   d. the people

3. What was the main weakness of the Articles of Confederation, which was remedied by the Constitution?
   a. no limited government
   c. no strong national government
   b. no judicial review
   d. no republican government

4. Which term refers to government managed by elected representatives?
   a. monarchy
   c. democracy
   b. republic
   d. aristocracy

5. Why is the separation of powers so important in government?
   a. so that the separate branches of government can do their work efficiently
   b. so that laws are made in accordance with the Constitution
   c. so that the people are guaranteed the rights specified in the Constitution
   d. so that no branch of the government becomes too powerful

6. Which phrase indicates the division of powers between the national government and state governments?
   a. judicial system
   c. constitutional system
   b. federal system
   d. republican system

7. What does the Bill of Rights provide for each citizen of the United States?
   a. the guarantee of safety from foreign invasion
   b. the right to own property
   c. the guarantee of certain basic rights
   d. a listing of all the rights to which he is entitled

Quiz Answers

1. **d**   5. **d**
2. **d**   6. **b**
3. **c**   7. **c**
4. **b**

Answer Key

Focus for Thought (page 208)

1. *Which had more power under the Articles of Confederation—the states or the national government?*

the states

2. *What major accomplishment was achieved in 1783 by the government under the Articles of Confederation?*

the Treaty of Paris was signed

3. a. *What plan provided for the dividing and selling of lands bounded by the Ohio River, the Mississippi River, and the Great Lakes?*

the Land Ordinance of 1785

   b. *What plan provided an orderly pattern for adding more states to the original thirteen?*

the Northwest Ordinance of 1787

4. a. *What was the main problem with the Articles of Confederation?*

The Articles made the national government too weak to govern the nation effectively.

   b. *What was the reason for this problem?*

The framers were afraid that a strong national government would be a threat to freedom.

5. *Due to the weakness of the Confederation, what problems did the United States experience in the following areas?*

   a. *in unity*

Each state was more concerned about its own interests than about the welfare of the nation. The states taxed each other on interstate commerce, and they considered fighting each other when disputes arose. The new nation was heading toward lawless confusion.

   b. *with foreign nations*

The United States received little respect from other nations. For example, the British closed the West Indies to American trade, and refused to withdraw from some forts in the Northwest Territory. Spain disputed with the United States about the boundary of Florida and about trade on the Mississippi River. Pirates in the Mediterranean Sea preyed freely on United States trading ships. The government could do little about these matters.

   c. *in finances*

Congress had no power to levy taxes and therefore had no money to

pay its debts. Congress printed paper money, but it quickly lost value. Wage earners were especially discontented, for their pay was almost worthless.

Focus for Thought (page 212)

6. *Why was the Constitutional Convention held in secret?*

   The delegates did not want public opinion to influence their work before it was finished. Also, they wanted everyone to feel free to speak his opinion or change his mind. They wanted to avoid distractions.

7. *The delegates wanted a new government that would not be plagued by the weaknesses of the Confederation. What kind of government would that be?*

   The new government had to be stronger than the states. It needed authority to take the actions necessary for exercising its powers.

8. a. *How would states be represented in Congress under the Virginia Plan? under the New Jersey Plan?*

   Under the Virginia Plan, the states would be represented according to their population. Under the New Jersey Plan, each state would be represented equally.

   b. *What was the main objection to each plan?*

   Virginia Plan: Small states thought they would have too little voice in the new government because of their lower population. Others thought the Virginia Plan made the national government too strong. New Jersey Plan: Large states thought they would not be represented fairly, since they would have only as much power in Congress as the smaller states.

9. *How did the Great Compromise settle the issue of representation?*

   It was agreed that there would be a House of Representatives in which representation was according to population, and a Senate in which representation was according to states.

10. *Explain how two other issues were settled with compromises.*

    (Any two of the following.)

    The slavery issue: The Three-Fifths Compromise said that for purposes of Congressional representation, only three-fifths of the slaves would be counted. (It was agreed that Congress could not end the slave trade before 1808.)

    The trade issue: The Commerce and Slave Trade Compromise stated that Congress could control foreign trade, but it could not tax exports and could not end the slave trade before 1808.

    Election of presidents: The president was not to be elected directly by the people, but indirectly by the Electoral College.

11. a. *What was the position of the Federalists regarding the Constitution?*
Federalists approved of the Constitution because it seemed to be the answer to the problems of the Confederation government.
b. *What was the position of the Anti-Federalists?*
Anti-Federalists believed that the Constitution gave the national government too much power. They believed a bill of rights should be added.

Focus for Thought (page 217)

12. *Explain what is meant by a federal system of government.*
Powers are divided between the national government and the state governments. The national government has authority over national matters, and state governments have authority over local matters.
13. a. *What are two characteristics of a republic?*
A republic is controlled by the people, and its government is managed by elected representatives.
b. *How is a republic different from a pure democracy?*
In a republic, the government is managed by elected representatives, whereas in a pure democracy, all the people participate directly in government.
14. *What is the reason for separation of powers?*
to keep any one person or group from becoming too powerful
15. *Name the branch of federal government described by each sentence.*
   a. *It makes laws.* **legislative**
   b. *It is headed by a president and a vice president.* **executive**
   c. *It consists of district courts, circuit courts of appeals, and the Supreme Court.* **judicial**
   d. *It enacts and enforces laws.* **executive**
   e. *It decides how laws apply to specific cases.* **judicial**
   f. *It consists of the House of Representatives and the Senate.* **legislative**
16. *Describe two ways that government branches can check each other's powers.*
(Any two.) The president can veto laws passed by Congress. The president can appoint judges. The Senate must approve judges appointed by the president. Congress can override vetoes. Congress can impeach the president. The Supreme Court can declare laws unconstitutional.
17. a. *What is the purpose of the Bill of Rights?*
to guarantee certain rights to all citizens of the United States
b. *When was it added to the Constitution?*
in 1791

18. *Answer with the number of an amendment shown in the text. Which amendment*
   a. *would prohibit punishment by crucifixion?* **Amendment 8**
   b. *prevents a person from being retried for an offense after he has once been tried and found innocent?* **Amendment 5**
   c. *grants Christian publishers the right to freely publish and distribute literature?* **Amendment 1**
   d. *prohibits an officer of the law from entering someone's house without having specific authority?* **Amendment 4**
   e. *grants the right to a trial by jury?* **Amendment 6**
   f. *prohibits the government from taking a person's property without paying for it?* **Amendment 5**
   g. *grants freedom of conscience?* **Amendment 1**
   h. *permits an accused person to gather witnesses in his defense?* **Amendment 6**
   i. *requires that a trial be held in the same local area where the offense was committed?* **Amendment 6**
   j. *freely permits orderly religious gatherings?* **Amendment 1**

HISTORICAL HIGHLIGHTS (pages 218–220)

A. Matching: Names

One answer in this set will be used twice.
   a. *Alexander Hamilton*   f. *John Jay*
   b. *Benjamin Franklin*   g. *Old Northwest*
   c. *Constitutional Convention*   h. *Roger Sherman*
   d. *George Washington*   i. *Shays's Rebellion*
   e. *James Madison*

h   1. *Proposed the Great Compromise during the Constitutional Convention.*
b   2. *Suggested prayer during the Constitutional Convention.*
a, e, f 3. *Authors of the Federalist Papers (three answers).*
d   4. *Chairman who stabilized the Constitutional Convention.*
e   5. *"Father of the Constitution."*
i   6. *Uprising against high taxes and foreclosure on farms in Massachusetts.*
c   7. *Meeting that produced the Constitution.*
g   8. *Region bounded by the Ohio River, the Mississippi River, and the Great Lakes.*

B. Matching: Terms 1

a. *Cabinet*

b. *checks and balances*

c. *chief justice*

d. *confederation*

e. *Congress*

f. *constitution*

g. *Electoral College*

h. *executive branch*

i. *federal*

j. *Founding Fathers*

k. *House of Representatives*

l. *judicial branch*

m. *legislative branch*

n. *president*

o. *republic*

p. *Senate*

q. *separation of powers*

r. *Supreme Court*

q 1. *Dividing of government into three branches.*

m 2. *Division of government that proposes new laws.*

c 3. *Head judge of the Supreme Court.*

d 4. *Weak union in which states have more power than the national government.*

i 5. *Kind of government system with powers divided between the states and the national government.*

n 6. *Head of the executive branch.*

f 7. *Written plan of government.*

a 8. *Group appointed as advisers to the president.*

h 9. *Division of government that enacts and enforces laws.*

b 10. *Methods by which branches of government limit each other's powers.*

o 11. *Government managed by elected representatives.*

l 12. *Division of government that decides whether laws have been broken or whether laws are constitutional.*

e 13. *Federal lawmaking body that includes the Senate and the House of Representatives.*

r 14. *Highest judicial body in the nation.*

g 15. *Group of men who elect the president.*

k 16. *Part of Congress with states represented proportionately.*

p 17. *Part of Congress with states represented equally.*

j 18. *Men who framed the Constitution of the United States.*

C. Matching: Terms 2

a. *Anti-Federalists*

b. *bicameral*

c. *elastic clause*

d. *Federalists*

e. *impeach*

f. *judicial review*

g. *Preamble*

h. *ratification*

i. *unicameral*

j. *veto*

k. *Articles of Confederation*

l. *Bill of Rights*

m. *Commerce and Slave Trade Compromise*

n. *Federalist Papers*

o. *Great Compromise*

p. *New Jersey Plan*

q. *Northwest Ordinance of 1787*

r. *Three-fifths Compromise*

s. *Virginia Plan*

o   1. *Proposal that settled the issue of representation.*

d   2. *People who supported the new Constitution.*

b   3. *Having a legislature with two houses.*

g   4. *Introduction to the Constitution.*

r   5. *Proposal that settled the issue of counting slaves for representation.*

k   6. *Unsatisfactory plan for governing the United States.*

j   7. *To reject a proposed law.*

e   8. *To bring to trial for misconduct in office.*

s   9. *Proposal calling for states to have proportionate representation in Congress.*

p 10. *Proposal calling for states to have equal representation in Congress.*

m 11. *Proposal about control of trade and slavery.*

a 12. *People who opposed the new Constitution.*

q 13. *Law that provided a plan of government and statehood for new territories.*

i 14. *Having a legislature with only one house.*

n 15. *Series of articles defending the Constitution.*

h 16. *The act of giving formal agreement to.*

f 17. *Action in which a court examines a law to determine whether it is constitutional.*

c 18. *Statement in the Constitution saying that Congress may assume powers not specifically mentioned in the Constitution.*

l 19. *First ten amendments to the Constitution, which guarantee certain freedoms.*

D. Principles From the Preamble to the Constitution

Match the letters of the phrases from the Preamble to the sentences below.

a. *"We the People of the United States"*

b. *"In Order to form a more perfect Union"*

c. *"Establish Justice"*

d. *"Insure domestic Tranquility"*
e. *"Provide for the common defense"*
f. *"Promote the general Welfare"*
g. *"Secure the Blessings of Liberty to ourselves and our Posterity"*

c 1. *The court will decide who is at fault.*
f 2. *Paper money is a convenient way to pay for purchases.*
a 3. *The citizens, not a king, are the final authority.*
e 4. *The army, navy, and air force are responsible to protect the nation.*
d 5. *People are arrested for starting a riot.*
g 6. *The freedoms enjoyed in the United States have continued for many years.*
b 7. *The Articles of Confederation did not provide for a strong national government.*

E. The Bill of Rights

To which amendment shown in this chapter could a citizen of the United States appeal if he were to face the following situations? Answer with the number of that amendment.

4 1. *A search warrant that does not describe the objects to be found in the search.*
8 2. *A $10,000 fine for the first offense of driving without a license.*
6 3. *Conviction of a crime without a public trial by jury.*
1 4. *Denial of military exemption because of religious beliefs.*
5 5. *Using force and threats against a person accused of robbery, to make him tell where he hid the stolen goods.*

F. Deeper Discussion

1. *The framing of the Constitution involved much compromise (two disagreeing parties each yielding so that agreement can be reached). When is compromise right, and when is it wrong?*
   Compromise is right when the point of disagreement is not a matter of right or wrong, as were many issues relating to the Constitution. For example, the matter of representation in Congress was a nonmoral issue. But compromise is wrong when people sacrifice Biblical principles for the sake of harmony with others.

2. *Why did God allow the work of the Founding Fathers to succeed even though they were worldly-minded men?*
   God's Word says, "Them that honour me I will honour" (1 Samuel 2:30). The Lord allowed the work of the Founding Fathers to succeed because the Constitution honors Biblical principles such as justice, respect for all men, and separation of church and state.

3. *Read Ecclesiastes 8:11. What else in addition to law is necessary for man to live in an orderly society?*
the enforcement of law (or the prompt punishment of lawbreakers)

G. Chronology and Geography

Note: Students will be tested on the dates in number 1 below.

1. *Explain why each date is important.*
   a. *1781* **year when the Articles of Confederation were ratified**
   b. *1787* **year of the Constitutional Convention (also the Northwest Ordinance)**
   c. *1789* **year when Constitutional government began**
   d. *1791* **year when the Bill of Rights was added to the Constitution**
2. *Consider the large size of the United States.*
   a. *How would the size contribute to the difficulty of governing the nation under a weak national government?*
   Conflicts are sure to arise because of the many diverse regions in the United States. A weak central government would not be able to deal with these conflicts.
   b. *Why would the size make a pure democracy impractical?*
   Because of the great traveling distances and large numbers of people involved, a pure democracy would be completely impractical.
3. *Trace the outline of Map A again, and label it "The States of the United States."*
   a. *Trace the borders of the original thirteen states. (Draw their present borders, even though some states originally included more area.)*
   b. *Label the original thirteen states. (Write the names of small states outside the United States border and draw arrows to their locations.)*
   c. *Color the original thirteen states (present areas only) all the same color. In Chapters 12, 16, 19, and 26, you will use other colors for states admitted in later periods.*
   d. *Memorize the names and locations of these states.*
   (Individual work. Periodically test the students' memorization of the states by requiring them to fill in blank maps with the states they have studied so far. You may make copies of Map A for this purpose.)

So Far This Year (page 221)

Write whether each statement is true *(T)* or false *(F)*.

T   1. *The French and Indian War began in 1754 and ended in 1763.*

F   2. *Mennonites first arrived in America in 1607.*

F   3. *The Constitution was adopted on July 4, 1776.*

T   4. *The Second Continental Congress declared independence from Great Britain.*

T   5. *Americans who supported Great Britain in the Revolution were called Loyalists.*

F   6. *Conflicting claims over the Hudson Bay led to the French and Indian War.*

F   7. *The battle at Fort Duquesne was the decisive battle of the French and Indian War.*

F   8. *Thomas Jefferson wrote a stirring pamphlet called* Common Sense *that promoted American independence.*

T   9. *The French and Indian War is important in the history of North America because the French were removed as a North American power.*

T 10. *The Americans and British disagreed about Parliament's authority over the colonies.*

F 11. *The Battle of Lexington was the turning point in the Revolution.*

F 12. *The Battle of Saratoga was the last major battle of the Revolution.*

T 13. *General Cornwallis was the British general whose defeat ended the Revolution.*

F 14. *The nonresistant groups were Tories.*

F 15. *At the end of the American Revolution, the British gained all the land from the Atlantic to the Mississippi and from Canada to Florida.*

T 16. *Nonresistant people prepared for the French and Indian War by having the* Martyrs Mirror *published in German.*

F 17. *An issue that nonresistant people faced in the French and Indian War was the Oath of Allegiance.*

F 18. *The Treaty of Paris ended the Revolutionary War in 1763.*

T 19. *John Cabot explored the northeastern coast of North America for England in 1497.*

F 20. *Jacques Cartier explored the St. Lawrence River area for France in 1524.*

UNIT 4: TIMES OF GROWTH, 1790–1850

11 National Beginnings

George Washington becomes president;
French Revolution begins   1789

1790

Bill of Rights added to Constitution;
Vermont becomes a state; first
Bank of the United States   1791

Washington re-elected; Kentucky
becomes a state   1792

Neutrality Proclamation 1793

Jay Treaty with Britain 1794

Whiskey Rebellion 1794

Pinckney Treaty with Spain 1795

Tennessee becomes a state;
John Adams elected president 1796

XYZ Affair 1797–1798

Alien and Sedition Acts 1798

1800   Capital moved to Washington, D.C.;
Thomas Jefferson elected president 1800

Louisiana Purchase;
Ohio becomes a state **1803**

Jefferson re-elected; *Addresses to Youth*
published by Christian Burkholder 1804

Lewis and Clark expedition 1804–1806

Embargo Act; *Leopard-Chesapeake* incident 1807

James Madison elected president 1808

1810

War of 1812 begins; Madison re-elected **1812**

Oliver Hazard Perry wins Battle of Lake Erie 1813

Washington, D.C. burned; Treaty of Ghent signed **1814**

Battle of New Orleans 1815

"How say ye, We are mighty and strong men for the war?"

Jeremiah 48:14

1820

Unit 4: Times of Growth, 1790–1850

Chapter 11 (pages 222–243)

NATIONAL BEGINNINGS

Chapter Objectives

- To learn how the United States government was established, what problems the new government faced, and how they were dealt with.
- To learn about the first political parties in America and what they stood for.
- To learn about the Louisiana Purchase and the Lewis and Clark expedition.
- To understand the causes, course, and significance of the War of 1812.

To the Teacher

Be impartial when discussing political parties. We as Christians do not identify with a particular party because we do not vote or see the government as the solution to man's basic needs. Although any party may have strong points and weak points, and although one may seem better overall than another, no political party has the solutions to man's basic spiritual problems.

The Federalists operated on the belief that only the rich, wise, and good can lead a nation, and that ordinary citizens should defer to the opinions and leadership of their "betters." They predicted ruin if the common people as led by Jefferson should take control. Their beliefs led to their decline after the election of 1800.

The presidency of Thomas Jefferson led the nation in a new direction. He believed in the ability of the common people to give valuable direction to the government. Also, he believed that people could manage their own affairs without interference from the government. He helped to promote democracy, which led to the "common man" emphasis of Andrew Jackson in 1828 (discussed in the next chapter).

An important factor in the War of 1812 is that the United States did not want to be bound by the trade rules of other nations. Obeying foreign trade laws was like being independent in name but not in fact. After all, the Revolution had also been fought partly over trade. So the War of 1812 is considered as "the second war of independence," and in this it did partly succeed. Remember to be impartial in discussing this war.

The matter of Mennonites and the Great Awakening is a bit difficult to handle. Because of the coldness and deadness in the Mennonite Church at that time, it is easy to understand why pietism held a strong appeal for those who wanted more spiritual church life. However, the pietists failed to uphold New Testament doctrines like separation and nonresistance; so their road led to apostasy. The Mennonites did need to return to Scriptural church life, but pietism was not the way. *Addresses to Youth* provided a Biblical perspective on many issues; yet in some parts of the book, Christian Burkholder called for loyalty to the Mennonite Church without addressing the great spiritual needs in the church.

Note on chapter test: There is a single test for Chapters 11 and 12.

Christian Perspectives

- Nonresistant Christians must not get involved in political parties and systems. We are in the world, but we are not part of its political system (John 18:36).
- Political leaders often deviate from their professed principles. If it is to their advantage, they will operate on principles of the opposite party. In Matthew 5:37, Jesus teaches us to let our yea be yea and our nay be nay.
- The Christian's view of war is directly opposed to the world's view. To the Christian, war always reveals men's folly. This is especially true of the War of 1812, in which the fighting had little to do with resolving the issues contributing to the war.
- Nonresistant Christians must not be nationalistic. Eternal principles must always be esteemed more highly than one's country. By being separated from the political system, Christians can love all men—even the enemies of their country.
- While the world struggles on toward destruction, God's church continues its work in the world.

Further Study

- Political parties in America: their history, their basic principles, and the changes in those principles over the years.
- The Lewis and Clark expedition.
- The War of 1812. (You might also study specific aspects of the war, such as the burning of Washington, D.C., the Battle of New Orleans, or the Canadian viewpoint on the war.)
- The lives of presidents discussed in this chapter.

Chapter 11 Quiz

1. Which political party favored a loose interpretation of the Constitution and a strong national government?

_____

2. Which political party favored a strict interpretation of the Constitution and a weak national government? (Give the full name of the party.)

_____

3. Name the two men who explored the Louisiana Purchase from 1804 to 1806.

_____

4. Name the first secretary of the treasury, who helped the United States to become established financially.

_____

5. Give the beginning and ending years for the War of 1812.

_____

6. Name in order the first four presidents of the United States.

_____

_____

Quiz Answers

1. **Federalists**
2. **Democratic-Republicans**
3. **Meriwether Lewis and William Clark**
4. **Alexander Hamilton**
5. **1812 and 1815**
6. **George Washington, John Adams, Thomas Jefferson, James Madison**

Answer Key

Focus for Thought (page 230)

1. *Name the first three departments in the executive branch, along with their functions and their secretaries.*

   Department of State; dealing with foreign nations; Thomas Jefferson
   Department of War; defending the nation; Henry Knox
   Department of the Treasury; controlling revenue and spending; Alexander Hamilton

2. *Copy and complete the following table to compare the first two political parties.*

Party	Things Favored by Party	Leaders
Federalists	**Hamilton's plans** **Strong federal government** **Loose interpretation of the Constitution** **Businessmen, bankers, manufacturers** **Great Britain**	**Alexander Hamilton**
Democratic-Republicans	**Opposition to Hamilton's plans** **Weak federal government** **Strict interpretation of the Constitution** **Farmers, craftsmen** **France**	**Thomas Jefferson** **James Madison**

3. a. *How did President Washington avoid going to war to help France?*

   He issued the Neutrality Proclamation.

   b. *How was war avoided with Great Britain?*

   The Jay Treaty was negotiated.

4. *What benefits did the Pinckney Treaty give the United States?*

   It allowed American merchants to trade on the Mississippi and to use New Orleans as a port of deposit. Spain also recognized the American claims to lands east of the Mississippi.

5. *Why did the Alien and Sedition Acts make the Federalists unpopular?*

   These acts caused many Americans to think that the Federalist Party was becoming too strong and was threatening their freedoms.

6. *Name in order the four states added to the Union between 1790 and 1805, and the year of admission for each.*

   Vermont—1791; Kentucky—1792; Tennessee—1796; Ohio—1803

Focus for Thought (page 235)

7. *What were some important changes that President Jefferson made in the federal government?*

   He allowed the Alien and Sedition Acts to expire and repealed the excise taxes. He reduced the number of government workers and decreased the size of the military. He lowered expenses and reduced the government debt.

8. a. *How did President Jefferson compromise his principles to buy Louisiana?*

   He believed in a strict interpretation of the Constitution, but it did not specifically provide for purchasing territory. He had to interpret the Constitution loosely in order to make the Louisiana Purchase.

   b. *How was the Louisiana Purchase valuable to the United States?*

   It doubled the size of the United States. All or parts of thirteen new states were made from it.

9. *What were some fruits of the Lewis and Clark expedition?*

   a wealth of information about the Louisiana region, discovery of passes through the Rockies, friendship with various Indian tribes, proof that there is no direct water route to the Pacific Ocean, detailed maps and scientific reports about the territory

10. a. *What was the purpose of the Embargo Act?*

    to deprive the warring nations of needed American goods

    b. *Why was this act a failure?*

    It had little effect on Britain and France, but it was disastrous to America.

Focus for Thought (page 240)

11. *Explain how each of the following contributed to war with Britain.*

    a. *trade*

    The British and French had been seizing American merchant ships and restricting United States trade.

    b. *problems with the Indians*

    Settlers west of the Appalachians blamed Britain for the conflict, believing the British had stirred up the Indians and provided them with weapons. They believed that their troubles with the Indians would cease if the British were driven out.

    c. *war hawks*

    The war hawks strongly promoted war with Britain. They also believed that by going to war, the United States could take Canada from the British and Florida from Spain.

12. a. *Why did the Americans attack Canada?*
They attacked the British by land in Canada because the British navy was much stronger than the American navy. (Also, they wanted to capture Canada and add it to the United States.)
b. *What were the results?*
None of the Americans' plans succeeded. Instead of taking Canada, the Americans found themselves defending their Northwest Territory against the British.

13. a. *What major battle was fought after the War of 1812 officially ended?*
the Battle of New Orleans
b. *What American general became famous because of this battle?*
Andrew Jackson

14. *What two provisions were included in the Treaty of Ghent?*
Things were restored as they had been before the war. The two sides agreed to stop fighting.

15. *Give four effects of the War of 1812.*
(Any four.) Canadians were embittered, but European nations gained respect for the United States. Relations with Britain improved. Nationalism increased, manufacturing grew, and westward expansion increased.

HISTORICAL HIGHLIGHTS (pages 240–242)

A. Matching: People

a. *Alexander Hamilton*
b. *Daniel Boone*
c. *George Washington*
d. *Henry Clay*
e. *James Madison*
f. *John Adams*
g. *John C. Calhoun*
h. *John Jay*
i. *John Marshall*
j. *Meriwether Lewis and William Clark*
k. *Napoleon Bonaparte*
l. *Sacajawea*
m. *Tecumseh*
n. *Thomas Jefferson*
o. *William Henry Harrison*
p. *Zebulon Pike*

b   1. *Opened the Wilderness Road to Kentucky.*
i   2. *Chief Justice who strengthened the Supreme Court by establishing judicial review.*
m   3. *Tried to create an Indian confederacy.*
a   4. *Federalist leader and first secretary of the treasury.*
o   5. *Defeated Indians at Tippecanoe.*

c   6. *First president; served from 1789 to 1797.*

n   7. *Leader of Democratic-Republican Party; third president; served from 1801 to 1809.*

j   8. *Explored the Louisiana Purchase from 1804 to 1806.*

p   9. *Tried to climb a mountain in Colorado, now named after him.*

d, g 10. *War hawks (two answers).*

k 11. *French leader who sold Louisiana to the United States.*

e 12. *President during the War of 1812; served from 1809 to 1817.*

h 13. *First chief justice of the Supreme Court.*

f 14. *Second president; a Federalist; served from 1797 to 1801.*

l 15. *Indian woman who helped to guide the Lewis and Clark expedition.*

B. Matching: Terms

a. *bond*

b. *chief justice*

c. *excise tax*

d. *impress*

e. *judicial review*

f. *loose interpretation*

g. *strict interpretation*

h. *tariff*

i. *war hawks*

j. *Democratic-Republicans*

k. *Department of State*

l. *Department of the Treasury*

m. *Department of War*

n. *Federalists*

o. *Whiskey Rebellion*

l   1. *Part of government in charge of revenue and spending.*

o   2. *Resistance to paying taxes in western Pennsylvania in 1794.*

f   3. *Idea that the government should be free to assume powers not specifically described in the Constitution.*

i   4. *Bold young congressmen who promoted war.*

d   5. *To force into military service.*

m   6. *Part of government responsible for defending the nation.*

b   7. *Head judge of the Supreme Court.*

g   8. *Idea that the government should exercise only the powers specifically described in the Constitution.*

e   9. *Power of the Supreme Court to declare a Congressional law unconstitutional.*

j 10. *Party in favor of strict interpretation of the Constitution.*

n 11. *Party in favor of loose interpretation of the Constitution.*

c 12. *Tax levied on certain domestic products.*

k 13. *Part of government dealing with foreign nations.*

a 14. *Certificate of debt to be paid back with interest.*

h 15. *Tax levied on certain imports, often to protect domestic industries.*

C. Matching: Names

a. *Alien and Sedition Acts*   e. *Jay Treaty*
b. *Bank of the United States*   f. Marbury v. Madison
c. *Embargo Act*   g. *Pinckney Treaty*
d. *Federalist Era*   h. *Treaty of Ghent*

d 1. *Period when George Washington and John Adams were in office.*
g 2. *Treaty that settled issues with Spain in 1795.*
f 3. *Case that established the power of the Supreme Court to declare laws unconstitutional.*
e 4. *Treaty that settled issues with Britain in 1794.*
c 5. *Law that stopped all exports.*
a 6. *Laws that limited rights of foreigners and forbade criticism of the government.*
h 7. *Treaty that ended the War of 1812.*
b 8. *Institution for depositing and borrowing government funds.*

D. Deeper Discussion

1. *What are some contrasts between the French Revolution and the American Revolution?*
   The American Revolution was not nearly as violent and radical as the French Revolution (especially the Reign of Terror). The French Revolution became anti-Christian, whereas the American Revolution was led by men who recognized some Bible principles. The French Revolution led to the dictatorship of Napoleon, whereas the American Revolution led to the founding of a stable republic.

2. *How did the Alien and Sedition Acts violate the Bill of Rights?*
   These acts violated the First Amendment, which guarantees the freedoms of speech and the press.

3. *Were the Americans justified in their claim that the British stirred up the Indians? Explain.*
   As long as the British maintained their forts around the Great Lakes, they definitely supported the Indians. The fact that Tecumseh was killed in the Battle of the Thames shows that the British and the Indians were helping each other. On the other hand, the Americans themselves had done much to stir up the Indians as settlers continually moved into Indian territory. Perhaps the Americans had only themselves to blame.

4. *What lessons can be learned from the following facts about the War of 1812?*
   a. *The main issues faded soon after the war started.*

   Patience is a virtue. Men plunged into war without considering its full costs. Just a little more deliberation and waiting might have prevented war, as exemplified by Washington in 1795 and by Adams in 1798.

   b. *The Battle of New Orleans was fought after the Treaty of Ghent had been signed.*

   Since faster communication could have changed the outcome, this fact emphasizes the need for good communications. It also shows how foolish war is, and what a tragic destruction of lives and property is caused by war.

5. *Contrast pietism with a proper emphasis on obedience in the Christian walk of life.*

   Pietism puts emphasis on emotions and personal experience, but the emphasis on obedience points to the Bible and the church as a higher authority. Emphasizing obedience shows that the outward walk is as important as the inner beliefs.

6. *Read John 18:36 and 2 Corinthians 5:20. If God's children apply the truths of these Scriptures, can they be nationalistic? Explain.*

   No. Christians are grateful for their governments that maintain order, but their highest loyalty is to God. Since nationalism promotes loyalty to one's country above all else, Christians cannot be nationalistic.

E. Chronology and Geography

1. *Trace the outline of Map A again, and label it "Territorial Growth of the United States." (You will use this map again in Chapters 12 and 14.)*
   a. *Draw boundary lines to show the area included in the Louisiana Purchase. Label this area, but do not color it yet.*
   b. *Draw the border as it was between Florida and the Spanish territory at the time of the Louisiana Purchase. Also draw a line from the northern end of the Mississippi River straight north to the present border between the United States and Canada. Label the area north of Florida and east of the Louisiana Purchase "The United States in 1783." Color this area.*

   (Individual work.)

2. *On your map entitled "Exploration of North America," draw brown lines to trace the route of Lewis and Clark. Label the route.*
   (Individual work.)

3. *Using the map "Regions of the United States" in Chapter 1, describe the regions that Lewis and Clark explored.*
   Lewis and Clark traveled across the western part of the Central Plains, through the high and rugged Rocky Mountains, across the Columbia Plateau, through the Cascade and Coast Ranges, and down to the Pacific Ocean.

4. *Name the states of which all or part were formed from the Louisiana Purchase.*
   Arkansas, Missouri, Iowa, Nebraska, South Dakota, Louisiana, Minnesota, Oklahoma, Kansas, Colorado, Wyoming, North Dakota, Montana
   (Note to teacher: The first four states listed above were completely formed from the Louisiana Purchase. South Dakota was nearly all formed from it too.)

5. *From memory, list the presidents of this chapter in order, along with the dates for their terms of office. Give two sets of dates if a president served two terms. (Note that election years are divisible by 4, such as 1800, 1804, and so on. Also remember that an elected president's term begins in the year after the election.)*
   (Memorizing the presidents and their years in office is an optional exercise. You may wish to assign it to more able students or for extra credit.)
   (1) George Washington, 1789–1793, 1793–1797
   (2) John Adams, 1797–1801
   (3) Thomas Jefferson, 1801–1805, 1805–1809
   (4) James Madison, 1809–1813, 1813–1817

So Far This Year (page 243)

A. Completion (1)

Write the correct name or term for each description.

Ponce de León
1. *Man who discovered Florida in 1513 while seeking the Fountain of Youth.*

Francisco Coronado
2. *Explorer who sought the Seven Cities of Cíbola, 1540–1542.*

Hernando de Soto
3. *Explorer who discovered the Mississippi River, 1539–1543.*

John Smith
4. *Leader of Jamestown who established a policy of "no work, no food."*

Roger Williams
5. *Founder of Rhode Island who insisted on freedom of conscience.*

Lord Baltimore
6. *Founder of Maryland.*

William Penn
7. *Quaker who received a land grant as payment for a debt.*

James Oglethorpe
8. *Trustee leader in the founding of Georgia.*

George Whitefield, Jonathan Edwards
9. *Two leaders of the colonial Great Awakening.*

legislative
10. *Branch of government that makes laws.*

judicial
11. *Branch of government that decides cases about laws.*

executive
12. *Branch of government that enacts and enforces laws.*

House
13. *Part of legislative branch with states represented proportionately.*

Senate
14. *Part of legislative branch with states represented equally.*

Electoral College
15. *Group of men who elect the president.*

B. Completion (2)

Write the correct term or date that belongs on each blank.

16. *Under the Constitution, the American government is divided into three branches. This is according to the principle of* **separation of powers***.*

17. *The president may reject, or* **veto***, a proposed law that Congress has passed.*

18. *Congress may* **impeach** *a president, or bring him to trial for misconduct in office.*

19. *The Constitution provides ways for government branches to limit each other's power. These limits are called* **checks and balances**.
20. *In a* **federal** *system, government powers are divided between the states and the national government.*
21. *A written plan of government is called a* **constitution**.
22. *The Constitutional Convention was held in the year* **1787**.
23. *The United States government under the Constitution began in the year* **1789**.
24. *The first ten amendments to the Constitution, added in 1791, are called the* **Bill of Rights**.
25. *Since the United States government has no king, it is called a* **republic**.
26. *The man called the "father of the Constitution" was* **James Madison**.
27. *A form of manorialism, transplanted to New France, was the* **seigneurial system**.
28. *The Spanish used a* **mission** *system to convert and civilize the Indians, and to fortify their frontiers against enemies.*

C. Matching: Dates

Write the letter of the correct date for each description.

d 29. *Year when Georgia was founded.*   a. *1607*
b 30. *Year when Plymouth was founded.*   b. *1620*
a 31. *Year when Jamestown was founded.*   c. *1681*
c 32. *Year when Pennsylvania received a charter.*   d. *1733*

12 National Progress

1. THE ERA OF GOOD FEELINGS

Growth of Nationalism

Treaties With Other Nations

The Monroe Doctrine

Sectionalism and the Missouri Compromise

A Troubled Presidency

2. THE AGE OF JACKSON

Jacksonian Democracy

The Nullification Crisis

Indian Removal

Economic Developments

3. THE RISE OF THE WHIGS

The Whig Party

The Van Buren Administration

The Whigs in Power

"And it shall come to pass, if thou shalt hearken diligently unto the voice of the LORD thy God, . . . that the LORD thy God will set thee on high above all nations of the earth."

Deuteronomy 28:1

Timeline

1810

Treaty of Ghent signed **1814**

James Monroe elected president; Clay's American System proposed 1816

Panic of 1819; Adams-Onis Treaty (Transcontinental Treaty) 1819

Missouri Compromise passed; Monroe re-elected 1820 — **1820**

Monroe Doctrine proclaimed **1823**

John Quincy Adams elected president 1824

Andrew Jackson elected president 1828

1830

Nullification crisis; Jackson re-elected 1832

Seminole War 1835–1842

Martin Van Buren elected president 1836

Panic of 1837

1840 William Henry Harrison elected president 1840

William Henry Harrison dies; John Tyler takes office 1841

Webster-Ashburton Treaty negotiated 1842

James K. Polk elected president 1844

1850

Chapter 12 (pages 244–261)

NATIONAL PROGRESS

Chapter Objectives

- To understand the major periods of early American political history, such as the Era of Good Feelings and the Age of Jackson.
- To understand the purpose of the Monroe Doctrine.
- To grasp the issues of sectionalism.
- To understand the tensions between white men and Indians, and how they were dealt with.
- To understand how the Whig Party came to power and how it governed.
- To learn about economic policies during the first half of the 1800s.

To the Teacher

As the history of this period demonstrates, rapid change and growth often produces contention and strife. The name Era of Good Feelings can properly be applied only to the early years of James Monroe's presidency because sectional strife soon appeared, even though there was only one political party. The strengths and weaknesses of the sections could have been mutually beneficial; instead, strife developed because each section tried to use federal government policies for its own benefit. For example, the North promoted high tariffs while the South tried to protect slavery. Nevertheless, many people still held strong feelings of loyalty toward the Union, as illustrated by Webster's speech in the Webster-Hayne debates.

A strong federal government and broad interpretation of the Constitution versus limited government and strict interpretation were the issues that continued to draw the lines between opposing political parties. The Republicans split into National Republicans (who later became Whigs) and Democratic-Republicans (Democrats) on these issues. Andrew Jackson believed in limited government and strict interpretation, but he did not support states' rights. States' rights was an extreme position in which the federal government was viewed more as the old Confederation had been—simply as an alliance of sovereign states.

Protective tariffs may have benefited the new manufacturing enterprises after the War of 1812, but high tariffs generally are harmful to business. When a business is protected by government policies, it can charge higher prices without having to deal with normal market pressures to be more efficient. A common result is that an inefficient producer is subsidized at the expense of the consumer. Free trade and competition usually provide the best products at the best prices.

Jacksonian democracy was rooted in the idea that man has the native ability to improve himself. An outgrowth of this idea was that even a common man such as Andrew Jackson could become president of the nation. The Constitution outlined a republican form of government, which the Founding Fathers had thought would be headed by educated, wealthy men such as themselves. But Jeffersonian democracy sowed the seeds of a government "of the people, by the people, and for the people"; and Jacksonian democracy bore the fruit.

Note on chapter test: There is a single test for Chapters 11 and 12.

Christian Perspectives

- God sometimes sets up the "basest of men" (Daniel 4:17). Andrew Jackson was the first president to have married a divorced woman, and in other ways also he was not respectable. Yet God chose to set him up as the president.
- Proverbs 22:2 says, "The rich and poor meet together: the LORD is the maker of them all." In this sense, the "common man" idea of equality is true, that God created all men of equal worth. This does not mean that all have equal abilities or opportunities, or that most people will automatically choose right.
- God allowed the white race to overpower the Indian race, even though we cannot fully understand His purposes in doing so. God said in Ezekiel 18:4, "All souls are mine"; and in Acts 10:34, "God is no respecter of persons." Missionaries to the Indians are one of the bright spots in the generally dark picture of relations between white men and Indians.
- Cycles of economic prosperity and depression illustrate that riches are uncertain (1 Timothy 6:17) and deceitful (Mark 4:19), and that they "fly away" (Proverbs 23:5). The Christian must recognize these things and put his trust in God rather than in material wealth. He must not be a reckless spender or a hopeless debtor, but a wise steward of God's gifts.

Further Study

- The lives of the presidents discussed in this chapter and of noted men such as Henry Clay, Daniel Webster, and John C. Calhoun.
- The issues of sectionalism.
- The Monroe Doctrine.
- Indian removal and Indian wars.

Chapter 12 Quiz

T F 1. The Era of Good Feelings was a time of national unity and harmony during the presidency of Andrew Jackson.

T F 2. The Whigs were a political party that opposed Andrew Jackson.

T F 3. Andrew Jackson agreed that South Carolina should be able to nullify federal laws.

T F 4. The Monroe Doctrine declared that European nations should stay out of American affairs and that the United States would stay out of European affairs.

T F 5. Jacksonian democracy included the idea that common people were able to participate in government.

T F 6. One issue of sectionalism was slavery.

T F 7. According to states' rights, the federal government should be supreme over the states.

T F 8. John Quincy Adams was the son of a former president.

T F 9. John Tyler was the first president to die in office.

T F 10. The Panic of 1837 occurred during Martin Van Buren's presidency.

T F 11. Indian removal was done to open new lands for cotton growing.

T F 12. Andrew Jackson opposed the Bank of the United States because he believed it favored the wealthy and was unconstitutional.

Quiz Answers

1. **F**	4. **T**	7. **F**	10. **T**
2. **T**	5. **T**	8. **T**	11. **T**
3. **F**	6. **T**	9. **F**	12. **T**

Answer Key

Focus for Thought (page 251)

1. *Why were the first years of James Monroe's presidency called the Era of Good Feelings?*
   A new spirit of nationalism and unity prevailed in the United States. One reason was that there was only one political party.

2. *Why did conflict arise over the Bank of the United States?*
   People thought the bank was the reason for financial hard times. They thought the bank made the federal government too strong.

3. *Why was the Transcontinental Treaty (alternate name for the Adams-Onís Treaty) especially significant?*

This treaty foreshadowed the nation's expansion to the Pacific Ocean.

4. *Explain in your own words each of the three points of the Monroe Doctrine.*
European nations were not to establish any new colonies in America. European nations were to stay out of the affairs of the independent American nations. Americans would stay out of the affairs of European nations.

5. *The following table shows four main issues that contributed to sectionalism. Copy the table and fill it in by writing whether each section favored (F) or opposed (O) that issue. If support in a section was mixed, write M.*

	North	*South*	*West*
Cheap land	**O**	**O**	**F**
National bank	**F**	**O**	**O**
Protective tariffs	**F**	**O**	**M**
Slavery	**O**	**F**	**M**

6. *How did the Missouri Compromise settle the issue of slavery in Missouri and in the rest of the Louisiana Territory?*
Maine joined the Union as a free state and Missouri as a slave state. In the rest of the Louisiana Territory, slavery was forbidden north of a line drawn at 36°30' N, but it was permitted south of that line.

Focus for Thought (page 256)

7. *What were the two main ideas of Jacksonian democracy?*
One was the idea that common people were able to participate in government. The other was the idea that the government should consider all citizens to be equal.

8. *Why did the South oppose protective tariffs?*
The South believed that the tariffs benefited the North at the expense of the other states. Since Southerners imported many goods, they either had to pay higher prices for imports because of the tariff or pay higher prices to northern factories.

9. a. *On what basis did South Carolina say that a federal law could be nullified?*
on the basis of states' rights (the idea that the states are supreme over the federal government)
b. *How would nullification have affected the United States?*
It would have led to chaos and breakup of national unity.

10. a. *Around 1830, why did many white people want to move the Indians to lands across the Mississippi?*
   Many Indians lived on good cotton-growing land. (Another reason was that gold had been discovered on Indian land in Georgia.)
   b. *What was the Trail of Tears?*
   the journey of the Cherokees who were forced to move to Oklahoma
11. *Why did President Jackson oppose the Bank of the United States?*
   He believed that it had too much power, that it gave special privileges to the wealthy, and that it was unconstitutional.
12. *Explain what brought on the Panic of 1837.*
   After the Specie Circular was issued, people tried to exchange their paper money for gold and silver coins (specie). Banks were forced to close because they had too little specie for all the paper money. Many people had worthless paper money, and land values fell so much that many people owed more on their land than it was worth.

Focus for Thought (page 259)

13. a. *How did the Whigs receive their name?*
   They opposed "King Andrew" just as Whigs had opposed King George III in the American Revolution.
   b. *What things did they favor?*
   a national bank, high tariffs, and a strong federal government
14. *Why did President Van Buren do little to relieve the depression after the Panic of 1837?*
   He thought the depression should be relieved by the people and the states. (He believed in little government interference in business affairs and strict interpretation of the Constitution.)
15. *What things did the Whigs do to help William Henry Harrison win election as president?*
   They organized a strong campaign that used speeches, parades, songs, and the slogan "Tippecanoe and Tyler too!"
16. *Why did William Henry Harrison serve such a brief term as president?*
   He caught a severe cold after giving a long inaugural address on a cold, drizzly day. The cold developed into pneumonia, from which he died after a month in office.
17. a. *What uncertainty surrounded Tyler's administration?*
   whether Tyler was really the president or whether he was merely acting as president

b. *Why did Tyler's own party (the Whigs) turn against him?*
Tyler vetoed two bills for a national bank, which the Whigs supported.

18. *What borders were established by the Webster-Ashburton Treaty?*
the border between Canada and Maine, and the United States–Canadian border between Lake Superior and the Lake of the Woods

HISTORICAL HIGHLIGHTS (pages 259–261)

A. Matching: Presidents

You will use each answer twice.

a. *James Monroe*
b. *John Quincy Adams*
c. *Andrew Jackson*

d. *Martin Van Buren*
e. *William Henry Harrison*
f. *John Tyler*

e 1. *First president to die in office.*
b 2. *Son of a former president.*
f 3. *President when Webster-Ashburton Treaty was negotiated.*
c 4. *President who represented the common man.*
b 5. *President during a split in the Democratic-Republican Party.*
d 6. *President during the Panic of 1837.*
f 7. *First vice president to fill the position of a president who died in office.*
a 8. *President during the Era of Good Feelings.*
e 9. *First Whig president.*
d 10. *President who had served as vice president under Andrew Jackson.*
a 11. *President who issued a statement against European interference in America.*
c 12. *President who had thousands of Indians moved west.*

B. Matching: Terms

a. *Adams-Onís Treaty*
b. *American System*
c. *Era of Good Feelings*
d. *foreign policy*
e. *Independent Treasury Act*
f. *Missouri Compromise*
g. *Monroe Doctrine*
h. *nullify*
i. *protective tariff*
j. *secede*

k. *sectionalism*
l. *Seminole War*
m. *Specie Circular*
n. *spoils system*
o. *states' rights*
p. *Trail of Tears*
q. *Transcontinental Treaty*
r. *Webster-Ashburton Treaty*
s. *Whigs*

j   1. *To withdraw formally from an organization.*

f   2. *Agreement about slavery in the Louisiana Territory.*

r   3. *Treaty that settled disagreements over boundaries with Canada.*

g   4. *Proclamation stating (1) that America was no longer to be colonized by European nations, (2) that European nations were not to interfere in the affairs of American nations, and (3) that the United States would not interfere in the affairs of European nations.*

b   5. *Henry Clay's plan for a tariff to protect manufacturers, finance internal improvements, and establish a national bank.*

l   6. *Struggle between the United States and Osceola and his tribe over Indian removal to lands in the West.*

s   7. *Political party that opposed Andrew Jackson.*

c   8. *Time of national unity and harmony, with only one political party.*

p   9. *Journey of Cherokee Indians who were forced to move west.*

a, q   10. *Treaty with Spain that gained Florida and established borders (two answers).*

h   11. *To set aside; declare void.*

o   12. *Idea that states have more power than the federal government.*

e   13. *Law by which government money was separated from private banks.*

m   14. *Statement that only gold and silver would be accepted for government lands.*

d   15. *The manner of a nation or national leader in relating to other nations.*

n   16. *Practice in which the winner of an election rewards his supporters with government positions.*

i   17. *High tax on imports, designed to limit competition from foreign merchants.*

k   18. *Devotion to the interests of a local region rather than the whole nation.*

C. True or False

Write whether each statement is true *(T)* or false *(F)*.

F   1. *Andrew Jackson promoted many of the same ideas as the Federalist Party had.*

T   2. *Andrew Jackson was honored by the common people because he identified with them.*

T   3. *Jackson vigorously exercised the powers of the presidency.*

F   4. *Jackson closed the Bank of the United States because it interfered with the economic stability of the nation.*

F   5. *Jackson supported states' rights and sided with South Carolina on the issue of nullification.*

T   6. *The Whig Party was more like the Federalists than like the Democratic-Republicans.*

F   7. *Martin Van Buren thought the federal government should make strong efforts toward economic improvement after the Panic of 1837.*

D. Deeper Discussion

1. *Could the young United States have enforced the Monroe Doctrine at the time it was proclaimed? Explain.*

   Probably not. The new nation was in financial hardship, and its military forces were weak. British support of the Monroe Doctrine probably did more than the United States policy to prevent European interference.

2. a. *In what ways might protective tariffs be helpful?*

   Tariffs produce revenue for the government, and they help to protect businesses from foreign competition, thus maintaining jobs and production.

   b. *How might they be harmful?*

   With tariffs, inefficient businesses do not have the foreign competition that would stimulate them to greater efficiency. Consumers must also pay higher prices for goods—either to the marginal producer or for imported goods. At worst, protective tariffs have led to wars over trade.

3. *What would happen if any state could declare a national law null and void?*

   National unity would be destroyed and chaos would result. This actually happened when the Southern states seceded in the 1860s, and it led to the Civil War. A balance must be maintained between federal and state powers.

4. a. *What were the underlying causes of sectionalism?*

   Some causes were the different ways of living and of making a livelihood. For example, manufacturing flourished in the Northeast but agriculture prospered in the South. Each section favored its own interests above those of other sections. Consequently, people in each section supported government policies that were most profitable for themselves.

   b. *In what ways could the sections actually have helped each other?*

   Each section could have specialized in what it could produce best, and then traded with the other sections so that all would have their needs supplied. Especially with transportation on the Mississippi, the West could have become closely linked to the South. But instead, the Northeast became strongly tied to the West by means of canals and railroads, and the South was more and more isolated. (Many Northerners did not want to buy products made by slave labor.)

5. *How might Jackson's economic policies have contributed to the Panic of 1837?*
By putting the Bank of the United States out of business, Jackson destroyed the economic stability that the bank gave to the national economy. Moreover, with government money in wildcat banks, those banks made loans too freely, especially in the form of paper bank notes. When Jackson then issued the Specie Circular, a panic resulted because people could not redeem the bank notes in gold and silver.
A point not mentioned in the text is the distribution of surplus government funds from the sale of lands. The vast amount of money distributed to the states in this way encouraged reckless borrowing and spending. When this flow of money ended, many states defaulted on their financial obligations.

6. *The Bible says that people are not to "trust in uncertain riches" or to lay up treasures on earth, "where moth and rust doth corrupt, and where thieves break through and steal."*
   a. *How do the economic events of the Jacksonian Era, especially the panics of 1819 and 1837, demonstrate the truth of these verses?*
   The prosperity of the Jacksonian Era ended suddenly after the Specie Circular was issued. This illustrates how riches can "fly away" in a short time.
   b. *How should Christians respond? (See 1 Timothy 6:17–19 and Matthew 6:19, 20, 33.)*
   Instead of trusting in riches, Christians should trust in God, share their blessings with others, and seek first "the kingdom of God, and his righteousness."

E. Chronology and Geography

1. *On your map entitled "The States of the United States," draw the borders of the eleven states admitted between 1791 and 1821. The admission dates for these new states are given on the maps on pages 234, 248, and 250.*
   a. *Label the states with their names and dates of admission.*
   b. *Color these eleven states a different color from the original thirteen states.*
   c. *Start a legend showing what each color represents.*
   d. *Memorize the names and locations of these states.*
   (Individual work.)

2. *Do the following on your map entitled "Territorial Growth of the United States." (See maps on pages 248 and 259 for the location of the treaty lines.)*
   a. *Draw and label the British Treaty Line of 1818.*
   b. *Draw and label the Spanish Treaty Line of 1819.*
   c. *Label the area south of the British Treaty Line that was ceded by Britain in 1818. Color it a different color from the one you used for the United States in 1783.*
   d. *Label East Florida and West Florida. Use a third color to color them.*
   e. *Use a different color to color the remainder of the Louisiana Purchase after the treaties of 1818 and 1819.*
   f. *Draw and label the Webster-Ashburton Line, and color the area Britain ceded in 1842.*
   (Individual work.)
3. *Memorize the names of the first ten presidents in order.*
   (Optional exercise.)

   (1) George Washington   **(6) John Quincy Adams**
   (2) John Adams   **(7) Andrew Jackson**
   (3) Thomas Jefferson   **(8) Martin Van Buren**
   (4) James Madison   **(9) William Henry Harrison**
   (5) James Monroe   **(10) John Tyler**

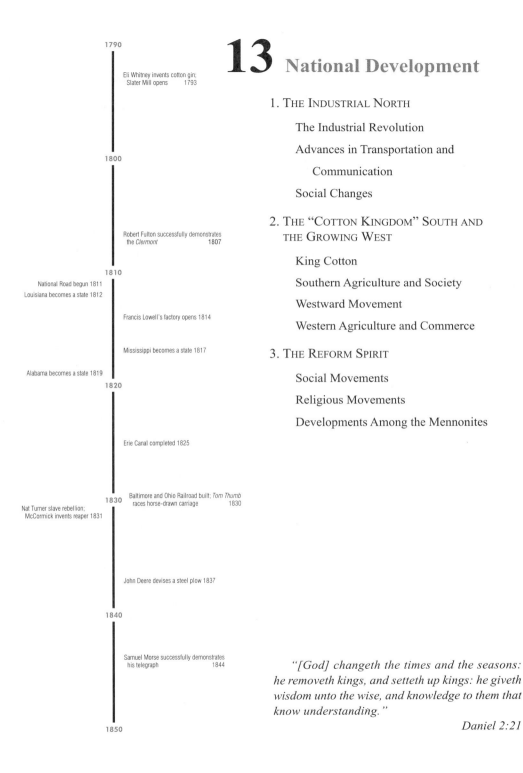

1790

Eli Whitney invents cotton gin;
Slater Mill opens   1793

1800

Robert Fulton successfully demonstrates
the *Clermont*   1807

1810

National Road begun 1811
Louisiana becomes a state 1812

Francis Lowell's factory opens 1814

Mississippi becomes a state 1817

Alabama becomes a state 1819

1820

Erie Canal completed 1825

Baltimore and Ohio Railroad built; *Tom Thumb*
1830   races horse-drawn carriage   1830

Nat Turner slave rebellion;
McCormick invents reaper 1831

John Deere devises a steel plow 1837

1840

Samuel Morse successfully demonstrates
his telegraph   1844

1850

13 National Development

1. THE INDUSTRIAL NORTH

The Industrial Revolution

Advances in Transportation and
Communication

Social Changes

2. THE "COTTON KINGDOM" SOUTH AND THE GROWING WEST

King Cotton

Southern Agriculture and Society

Westward Movement

Western Agriculture and Commerce

3. THE REFORM SPIRIT

Social Movements

Religious Movements

Developments Among the Mennonites

*"[God] changeth the times and the seasons:
he removeth kings, and setteth up kings: he giveth
wisdom unto the wise, and knowledge to them that
know understanding."*

Daniel 2:21

Chapter 13 (pages 262–289)

NATIONAL DEVELOPMENT

Chapter Objectives

- To study the profound changes that shaped American society in the period from 1800 to 1850.
- To learn about developments in commerce, industry, agriculture, transportation, and communication in the first half of the 1800s.
- To understand the role of cotton and slavery in the South, and to gain a Biblical perspective on slavery.
- To learn about the great westward movement of Americans in the first half of the 1800s.
- To learn about the reform movements and religious confusion of the period from 1800 to 1850.
- To learn about developments among Mennonites in the United States during the early 1800s.

To the Teacher

This chapter briefly covers the most important facets of life in the early 1800s. You can make the text come alive by providing outside information about this period, especially from books written by people of those times. *Freedom's Ferment*, by Alice F. Tyler, covers a broad range of religious and social movements, while *The Transportation Revolution*, by George R. Taylor, covers developments in transportation and industry.

Some sources may overemphasize the effects of the Industrial Revolution on workers. While it is true that working conditions were sometimes poor, we must remember that people on farms also worked hard for long hours. Wanting to work only ten hours a day was considered laziness! Whatever its drawbacks, industrialization did contribute to a higher standard of living. On the other hand, it also contributed to slums, moral decay, and religious confusion. The fact remains that technology increases man's capacity for evil; only God can make man better.

The slave system was debilitating and demoralizing. It kept the black people from developing their abilities; and even worse, it held them in such a state of inferiority that the resulting mentality still causes struggles today. Slavery gave the planters much time to indulge in idle pursuits, and it made tyrants of many. Southern defense of slavery amounted to rationalizing its evils. This is especially true when we consider that many Southerners stood ready to end slavery before the cotton gin was invented. But their attitudes hardened when slaves became "necessary" for large-scale cotton production. The tenor of the New Testament is opposed to human bondage. Thus a person could be a Christian slave but hardly a Christian slaveholder.

While the early reforms did some good, we do need to understand their motivation. Social reforms were based on the idea that man is able to improve by his own effort, and religious reforms were often based on postmillennialism—the idea that Christ will come to reign on earth after it has been sufficiently improved. Romanticism was a philosophy (expressed in art and in literature such as that of Nathaniel Hawthorne) that emphasized emotion and imagination rather than the reason and logic of the Enlightenment. Romanticists "championed the freedom of the human spirit" as well as greater freedom of thought and expression, and they idealized nature. They believed in the "rights and dignity of the individual." For Bible-believing Christians, these social and religious movements belonged to the world, not the church. It is not hard to understand why Mennonites of that time rejected the innovations of the reformers, both social and religious.

Note on chapter test: There is a single test for Chapters 13 and 14.

Christian Perspectives
- Man takes pride in his technology, but he is unable to improve his wicked heart (Genesis 6:5; Jeremiah 17:9; Romans 3:23).
- All men are created equal (Acts 17:26), and God is no respecter of persons (Acts 10:34; Philippians 2:3). The Christian must respect the worth and dignity of everyone, including people who are slaves, immigrants, or of a different religion.
- The Bible assumes the existence of slavery and nowhere condemns it as such. However, slavery is morally wrong according to the Golden Rule (Luke 6:31). Masters who become rich at the expense of others face a fearful penalty (James 5:1–6). Slaves were to be obedient and respectful to masters (Ephesians 6:5–8; Colossians 3:22; Titus 2:9, 10), and masters were to be considerate of their slaves (Ephesians 6:9; Colossians 4:1).
- Strong drink is not for people professing godliness (Proverbs 23:29–35).
- Parents, not the state, are responsible for educating their children (Ephesians 6:4). Today many concerned parents meet this responsibility by having their children educated in Christian schools.
- True spirituality is evident in a life of holiness, not in an emotional frenzy as in the camp meeting revivals. Also, acceptable worship is decent and orderly (1 Corinthians 14:23–40).
- Any person who claims a revelation contrary to Scriptural teaching is a false prophet. Joseph Smith was one of these (Galatians 1:8, 9; Jude).

Further Study
- The Industrial Revolution and men who contributed to it, such as Samuel Slater, Eli Whitney, and Francis Lowell.

- The Erie Canal and the canal era.
- The stories of noted inventors and their inventions, such as James Watt and the steam engine, Robert Fulton and the steamboat, and Samuel F. B. Morse and the telegraph.
- The westward movement in America.
- The movements in the early 1800s to promote temperance, educational reform, and the abolition of slavery.
- The religious movements of the early 1800s and their effects on the Mennonites.

Chapter 13 Quiz

Write the correct name or term for each description.

1. The change from producing handmade goods at home to producing machine-made goods in factories.

2. The elimination of slavery.

3. The movement to stop the use of strong drink.

4. Inventor of the cotton gin.

5. Man who brought textile manufacturing to America.

6. Inventor of the mechanical reaper.

7. Evangelist who used new methods to win converts.

8. Term for a traveling preacher in the West.

9. Inventor of the telegraph.

Quiz Answers

1. **Industrial Revolution**
2. **abolition**
3. **temperance**
4. **Eli Whitney**
5. **Samuel Slater**

6. **Cyrus McCormick**
7. **Charles Finney**
8. **circuit rider**
9. **Samuel F. B. Morse**

Answer Key

Focus for Thought (page 272)

1. *What was the Industrial Revolution?*
   the change from producing handmade goods at home to producing machine-made goods in factories

2. *What contributions did Eli Whitney and Francis Lowell make to the growth of industry?*
   Eli Whitney began the use of interchangeable parts. Francis Lowell built the first factory to do all the steps of manufacturing at one place.

3. *What were two reasons for the rapid growth of industry in the North?*
   (Any two.) The land was not as profitable for agriculture as in other places. Iron ore and other raw materials were available there. Abundant energy was available to power the factories. Many natural harbors made shipping easy.

4. *Why did railroads put canals out of business?*
   Trains could travel faster and go to more places than canal boats could.

5. *What were two great improvements that resulted from use of the telegraph?*
   Rail travel was safer because of better communications. News could be spread quickly over the country.

6. *Name and describe three social changes that accompanied the industrial changes in the North.*
   A new type of worker—Workers concentrated on just one step in the manufacturing process, and they repeated the same routine over and over.
   Growth of cities—Many people moved to cities to work in factories. Large slum areas developed.
   Increased immigration—Many poor immigrants worked in factories of the North.

7. *For what reasons were immigrants despised by some Americans?*
   Immigrants worked willingly for little pay, which kept wages low for everyone. Most immigrants were Roman Catholic at a time when most Americans were Protestant.

Focus for Thought (pages 280, 281)

8. a. *When was the cotton gin invented, and by whom?*
in 1793; by Eli Whitney

b. *What effects did it have?*
Cotton growing spread rapidly, and slaves became highly valuable because slave labor seemed to provide the only way to make cotton raising profitable. Slavery became firmly established in the South.

9. *What were the three characteristics of a Southern plantation?*
vast fields and large-scale production, a staple crop that provided the main income, and slave labor

10. a. *How was slavery a hindrance to the South?*
It hindered the industrial development because planters invested their money in land and slaves rather than in factories, stores, and other improvements.

b. *Why was it demeaning to the slaves?*
They had to work for a master rather than for themselves, and they lacked freedom and opportunities to develop their education and abilities. Slave families were often divided.

11. *What are two ways that small farmers in the South were different from planters?*
(Any two.) Small farmers raised food crops, such as corn. They raised only a little cotton. In general, they worked their own land instead of using slaves.

12. *By what two means did many pioneers move west in the early 1800s?*
by Conestoga wagons, by flatboats or steamboats

13. *What two inventions boosted agricultural production, and who invented them?*
a plow with a polished iron moldboard and a steel share, invented by John Deere; the mechanical reaper, invented by Cyrus McCormick

Focus for Thought (pages 285, 286)

14. *Describe two things that supporters of the temperance movement did to promote their cause.*
(Any two.) They organized temperance societies. They published books and pamphlets denouncing strong drink. They tried to have alcoholic beverages outlawed.

15. *Some reformers worked to make education available to everyone.*
a. *In what ways did these reformers think this would improve society?*
They thought people could better provide for themselves and participate

in elections and government. They believed education would help to reduce crime.

b. *What shift in the education of children did public schools help to bring about?*

The education of children shifted from being a responsibility of parents and churches to being a responsibility of the state.

16. a. *What are two ways in which abolitionists worked against slavery?*

(Any two.) Some made efforts to send freed slaves to Africa. They opposed slavery in speech and writing. They helped slaves to escape from their masters.

b. *How did nonresistant Christians view the actions of the abolitionists?*

They agreed that slavery was not right, but they considered it wrong to use force in opposing slavery.

17. *How did circuit riders and camp meetings bring the Gospel to settlers in the West?*

Circuit riders traveled about, preaching to rural families. In camp meetings, thousands of settlers gathered to hear the Gospel.

18. *What are two lasting effects that the Second Great Awakening had on the United States?*

(Any two.) Foreign mission work increased. The American Tract Society and the American Bible Society were founded. The Sunday school movement began. Several false religions began.

19. *How did a new kind of singing come into the Mennonite Church in the middle 1800s?*

Joseph Funk introduced the use of shaped notes and held singing schools that promoted singing in harmony.

HISTORICAL HIGHLIGHTS (pages 286–287)

A. Matching: People

a. *Adoniram Judson*

b. *Charles Finney*

c. *Cyrus McCormick*

d. *Eli Whitney*

e. *Francis Lowell*

f. *Frederick Douglass*

g. *Horace Mann*

h. *James Watt*

i. *John Deere*

j. *John Greenleaf Whittier*

k. *John Oberholtzer*

l. *Joseph Funk*

m. *Joseph Smith*

n. *Noah Webster*

o. *Robert Fulton*

p. *Samuel F. B. Morse*

q. *Samuel Slater*

r. *William Lloyd Garrison*

c 1. *Inventor of the mechanical reaper.*

g 2. *Promoter of educational reform.*

p 3. *Inventor of the telegraph.*

a 4. *"Father of American missions."*

h 5. *Built first practical steam engine.*

d 6. *Inventor of the cotton gin; used interchangeable parts.*

m 7. *Founder of the Mormons.*

j 8. *Abolitionist poet.*

q 9. *Brought Industrial Revolution to America by building textile machines from memory.*

n 10. *Published the "blue-backed speller."*

i 11. *Invented a steel plow for use on the prairie.*

o 12. *Built the* Clermont, *the first successful steamboat.*

b 13. *Evangelist who used new methods to win converts.*

r 14. *Extreme abolitionist who published* The Liberator.

k 15. *Mennonite leader who favored greater leniency.*

f 16. *Former slave who spoke out against slavery.*

l 17. *Virginia Mennonite who devised shaped notes and held singing schools.*

e 18. *Built the first factory to make raw cotton into cloth at one place.*

B. Matching: Terms 1

a. *abolition*

b. *breaking plow*

c. *camp meeting*

d. *circuit rider*

e. *cotton gin*

f. *girdling*

g. *interchangeable parts*

h. *plantation*

i. *"planter aristocracy"*

j. *slave code*

k. *temperance movement*

l. *turnpike*

i 1. *Small group of rich men who controlled the South.*

a 2. *Elimination of slavery.*

f 3. *Removing a strip of bark around a tree to kill it.*

b 4. *Large, heavy implement used to turn over prairie sod.*

k 5. *Effort to stop the use of strong drink.*

d 6. *Minister who traveled about, preaching to pioneers.*

c 7. *Evangelistic gathering held outdoors or in a tent.*

l 8. *Road for which users pay toll.*

h 9. *Large farm that produced one main crop and used slave labor.*

g 10. *Parts that can be interchanged because they are made exactly alike.*

j 11. *Set of laws placing restrictions on slaves.*

e 12. *Device for removing seeds from cotton.*

C. Matching: Terms 2

a. *American Colonization Society*   e. *Industrial Revolution*
b. *Conestoga wagon*   f. *McGuffey reader*
c. *Cotton Kingdom*   g. *National Road*
d. *Erie Canal*   h. *Second Great Awakening*

h   1. *Religious revival that began in the late 1790s.*
e   2. *Change from producing handmade goods at home to producing machine-made goods in factories.*
c   3. *Name given to the South because it depended on cotton.*
g   4. *Route extending from Cumberland to Vandalia.*
b   5. *Canvas-topped vehicle used by pioneers moving west.*
a   6. *Association with the goal of moving freed blacks to Africa.*
f   7. *Reading text used in schools of the 1800s.*
d   8. *Waterway that joined Lake Erie to the Hudson River and diverted western trade to New York City.*

D. Deeper Discussion

1. a. *What were some benefits of the Industrial Revolution?*
It allowed the production of more and better goods for lower prices. It raised the standard of living. It made life more pleasant.
b. *What were some detriments?*
It brought the growth of city slums (and the decline of morals that is common in cities). It caused poor working and living conditions for some workers.

2. a. *How did slavery degrade the blacks?*
Slavery kept blacks in a state of bondage, in which they were considered inferior to whites (whereas the Bible teaches that all men are equal before God). They were forced to do work for which their masters received the benefits. They lacked freedom and opportunities to develop their education and abilities.
b. *How was it degrading to the slaveholders?*
They had time for idle pleasures while the slaves did their work. Often the masters became tyrants who treated their slaves harshly.
c. *How did slavery hinder the South?*
Industry lagged because planters invested their money in land and slaves rather than in factories, stores, and internal improvements. With power held by a small group of rich men, the South could not benefit from the broad range of abilities in the population as a

whole. The South was less productive than the North because slave labor was inefficient.

3. *Why can man not solve spiritual and social problems by using his own intellect and abilities?*

Spiritual and social problems are generally the results of man's evil nature. Since man's greatest need is spiritual, he cannot improve himself or others by using his natural powers. The only true solution is God's solution: repenting from sin and receiving salvation by faith in Christ.

4. *Can national evils be overcome by making laws against them? Explain.*

No. Laws cannot deal with the basic sinfulness of man's heart. For example, if strong drink is outlawed, people will drink in secret. However, laws are necessary to restrain and control evil. If there were no laws against drugs like cocaine, no doubt much chaos and violence would result. But man's laws will never reform unrighteous people. Only the new birth can do that.

5. *How have time and experience shown that the expectations of Horace Mann and the educational reformers were wrong?*

Public education has been a dismal failure. Even though education is now available to everyone, crime and other social evils have not diminished. Because of moral decline, all manner of evil philosophies have come into the schools.

6. a. *Give evidence from this chapter of the religious confusion in the United States during the first half of the 1800s.*

Many people followed deceivers such as William Miller and Joseph Smith. Various social experiments to establish utopias drew away many. People engaged in emotional excess in the camp meeting revivals. These facts indicate that people longed for truth and leadership but were confused as to what the truth was.

b. *Why did Mennonites reject many of the religious innovations of this time?*

Mennonites rejected the innovations because of the way many of them were conducted and because of their effects. Mennonites emphasized the "old foundations" of discipleship, suffering for Christ, and separation from the world. To identify with the new ways would in many cases have been to identify with the world.

7. *How did the camp meetings in the West deviate from Scriptural principles for worship as given in 1 Corinthians 14:23–33, 40?*

In these meetings, many people lost control of their emotions. Religious hysteria brought improper and disorderly conduct, whereas "God is not the author of confusion" and wants all things to be done "decently and in order." Our worship is to be edifying, not just an emotional experience.

E. Chronology and Geography

Describe how the frontier moved westward from the mid-1700s to the mid-1800s.

Before the Revolution, the frontier was up to the Appalachian Mountains and just across the Appalachians. After the Revolution, Americans began to settle in Ohio, Kentucky, and Tennessee. After the War of 1812, the frontier included territories like Indiana, Illinois, Alabama, and Mississippi; and later it extended to the west bank of the Mississippi (Missouri).

So Far This Year (page 288)

A. Matching: Terms 1

b   1. *Time of national unity and harmony.*

h   2. *Agreement that ended the War of 1812.*

f   3. *Agreement that settled differences with Spain in 1795.*

d   4. *Agreement that settled a slavery problem.*

a   5. *Agreement that gained Florida in 1819.*

c   6. *Agreement that settled differences with Britain.*

e   7. *Declaration about involvement of European and American nations in each other's affairs.*

g   8. *Assembly that declared independence.*

i   9. *Agreement that ended the American Revolution.*

a. *Adams-Onís Treaty*
b. *Era of Good Feelings*
c. *Jay Treaty*
d. *Missouri Compromise*
e. *Monroe Doctrine*
f. *Pinckney Treaty*
g. *Second Continental Congress*
h. *Treaty of Ghent*
i. *Treaty of Paris*

B. Matching: Terms 2

h   10. *Practice in which the winner of an election rewards his supporters with government positions.*

j   11. *Political party that opposed Andrew Jackson.*

i   12. *Idea that states are supreme over the federal government.*

b   13. *Political party that favored loose interpretation and strong government.*

g   14. *Devotion to the interests of a local region rather than the whole nation.*

c   15. *Supreme Court's power to declare a law unconstitutional.*

e   16. *System in which lords owned land and serfs farmed it for them.*

a   17. *Political party that favored strict interpretation and limited government.*

d   18. *Supporters of Great Britain.*

f   19. *Persons favoring independence.*

a. *Democratic-Republicans*
b. *Federalists*
c. *judicial review*
d. *Loyalists*
e. *manorialism*
f. *patriots*
g. *sectionalism*
h. *spoils system*
i. *states' rights*
j. *Whigs*

C. Completion: People and Places

Write the correct name for each description.

Alexander Hamilton
20. *Federalist leader and first secretary of the treasury.*

Daniel Boone
21. *Man who opened the Wilderness Road to Kentucky.*

Meriwether Lewis, William Clark
22. *Two men who explored the Louisiana Purchase from 1804 to 1806.*

John Marshall
23. *Chief justice who strengthened the Supreme Court.*

Cornwallis
24. *British general whose defeat ended the Revolution.*

George Washington
25. *Patriot general in command of the entire American army.*

Saratoga
26. *Battle that was the turning point in the Revolution.*

Lexington (and Concord)
27. *Location of the beginning battle of the Revolution.*

Yorktown
28. *Location of the last major battle of the Revolution.*

Ohio River valley
29. *Place where conflicting claims led to the French and Indian War.*

Quebec
30. *Site of the decisive battle in the French and Indian War.*

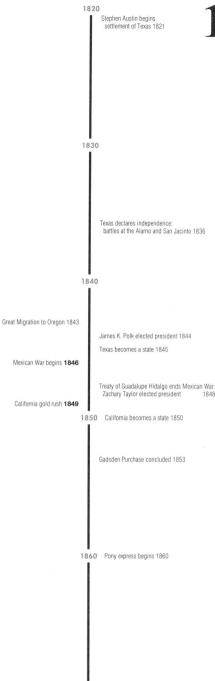

1820

Stephen Austin begins
settlement of Texas 1821

1830

Texas declares independence;
battles at the Alamo and San Jacinto 1836

1840

Great Migration to Oregon 1843

James K. Polk elected president 1844

Texas becomes a state 1845

Mexican War begins **1846**

Treaty of Guadalupe Hidalgo ends Mexican War;
Zachary Taylor elected president   1848

California gold rush **1849**

1850   California becomes a state 1850

Gadsden Purchase concluded 1853

1860   Pony express begins 1860

1870

14 National Expansion

1. TEXAS AND THE MEXICAN WAR

    The Story of Texas

    Expansionist Fever

    The Mexican War

    Events After the War

2. THE OREGON TERRITORY

    Oregon Fever

    The Oregon Trail

    Progress Toward Statehood

3. CALIFORNIA AND THE GOLD RUSH

    Discovery of Gold

    The Gold Rush

    Statehood of California

*"Wait on the LORD, and keep his way, and he shall
exalt thee to inherit the land."*

Psalm 37:34

Chapter 14 (pages 290–311)

NATIONAL EXPANSION

Chapter Objectives

- To learn how Texas became an independent nation and later a state of the United States.
- To understand the expansionism of the 1840s in terms of manifest destiny.
- To gain an understanding of the Mexican War and its effects.
- To learn how the Oregon Territory was settled and became part of the United States.
- To learn about the gold rush to California, and how California became a state.

To the Teacher

As the book progresses in American history, facts and concepts from earlier chapters will be increasingly involved in understanding the current chapters. To give students a proper comprehension, show how events are related to the earlier chapters. For example, the story of Texas, New Mexico, and California relates closely to Chapter 4 on Spanish colonization.

Geography is important in this chapter. Make sure students have a picture of the general geographic setting, especially the West in relation to California and Oregon. Make it clear that the westward movement discussed in this chapter is to the Far West, whereas that of earlier chapters related to what we today call the Midwest.

The Mexican War can be portrayed in a bad light. But as usual, there are two sides to every story. For example, the United States did send John Slidell to negotiate with Mexico; but because the Mexican government was so unstable, he was rebuffed. Present the facts without trying to decide who was good or bad, and remember that God has a purpose in what He allows.

Note on chapter test: There is a single test for Chapters 13 and 14.

Christian Perspectives

- Although God allowed the United States to expand to the Pacific Ocean, that does not mean He had a spiritual mission for the nation. God regards the nations as beasts (Daniel 7, 8), and beastly conduct is evident in the Mexican War. But God did bless the United States for recognizing basic principles of justice and right.
- Many mountain men, fur traders, and explorers lived loose, wicked lives, especially at rendezvous times. (Jedediah Smith was an exception.) Their contribution is recognized in the text because of their important role in opening the Far West.
- The Oregon-bound pioneers exhibited courage and fortitude on the Oregon

Trail. Marcus Whitman, later killed by Indians, is an example of sacrifice for the cause of the Gospel. Many others made similar sacrifices.

- The California gold rush was driven by rank covetousness. Many of the forty-niners lost everything they had, even their lives; or if they did get rich, they squandered their new-found wealth. These people experienced the truth of Proverbs 28:22: "He that hasteth to be rich hath an evil eye, and considereth not that poverty shall come upon him."

Further Study

- The Alamo and its defenders.
- The war of independence for Texas, and the life of Sam Houston.
- Events of the Mexican War.
- Mountain men and explorers such as Jedediah Smith.
- The Oregon Trail and experiences of the travelers. (See *Seven Alone* or *On to Oregon* for the story of young John Sager and his family, who were with the party led by George and Jacob Donner.)
- The California gold rush and how miners obtained gold.
- The pony express.
- The story of missionaries in Oregon, such as the Whitmans.

Chapter 14 Quiz

1. The idea that the United States should spread until it reached from coast to coast is called
   a. Mexican Cession.   c. Oregon fever.
   b. manifest destiny.   d. California gold rush.

2. A term that refers to land gained by the Mexican War is
   a. Gadsden Purchase.   c. Mexican Cession.
   b. manifest destiny.   d. Treaty of Guadalupe Hidalgo.

3. A term that refers to the hardy fur traders and explorers of the West is
   a. forty-niners.   c. prospectors.
   b. rendezvous.   d. mountain men.

4. The expansionist president who served from 1845 to 1849 was
   a. James Polk.   c. Zachary Taylor.
   b. Sam Houston.   d. Winfield Scott.

5. The man who began colonizing Texas was
   a. John Sutter.   c. Sam Houston.
   b. Stephen Austin.   d. Marcus Whitman.

6. The missionary who encouraged settlement of Oregon was
   a. Marcus Whitman.   c. John Sutter.
   b. John Frémont.   d. Stephen Austin.

7. The man near whose fort gold was discovered was
   a. John Frémont.   c. John Sutter.
   b. James Marshall.   d. Stephen Kearny.

8. A mail system to connect California with the East was the
   a. gold rush.   c. Oregon Trail.
   b. pony express.   d. forty-niners.

9. The treaty that ended the Mexican War was the
   a. joint occupation.   c. Treaty of Guadalupe Hidalgo.
   b. Gadsden Purchase.   d. Mexican Cession.

Quiz Answers

1. **b**   6. **a**
2. **c**   7. **c**
3. **d**   8. **b**
4. **a**   9. **c**
5. **b**

Answer Key

Focus for Thought (page 298)

1. *Give several answers to each question.*

   a. *Why were Americans eager to settle Texas?*

   The land was rich, vast, and sparsely populated. Mexico held only weak control over the region, and Mexico wanted more settlers. The land was cheap. The South saw in Texas a way to expand slavery and influence.

   b. *Why did American settlers in Texas want to be independent?*

   The settlers were required to become Mexican citizens, join the Catholic Church, and free their slaves. They were different from Mexicans in their language and way of life. They wanted to be free from the harsh rule of Santa Anna.

2. a. *What happened at the Alamo?*

   The Alamo was an old mission where a force of Texan soldiers found refuge. Santa Anna's troops besieged the Texans, forced their way into the Alamo, and killed all the defenders.

   b. *How did Texas gain independence soon after the incident there?*

   The Texans defeated the Mexican army at San Jacinto and captured Santa Anna. Then they forced Santa Anna to sign a treaty granting independence to Texas.

3. *What did the Texans name their new nation, and how long was it an independent republic?*

   the Lone Star Republic; ten years

4. a. *What was meant by* manifest destiny?

   It was the belief that the United States was clearly destined by God to spread over the whole North American continent (as the "great center from which civilization, religion, and liberty should radiate").

   b. *How was this idea expressed in the 1800s?*

   The United States expanded significantly by gaining various new territories (such as Texas, the Mexican Cession, and the Gadsden Purchase).

5. *What were three disputes that contributed to the Mexican War?*

   (Any three.) The Mexican government had never recognized the treaty signed by Santa Anna (or the independence of Texas). Mexico and the United States disputed over the boundary of Texas. Mexico had not paid the debt owed to some citizens of the United States. John Slidell had not been able to negotiate with the Mexicans. General Taylor advanced to the Rio Grande, which Mexicans believed was their territory.

6. *List the provisions of the Treaty of Guadalupe Hidalgo.*
Mexico recognized the border of Texas at the Rio Grande. Mexico gave land (the Mexican Cession) to the United States. The United States paid Mexico $15 million and also reimbursed American citizens the $3.25 million that Mexico owed them.

7. *What were three effects of the Mexican War?*
(Any three.) The Americans gained a vast stretch of land. They gained the ill feelings of the Mexicans. The question of slavery in new territories was reopened. The Mexican War contributed to the Civil War.

Focus for Thought (page 303)

8. *How did the mountain men contribute to interest in the Far West?*
They explored new regions, developed trails, and found passes by which to cross the mountains. John Frémont wrote a book that became a guide for people traveling west. Also, mountain men often guided groups of pioneers moving west.

9. a. *Why did missionaries go to Oregon?*
to evangelize the Indians there

   b. *How did Marcus Whitman influence settlers to move there?*
He wrote letters promoting the bounties of the land, and he led one group of pioneers to Oregon.

10. *On the Oregon Trail, why did pioneers need to*
   a. *travel light?*
because of the steep mountains they had to cross (and because of the great distance to be traveled)

   b. *work together?*
They worked together to overcome the difficulties and hazards of the trail. For example, at night, they formed a tight circle with their wagons to defend themselves against Indians and wild animals, and to corral their livestock.

   c. *keep moving?*
in order to cross the high western mountains before winter

11. a. *How was the Oregon Country divided between the United States and Great Britain?*
It was divided at 49° N except that the British retained all of Vancouver Island.

   b. *What modern states contain land that was part of this territory?*
Washington, Oregon, and Idaho

Focus for Thought (page 308)

12. *What three main routes did miners from the East take to travel to California?*
They traveled by land routes, including the Old Spanish Trail and the Oregon Trail; by sailing around South America; or by sailing to Panama, crossing the isthmus, and sailing to California.

13. *Give several details of life in California during the gold rush.*
(Sample answers.) The miners had to work very hard to obtain gold. Fighting, robbery, and murder increased. Many miners spent their gold on strong drink and riotous living. Prices rose exorbitantly. Serving the needs of the miners was often more profitable than mining.

14. *How did California become a state so quickly?*
So many people flocked to California that it soon had more than the sixty thousand people necessary to become a state.

15. a. *Why was the pony express established, and how did it operate?*
It was established because travel and communication were slow and difficult between California and the rest of the nation. Stagecoaches required twenty days or more to make the trip.
Horsemen galloped from one station to another, changing horses at each station. In this way mail could travel between Missouri and California in about ten days.
b. *How long did it last, and why did it end?*
The pony express lasted for eighteen months. It ended when telegraph lines linked California to the rest of the nation.

HISTORICAL HIGHLIGHTS (pages 308–311)

A. Matching: People

a. *Davy Crockett*

b. *James K. Polk*

c. *Jedediah Smith*

d. *Jim Bowie*

e. *John Frémont*

f. *John Sutter*

g. *Kit Carson*

h. *Marcus Whitman*

i. *Sam Houston*

j. *Santa Anna*

k. *Stephen Austin*

l. *Stephen Kearny*

m. *Winfield Scott*

n. *Zachary Taylor*

a, d 1. *Men who died in defending the Alamo (two answers).*

n 2. *General in the Mexican War who was elected president in 1848.*

i 3. *First president of the Lone Star Republic.*

g   4. *Well-known mountain man.*

k   5. *Man who began colonizing Texas.*

c   6. *Discoverer of South Pass; first American known to enter California by land.*

l   7. *General who conquered New Mexico and California in the Mexican War.*

m   8. *General who conquered Mexico City in the Mexican War.*

b   9. *Expansionist president when United States gained Texas and California.*

h   10. *Missionary to Indians in Oregon who promoted settlement there.*

f   11. *Man near whose fort gold was discovered.*

e   12. *Captain who led a revolt in California and wrote a book about the West.*

j   13. *Harsh ruler and military leader of Mexico.*

B. Matching: Terms

a. *Bear Flag Republic*   h. *mountain men*

b. *forty-niners*   i. *Oregon Trail*

c. *Free-Soil Party*   j. *pony express*

d. *Gadsden Purchase*   k. *prospectors*

e. *Lone Star Republic*   l. *rendezvous*

f. *manifest destiny*   m. *Treaty of Guadalupe Hidalgo*

g. *Mexican Cession*

f   1. *Idea that the United States was intended to spread over the whole North American continent.*

h   2. *Hardy fur traders and explorers in the West.*

j   3. *Improved system for delivering mail to California.*

a   4. *Name given to California when it became independent.*

d   5. *Land obtained from Mexico to build a southern railroad.*

i   6. *Route used by settlers traveling to the Northwest.*

b   7. *People who rushed to find gold in 1849.*

g   8. *Land gained through the Mexican War.*

c   9. *Political party that opposed slavery in 1848.*

l   10. *Meeting place for fur traders to sell their furs and buy supplies.*

m   11. *Agreement that ended the Mexican War in 1848.*

k   12. *People who seek valuable minerals.*

e   13. *Name used for independent Texas.*

C. Matching: Places

a. *Alamo*

b. *Buena Vista*

c. *Fort Laramie*

d. *Great Salt Lake*

e. *Oregon Territory*

f. *Platte River*

g. *Rio Grande*

h. *San Jacinto*

i. *Snake River*

j. *South Pass*

k. *Sutter's Fort*

l. *Vancouver Island*

m. *Walla Walla*

n. *Willamette River valley*

o. *49° N latitude*

k   1. *Place in central California near which gold was found.*

d   2. *Body of water in Utah.*

o   3. *Border between the United States and Canada to the Pacific.*

b   4. *Place in northern Mexico where Zachary Taylor defeated the Mexicans.*

n   5. *Final destination of Oregon settlers.*

l   6. *Land extending south of 49° N and remaining entirely British.*

h   7. *Location of the battle that won independence for Texas.*

m   8. *Fort near the Whitman Mission.*

c   9. *Stopping place in Wyoming, along the Oregon Trail.*

f 10. *River in present-day Nebraska that the Oregon Trail followed for almost 600 miles (966 km).*

a 11. *Old mission near San Antonio, Texas, that fell to the Mexicans.*

j 12. *Place where the Oregon Trail crossed the Rockies.*

g 13. *River that formed the disputed boundary between Texas and Mexico.*

e 14. *Area from which the states of Oregon, Washington, and Idaho were formed.*

i 15. *River that the Oregon Trail followed across Idaho.*

D. Multiple Choice

Write the letter of the best answer.

1. *What was the main attraction that drew American settlers to Oregon?*

   a. *freedom of religion*

   c. *social discontent*

   b. bounty of the land

   d. *gold*

2. *Why did the United States obtain so much territory during the presidency of James Polk?*

   a. *The United States bought land through the Mexican Cession.*

   b. *The United States made the Gadsden Purchase.*

   c. *The mountain men opened the West by exploring it.*

   d. The president and many others believed in manifest destiny.

3. *Why was Texas not accepted into the United States when it first applied for admission?*
   a. *The president of that time did not support manifest destiny.*
   b. *Texas had rebelled against the Mexican government.*
   c. There was conflict over slavery in Texas, and fear that war would break out with Mexico.
   d. *Texas was part of the Mexican Cession.*
4. *Which one of the following was included in the Mexican Cession?*
   a. *Gadsden Purchase*   c. *Texas*
   b. California   d. *Oregon Country*
5. *What was Marcus Whitman's greatest contribution to gaining the Oregon Country for the United States?*
   a. *He conducted a successful mission among the Indians there.*
   b. *He persuaded authorities that the British and the Americans should occupy the area jointly.*
   c. He influenced many United States settlers to move into the area.
   d. *He encouraged the mountain men to keep the British out of the area.*

E. Deeper Discussion

1. *Why did Americans believe in manifest destiny?*
   Americans considered their nation as the "great center from which civilization, religion, and liberty should radiate," and this led naturally to the idea that the United States was clearly destined by God to spread over the whole North American continent. Manifest destiny seemed to be supported by the pioneers' success in subduing the wilderness, by the steady westward expansion, and by the advances of technology.
2. *Why did the Mexicans hold ill feelings toward the United States after the Mexican War?*
   The Mexicans must have felt that the Americans had bullied them for their land; when they could not buy it, they fought for it. The Mexicans had given up a large part of their territory. They probably feared that the United States might sometime try to take all of Mexico.
3. *How did the Mexican War contribute to the Civil War?*
   Because land was gained by the Mexican War, the question about slavery in new territories again came up. This question was one of the main issues leading to the Civil War. Also, many of the men and officers who fought in the Mexican War gained experience and learned lessons that they later used in the Civil War.

4. *What contributed to the lawlessness and violence of the mining towns in California during the gold rush?*

One factor was the absence of established government in California; each man had to take care of himself. Another factor was the greed of the miners, who would do almost anything to achieve their desire. Still another was the character of many who came; they were not industrious citizens with families, but often the dishonest, lawless, and unattached. This was not true of all forty-niners, of course, but the many unscrupulous men did contribute to the lawless environment. When man's baser passions rule without restraint, as in the desire for quick wealth and strong drink, lawlessness and violence are sure to follow.

5. *Using a topical Bible, look up New Testament references to gold and riches. How should the Christian relate to a gold rush?*

According to passages such as 1 Timothy 6 and Matthew 6, the Christian is not to trust in material riches, which will pass away. He is rather to trust in God, seek first the kingdom of God, and be content with what he has. The Bible also describes covetousness as idolatry; a gold rush is the epitome of covetousness. Instead of taking part in a gold rush, the Christian awaits a crown in heaven that will not fade away.

F. Chronology and Geography

1. *On your map entitled "Territorial Growth of the United States," draw lines showing the Texas Annexation, the Mexican Cession, the Gadsden Purchase, and the Oregon Territory. Label these areas, and color each a different color.* **(Individual work.)**

2. *On a large map of the United States, follow the route of the Oregon Trail through the present states. (A map in an encyclopedia or a road atlas may help.) Note also the California Trail, as well as the alternate routes at various places. Do modern highways follow the same routes? Over what kind of terrain did the Oregon Trail pass?*

Modern highways often do follow the old trail routes. One is Interstate 80, passing by the Great Salt Lake and going through the Great Salt Lake Desert and through the Sierras. U.S. Route 30 also follows part of the Oregon Trail. The land was certainly difficult to travel across, with rugged terrain, steep mountains, and dry deserts.

3. *Answer these questions.*

   a. *What were the advantages and disadvantages of each of the three routes to California?*

The overland routes were shortest, but they were difficult and dangerous because of mountains, deserts, and attacks by Indians and robbers. The route around South America was easier but more expensive, and it involved some nine or ten months of hazardous sailing. The route across Panama was shorter than sailing around South America, but travelers faced the danger of diseases carried by insects in Panama.

   b. *Why was the Pacific coast settled before other areas of the West?*

Most of the West between Missouri and the Pacific Coast was a dry region, which at that time was called the Great American Desert. The lure of gold in California and rich soil in Oregon motivated people to cross this dry land and settle the Pacific Coast.

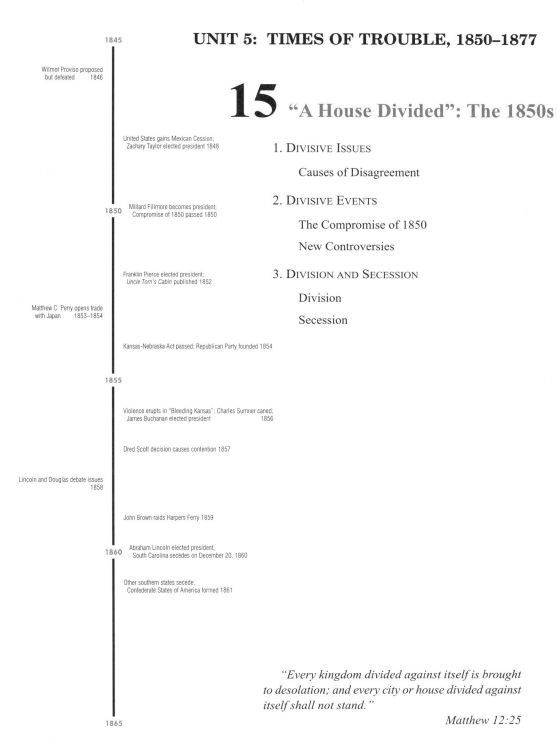

1845

Wilmot Proviso proposed
but defeated   1846

United States gains Mexican Cession;
Zachary Taylor elected president 1848

1850   Millard Fillmore becomes president;
Compromise of 1850 passed 1850

Franklin Pierce elected president;
Uncle Tom's Cabin published 1852

Matthew C. Perry opens trade
with Japan   1853–1854

Kansas-Nebraska Act passed; Republican Party founded 1854

1855

Violence erupts in "Bleeding Kansas"; Charles Sumner caned;
James Buchanan elected president   1856

Dred Scott decision causes contention 1857

Lincoln and Douglas debate issues
1858

John Brown raids Harpers Ferry 1859

1860   Abraham Lincoln elected president;
South Carolina secedes on December 20, 1860

Other southern states secede;
Confederate States of America formed 1861

1865

15 "A House Divided": The 1850s

1. DIVISIVE ISSUES

Causes of Disagreement

2. DIVISIVE EVENTS

The Compromise of 1850

New Controversies

3. DIVISION AND SECESSION

Division

Secession

*"Every kingdom divided against itself is brought
to desolation; and every city or house divided against
itself shall not stand."*

Matthew 12:25

Unit 5:   Times of Trouble, 1850–1877

Chapter 15 (pages 312–331)

"A HOUSE DIVIDED": THE 1850S

Chapter Objectives

- To see how slavery and related issues caused disagreement between the North and the South.
- To understand the nature and the effects of attempts to settle the slavery question, such as the Compromise of 1850 and the Kansas-Nebraska Act.
- To see how bitter feelings and violence produced a climate that led to war.
- To understand specific events that drove apart the North and South, such as reaction to the Fugitive Slave Law, the Dred Scott decision, John Brown's raid, and the election of Abraham Lincoln as president.
- To learn how the Southern states seceded and formed the Confederacy.

To the Teacher

This chapter should help to clear the misconception that slavery was the sole cause of the Civil War. The root causes went deeper than slavery, to issues such as states' rights, economics, national expansion, and way of life. Yet slavery related to all of these. The Southern economy and way of life depended on slavery. Consequently, Southerners became stronger and stronger in their defense of slavery, and they turned to the doctrine of states' rights to uphold their view.

Point out that this chapter shows how the differences eventually led to secession and war. At the time, however, this progression was not as clear as we can see it in retrospect. Life went on normally in most places. People raised crops, operated businesses, and moved westward. But clouds of gloom thickened over the Union as the decade wore on.

Another important lesson from this chapter is that violence begets violence. As the North and the South moved toward more radical positions, tempers flared and violence erupted. Many people took a more moderate stance on the issues, but radicals on both sides stirred up strife with grievous words and actions. "Bleeding Kansas," the caning of Sumner, and John Brown's raid stand out as examples of this.

Who was to blame—North or South? Some have emphasized that radical Northern abolitionists, such as John Brown, caused the division. Yet radicals in the South, such as Edmund Ruffin, were just as strong in their insistence on slavery and secession. No doubt the Northerners did try to force their views upon the South, as in the tariff question; and so the South feared that they would also impose their views about slavery. As in most conflicts, both sides were to blame; but even today, many writers take one side or the other. Two points should be kept in mind. First, the Northern view had a moral basis—it was wrong to consider blacks inferior and make slaves of them. Second, the North did not expel the Southern states; they made the decision to secede.

Could a minority, denied their way in the political process, demonstrate their grievance by leaving the Union? It was basically a question of states' rights versus national government sovereignty. The South believed that the states had formed the Union and therefore could withdraw from it. The Republicans of the North believed that the Union was perpetual and could not be dissolved. The Constitution was silent on the issue, though it did call for a "more perfect" union. Dispute over the question was settled only by the Civil War, which basically ended the idea that states could secede and which clearly established the federal government's sovereignty over the states.

Note on chapter test: There is a single test for Chapters 15 and 16.

Christian Perspectives

- "Grievous words stir up anger" (Proverbs 15:1). Many grievous words were spoken during these years, and the anger they stirred up produced division and war.
- Strife comes from pride and from the "lusts that war in your members" (Proverbs 13:10; James 4:1–6).
- Violence begets more violence (Matthew 26:52).
- God has created all men equal. No race is superior to another (Acts 10:34; Galatians 3:28).
- Things done in haste and anger, such as John Brown's raid, often have a bitter end (Proverbs 14:29; Ecclesiastes 7:9).

Further Study

- The Underground Railroad. (*Levi Coffin and the Underground Railroad* gives information about the life of Levi Coffin.)
- John Brown and the raid on Harpers Ferry.
- The Dred Scott case.
- Harriet Beecher Stowe and *Uncle Tom's Cabin*. (The author never visited the Deep South, but she did witness some scenes described in the book.)

Chapter 15 Quiz

Write the correct name or term for each description.

1. Author of *Uncle Tom's Cabin*.

_____

2. Black man whose appeal for freedom was rejected by the Supreme Court.

_____

3. President of the Confederate States of America.

_____

4. Republican who won the presidency in 1860.

_____

5. Man who planned to free the slaves through an armed uprising.

_____

6. Northern Democrat who promoted popular sovereignty and ran for president in 1860.

_____

7. Man who was called the "president of the Underground Railroad."

_____

8. Proposal that allowed slavery to spread into new areas in the Louisiana Territory.

_____

9. Idea that people living in an area should decide for themselves about slavery.

_____

10. Proposal introduced after California requested admission as a free state.

_____

Quiz Answers

1. **Harriet Beecher Stowe**
2. **Dred Scott**
3. **Jefferson Davis**
4. **Abraham Lincoln**
5. **John Brown**
6. **Stephen Douglas**
7. **Levi Coffin**
8. **Kansas-Nebraska Act**
9. **popular sovereignty**
10. **Compromise of 1850**

Answer Key

Focus for Thought (page 315)

1. *Compare the North and the South before 1860. Name the section that*
   a. *was more agricultural.* **South**
   b. *had more people.* **North**
   c. *emphasized states' rights.* **South**
   d. *had fewer people, even though counting three-fifths of the blacks.* **South**
   e. *favored a strong federal government.* **North**
   f. *had earlier dominated the federal government through the Democratic Party.* **South**
   g. *was more industrial and favored tariffs.* **North**

2. *Explain how slavery related to*
   a. *states' rights.*
   Southerners thought the federal government had no authority to forbid slavery in new territories, but Northerners believed the federal government did have this authority.
   b. *differing economies of North and South.*
   The Northern economy was based on manufacturing and trading whereas the Southern economy was based on producing cotton by slave labor. Abolishing slavery would have little effect on the North, but it would threaten the whole economic system of the South.
   c. *control of the federal government.*
   Southerners had to maintain control of the federal government in order to maintain slavery.

Focus for Thought (page 321)

3. a. *What was the Wilmot Proviso?*
   a proposal to forbid slavery in the Mexican Cession
   b. *How was the South able to defeat it?*
   The South defeated it in the Senate, where their power was equal to that of the North.

4. *What caused the dispute in 1850 over slavery?*
   It was caused by California's request to be admitted as a free state, which would have upset the balance in the Senate.

5. *Give the four provisions of the Compromise of 1850. After each, write N if it favored the North, S if it favored the South, or C if it was a compromise to satisfy both sides.*
   (1) Allow California to enter as a free state.—N

(2) Divide the rest of the Mexican Cession into New Mexico Territory and Utah Territory, and let the settlers there decide the issue of slavery for themselves.—S

(3) End the slave trade, but not slavery itself, in Washington, D.C.—C

(4) Enact a Fugitive Slave Law that would provide for runaway slaves to be returned to their masters.—S

6. *What significant agreement was made with Japan in 1854?*
The Japanese agreed to open two ports for trade with American merchants.

7. *In what ways did the Fugitive Slave Law bring division?*
Northerners considered it wrong to return blacks to slavery, and some states even passed personal liberty laws. This caused the South to accuse them of failing to keep their part of the agreement.

8. a. *How did* Uncle Tom's Cabin *help to increase Northern sympathy for black slaves?*
The book portrayed the slaves as normal humans.

   b. *How did Southerners respond to the book?*
Southerners said the book gave an unfair picture of slavery.

9. a. *How did the Kansas-Nebraska Act open additional land for slavery?*
This act permitted slavery in a part of the Louisiana Purchase that had been closed to slavery by the Missouri Compromise. It also supported popular sovereignty, which would allow slavery to spread into the new territories.

   b. *What were two effects of this act?*
(Any two.) The act caused strong protest in the North. It opened all new territories to slavery. It divided the Union more sharply than ever. It led to violence in Kansas between proslavery and antislavery forces.

Focus for Thought (pages 325, 326)

10. *What modern political party was founded in the 1850s?*
the Republican Party

11. *What incident of violence occurred in Congress because of the slavery issue?*
the caning of Charles Sumner

12. *Give the basis on which*
   a. *Dred Scott sued for his freedom.*
He had lived in free territory for a time.
   b. *the Supreme Court dismissed Scott's case.*
Scott was not a citizen of the United States.

c. *the Supreme Court ruled that the Missouri Compromise was unconstitutional.* **By prohibiting slavery, this law violated slaveholders' property rights.**

13. *What were the Northern and Southern viewpoints on John Brown's raid?*
Some in the North considered John Brown a martyr. Southerners considered the raid an example of the extreme measures that abolitionists would use to free the slaves.

14. a. *Which Southern states seceded before Abraham Lincoln became president?*
South Carolina, Mississippi, Florida, Alabama, Georgia, Louisiana, and Texas

b. *Which ones waited to see what Lincoln would do as president?*
Virginia, North Carolina, Tennessee, and Arkansas

c. *What government did the seceded states form, and who became their president?*
They formed the Confederate States of America, with Jefferson Davis as their president.

15. *Why did President Buchanan take no action against the Southern states that seceded?*
He thought the federal government had no authority to take action.

HISTORICAL HIGHLIGHTS (pages 326–328)

A. Matching: People

a. *Abraham Lincoln*
b. *Charles Sumner*
c. *Dred Scott*
d. *Franklin Pierce*
e. *Harriet Beecher Stowe*
f. *Henry Clay*
g. *James Buchanan*

h. *Jefferson Davis*
i. *John Brown*
j. *Levi Coffin*
k. *Matthew C. Perry*
l. *Millard Fillmore*
m. *Roger Taney*
n. *Stephen Douglas*

e 1. *Author of Uncle Tom's Cabin.*
h 2. *President of the Confederate States of America.*
c 3. *Black man whose appeal for freedom was rejected by the Supreme Court.*
b 4. *Senator who was caned by Preston Brooks.*
j 5. *"President of the Underground Railroad."*
f 6. *Introduced the Compromise of 1850.*
l 7. *President when the Compromise of 1850 passed.*
m 8. *Chief Justice of Supreme Court who wrote for the majority in the Dred Scott decision.*

i 9. *Planned to free slaves through an armed uprising.*

a 10. *Republican who won the presidency in 1860.*

g 11. *United States president when Southern states began to secede.*

n 12. *Promoter of popular sovereignty; Northern Democratic candidate for the Senate in 1860.*

d 13. *President when Japan opened ports to Americans.*

k 14. *Gained permission for the United States to trade with Japan.*

B. Matching: Terms

a. *Compromise of 1850*

b. *Confederate States of America*

c. *Fugitive Slave Law*

d. *Kansas-Nebraska Act*

e. *popular sovereignty*

f. *Republican Party*

g. Uncle Tom's Cabin

h. *Underground Railroad*

i. *Wilmot Proviso*

f 1. *Political group that opposed the spread of slavery.*

c 2. *Requirement stating that runaway slaves must be returned.*

h 3. *Secret system for helping slaves escape to Canada.*

d 4. *Proposal that allowed slavery to spread into new areas.*

g 5. *Book that strengthened antislavery feelings in the North.*

b 6. *States that seceded from the Union.*

i 7. *Proposal to forbid slavery in the Mexican Cession.*

a 8. *Proposal introduced after California requested admission as a free state.*

e 9. *Idea that people living in an area should decide for themselves about slavery.*

C. Multiple Choice

Write the letter of the best answer.

1. *How did abolitionists help to move the nation toward the Civil War?*

   a. They aroused ill feelings between the North and the South.

   b. *They caused the slaves to become restless and rebellious.*

   c. *They promoted sending black slaves back to Africa.*

   d. *They opposed the idea that blacks were inferior beings.*

2. *Why did the Compromise of 1850 fail to overcome the sharp disunity in the nation?*

   a. *It failed to deal with the major points of conflict.*

   b. *The South was not satisfied with the final decision.*

   c. *It favored one side.*

   d. It did not settle the bitter dispute over slavery.

3. *In what way did popular sovereignty extend slavery?*
    a. *It allowed slavery to spread into any part of the nation.*
    b. *It allowed the Dred Scott decision to take effect.*
    c. It allowed slavery to spread into new areas if the people there wanted it.
    d. *It allowed the South to vote for the extension of slavery.*
4. *What issue prompted the rise of the Republican Party?*
    a. *the Compromise of 1850*   c. *the Dred Scott decision*
    b. the Kansas-Nebraska Act   d. *John Brown's raid*
5. *Which concept eventually climaxed in Southern secession?*
    a. *popular sovereignty*   **c. states' rights**
    b. *nullification*   d. *aristocracy*
6. *What was the immediate cause for some Southern states to secede from the Union?*
    a. Abraham Lincoln, the Republican candidate, won the presidential election.
    b. *Southerners were tired of being harassed by abolitionists.*
    c. *Southerners wanted Jefferson Davis to be their president.*
    d. *The Compromise of 1850 did not work.*

D. Deeper Discussion

1. a. *Explain popular sovereignty.*
    Under popular sovereignty, citizens in a territory could decide for themselves whether they wanted slavery there.
    b. *How did Senator Douglas think popular sovereignty would defuse the slavery quarrel?*
    He thought if each territory could decide for itself, the question would be settled without further controversy. Since the people in each territory would have exactly what they wanted, the United States could continue its westward expansion without hindrance.
    c. *Why did it fail to work that way?*
    It did not work that way because both proslavery and antislavery groups tried to use popular sovereignty to further their cause. In Kansas, for example, the contest to establish or outlaw slavery led to violence instead of peaceful progress. Also, popular sovereignty ignored the keeping of a balance between free states and slave states in the Senate.

2. *How did the Dred Scott decision favor the South's view of slavery?*

This decision endorsed the idea that slaves were property rather than citizens, and therefore less than human. It also supported the idea that the federal government could not stop the spread of slavery into new territories.

3. *How did the South justify its secession?*

The South believed in states' rights—that the nation was a union of sovereign states which had more power than the federal government. Since the United States government did not respect the wishes of the Southern states, they felt justified in seceding.

4. a. *What changes did the Confederate States of America make to the United States Constitution?*

They changed the Constitution to allow slavery and to clearly define the states as sovereign. (Apparently they forgot what the nation had experienced under the Articles of Confederation—that a union of sovereign states does not work.)

b. *Why did they make these changes?*

In the United States Constitution, slavery was tolerated (as by the Three-fifths Compromise) but not specifically allowed. And the Constitution provided for mixed sovereignty, with some powers belonging to the states and others to the federal government. The Confederates' changes would ensure that their nation would keep slavery and maintain states' rights.

5. *Galatians 5:15 says, "But if ye bite and devour one another, take heed that ye be not consumed one of another." Explain how this warning went unheeded by the North and the South.*

Each side "bit and devoured" the other with words and even with actions, as in "Bleeding Kansas" and John Brown's raid. This eventually led to a war in which the North and South "consumed" one another.

E. Chronology and Geography

1. *The following list gives events leading to the secession of the Southern states. Arrange the list in the proper order, and supply the date for each event.*

Charles Sumner caned

Compromise of 1850 passed

Dred Scott decision causes contention

Fugitive Slave Law enacted

John Brown raids Harpers Ferry
Kansas-Nebraska Act passed
Lincoln and Douglas debate issues
Lincoln elected president
Other Southern states secede
Republican Party founded
South Carolina secedes on December 20
Uncle Tom's Cabin *published*
Violence erupts in "Bleeding Kansas"
Wilmot Proviso proposed but defeated

1846—Wilmot Proviso proposed but defeated
1850—Compromise of 1850 passed
1850—Fugitive Slave Law enacted
1852—*Uncle Tom's Cabin* published
1854—Kansas-Nebraska Act passed
1854—Republican Party founded
1856—Violence erupts in "Bleeding Kansas"
1856—Charles Sumner caned
1857—Dred Scott decision causes contention
1858—Lincoln and Douglas debate issues
1859—John Brown raids Harpers Ferry
1860—Lincoln elected president
1860—South Carolina secedes on December 20
1861—Other Southern states secede

2. a. *List the seven original states of the Confederacy in the order of secession.*
South Carolina, Mississippi, Florida, Alabama, Georgia, Louisiana, Texas
b. *Where was the first capital of the Confederacy?*
Montgomery, Alabama
c. *Which four slave states did not secede immediately?*
Virginia, North Carolina, Tennessee, Arkansas
d. *Why might they have waited longer to secede?*
They waited to see how Lincoln would treat the states that had already seceded. They may have had closer ties to the North. They probably did not depend on slavery as much as some of the other states did.

So Far This Year (pages 329, 330)

A. Multiple Choice

Write the letter of the correct answer for each description.

1. *Idea that the United States should spread over the whole North American continent.*
   a. *Mexican Cession*
   b. manifest destiny
   c. *Oregon fever*
   d. *California gold rush*

2. *Land gained by the Mexican War.*
   a. *the Gadsden Purchase*
   b. *manifest destiny*
   c. the Mexican Cession
   d. *the Treaty of Guadalupe Hidalgo*

3. *Hardy fur traders and explorers of the West.*
   a. *forty-niners*
   b. *rendezvous*
   c. *prospectors*
   d. mountain men

4. *Expansionist president from 1845 to 1849.*
   a. James Polk
   b. *Sam Houston*
   c. *Zachary Taylor*
   d. *Winfield Scott*

5. *Man who began colonizing Texas.*
   a. *John Sutter*
   b. Stephen Austin
   c. *Sam Houston*
   d. *Marcus Whitman*

6. *Missionary who encouraged settlement of Oregon.*
   a. Marcus Whitman
   b. *John Frémont*
   c. *John Sutter*
   d. *Stephen Austin*

7. *Man near whose fort gold was discovered.*
   a. *John Frémont*
   b. *James Marshall*
   c. John Sutter
   d. *Stephen Kearny*

8. *Mail system connecting California to the East.*
   a. *gold rush*
   b. pony express
   c. *Oregon Trail*
   d. *forty-niners*

9. *Treaty that ended the Mexican War.*
   a. *joint occupation*
   b. *Gadsden Purchase*
   c. Treaty of Guadalupe Hidalgo
   d. *Mexican Cession*

10. *Area from which the states of Oregon, Washington, and Idaho were formed.*
    a. *Mexican Cession*   c. *Gadsden Purchase*
    b. Oregon Territory   d. *California Territory*

11. *President elected in 1848, who had been a general in the Mexican War.*
    a. Zachary Taylor   c. *Winfield Scott*
    b. *James Polk*   d. *Sam Houston*

12. *General who conquered Mexico City in the Mexican War.*
    a. *Stephen Kearny*   c. *Zachary Taylor*
    b. *Santa Anna*   **d. Winfield Scott**

13. *River that formed the disputed boundary between Texas and Mexico.*
    a. *Platte River*   **c. Rio Grande**
    b. *Snake River*   d. *Colorado River*

14. *Discoverer of the South Pass and first American known to enter California by land.*
    a. *Kit Carson*   c. *John Frémont*
    b. *Jim Bridger*   **d. Jedediah Smith**

15. *Old mission near San Antonio, Texas, that fell to the Mexicans.*
    a. the Alamo   c. *Buena Vista*
    b. *San Jacinto*   d. *Fort Laramie*

16. *People with whom the Oregon Country was shared from 1818 to 1846.*
    a. *Spanish*   c. *Russians*
    b. British   d. *French*

B. Matching: Terms 1

b 17. *Traveling preacher in the West.*   a. *abolition*

g 18. *Effort to stop the use of strong drink.*   b. *circuit rider*

c 19. *Machine for removing seeds from cotton.*   c. *cotton gin*

a 20. *Elimination of slavery.*   d. *Cotton Kingdom*

d 21. *Region dependent on cotton.*   e. *Industrial Revolution*

f 22. *Large farm that produced one main crop and used slave labor.*   f. *plantation*

e 23. *Change from producing handmade goods at home to producing machine-made goods in factories.*   g. *temperance movement*

C. Matching: Terms 2

h 24. *Government divided into three branches.*

f 25. *Branch of government that makes laws.*

g 26. *Government by elected representatives.*

a 27. *Ways by which government branches limit each other.*

b 28. *Group of men who elect the president.*

c 29. *Branch of government that enacts and enforces laws.*

d 30. *Government divided between states and national government.*

e 31. *Branch of government that decides cases about laws.*

a. *checks and balances*

b. *Electoral College*

c. *executive*

d. *federal*

e. *judicial*

f. *legislative*

g. *republic*

h. *separation of powers*

D. Completion

Write the correct name or date for each description.

Samuel F. B. Morse   32. *Inventor of the telegraph.*

Samuel Slater   33. *Brought textile manufacturing to America.*

Eli Whitney   34. *Inventor of the cotton gin.*

Noah Webster   35. *Published the "blue-backed speller."*

Robert Fulton   36. *Built the first successful steamboat.*

1846–1848   37. *Years of the Mexican War.*

1787   38. *Date for the Constitutional Convention.*

1791   39. *Date when the Bill of Rights was added to the Constitution.*

1789   40. *Date when the United States government under the Constitution began.*

1861

March 4	Lincoln inaugurated
April 12	Fort Sumter fired upon
July 21	First Battle of Bull Run

1862

February 6	Fall of Fort Henry
February 16	Fall of Fort Donelson
March–July	Peninsular Campaign
March 9	Battle between *Monitor* and *Merrimack*
April 6–7	Battle of Shiloh
April 25	Fall of New Orleans
August 29–30	Second Battle of Bull Run
September 17	Battle of Antietam
September 22	Emancipation Proclamation issued
December 13	Battle of Fredericksburg
January 1 **1863**	Emancipation Proclamation becomes effective
May 1–4	Battle of Chancellorsville
July 1–3	Battle of Gettysburg
July 4	Fall of Vicksburg
November 19	Gettysburg Address

1864

May–June 1864	Wilderness Campaign
May 5–6	The Battle of the Wilderness
May 8–19	Battle of Spotsylvania Court House
June 3–12	Battle of Cold Harbor
June 20, 1864–April 2, 1865	Siege of Petersburg
September 2	Fall of Atlanta
September 19–October 19	Sheridan's raid
November 8	Lincoln re-elected
November 15–December 21	Sherman's March to the Sea
December 21 **1865**	Fall of Savannah
April 2	Fall of Richmond
April 9	Lee surrenders at Appomattox Court House
April 14	Lincoln assassinated

1866

16 The Civil War

1. The Civil War, Part 1: 1861–1862

The War Begins, 1861

The South Endures, 1862

2. The Civil War, Part 2: 1863–1865

The Tide Turns, 1863

The North Strikes Hard, 1864

The War Ends, 1865

3. Costs and Results of the Civil War; Experiences of Nonresistant People

Costs of the Civil War

Results of the War

Nonresistance in the North

Nonresistance in the South

Nonresistance Asserted

"And, behold, every man's sword was against his fellow, and there was a very great discomfiture."
1 Samuel 14:20

Chapter 16 (pages 332–352)

THE CIVIL WAR

Chapter Objectives

- To learn about the goals of the North and the South in the Civil War, and about the resources of each side.
- To study the general course of the Civil War.
- To comprehend some of the costs and results of the Civil War.
- To learn about the tests of nonresistance in the North and South.

To the Teacher

The Civil War is surrounded by much patriotic fervor, as well as controversy. Be careful not to take sides, but to present the goals of each side and the basis for those goals. For example, since Lincoln believed that the Union was perpetual, the North fought to keep the Union intact. While both the North and the South believed that God was on their side, it is better to say that God overruled in the affairs of men to accomplish His sovereign purposes. For example, the war raged four years even though the North was much stronger than the South.

Be sure students realize that the Civil War was not fought primarily to settle the slavery question, but rather to determine whether the Union would be preserved or dissolved. Only when Lincoln issued the Emancipation Proclamation did slavery officially become part of the cause. In addition to changing the war into a moral crusade against slavery (for Northerners), the proclamation was also important in preventing British recognition of the Confederacy; for the British had outlawed slavery and did not want to go on record as endorsing it.

See that the students understand the test that a military draft is to those who uphold Biblical nonresistance. Show the costs of the war as the bitter fruit of enmity and strife. Lincoln's assassination was only the first fruits of many years of bitter harvests to come. Also present clearly the far-reaching consequences of the Civil War.

Much has been written on the experiences of nonresistant people during the Civil War. Some Christians were unprepared spiritually for the trials, but many stood true to their faith. Be sure to uphold the doctrine of nonresistance and draw lessons that challenge our own faith.

Note on chapter test: There is a single test for Chapters 15 and 16.

Christian Perspectives

- War brings much division, bitterness, hardship, and destruction.
- War has negative moral consequences.
- God does not take sides in men's wars. Rather, He overrules so that His will is accomplished (Psalm 19:9; Ecclesiastes 9:11).

- God sometimes allows circumstances that test His people's faith, but He is always faithful (Hebrews 13:6).
- Jesus' followers do not take part in carnal warfare (Matthew 26:52; John 18:36).

Further Study

- Major battles of the Civil War, such as the ones at Shiloh, Antietam, and Gettysburg.
- The lives of Abraham Lincoln and Robert E. Lee.
- Nonresistance during the Civil War. (*War-torn Valley* describes the experiences of Mennonites in the Shenandoah Valley.)

Quiz Answers

1. **l**	6. **n**	11. **q**	16. **a**
2. **k**	7. **e**	12. **i**	17. **m**
3. **p**	8. **b**	13. **d**	18. **h**
4. **j**	9. **r**	14. **c**	
5. **o**	10. **g**	15. **f**	

Note: If you give the following quiz orally, write the lettered choices on the chalkboard.

Chapter 16 Quiz

One choice will not be used.

a. Appomattox Court House
b. First Battle of Bull Run
c. David Farragut
d. Emancipation Proclamation
e. Fort Sumter
f. Gettysburg
g. Philip Sheridan
h. Richmond
i. Robert E. Lee
j. Stonewall Jackson

k. Thirteenth Amendment
l. Ulysses S. Grant
m. Vicksburg
n. West Virginia
o. William T. Sherman
p. April 12, 1861
q. January 1, 1863
r. April 9, 1865
s. April 14, 1865

_____ 1. Chief Union general at the end of the Civil War.

_____ 2. Means by which slavery was outlawed permanently.

_____ 3. Date when the Civil War began.

_____ 4. Confederate general shot by his own men at Chancellorsville.

_____ 5. Union general who led a destructive March to the Sea.

_____ 6. New state formed from Virginia.

_____ 7. Place where the Civil War began.

_____ 8. Battle that showed the war would be long and hard.

_____ 9. Date when the Civil War ended.

_____ 10. Union general who devastated the Shenandoah Valley.

_____ 11. Date when the Emancipation Proclamation went into effect.

_____ 12. Chief general of the Confederate armies.

_____ 13. Statement declaring that slaves in the Confederacy were free.

_____ 14. Union naval commander who took New Orleans and Mobile.

_____ 15. Town known as the "high-water mark of the Confederacy."

_____ 16. Place where Lee surrendered to Grant.

_____ 17. Stronghold whose fall allowed Union control of the Mississippi.

_____ 18. Confederate capital.

Answer Key

Focus for Thought (page 339)

1. *On what basis did Lincoln consider secession to be illegal?*
   Lincoln believed that the Union was perpetual.

2. a. *What two things was the South hoping to do in the Civil War?*
   The South hoped to win enough battles so that the North would grow weary of fighting and give up. The South also hoped to gain assistance from foreign nations.

   b. *What were the three points in the plan of the North?*
   The North planned to blockade Southern ports so that cotton could not be shipped out or supplies be brought in, to divide the South by taking control of the Mississippi River, and to capture the Confederate capital of Richmond.

3. *What were the advantages*
   a. *of the North?*
   The North had many more people. It also had most of the factories and railroads.

   b. *of the South?*
   The South was defending its own territory. Confederates knew the land better. Their generals were more capable.

4. *Name the border states in the war, and also the new state that emerged.*
   Border states: Delaware, Maryland, Kentucky, Missouri. New state: West Virginia

5. *What two effects did the Battle of Antietam have?*
   This battle repelled Lee's invasion of the North in 1862. The victory provided Lincoln the opportunity he sought for delivering the Emancipation Proclamation.

6. a. *What was the provision of the Emancipation Proclamation?*
   It declared freedom for all the slaves in states still rebelling against the United States on January 1, 1863.

   b. *In what three ways did it help the Northern cause?*
   It kept the British from recognizing the Confederacy as a nation. It gave Northerners a new zeal for fighting—to end slavery. It strengthened the Union forces by allowing blacks to serve as soldiers.

Focus for Thought (page 346)

7. *Why is Gettysburg known as the "high-water mark of the Confederacy"?*
   After the defeat at Gettysburg, the Confederacy declined steadily

until it was totally defeated.

8. *Why was the fall of Vicksburg a major triumph for the North?*
With this victory, the North gained control of the Mississippi and divided the South.

9. a. *How did the Northern aim of the war change in 1864?*
It changed from merely forcing the South back into the Union, to completely crushing the South.
b. *Give one example of how this was carried out.*
(Any one.) Grant's drive to conquer Richmond in the Wilderness Campaign; Sheridan's raid; Sherman's March to the Sea

10. a. *Why did Grant order the destruction of the Shenandoah Valley in 1864?*
The Shenandoah Valley supplied much food for Southern armies, in addition to being a hideout for Confederate raiding bands.
b. *What were the results?*
Sheridan's men destroyed houses, barns, mills, crops, and stores of hay and grain. Hundreds of innocent people suffered in this destruction.

11. *What did Sherman's men do on their March to the Sea?*
They destroyed almost everything in a swath 50 miles (80.5 km) wide, burning houses and other buildings, taking anything they wanted, and tearing up railroad tracks.

12. a. *Where and when did General Lee surrender to General Grant?*
at Appomattox Court House on April 9, 1865
b. *Give two details of Grant's generous terms of surrender.*
(Any two.) Confederate soldiers would be paroled and allowed to return to their homes. They could take their horses along for planting crops. Grant promised food for Lee's soldiers.

13. a. *When and how was Lincoln assassinated?*
Lincoln was assassinated on April 14, 1865, when an actor named John Wilkes Booth shot him from behind.

13. b. *How was Lincoln's death a great loss for the South?*
After Lincoln's death, restoration of the Southern states was in the hands of men less charitable than Lincoln.

Focus for Thought (page 351)

14. *What were some effects of the Civil War*
a. *on the South?*
Southern cities lay in ruins, bridges were burned, and railroads were destroyed. Many Southern men had been killed or wounded in the

war. The South had shortages of many basic items. Confederate paper money lost most of its value.

b. *on the North?*

The North suffered little in comparison with the South. Northern factories had steadily produced war supplies. There was some inflation, but not as much as in the South. An income tax was imposed.

15. *Name three major results of the war.*

The war led to the end of slavery, established federal supremacy, and caused a need for reconstruction.

16. *In what ways did nonresistant people respond to the draft*

a. *in the North?*

Some petitioned the government to recognize their conscientious objection. Some paid the commutation fee of $300. Some hired a substitute to fight for them (though others considered this wrong). Some moved to Canada, went into hiding, or claimed physical disability.

b. *in the South?*

Some became cooks or wagon drivers in the army. Some went into hiding. Some tried to escape into West Virginia or Pennsylvania. Some paid a commutation fee of $500 or hired a substitute.

17. *Besides hardships relating to the draft, what sufferings did the war bring to nonresistant people*

a. *in the North?*

Mennonites and Dunkers suffered when Lee invaded the region around Gettysburg. The Confederates took livestock, food, crops, fences, and money. A few people suffered threats to their lives, as Michael Hege, and at least one—Isaac Strite—was killed.

b. *in the South?*

Nonresistant people in the Shenandoah Valley suffered severe hardships when their houses, barns, and crops were destroyed or plundered in Sheridan's raid. There was also an epidemic of diphtheria.

18. *What was done by Mennonite leaders of the 1860s to strengthen the church's stand on nonresistance?*

John Funk published *Warfare, Its Evils, Our Duty* and also the *Herald of Truth*. John Brenneman published *Christianity and War*.

HISTORICAL HIGHLIGHTS (pages 351–353)

A. Matching: People

a. *Clara Barton*
b. *David G. Farragut*
c. *George McClellan*
d. *George Meade*
e. *George Pickett*
f. *John Funk*

g. *John Wilkes Booth*
h. *Philip Sheridan*
i. *Robert E. Lee*
j. *Stonewall Jackson*
k. *Ulysses S. Grant*
l. *William T. Sherman*

e   1. *Led a Confederate charge against Union forces at Gettysburg.*
h   2. *Devastated the Shenandoah Valley in 1864.*
c   3. *Union general in Battle of Antietam; Lincoln's opponent in election of 1864.*
k   4. *Chief Union general at the end of the Civil War.*
b   5. *Conquered New Orleans and Mobile for the Union.*
g   6. *Assassinated President Lincoln.*
l   7. *Conquered Atlanta and led the destructive March to the Sea.*
d   8. *Commander of Union armies at Gettysburg.*
j   9. *Noted Confederate general who was shot by his own men.*
f 10. *Published the* Herald of Truth *and a pamphlet on nonresistance.*
a 11. *Cared for wounded soldiers and helped to found American Red Cross.*
i 12. *General of the Confederate armies whose surrender brought the war to an end.*

B. Matching: Terms

a. *border states*
b. *commutation fee*
c. *Confederates*
d. *conscientious objectors*
e. *draft*
f. *Emancipation Proclamation*
g. *Federals*

h. *Gettysburg Address*
i. *ironclad*
j. *Pickett's Charge*
k. *"Rebels"*
l. *Thirteenth Amendment*
m. *Union*
n. *"Yankees"*

d   1. *People who believe it is wrong to take part in warfare.*
a   2. *Delaware, Maryland, Kentucky, Missouri.*
c, k   3. *Terms for Southern soldiers (two answers).*
g, m, n 4. *Terms for Northern soldiers (three answers).*
e   5. *Compulsory enrollment in a military force.*
b   6. *Money paid to avoid military service.*
f   7. *Statement declaring that slaves in the Confederacy were free.*

i   8. *New type of ship that changed naval warfare.*

l   9. *Measure that permanently outlawed slavery.*

j   10. *Attack on the Union army at Gettysburg.*

h   11. *Speech given in the dedication of a cemetery at Gettysburg.*

C. Matching: Places and Dates

a. *Antietam*

b. *Appomattox Court House*

c. *Atlanta*

d. *First Battle of Bull Run*

e. *Chancellorsville*

f. *Fort Sumter*

g. *Gettysburg*

h. *Richmond*

i. *Savannah*

j. *Shenandoah Valley*

k. *Shiloh*

l. *Vicksburg*

m. *West Virginia*

n. *April 12, 1861*

o. *January 1, 1863*

p. *April 9, 1865*

q. *April 14, 1865*

c   1. *City whose capture aided Lincoln's re-election in 1864.*

n   2. *Date when the Civil War began.*

g   3. *Battle that was a turning point in the war.*

a   4. *Victory that gave Lincoln an occasion to issue the Emancipation Proclamation.*

i   5. *City at the end of Sherman's destructive March to the Sea.*

p   6. *Date when the Civil War ended.*

j   7. *Area destroyed by Sheridan's raid, where Mennonites lived.*

e   8. *Battle where Stonewall Jackson lost his life.*

o   9. *Date when Lincoln declared that the slaves in the Confederacy were free.*

f   10. *Place where the Civil War began.*

b   11. *Place where Lee surrendered to Grant.*

d   12. *Battle showing that the war would be long and hard.*

m   13. *New state formed from Virginia.*

k   14. *Bloody battle in Tennessee.*

h   15. *Confederate capital.*

l   16. *Mississippi stronghold whose fall directly followed the Battle of Gettysburg.*

q   17. *Date of Lincoln's assassination.*

D. Deeper Discussion

1. *Explain why the Civil War lasted four years even if the North had definite advantages over the South.*

   It took time for Northern strategies to do their work, especially the blockade of Southern ports. Also, Northern generals such as

McClellan and Meade proved ineffective, while Southern generals like Lee and Jackson showed themselves brilliant in battle. Southern armies fought to defend their homeland, as well as to gain independence from the Union—in a spirit much like that of patriots in the American Revolution. But there was possibly a deeper reason: God may have been judging the nation for its great injustices against the black people.

2. *In relation to the Civil War, Lincoln quoted Psalm 19:9: "The judgments of the LORD are true and righteous altogether." What is the connection?*
Lincoln was suggesting that the Civil War was God's just judgment on the nation for allowing slavery. God overrules in the affairs of men to accomplish His will, which is always "true and righteous altogether." Man may pervert judgment, as in the Dred Scott decision, but God's judgments are always righteous. God will judge any nation that turns away from Him.

3. a. *Why did the Emancipation Proclamation declare freedom only for slaves in the Confederacy?*
Lincoln was seeking to avoid antagonizing the border states. He was also hoping to keep the British from supporting the Confederacy, since they opposed slavery.

   b. *Why did Lincoln wait until after a Union victory to issue the proclamation?*
Issuing the proclamation after a defeat could have made it look like a desperate bid for the help of slaves to win the war. This would have given Lincoln's opponents an opportunity to discredit him.

4. *How was Lincoln's assassination a blow to the South as well as to the North?*
The North lost a strong leader. The South also lost because Lincoln wanted to reconcile the South rather than punish it. This was demonstrated by Lincoln's directions for the terms of surrender.

5. *What are some factors that made the Civil War especially destructive and tragic.*
One factor was the divisive nature of the war. Friends fought friends, father fought son, and brother fought brother. The issues of the war, such as slavery, states' rights, and preservation of the Union, stirred powerful passions that issued into fanaticism. Another factor was the destructive nature of this first of "modern wars." New, more potent weapons (such as repeating rifles and cannons loaded with canisters) resulted in greater loss of life. This was

especially true when the new weapons were used at the same time as old tactics such as frontal assaults. The concept of "total war" also increased the destruction of life and property.

E. Chronology and Geography

1. *On your map entitled "The States of the United States," draw the borders of the eleven states admitted between 1836 and 1863. (See maps on pages 317 and 334.)*
   a. *Label the states with their names and dates of admission.*
   b. *Color these states a different color, and add this color to the legend.*
   c. *Memorize the names and locations of these states.*
   (Individual work.)
2. a. *List the eleven states that joined the Confederacy.*
   Virginia, North Carolina, South Carolina, Tennessee, Arkansas, Georgia, Alabama, Mississippi, Louisiana, Texas, Florida
   b. *How many states did the Union retain?*
   It retained twenty-four states, including Kansas, the five border states, and West Virginia. (There were twenty-five Union states after Nevada joined in 1864.)
   c. *In general, which of the three sections of the country stayed in the Union, and which seceded?*
   The North and the West stayed, and the South seceded.
3. a. *How did fighting on their own land give Southerners an advantage in the Civil War?*
   Southern soldiers knew the land better. They could supply their men more easily, and they could take advantage of the terrain for cover and for movements.
   b. *How did it become a disadvantage by the end of the war?*
   Since most fighting was done in the South, most of the destruction in the war occurred there. The North suffered little destruction in comparison.
4. *Why did the Union's capture of Vicksburg weaken the South?*
   The Mississippi was of major importance for trade. Also, the Mississippi divided the South, so that Northern control of the waterway isolated Confederate states west of it. This control gave the North a base for making further attacks in the South.

5. *Place the following events in chronological order, giving the date for each one. The time line for this chapter may help you.*

Battle of Antietam	*Fall of Vicksburg*
Battle of Chancellorsville	*First Battle of Bull Run*
Battle of Gettysburg	*Gettysburg Address*
Battle of Shiloh	*Lincoln's assassination*
Battle of the ironclads	*Lincoln's re-election*
Emancipation Proclamation	*Sheridan's raid*
Fall of Atlanta	*Sherman's March to the Sea*
Fall of Richmond	*Surrender at Appomattox Court House*

 (1) **First Battle of Bull Run (July 21, 1861)**

 (2) **Battle of the ironclads (March 9, 1862)**

 (3) **Battle of Shiloh (April 6–7, 1862)**

 (4) **Battle of Antietam (September 17, 1862)**

 (5) **Emancipation Proclamation (September 22, 1862)**

 (6) **Battle of Chancellorsville (May 1–4, 1863)**

 (7) **Battle of Gettysburg (July 1–3, 1863)**

 (8) **Fall of Vicksburg (July 4, 1863)**

 (9) **Gettysburg Address (November 19, 1863)**

(10) **Fall of Atlanta (September 2, 1864)**

(11) **Sheridan's raid (September 19–October 19, 1864)**

(12) **Lincoln's re-election (November 8, 1864)**

(13) **Sherman's March to the Sea (November 15–December 21, 1864)**

(14) **Fall of Richmond (April 2, 1865)**

(15) **Surrender at Appomattox Court House (April 9, 1865)**

(16) **Lincoln's assassination (April 14, 1865)**

17 Reconstruction

1860

Emancipation Proclamation becomes effective (January 1) 1863

Andrew Johnson becomes president 1865

1865 Civil War ends (April 9); Lincoln assassinated (April 14) **1865**

Reconstruction Act passed; United States purchases Alaska 1867

Fourteenth Amendment ratified 1868

Johnson impeached and acquitted; Ulysses S. Grant elected president 1868

1870 Last of Southern states readmitted; Fifteenth Amendment ratified 1870

Ku Klux Klan Act passed 1871

Amnesty Act passed; Grant re-elected 1872

1875

Rutherford B. Hayes elected president 1876

Compromise of 1877 approved; Reconstruction ends 1877

1880

"A brother offended is harder to be won than a strong city: and their contentions are like the bars of a castle."

Proverbs 18:19

Chapter 17 (pages 354–377)

RECONSTRUCTION

Chapter Objectives

- To understand Presidential Reconstruction and Congressional Reconstruction.
- To learn about the difficult conditions that blacks faced after the Civil War.
- To study the impeachment of President Johnson.
- To learn about the three amendments of the Constitution that relate to the Civil War.
- To learn about changes in the South after Reconstruction.

To the Teacher

A number of factors made Reconstruction a difficult period for the United States. On the one hand, President Johnson wanted to restore the South without much recrimination. This approach made it easy for Southern states to be readmitted to the Union. On the other hand, the Radical Republicans wanted to punish and completely restructure the South so that it would be impossible for the Old South ever to rise again. They believed that the South was refusing to accept the results of the war, and therefore must be forced to accept them. Otherwise, they feared the Civil War had been fought in vain. The conflict between the two sides grew so strong that it led to much violence and to the impeachment of President Johnson.

Another difficulty was the desperate conditions of the freedmen. Whites could say that the freedmen were illiterate, irresponsible, and so on; but what can be expected of people who had been oppressed as they had been? The freedmen did need help—in the material, political, and educational realms—but how far should the government go in helping them? The Freedmen's Bureau was a good attempt, yet it involved the dangers of dependence on handouts and too much government intervention. Many private organizations also helped the blacks, as was the case of the Hampton Institute, where Booker T. Washington studied.

Be aware that historians' perspective of the Reconstruction has changed over the years. According to the "Dunning School" of around 1900, Reconstruction was a total failure and redemption was just that—redemption from an evil. More recent scholars (since 1950) have viewed the Radicals as having the right intentions and the blacks as suffering oppression by whites. In this latter view, Reconstruction ended too soon and was not revived until the more recent civil rights movement. In any case, historians on either side have overemphasized certain aspects of Reconstruction.

This text seeks to avoid controversial issues and simply present what happened. It also tries to show how each side viewed the situation. For example, the Reconstruction governments may have been corrupt, but they also did some good.

Carpetbagger and *scalawag* are terms of contempt, but some of these people did have good motives. It is easy to sympathize with the poor freedmen and to feel bitter about the injustices perpetrated against blacks, both during and after Reconstruction. But we must remember that "vengeance is mine; I will repay, saith the Lord" (Romans 12:19).

Be sure you understand the impeachment process and the electoral process so that you can properly grasp the trial of Johnson and the election of Hayes. In the latter case, a special electoral commission was appointed to decide who was the winner, and its decision was to be final unless both houses of Congress voted otherwise. But the commission had one more Republican than Democrat; this is why the issue was still not settled even after the commission voted for Hayes.

Note on chapter test: Chapter 17 has its own test.

Christian Perspectives

- Racial discrimination is wrong. God is no respecter of persons, white or black (Acts 10:34).
- God will avenge all injustices, for He notices all (Ecclesiastes 5:8; Romans 12:19).
- It is impossible to change social attitudes, such as between whites and blacks, by force of law. The only real solution is the new birth and God's love in the heart.
- Moral corruption destroys people and nations (Deuteronomy 16:19; Proverbs 14:34; 17:23).
- The government has a responsibility to suppress evil (Romans 13:4).

Further Study

- The lives of Booker T. Washington and George Washington Carver.
- The lives and administrations of Hayes, Johnson, and Grant.
- The Ku Klux Klan.
- Experiences of blacks after the Civil War.

Chapter 17 Quiz

Write the correct name or term for each description.

1. Northerners who went south to help in Reconstruction.

2. Southern whites who took part in the Reconstruction governments.

3. Former slaves.

4. Constitutional amendment that granted citizenship to blacks.

5. System in which farm workers rent cropland and use a share of the crops to pay the rent.

6. Constitutional amendment that granted all citizens the right to vote.

7. Rebuilding and restoration of the South after the Civil War.

8. President who was impeached in 1868.

9. Former Civil War general who became president.

10. President appointed after a disputed election and the Compromise of 1877.

Quiz Answers

1. **carpetbaggers**
2. **scalawags**
3. **freedmen**
4. **Fourteenth Amendment**
5. **sharecropping**
6. **Fifteenth Amendment**
7. **Reconstruction**
8. **Andrew Johnson**
9. **Ulysses S. Grant**
10. **Rutherford B. Hayes**

Answer Key

Focus for Thought (page 360)

1. *Give three reasons why Reconstruction was needed.*

   The South had suffered much destruction in the war. The freedmen needed help to become responsible citizens. The Southern states needed to be restored to the Union.

2. *What were the two main points in Lincoln's ten percent plan?*

   Most Southerners would be pardoned and restored to citizenship if they took an oath of loyalty to the United States. After this oath was taken by 10 percent of the 1860 (pre-Civil War) voters in a state, that state could form a new government.

3. a. *How was President Johnson's plan similar to Lincoln's?*

   It was lenient to the South.

   b. *How was it different?*

   It omitted the ten-percent provision. It required wealthy Southerners to make individual applications for pardons.

4. *For what reasons did the Radical Republicans oppose President Johnson's plan for Reconstruction?*

   They thought it was too lenient on Southern whites, whom they viewed as unrepentant rebels. They feared that if the same Southern leaders continued in power, they would keep the freedmen from becoming equal with whites. The representatives sent to Congress in 1865 by Southern states included many officials from the Confederacy.

5. a. *What difficulties were blacks facing in the South?*

   Blacks were insulted, whipped, and even killed by whites, for such things as not removing a hat or for using disrespectful language. They faced legal discrimination through the black codes. They found it hard to support themselves, and many were trapped in sharecropping.

   b. *How did the sharecropping system work?*

   Planters divided their vast lands into small plots each rented by a black family. A planter often provided cabins, tools, and seeds while the black families raised the crops. The black family paid their rent by giving the owner a share of the harvest.

6. *What did the Freedmen's Bureau accomplish?*

   It gave food, clothing, medicine, and seeds to poor people in the South. It helped freedmen get jobs and provided schools for them. It tried to provide justice for blacks through a special court system.

7. *What are the terms of the Fourteenth Amendment?*

It states that all persons (except Indians) born in the United States are citizens. It prohibits states from depriving any citizen of his rights.

Focus for Thought (page 366)

8. *What were some provisions of the Reconstruction Act of 1867?*

The South was divided into five military districts each governed by a Union general. Soldiers kept order and enforced civil rights. Each state was to write a new constitution including a guarantee that blacks could vote. When a state had ratified the Fourteenth Amendment and Congress had approved its constitution, it could be readmitted to the Union and military rule would end.

9. *Name and describe each of the three groups who were involved in the Reconstruction governments.*

Freedmen gained the right to vote and hold government offices. (They usually voted Republican.) Carpetbaggers were Northerners who had come to aid the South or to profit from the Reconstruction. Scalawags were Southern whites who joined the Republican Party.

10. a. *What were some accomplishments of the Reconstruction governments?*

They improved local governments, allowed more people to vote, provided more schools, repaired war damages, and encouraged the building of hospitals and factories.

b. *What were some of their problems?*

Taxes were raised, which angered many whites. The states went deeply into debt. Some money was wasted through corruption.

11. a. *Why was President Johnson impeached?*

Johnson had deliberately violated the Tenure of Office Act (which Congress had passed to restrict the president).

b. *How did his acquittal help to maintain the balance between the branches of the United States government?*

If Johnson had been removed from office, it could easily have started a practice of impeaching any president who did not agree with Congress.

c. *What major purchase was made during Johnson's presidency?*

the purchase of Alaska from Russia for $7.2 million

12. *What is the main provision of the Fifteenth Amendment?*

It preserves the right of blacks to vote, saying that no citizen can be denied voting privileges because of his race.

Focus for Thought (page 371)

13. a. *What were the goals and methods of secret societies such as the Ku Klux Klan?*

The secret societies wanted to overthrow the Republican governments and restore white supremacy. They accomplished these goals through terror and violence. They whipped and killed many blacks. They tried to keep blacks from voting.

b. *How did the government control the Ku Klux Klan?*

Congress passed the Ku Klux Klan Act, which declared that if states did not punish the ones guilty of violence, the federal government would. President Grant sent soldiers to keep order in South Carolina.

14. a. *What two things enabled Southern whites to "redeem" their state governments?*

Young citizens who had not taken part in the Confederacy began to vote. The Amnesty Act allowed most ex-Confederates to vote and hold office.

b. *What did the new governments do?*

They tried to undo the changes made by Reconstruction governments. They lowered taxes, reduced government spending, and made efforts to reduce the power of blacks.

15. *How did the Compromise of 1877 end Reconstruction?*

In this compromise, Hayes promised to let the states have home rule rather than using federal troops to intervene. Reconstruction ended after the federal troops were withdrawn.

16. *Name four important ways that the South changed after Reconstruction.*

(Any four.) Southern agriculture changed from large plantations to small farms. The South developed more factories, such as steel, lumber, and textile mills. The South solidly supported the Democratic Party. Discrimination against blacks continued or increased, especially through Jim Crow laws. A middle class of blacks developed.

HISTORICAL HIGHLIGHTS (pages 371–375)

A. Matching: People

a. *Andrew Johnson*   f. *Hiram Revels*
b. *Booker T. Washington*   g. *Rutherford B. Hayes*
c. *Edmund Ross*   h. *Samuel Tilden*
d. *Edwin Stanton*   i. *Ulysses S. Grant*
e. *George Washington Carver* j. *William Seward*

j 1. *Johnson's secretary of state who purchased Alaska from Russia.*
a 2. *Lincoln's vice president; impeached when he was president.*
d 3. *Secretary of war who was dismissed by President Johnson.*
i 4. *President whose two terms were marked by corruption.*
c 5. *Man whose vote saved President Johnson from being found guilty.*
h 6. *Democratic candidate in disputed election of 1876.*
b 7. *Black leader who founded Tuskegee Institute and helped his people.*
g 8. *President elected by the Compromise of 1877, which aided redemption.*
f 9. *First black man elected to the United States Senate.*
e 10. *Black scientist who encouraged Southern farmers to grow peanuts.*

B. Matching: Terms 1

a. *black codes*   h. *Freedmen's Bureau*
b. *carpetbaggers*   i. *Radical Republicans*
c. *Civil Rights Act*   j. *Reconstruction*
d. *discrimination*   k. *Reconstruction Act*
e. *Fourteenth Amendment*   l. *scalawags*
f. *Fifteenth Amendment*   m. *sharecropping*
g. *freedmen*   n. *ten percent plan*

h 1. *Government agency that aided former slaves after the war.*
b 2. *Northerners who went south after the Civil War to help in Reconstruction.*
e 3. *Constitutional amendment that guarantees the rights of black people.*
c 4. *Law that defined citizenship and provided equal benefit of the law for all citizens.*
f 5. *Constitutional amendment granting all citizens the right to vote.*
n 6. *President Lincoln's plan for restoring the Southern states.*
i 7. *Group that wanted to punish and reform the South.*
m 8. *System in which farm workers rent cropland and use a share of the crops to pay the rent.*
l 9. *Southern whites who took part in Reconstruction governments.*

g 10. *Former slaves.*

a 11. *Laws that restricted blacks and kept them subordinate to whites.*

j 12. *Rebuilding and restoration of the South after the Civil War.*

d 13. *Action based on prejudice against a person.*

k 14. *Law that provided military control to enforce Reconstruction.*

C. Matching: Terms 2

a. *Amnesty Act*	h. *redeem*
b. *civil rights*	i. *segregation*
c. *Force Acts*	j. *Seward's Folly*
d. *home rule*	k. *solid South*
e. *Jim Crow laws*	l. *Tenure of Office Act*
f. *Ku Klux Klan*	m. *white supremacy*
g. *poll*	

d 1. *Policy allowing Southern states to deal with their own affairs.*

m 2. *Belief that whites are superior to blacks.*

g 3. *Voting place.*

k 4. *Dependable Southern support of Democrats after redemption.*

h 5. *To restore government control by whites to a Southern state.*

f 6. *Secret society that terrorized blacks.*

l 7. *Law forbidding dismissal of Cabinet members without Senate approval.*

c 8. *Laws containing measures for dealing with groups that terrorized blacks.*

e 9. *Laws requiring segregation of blacks and whites after Reconstruction.*

a 10. *Law restoring to most ex-Confederates the right to vote and hold office.*

i 11. *Social separation based on race.*

j 12. *Term for Alaska.*

b 13. *Freedoms and privileges belonging to all citizens.*

D. Multiple Choice

Write the letter of the best answer.

1. *Which of the following was* not *lost by the South?*
   a. religious freedom   c. *family members*
   b. *slaves*   d. *wealth*

2. *Why did Radicals resist the presidential plans for Reconstruction?*
   a. *They considered those plans unconstitutional.*
   b. *The president wanted Congress to control Reconstruction.*
   c. They wanted to punish and reform the South.
   d. *They thought Southerners themselves should take charge of Reconstruction.*

3. *What two goals did the Radicals have for the South?*

   a. Blacks and whites would be equal.

   b. *Sharecropping would continue for blacks and landowners.*

   c. *Carpetbaggers and scalawags would rebuild the war-torn areas.*

   d. *Southern states would be restored to the Union as soon as possible.*

   e. Republicans would have control of the Southern states.

4. *What goal did President Johnson have for the South?*

   a. *Blacks and whites would be equal.*

   b. *Southern plantations would be divided and given to the freedmen.*

   c. *The federal government would provide money for repairing war damages.*

   d. Southern states would be restored to the Union as soon as possible.

5. *For what reason did Southern states pass black codes?*

   a. *These codes helped the blacks to gain equality with whites.*

   b. *These codes aided the blacks economically.*

   c. These codes kept blacks in an inferior status.

   d. *The Ku Klux Klan promoted these codes.*

6. *In what two ways was the United States different after the Fourteenth Amendment was added to the Constitution?*

   a. *The slaves were productive as sharecroppers.*

   b. *The president could no longer veto legislation.*

   c. The federal government had more authority over the states.

   d. The law provided equal rights for blacks and whites.

7. *Which one of the following best describes the charges of impeachment against President Johnson?*

   a. *The charges grew out of personal dislike for the president.*

   b. The charges were based on a new law passed mainly to restrict the president.

   c. *The president had committed serious crimes worthy of punishment.*

   d. *The president was incapable of fulfilling the duties of his office.*

8. *Which political party did the carpetbaggers and scalawags represent?*

   a. Republican   b. *Democratic*

9. *What does the Fifteenth Amendment declare?*

   a. *No person may be held as a slave.*

   b. *Blacks and whites were equal before the law as citizens.*

   c. No citizen (including a black person) may be denied the right to vote.

   d. *Poll taxes and literacy tests may not be required for voting.*

10. *Which one of the following was* not *true of the Ku Klux Klan?*

    a. *It sought to reverse the changes that Reconstruction was bringing.*

    b. *Its members supported the Democratic Party.*

c. *It was devoted to white supremacy.*

d. **Its members frightened black people but did not actually harm them.**

11. *What contributed to government corruption during Reconstruction?*

a. *Whites were considered superior to blacks.*

b. **The Civil War had undermined the morals of the nation.**

c. *People had an unusually strong love for money.*

d. *Officeholders in Reconstruction governments were lazy and inefficient.*

12. *Why is the beginning of the Hayes administration considered the end of Reconstruction?*

a. **The federal government ended its direct involvement in rebuilding the South.**

b. *Hayes won the electoral vote but not the popular vote.*

c. *Redeemed governments greatly reduced taxes.*

d. *Segregation became the normal policy for race relations in the South.*

E. Deeper Discussion

1. *Which approach to Reconstruction—the presidential plan or the Congressional plan—yielded better results? Explain.*

   The presidential plan did provide a simple way to restore national unity. However, it allowed whites to continue treating blacks as inferior and to oppress them in many ways. It also failed to punish the South for seceding, and actually allowed many ex-Confederates to retain power. In many ways, Southerners could act almost as if they had won the war.

   The Congressional plan was better in that it made provisions for the needs of blacks and tried to gain equality for them. It also punished the South and reinforced the federal government's power over the states—though that power did tend to be excessive. Yet the Congressional plan generated bitterness and opposition, with the result that Southern whites ended Reconstruction as soon as possible by "redeeming" their states from federal control. Then the lives of blacks were much the same as when they had been slaves.

2. a. *Why did blacks need so much help after they were free?*

   Most blacks had always been under someone else's authority and therefore had little sense of initiative or responsibility. Blacks needed to learn how to support themselves and how to handle their new-found freedom. Since most were illiterate, they needed education; and since they owned hardly anything, they needed financial

help. Besides this, many Southern whites tried to keep the blacks in a state of inferiority.

b. *What more could have been done to help the freedmen make the transition from slavery to freedom?*

Perhaps a form of homesteading could have been offered to help the blacks obtain land. Private organizations could have offered more help. And it would certainly have been much better for the Southern people to voluntarily help the blacks than to be forced by the federal government to help them. But many Southerners wanted to suppress the blacks rather than help them.

c. *Was sharecropping a benefit or a hindrance to blacks? Explain.*

Benefit: Sharecropping provided a better life than slavery, for families were not broken up and sold at auctions, and the family could work together as a unit. It also gave blacks a chance to improve themselves financially, as some did.

Hindrance: Sharecropping often led blacks deeper and deeper into debt until they were hopelessly trapped in poverty.

3. a. *Why were blacks kept in an inferior position even though the Constitution gave them equal standing with whites?*

Laws cannot change people's attitudes. Since many Southern whites still considered blacks inferior, they found ways to evade the law or they resorted to terrorism.

b. *How did whites accomplish this?*

White people passed Jim Crow laws to restrict the blacks. They used poll taxes and literacy tests to keep blacks from voting. They established "separate but equal" facilities to keep blacks in an inferior position. They used lynching and other injustices to "keep blacks in their place."

4. a. *Read Psalm 12:5 and Ecclesiastes 3:16, 17 and 5:8. Who notices each injustice that is never avenged on earth?*

God notices, and He will remember each injustice. He never makes mistakes.

b. *What will finally be done about such injustices? (See Revelation 18:5, 6.)*

God will finally take vengeance on those who have escaped punishment on earth, unless they repent.

5. *How would the balance of power have been upset if President Johnson had been found guilty during his impeachment trial?*

If Johnson had been removed from office, it would have set a precedent by which a strong Congress could remove a president from

office simply for opposing its policies. This would have strengthened Congress and weakened the presidency, thus damaging the
delicate balance of power as established in the Constitution.

6. a. *In what respects did Reconstruction succeed?*
It succeeded in that Southern states were restored to the Union and
Southern industry made progress. Blacks gained legal equality,
became United States citizens, and received the right to vote.
Blacks also gained educational and economic opportunities.

b. *In what respects did it fail?*
It failed in that the South reverted to oppressing blacks as soon as
federal constraints were removed. It also failed to change people's
attitudes about racial issues, and prejudice remained. Much violence and turmoil occurred during Reconstruction. The South still
lagged behind the rest of the nation economically.

F. Chronology and Geography

1. *The following list gives some major events during the 1860s and 1870s.
Arrange the list in the proper order, and supply the date for each event.*

> *Amnesty Act passed*
> *Civil Rights Act passed*
> *Civil War ends*
> *Compromise of 1877 approved*
> *Disputed Hayes–Tilden election*
> *Emancipation Proclamation becomes effective*
> *Fourteenth Amendment ratified*
> *Fifteenth Amendment ratified*
> *Grant re-elected*
> *Johnson impeached and acquitted*
> *Ku Klux Klan Act passed*
> *Lincoln assassinated*
> *Reconstruction Act passed*
> *Reconstruction ends*
> *United States purchases Alaska*

1863—Emancipation Proclamation becomes effective
1865—Civil War ends
1865—Lincoln assassinated
1866—Civil Rights Act passed
1867—Reconstruction Act passed
1867—United States purchases Alaska

1868—Fourteenth Amendment ratified
1868—Johnson impeached and acquitted
1870—Fifteenth Amendment ratified
1871—Ku Klux Klan Act passed
1872—Amnesty Act passed
1872—Grant re-elected
1876—Disputed Hayes–Tilden election
1877—Compromise of 1877 approved
1877—Reconstruction ends

2. *Name the Southern states in the order they were redeemed, and give the year of redemption for each.*
Tennessee—1869; Virginia and North Carolina—1870; Georgia, 1871; Arkansas, Alabama, Texas—1874; Mississippi—1875; Louisiana, South Carolina, Florida—1877

3. *How did the South make better use of its resources after the war?*
The South built steel mills to use its iron ore, especially in Alabama. Lumber mills produced lumber from its vast forests, and cotton mills made cloth from its cotton. Raising new crops, such as peanuts, took advantage of the South's abundant farmland.

So Far This Year (pages 376, 377)

A. Matching: Climates

c 1. *Sunny and mild; good for growing oranges and olives.*

b 2. *Very warm and moist.*

e 3. *Wet and mild; found in Pacific valleys.*

d 4. *Cold climate in Canada and Alaska.*

a 5. *Climate of four seasons.*

a. *humid continental*
b. *humid subtropical*
c. *Mediterranean*
d. *subarctic*
e. *west coast marine*

B. Matching: Physical Features

f 6. *Drains about 40 percent of the United States.*

c 7. *Rocky region curving like a horseshoe around Hudson Bay.*

h 8. *Made up of the Coast Ranges, the Pacific ranges, and the Pacific valleys.*

i 9. *Region with high mountains extending from Canada to New Mexico; region includes Great Basin and plateaus.*

g 10. *Longest river in Canada.*

e 11. *Vast, treeless, grassy land stretching from the Mississippi to the Rockies.*

d 12. *Heartland of Canada in Ontario and Quebec.*

b 13. *Broad, flat region bordering the Gulf of Mexico and the ocean east of the United States.*

a 14. *Made up of the Piedmont, the Appalachian Mountains, and the Allegheny and Cumberland Plateaus.*

a. *Appalachian region*
b. *Atlantic Coastal Plain*
c. *Canadian Shield*
d. *Great Lakes-St. Lawrence Lowlands*
e. *Central Plains*
f. *Mississippi River*
g. *Mackenzie River*
h. *Pacific Coast*
i. *Rocky Mountain region*

C. Matching: Explorers

g 15. *Viking who explored the northeastern coast of North America around A.D. 1000.*

e 16. *"Admiral of the Ocean Sea" who discovered the New World in 1492.*

o 17. *Man who described the new lands as being a new world rather than part of the Orient.*

b 18. *Explorer of the northeastern coast of North American for England in 1497.*

a 19. *Explorer who discovered in 1513 that a great ocean lay west of America.*

l 20. *Captain of five ships, one of which became the first to sail around the world (1519–1522).*

h 21. *Explorer who claimed part of America for the Netherlands in 1609.*

p 22. *Explorer of the North American coast for France in 1524.*

c 23. *Explorer of the St. Lawrence River area for France in 1534.*

d 24. *The "father of New France."*

j 25. *Explorer who claimed for France the area drained by the Mississippi River.*

i, m 26. *Jesuits who explored part of the Mississippi River for France (two answers).*

f 27. *Explorer who sought the Seven Cities of Cíbola in the Southwest (1540–1542).*

n 28. *Explorer who discovered the Mississippi River.*

k 29. *Explorer who discovered Florida in 1513 while seeking the Fountain of Youth.*

a. *Vasco de Balboa*
b. *John Cabot*
c. *Jacques Cartier*
d. *Samuel de Champlain*
e. *Christopher Columbus*
f. *Francisco de Coronado*
g. *Leif Ericson*
h. *Henry Hudson*
i. *Louis Jolliet*
j. *Robert de La Salle*
k. *Ponce de León*
l. *Ferdinand Magellan*
m. *Jacques Marquette*
n. *Hernando de Soto*
o. *Amerigo Vespucci*
p. *Giovanni da Verrazano*

D. Completion

Write the correct name, term, or date that belongs on each blank.

30. *The idea that people living in an area should decide for themselves about slavery is called* **popular sovereignty**.

31. *The* **Thirteenth** *Amendment to the Constitution permanently outlawed slavery.*

32. *The* **Emancipation Proclamation** *declared that slaves in the Confederacy were free.*

33. *A secret system that aided escaping slaves was the* **Underground Railroad**.

34. *During the Civil War, Delaware, Maryland, Kentucky, and Missouri were called* **border states**.

35. **Jefferson Davis** *was president of the Confederate States of America.*

36. **Abraham Lincoln** *was president of the Union during the Civil War.*

37. **Ulysses S. Grant** *was the chief Union general at the end of the Civil War.*

38. **Robert E. Lee** *was the chief general of the Confederate armies.*

39. **John Brown** *tried to free the slaves through an armed uprising.*

40. **Harriet Beecher Stowe** *wrote a book called* Uncle Tom's Cabin.

41. **Dred Scott** *was a black man whose appeal for freedom was rejected by the Supreme Court.*

42. **Stonewall Jackson** *was a Confederate general shot by his own men at the Battle of Chancellorsville.*

43. **William T. Sherman** *was a Union general who led a destructive March to the Sea.*

44. *The town of* **Gettysburg** *became known as the "high-water mark of the Confederacy."*

45. **Fort Sumter** *was the place where the Civil War began.*

46. *The city that served as the Confederate capital was* **Richmond**.

47. **Vicksburg** *was the stronghold whose fall gave the Union control of the Mississippi.*

48. *The new state formed from a Confederate state during the Civil War was* **West Virginia**.

49. *An early battle that showed the Civil War would be long and hard took place at* **Bull Run**.

50. *The Civil War began in the year* **1861** *and ended in the year* **1865**.

18 The Development of Canada

1750

Quebec Act passed 1774

New Brunswick formed 1784
Mennonites settle in Canada 1786
Upper Canada and Lower Canada
formed by the Canada Act 1791

Alexander Mackenzie
explores to the Pacific 1793

1800

War of 1812 **1812–1814**

Rebellion of 1837
Durham Report submitted 1838

Province of Canada formed by the Act of Union
1841

Rebellion Losses Bill approved;
1850   Parliament buildings burned in Montreal 1849

Reciprocity Treaty implemented 1854

Quebec Conference held 1864
Rupert's Land and North West Territories
obtained; Red River Rebellion   1869
Manitoba Act passed 1870
British Columbia joins the Dominion 1871
Russian Mennonites arrive
in Manitoba   1874

Reciprocity Treaty ended by U.S.; Confederation approved;
British Columbia formed   1866
Dominion of Canada formed by the British North America Act
1867
Rupert's Land and North West Territories organized into
the Northwest Territories   1870
North West Mounted Police formed;
Prince Edward Island joins the Dominion 1873
North West Rebellion 1884–1885
Canadian Pacific Railway completed 1885

1900   Yukon Territory formed 1898

Saskatchewan and Alberta become provinces 1905

Newfoundland joins the Dominion 1949

1950

*"There is none holy as the LORD: for there is none
beside thee: neither is there any rock like our God."*
1 Samuel 2:2

2000   Nunavut becomes a territory 1999

Chapter 18 (pages 378–403)

THE DEVELOPMENT OF CANADA

Chapter Objectives

- To acquaint students with a broad scope of Canadian history from the late 1700s through the 1800s.
- To learn about the early settlement of Upper Canada (Ontario), especially Mennonite settlement.
- To understand the problems that Canadians faced as they struggled for more self-government, including difficulties between the French and English citizens.
- To learn how the Dominion of Canada was formed.
- To learn how the North West Mounted Police brought law and order to the Canadian West.
- To learn how Manitoba, British Columbia, and the remaining provinces became part of the Dominion of Canada.

To the Teacher

This chapter should lend an interesting perspective to a study of American history. Many "Yankees" know little or nothing about the history of their northern neighbor—so the main objective of this chapter is to familiarize United States pupils with that history. Unique aspects of Canadian history include the strongly British flavor of the country, the distinctly *un*revolutionary way in which the Canadians formed their nation, the British-French rivalry, and the Canadians' strong desire *not* to be assimilated into the United States.

Canadian history seems to be less coherent than United States history. The flow of events is harder to organize sequentially, so the overall scope may be harder to grasp. For example, in United States history, the student can think in terms of major events separated by periods of more common happenings: Revolution, Constitution, War of 1812, Civil War, and so on. In Canadian history, the main events are less clearly defined. For example, what is so memorable about the Canada Act that created Upper and Lower Canada in 1791, or about a report written by a British diplomat in 1838?

The important thing, then, is to grasp the developments toward which events were heading—something clearly visible only in hindsight. First, events moved Canada toward greater self-government as a colony of Great Britain. Then, Canada moved toward becoming a nation in its own right without being totally independent. From there, Canada expanded until it covered the northern half of the continent as we know it today. The later history of Canada is discussed briefly on pages 630 and 631.

Another thing to add interest will be to relate events to people. For example, the settlement of Mennonites in Ontario should help to enliven the discussion of early settlement. The lives of John A. Macdonald and other key figures in Canadian history add flavor. The Canadian West should also stir interest. So do some further study from an encyclopedia or other reference books on topics mentioned in "Further Study."

Since this chapter is not on United States history, it could be skimmed, eliminated, or assigned only to fast students. Just remember that Canadians think that people in the United States are woefully ignorant of Canadian history. So teach the chapter if you can.

Note on chapter test: Chapter 18 has its own test.

Christian Perspectives

- Those in a Christian brotherhood need to bear "one another's burdens, and so fulfil the law of Christ" (Galatians 6:2).
- The Family Compact illustrates the truth that power corrupts, and it demonstrates man's lust for power.
- Conflict develops between peoples when those on each side demand their own rights and forget about the rights of others. This is illustrated in the French–English rivalry, which surfaced in the various rebellions of the 1800s.
- Man's depravity causes him to corrupt others, as the whiskey traders did to the Indians (Genesis 6:5; Jeremiah 17:9; Habakkuk 2:15, 16; Romans 3:10–23).
- The government has a responsibility to keep law and order, as the Canadian government did through the Mounties, and as Governor Douglas did in the gold rushes of British Columbia (Romans 13:1–4).
- Dealing in wisdom works better than dealing by military might (Ecclesiastes 9:16, 18). This is demonstrated in the Canadian dealings with the Indians.

Further Study

- Mennonite colonists in Canada.
- The life of John A. Macdonald.
- The Canadian West, including details about the fur trade, the Métis, Louis Riel, the gold rushes in British Columbia, and the settlement of the western plains.

Chapter 18 Quiz

Write the correct name or term for each description.

1. Law that created the Dominion of Canada.

_____

2. People who left the United States to remain under British rule.

_____

3. Government controlled by the people rather than by aristocrats.

_____

4. First prime minister of Canada.

_____

5. Explorer who reached the Pacific by land when trying to find the Northwest Passage.

_____

6. Famous surveyor who explored the Columbia River.

_____

7. Produced a report that led to changes in Canadian government.

_____

8. Date when Canada became a nation.

_____

Quiz Answers

1. **British North America Act**
2. **(United Empire) Loyalists**
3. **responsible government**
4. **John A. Macdonald**
5. **Alexander Mackenzie**
6. **David Thompson**
7. **Lord Durham**
8. **July 1, 1867**

Answer Key

Focus for Thought (page 384)

1. *What were four important provisions of the Quebec Act?*

   The Quebec Act permitted French Canadians to exercise their religion freely. It allowed them to take part in the government. It allowed the seigneurial system and French civil laws to continue. It extended the borders of Quebec south to the Ohio River and west to the Mississippi River.

2. *What effects did the Loyalists have on the parts of Canada where they settled?*

   Loyalists in Nova Scotia wanted their own government, so the province of New Brunswick was established. Loyalists made western Quebec overwhelmingly English, and they also wanted their own government; so Quebec was divided into Upper Canada and Lower Canada.

3. a. *What was the aim of the Canada Act of 1791?*

   The British hoped that the French Canadians would be so impressed with British ways that they would give up their French ways.

   b. *Why was this aim not fulfilled?*

   The French continued to cling to their established culture and customs.

4. a. *What problem was experienced by Mennonites who bought land from Richard Beasley?*

   The Mennonites learned that their deeds were worthless because Beasley did not hold clear title to the land.

   b. *How did they solve the problem?*

   Mennonites in Lancaster, Pennsylvania, raised the $20,000 needed to gain a clear title.

5. *What were some ways that the War of 1812 affected Canada?*

   It brought greater prosperity because of increased British military spending. It gave Canadians a stronger sense of nationalism. Many Canadians became bitter because of invasions by United States armies.

Focus for Thought (page 389)

6. *Why did the French Canadians distrust the English-speaking settlers in Canada?*

   The French were afraid their language and culture might lose out to those of the English. They were also afraid of losing their farms to English industrialization.

7. *A two-part rebellion broke out in 1837.*

   a. *What sparked the rebellion in Upper Canada? in Lower Canada?*

   Upper Canada: In 1836, Sir Francis Bond Head dissolved the Reform-dominated Assembly and ordered a new election, which the Tories won because of his manipulation.

   Lower Canada: The English decided to move ahead without French cooperation, and the French-controlled Legislative Assembly was adjourned.

   b. *What were the results of these rebellions?*

   The rebels were defeated, and their two main leaders (Mackenzie and Papineau) fled to the United States. The British government investigated the problems in the Canadian colonies.

8. *What three things did the Durham Report recommend?*

   It recommended that the Canadian provinces be given more self-government, that their government be made more responsible, and that Upper and Lower Canada be joined into one province.

9. *Why was the passage of the Rebellion Losses Bill an important step in achieving responsible government?*

   The passage of this bill showed that the governor-general supported responsible government. It also demonstrated that the British Parliament would not intervene in the affairs of Canada, and also that Parliament approved Elgin's support of responsible government.

10. *Name and describe three factors that moved the Canadian provinces toward uniting as a nation.*

    Commerce: Because of changes in British and United States trade policies, it became clear that the Canadian provinces should unite to increase trade among themselves.

    Relations with the United States: Canadians worried that the United States might expand northward into their territory.

    Political problems: The equal number of French-speaking and English-speaking representatives caused deadlock in the Legislative Assembly.

11. *List the four original provinces in the Dominion of Canada, and the date when they officially became a self-governing nation.*

    Ontario, Quebec, Nova Scotia, and New Brunswick; July 1, 1867

Focus for Thought (page 397)

12. a. *What did Alexander Mackenzie hope to find in the Northwest?*

    the Northwest Passage

b. *What three rivers did he explore?*

the Slave River, the Mackenzie River, and the Peace River

13. *Describe how the Northwest Territories came to be part of the Dominion of Canada.*

The North West Company and the Hudson's Bay Company merged in 1821. In 1869, the Dominion purchased Rupert's Land from the Hudson's Bay Company and later gained possession of the land lying north, west, and south of Rupert's Land. The Dominion organized the two regions as the Northwest Territories.

14. *What did the Red River Rebellion gain for the Métis?*

It resulted in the Manitoba Act, which incorporated nearly all the Métis demands and granted them about 1.4 million acres (567,000 ha) of land.

15. *What were two important accomplishments of the North West Mounted Police?*

They stopped the whiskey trade in about a year. They made treaties by which the Indians received money and supplies in return for their land.

16. a. *Why can it be said that British Columbia had its beginnings in furs and gold?*

Furs were the first attraction in British Columbia. Later, two gold rushes drew thousands of people to the region.

b. *What did a transcontinental railroad have to do with British Columbia?*

To encourage British Columbia to join the Dominion of Canada, the Dominion promised to build a transcontinental railroad to British Columbia.

17. *What were the results of the North West Rebellion of 1885?*

The Métis received title to their lands. Resentment became stronger between French Canadians and the English citizens.

18. *List the four provinces that joined the Dominion after British Columbia, and the dates when they joined.*

Prince Edward Island—1873; Saskatchewan—1905; Alberta—1905; Newfoundland—1949

HISTORICAL HIGHLIGHTS (pages 398–402)

A. Matching: People

a. *Alexander Mackenzie*

b. *David Thompson*

c. *George Simpson*

d. *Isaac Brock*

e. *James Douglas*

f. *John A. Macdonald*

g. *Lord Durham*

h. *Joseph Howe*

i. *Louis J. Papineau*

j. *Louis Riel*

k. *Métis*

l. *Peter Pond*

m. *Simon Fraser*

n. *William L. Mackenzie*

f   1. *First prime minister of Canada.*

l   2. *Explorer who established the fur trade around Lake Athabasca.*

d   3. *Canadian colonel who defeated Americans in the War of 1812.*

j   4. *Métis leader of the Red River Rebellion and the North West Rebellion.*

i, n   5. *Reformers who led rebellions in 1837 (two men).*

h   6. *Leader of reform in Nova Scotia.*

b   7. *Famous surveyor who explored the Columbia River.*

m   8. *Explorer who in 1808 followed a river (later named after him) to the Pacific Ocean.*

g   9. *British noblemen who wrote a famous report that recommended responsible government for Canada.*

a   10. *Explorer who followed a river (later named after him) to the Arctic Ocean and also reached the Pacific by land in 1793.*

k   11. *People of mixed French and Indian ancestry.*

c   12. *Skillful director of the combined North West Company and Hudson's Bay Company.*

e   13. *Governor of British Columbia who built the Cariboo Road.*

B. Matching: Canadian Government

a. *Cabinet*

b. *Executive Council*

c. *House of Commons*

d. *Legislative Assembly*

e. *Legislative Council*

f. *Parliament*

g. *prime minister*

h. *Senate*

g   1. *Leader of the majority party in the House of Commons, and actual head of the Dominion government.*

c   2. *Elected law-making body in the Dominion government.*

e   3. *Upper house of the colonial government, its members appointed.*

b   4. *Council in the colonial government that assisted the governor.*

a   5. *Group of men assisting the prime minister in the Dominion government.*

f   6. *Legislative branch of the Dominion, including both upper and lower houses.*

d   7. *Lower law-making body of the colonial government, its members elected.*

h   8. *Upper law-making body of the Dominion, its members appointed.*

C. Matching: Terms 1

a. *Act of Union*   g. *Quebec Act*

b. *Canada Act*   h. *Rebellion of 1837*

c. *Durham Report*   i. *Reform Party*

d. *Family Compact*   j. *responsible government*

e. *oligarchy*   k. *Tories*

f. *Patriotes*   l. *United Empire Loyalists*

f   1. *Supporters of Papineau in the Rebellion of 1837.*

a   2. *United two provinces into the Province of Canada.*

e   3. *Rule by a small group of people.*

i   4. *Party that opposed the Family Compact.*

h   5. *Uprisings in Upper and Lower Canada against the Family Compact.*

l   6. *People who left the United States because they wanted to stay under British rule.*

g   7. *Law passed in 1774 that attempted to reconcile the French to British rule.*

b   8. *Divided the province of Quebec into Upper and Lower Canada.*

c   9. *Recommended changes in the government of the Canadian provinces.*

j 10. *Government controlled by the people rather than by aristocrats.*

k 11. *Another name for Loyalists.*

d 12. *Small group of wealthy men who controlled Canadian government.*

D. Matching: Terms 2

a. *British North America Act*   i. *North West Rebellion*

b. *confederation*   j. *Quebec Conference*

c. *fathers of the Confederation*   k. *Rebellion Losses Bill*

d. *Hudson's Bay Company*   l. *Reciprocity Treaty*

e. *Manitoba Act*   m. *Red River Rebellion*

f. *National Policy*   n. *Seventy-two Resolutions*

g. *North West Company*   o. *squatters*

h. *North West Mounted Police*   p. *voyageurs*

l   1. *Trade agreement with the United States.*

k   2. *Law that stirred up a riot and demonstrated support for responsible government.*

b   3. *Union of provinces under a single government.*

f   4. *Program that included tariffs, railroad construction, and settlement of the Northwest.*

o   5. *People who settle on unoccupied land without legal title to it.*

i   6. *Métis rebellion in 1885 in the Saskatchewan River valley.*

p   7. *Strong French Canadian canoe paddlers.*

e   8. *Law that created the province of Manitoba.*

m   9. *Métis rebellion in 1869 that led to the establishment of Manitoba.*

d, g 10. *Competing fur companies that merged in 1821 (two answers).*

a 11. *Law that created the Dominion of Canada.*

n 12. *Details for the Confederation drawn up at the Quebec Conference.*

h 13. *Men sent to stop the whiskey trade and to deal with the Indians.*

j 14. *Meeting where the Confederation was proposed and planned.*

c 15. *Men who worked out the plan for the Confederation.*

E. Matching: Places

a. *Alberta*

b. *Assiniboia*

c. *British Columbia*

d. *Canada East*

e. *Canada West*

f. *Canadian Pacific Railroad*

g. *Cariboo Road*

h. *Dominion of Canada*

i. *Lower Canada*

j. *Manitoba*

k. *New Brunswick*

l. *Newfoundland*

m. *Northwest Territories*

n. *Nova Scotia*

o. *Ontario*

p. *Ottawa*

q. *Prince Edward Island*

r. *Province of Canada*

s. *Quebec*

t. *Saskatchewan*

u. *Upper Canada*

k, n, o, s 1. *Provinces that formed the Dominion of Canada (four answers).*

e, u 2. *Other names for the province of Ontario (two answers).*

d, i 3. *Other names for the province of Quebec (two answers).*

c 4. *Province on the west coast; first settled through a gold rush.*

b 5. *Land in the Red River region.*

f 6. *Provided transcontinental travel.*

j 7. *Province that began through a rebellion.*

a, t 8. *Provinces that grew out of settlement of the plains (two answers).*

h   9. *Confederation of the British North American provinces.*

g   10. *Improved transportation during the gold rush in British Columbia.*

r   11. *Union of Upper and Lower Canada.*

q   12. *Small province that joined the Dominion in 1873.*

l   13. *Province that did not join the Dominion until 1949.*

m   14. *Rupert's Land and land north, west, and south of it; became part of Canada in 1869.*

p   15. *Capital of the Dominion of Canada.*

F. Matching: Dates

a. *1774*	d. *July 1, 1867*	g. *1873*	j. *1949*
b. *1791*	e. *1870*	h. *1898*	k. *1999*
c. *1841*	f. *1871*	i. *1905*	

h   1. *Yukon Territory formed after a gold rush.*

d   2. *Canada's birthday.*

g   3. *Prince Edward Island joins the Dominion.*

e   4. *Manitoba becomes a province.*

a   5. *Quebec Act passed.*

f   6. *British Columbia becomes a province.*

c   7. *Province of Canada formed by the Act of Union.*

k   8. *Nunavut formed from the Northwest Territories.*

b   9. *Upper Canada and Lower Canada formed by the Canada Act.*

i   10. *Alberta and Saskatchewan become provinces.*

j   11. *Newfoundland joins the Dominion.*

G. True or False

Write whether each statement is true *(T)* or false *(F)*.

F   1. *Every year the "wintering partners" traded with the voyageurs at Montreal.*

F   2. *The French people of Lower Canada were eager to adopt English ways and industrialize Canada.*

F   3. *The oligarchy of Upper Canada sought to introduce responsible government.*

T   4. *The Durham Report recommended responsible government.*

T   5. *Reciprocity with the United States helped Canada to prosper after 1854.*

T   6. *The Fraser River gold rush was noted for its law and order in contrast to the California gold rush.*

T   7. *The British Parliament created the nation called the Dominion of Canada.*

F   8. *The Dominion of Canada was to be independent of Great Britain.*

T   9. *Prime Minister John A. Macdonald promoted a transcontinental railroad to bind the provinces together.*

T 10. *The Red River Rebellion led to the formation of Manitoba.*

T 11. *The Mounted Police brought law and order to the prairies.*

F 12. *Louis Riel's execution helped to calm the strife between the French and English peoples of Canada.*

H. Deeper Discussion

1. a. *Why did Canada remain British?*

The Canadians appreciated British traditions and respected the authority of the monarch. This was largely due to the United Empire Loyalists and the heavy British immigration after the War of 1812.

b. *Why did it not revolt as the United States had, or join the United States?*

Canadians preferred slower change rather than revolt, and wanted to solve their problems by legal methods. Several times some Canadians wanted to join the United States, and the United States would have been only too willing to receive them; but most of the time, the Canadians made determined efforts to stay out of the United States. (One example is the War of 1812.) Confederation took place partly because the Canadians did not want to join the United States. John A. Macdonald, for one, strongly favored staying British and worked hard to keep Canada from being absorbed into the United States or becoming Americanized.

2. a. *How is government in the Dominion of Canada similar to that of the United States?*

The Dominion government is similar in that it is a federation of provinces, with both provincial governments and a federal government. Both have a bicameral (two-house) legislature.

b. *How is it different?*

It is different in that it follows the British model of having a Parliament. The Senate is appointed rather than elected. It has a House of Commons instead of a House of Representatives, and a prime minister from the majority party in the House of Commons instead of an elected president. At the time it was formed, the Dominion was not fully independent, but the British government retained control of some affairs; whereas the United States government is independent. (In 1982, Canada did gain the right to modify its constitution, the

British North America Act of 1867. The British monarch is still the head of state, but Canada is otherwise independent.)

3. a. *Why did the French not become assimilated into the British society of Canada?*

The French Canadians clung to their traditional ways. They saw the British as trying to take away their simple way of life and their Catholic religion.

b. *How did this help to make the Métis issue so divisive?*

Catholic French Canadians sympathized with the Métis, and English Canadians, who were Protestant, tended to oppose the Métis.

4. *Why were the Canadians so successful in their approach to the British Columbia gold rushes, the whiskey trade, and their relations with the Indians?*

The Canadians focused on law and order, which made people respect authority. They dealt with the Indians as citizens rather than as foreign nations to be fought by military force. The Canadian approach followed God's provisions for government.

5. *How does Habakkuk 2:15, 16 aptly describe the wickedness of the whiskey trade with the Indians?*

The whiskey traders sold whiskey to the Indians so they could enrich themselves and corrupt the Indians. God's judgment is pronounced on this kind of sinful behavior, and it certainly was shameful.

I. Chronology and Geography

1. *The following list gives major events in Canadian history. Arrange the list in the proper order, and supply the date for each event.*

   British Columbia formed

   British Columbia joins the Dominion

   Confederation approved

   Dominion of Canada formed by the British North America Act

   Durham Report submitted

   Manitoba Act passed

   Newfoundland joins the Dominion

   North West Rebellion

   Prince Edward Island joins the Dominion

   Province of Canada formed by the Act of Union

   Rebellion of 1837

   Red River Rebellion

   Saskatchewan and Alberta join the Dominion

1837—Rebellion of 1837
1838—Durham Report submitted
1841—Province of Canada formed by the Act of Union
1866—Confederation approved
1866—British Columbia formed
1867—Dominion of Canada formed by the British North America Act
1869—Red River Rebellion
1870—Manitoba Act passed
1871—British Columbia joins the Dominion
1873—Prince Edward Island joins the Dominion
1884–1885—North West Rebellion
1905—Saskatchewan and Alberta join the Dominion
1949—Newfoundland joins the Dominion

2. *On your map entitled "Exploration of North America," draw red lines to show the explorations of Mackenzie, Fraser, and Thompson. Label these lines.* **(Individual work.)**

3. *Trace Map B (including the borders of the provinces and territories) and label it "Provinces and Territories of Canada."*

   a. *Label the ten provinces and three territories. Give admission dates for the provinces that were admitted after 1867.*

   b. *Use four different colors to represent the following areas: (1) four original provinces, (2) provinces admitted from 1870 to 1873, (3) provinces admitted from 1905 to 1949, (4) three territories.*

   c. *Make a legend to show what each color represents.*

   d. *Memorize the names and locations of the provinces and territories.* **(Individual work.)**

19 The Last Frontier

1840

1860

Pikes Peak gold rush; Comstock Lode
discovered in Nevada   1859

Sioux War 1865–1867

Nevada becomes a state;
Sand Creek massacre in Colorado 1864

Transcontinental railroad completed;
George Westinghouse invents air brake 1869

Russian Mennonites settle in Kansas 1873–1874
Joseph Glidden invents barbed wire 1874

Black Hills gold rush 1875–1876

Colorado becomes a state;
Battle of the Little Bighorn 1876

1880

Time zones created 1883

Dawes Act passed 1887

Montana, Washington, North and
South Dakota become states 1889
Idaho and Wyoming become states;
Wounded Knee massacre   1890

Utah becomes a state 1896

1900

Oklahoma becomes a state 1907

Arizona and New Mexico become states 1912

1920

Indians become citizens 1924

Indian Reorganization Act passed 1934

1940

1. THE MINERS AND RAILROADERS

The Mining Frontier

The Transcontinental Railroad

2. THE INDIANS

The Indian Wars

Recognition for the Indians

3. THE CATTLEMEN AND HOMESTEADERS

The Cattle Kingdom

Homesteading in the West

"For he that will love life, and see good days, let him refrain his tongue from evil, and his lips that they speak no guile: let him eschew evil, and do good; let him seek peace, and ensue it."

1 Peter 3:10, 11

Unit 6: Times of Change, 1859–1920

Chapter 19 (pages 404–431)

THE LAST FRONTIER

Chapter Objectives

- To learn about some famous gold rushes in the West, and understand how the miners contributed to settling the last frontier of the United States.
- To see how the transcontinental railroad was constructed, and consider the effects of railroads on settlement of the West.
- To learn about the Indian wars and other dealings of the United States with Indians of the West.
- To study about the beginning, spread, and end of the cattle kingdom.
- To learn about the homestead laws and about the lives of homesteaders as they settled the West.

To the Teacher

This chapter covers the fascinating story of the "Wild West," a story that is glamorized and romanticized in western novels and movies. Although those materials are unsuitable for godly people, plenty of worthwhile facts and stories are available to add color and interest to the study of this era. Beware of showing admiration for the wild, free spirit of the West; rather, focus on the accomplishments of settling this last frontier. Use the same approach in discussing the transcontinental railroad, the cattle kingdom, and the homesteaders in the West.

One cannot help feeling sorry for the Indians. Although it is not proper to denounce the white man and extol the Indian, the white men's treatment of the Indians did leave much to be desired. Their wrong attitudes, broken promises, massacres—none of this can be excused on the basis that the Indians were guilty of the same things. But the facts of history cannot be changed, so you must simply portray the Indian wars as they were. Remember, however, that the text presents only a few of the most significant events, and many more battles and other incidents could be included. Also beware of distortion of facts; some books gloss over events that make whites look bad, while others play them up. The story is bad enough without trying to exaggerate it. The Indian wars show that the United States was a Christian nation in name only.

Note on chapter test: Chapter 19 has its own test.

Christian Perspectives

- Covetousness and ambition motivated the gold and silver rushes, while the Christian should live by the rule of "rather seek ye the kingdom of God" (Luke 12:15, 31, 34).

- Law and order provides the basis for a stable society (Romans 13:4).
- The Christian should respect others, seek the way of peace, keep his promises, and live for the good of others—unlike most of those who dealt with the Indians (Acts 10:34; Romans 12:16–21; 1 Peter 3:8–12).
- The Christian must trust God in His sovereignty, no matter what happens (Habakkuk 2:20; 3:17–19).
- God has given man the ability to do many things by using his ingenuity and energies, as in building the railroad, raising cattle, and settling the homesteads (Genesis 1:26–28).
- God exercises ultimate control over the affairs of man, as shown by the harsh winter that caused many cattle to die and by the natural disasters that plagued the homesteaders (Job 42:1–6; Ecclesiastes 7:14).

Further Study

- The transcontinental railroad.
- The Indian wars in the West.
- Cattle herding on the open range.
- The life of a homesteader.
- The experience of Russian Mennonites who settled in Kansas.

Scores of books and novels have been written about the Great American West, but many of these are unfit to read. True stories and historical accounts are much better for educational research.

Chapter 19 Quiz

T F 1. The Homestead Act allowed settlers to claim 160 acres (65 ha) of land for farming.

T F 2. The Union Pacific built the transcontinental railroad east from California.

T F 3. The Dawes Act authorized a transcontinental railroad.

T F 4. Joseph McCoy invented barbed wire in 1874.

T F 5. Joseph Glidden built stockyards at Abilene, Kansas.

T F 6. Promontory, Utah, was the place where the transcontinental railroad was joined in 1869.

T F 7. Sitting Bull and Crazy Horse were two Indian chiefs defeated at the Battle of the Little Bighorn.

T F 8. The colonel defeated at the Battle of the Little Bighorn was George Custer.

T F 9. The Chisholm Trail was the route of cattle herds moving north to Kansas.

T F 10. Wounded Knee was the place where one of the last Indian battles took place.

Quiz Answers

1. **T**		6. **T**	
2. **F**		7. **F**	
3. **F**		8. **T**	
4. **F**		9. **T**	
5. **F**		10. **T**	

Answer Key

Focus for Thought (page 414)

1. *How did miners help the West to become settled?*

   When miners rushed to an area to seek gold or silver, other people also flocked there. The result was often a permanent town or city in that area.

2. a. *How did vigilance committees mete out justice?*

   They meted out swift, stern justice, often by hanging. This was done by the miners themselves rather than by an established government.

   b. *What American tendency did this illustrate?*

   the tendency of Americans to govern themselves when there was no established government

3. *Why did prospecting by individuals give way to mining by large companies?*

   Large companies used machines to extract the gold and silver that individual prospectors could not reach. (Prospectors could not afford large mining machines.)

4. *Why was there a need for a transcontinental railroad?*

It was needed to link the eastern part of the nation to California and the other western settlements.

5. a. *What were some difficulties faced by the builders of the transcontinental railroad?*

Difficulties included the shipping of supplies, a shortage of workers, attacks from Indians, snowslides in the high mountains, making cuts or blasting tunnels through ridges, building trestles across ravines, and laying the tracks entirely by muscle power.

   b. *Where and when was the first transcontinental railroad completed?*

at Promontory, Utah, in May 1869

6. *What were three effects of railroads in the West?*

(Any three.) Railroads linked the remote sections of the West together. They improved travel, shipping, and mail delivery. They contributed to the growth of industries, such as steel companies. Time zones made things more convenient for society in general. Railroads promoted settlement of the West by advertising for immigrants to settle on their land grants.

Focus for Thought (page 420)

7. *What were three main causes of the Indian wars?*

(Any three.) The government placed the Indians on reservations, and greedy whites often settled on the land that had been promised to the Indians. Settlement of the West and destruction of the buffalo threatened the Indian way of life. Misunderstandings and bad attitudes brought war. Cultural differences played a large part in the struggle. A general reason was the greed of white men.

8. a. *Name the Indian tribes and their leader who camped at Sand Creek in 1864 after seeking peace with the whites.*

Cheyenne and Arapaho led by Black Kettle

   b. *Who attacked them, and how many Indians were killed?*

Colonel John Chivington and his men killed an estimated 450 Indians.

9. *How did the Sioux victory at the Battle of the Little Bighorn finally lead to their defeat?*

After this battle, the United States began attacking the Indians so forcefully that most of the Sioux surrendered within the next year.

10. a. *Why was Sitting Bull arrested in 1890?*

Some people blamed him for the Ghost Dance that many Indians were performing.

b. *Where did an Indian massacre take place soon afterward?*
at Wounded Knee

11. *Explain what the Dawes Act provided for the Indians, and why this law did not work well.*
It divided the reservations into farms for the Indian families. This did not work well, for the Indians were accustomed to functioning in tribal groups rather than as separate families.

12. *Besides the Dawes Act, what three things showed a change in white people's attitudes toward Indians?*
The government granted citizenship to all Indians in 1924. The Indian Reorganization Act of 1934 promoted a return to tribal organization among the Indians. Schools like the Carlisle Indian School tried to teach Indians how to function as individuals in American society.

Focus for Thought (page 427)

13. a. *Why were hides the main product of early ranches in Texas?*
Both the East and California were too far away to provide a market for beef.
b. *What caused this to change later?*
Railroads provided a way to send cattle to faraway markets.

14. *What were some difficulties that cowboys experienced as they drove cattle to a cattle town?*
Flooding rivers had to be forded. Wolves or thunderstorms could cause the cattle to stampede. Angry Indians or farmers might attack.

15. *Describe two things that brought an end to open-range cattle herding.*
Cattlemen began using barbed wire to fence off their land. The hard winter of 1886–87 ruined many cattlemen, with the result that ranchers began keeping smaller herds and raising hay to feed them in winter.

16. *What were some provisions of the Homestead Act?*
Any citizen of age twenty-one or older could file a claim for 160 acres (65 ha); married couples could claim 320 acres (130 ha). A settler had to live on the land for five years, make improvements such as building a claim shanty, and cultivate the land. A settler could also preempt land by buying it for $1.25 per acre.

17. a. *Describe some difficulties of homesteading.*
A homesteader had to build a dwelling with scarce materials. He had to dig a well by hand if no water was near. He had to break the sod and plant crops. Money was scarce. He faced natural calamities like fires, storms, and grasshopper plagues.

b. *What enabled the homesteaders to survive?*

Some helps for survival were new crops and technology, such as hard wheat, improved plows, windmills, and barbed wire. The homesteaders overcame by perseverance, hard work, and their God-given mental abilities.

18. a. *How was the settlement of Oklahoma carried out?*

There were two land rushes, one in 1889 and one in 1893.

b. *Who were the "sooners"?*

people who rushed in ahead of the appointed time to make their claims

HISTORICAL HIGHLIGHTS (pages 427–429)

A. Matching: People 1

a. *Charles Crocker*
b. *Charles Goodnight*
c. *George Custer*
d. *George Westinghouse*

e. *Joseph Glidden*
f. *Joseph McCoy*
g. *Nelson Miles*

e 1. *Man who invented barbed wire in 1874.*
c 2. *Colonel who lost the Battle of the Little Bighorn.*
d 3. *Man who invented the air brake for trains in 1869.*
b 4. *One of the first cattle ranchers in Texas.*
g 5. *Colonel who defeated the Sioux and Nez Perce during 1876 and 1877.*
f 6. *Man who built stockyards at Abilene, Kansas.*
a 7. *Railroad director who hired Chinese workers.*

B. Matching: People 2

a. *Black Kettle*
b. *Chief Joseph*
c. *Cochise*
d. *Crazy Horse*

e. *Geronimo*
f. *Red Cloud*
g. *Sitting Bull*

c 1. *Apache leader who went on a reservation in 1872.*
a 2. *Cheyenne and Arapaho leader whose people were massacred at Sand Creek.*
d, g 3. *Indian leaders at the Battle of the Little Bighorn (two answers).*
e 4. *Last great Apache leader, who surrendered in 1886.*
b 5. *Nez Perce leader who went on a long flight with his people before capture.*
f 6. *Sioux leader whose warriors killed all of Captain Fetterman's troops.*

C. Matching: Terms 1

a. *cattle town*   g. *open range*
b. *Central Pacific*   h. *reservation*
c. *Dawes Act*   i. *Union Pacific*
d. *Ghost Dance religion*   j. *vigilance committee*
e. *Indian Reorganization Act*   k. *winter of 1886–87*
f. *mother lode*   l. *work train*

d   1. *Belief that Indians and buffalo would come back.*
f   2. *Main vein of ore.*
a   3. *Place to which cattle were driven by cowboys.*
g   4. *Unfenced grazing land.*
l   5. *Main feature of efficient track-laying method.*
j   6. *Group that meted out swift and stern justice.*
c   7. *Law that divided Indian reservations into family farms.*
b   8. *Railroad that laid track east from California.*
h   9. *Place where Indians were compelled to live.*
k 10. *Helped to end open-range cattle herding.*
i 11. *Railroad that laid track west from Nebraska.*
e 12. *Law that promoted a return to tribal organization of Indians.*

D. Matching: Terms 2

a. *claim jumping*   f. *preempt*
b. *Homestead Act*   g. *public domain*
c. *homesteader*   h. *Second Treaty of Fort Laramie*
d. *"long drive"*   i. *sod house*
e. *Pacific Railroad Act*

g   1. *Land owned by the government.*
b   2. *Law that allowed settlers to claim 160 acres (65 ha) for farming.*
f   3. *To settle on (public land) so as to have the first chance to buy it.*
a   4. *Taking of land already claimed by someone else.*
e   5. *Law authorizing a transcontinental railroad.*
i   6. *Dwelling built with blocks of prairie turf.*
c   7. *Person who claimed land and settled on it for five years.*
h   8. *Indian treaty of 1868 with the Sioux.*
d   9. *The taking of cattle over a trail to a cattle town.*

E. Matching: Places

a. *Abilene*

b. *Black Hills*

c. *Chisholm Trail*

d. *Comstock Lode*

e. *Pikes Peak*

f. *Promontory*

g. *Wounded Knee*

c 1. *Route of cattle herds moving north to Kansas.*

g 2. *Place where last Indian war took place.*

f 3. *Place where transcontinental railroad joined.*

b 4. *Part of Dakota Territory promised to Indians, where a gold rush occurred.*

d 5. *Rich gold and silver strike in Nevada.*

a 6. *Famous cattle town in Kansas.*

e 7. *Place in Colorado where a gold rush occurred in 1859.*

F. Deeper Discussion

1. *How did the mining camps illustrate the tendency of Americans to govern themselves?*

   When a mining camp became large, the miners called a meeting and made laws to control disorder and violence. They did not wait for an organized government, but set up their own laws. One source says, "Making governments and building towns are the natural employments of the migratory Yankee. . . . Congregate a hundred Americans anywhere beyond the settlements, and they immediately lay out a city, frame a state constitution, and apply for admission into the Union, while twenty-five of them become candidates for the United States Senate" (quoted in *Westward Expansion,* by R. A. Billington).

2. a. *Why could Indians and whites seemingly not live together in peace?*

   The main source of conflict was land. Whites wanted the Indians' land for settlement, but Indians did not want to give up their land. Another source was the tendency of white men to look down on Indians and treat them as inferiors (though Indians also looked down on white men). Placing Indians on reservations was another source of conflict. Most Indians did not like to be settled in one place when they had been used to a nomadic lifestyle of hunting. Whites thought they knew what was best for the Indians and tried to force them to accept that, but the Indians resisted the white man's ways.

   b. *Why could the Indians not hold out against the whites?*

   The Indians were far outnumbered by white people. The weapons of whites were superior to the weapons of the Indians. The Indian

tribes often failed to unite in fighting against the whites. Some tribes frequently fought against each other, and some even aided white men in fighting other tribes.

3. a. *In Habakkuk 1:1–4, the prophet asked God how He could tolerate such violence and evil in the land. When God told Habakkuk that the Chaldeans would punish Judah, the prophet wondered how God could punish the Judeans by using people more wicked than they (1:12–17). How do Habakkuk's questions relate to the Indian wars?*

For the first question, we too might wonder how a holy God could allow the violence of the Indian wars to go unpunished. For the second question, we might wonder why the whites prevailed by the use of force and dishonesty, even though they were more accountable than the Indians.

   b. *What was God's answer to Habakkuk (2:14, 20) and Habakkuk's response to that (3:17–19)? How does this help us to put the Indian wars in proper perspective?*

God said that His dealings with men will spread the knowledge of His glory around the earth. God is sovereign, and man must "keep silence" before Him rather than questioning His ways. Habakkuk responded with a declaration of faith that he would trust God no matter what happened.

We may not understand everything, but that is only because of our finite vision. Although the Indian wars certainly reveal man's wickedness, they do not reflect in any way against God. This should cause us to fear God; for if He allowed the Indians to be removed, He can do the same with the white men.

4. *What made barbed wire so important in the West?*

Barbed wire provided a means to enclose the vast spaces of the West, since other fencing materials were scarce. Barbed wire gave the crop farmer a weapon against the cattle rancher, whose livestock trampled his fields. It allowed the cattle rancher to fence off his own water and pastures against other cattle, thus ending the open range. Barbed wire changed the whole ranching industry.

5. *Why did the boomtowns of the West become such dens of evil and violence?*

Many people who flocked to boomtowns came with dishonorable motives. The miners came for easy money, and they spent it freely on gambling and liquor. Criminals, gamblers, and others came to prey on the money that flowed in the mining towns and railroad towns. (The towns with railroad terminals were especially wicked.) Violence broke out because of greed, selfishness, and licentious living.

G. Chronology and Geography

1. *Match the states to the years of their admission into the United States. Some dates will be used more than once.*

   1889   a. *North and South Dakota*
   1912   b. *New Mexico*
   1876   c. *Colorado*   *1864*
   1864   d. *Nevada*   *1867*
   1912   e. *Arizona*   *1876*
   1896   f. *Utah*   *1889*
   1889   g. *Montana*   *1890*
   1889   h. *Washington*   *1896*
   1890   i. *Wyoming*   *1907*
   1907   j. *Oklahoma*   *1912*
   1890   k. *Idaho*
   1867   l. *Nebraska*

2. *Give the correct year for each item.*

   1862   a. *Homestead Act and Pacific Railroad Act.*
   1869   b. *Completion of transcontinental railroad.*
   1876   c. *Battle of the Little Bighorn.*
   1887   d. *Dawes Act.*

3. *On your map entitled "The States of the United States," draw the borders of the thirteen states admitted between 1864 and 1912. (See the map on page 426.)*

   a. *Label the states with their names and dates of admission.*
   b. *Color the states admitted between 1864 and 1896 one color, and those admitted in the 1900s another color. Add both colors to the legend.*
   c. *Memorize the names and locations of these states.*
   (Individual work.)

So Far This Year (pages 430, 431)

A. Matching

c   1. *Northerners who went south to help in Reconstruction.*

j   2. *System in which farm workers rent cropland and use a share of the crops to pay the rent.*

h   3. *Southern whites who took part in Reconstruction governments.*

g   4. *Rebuilding of the South after the Civil War.*

a   5. *Seward's Folly.*

i   6. *Social separation based on race.*

d   7. *Amendment that granted citizenship to blacks.*

e   8. *Amendment granting all citizens the right to vote.*

b   9. *Laws that restricted blacks.*

f 10. *Former slaves.*

a. *Alaska*
b. *black codes*
c. *carpetbaggers*
d. *Fourteenth Amendment*
e. *Fifteenth Amendment*
f. *freedmen*
g. *Reconstruction*
h. *scalawags*
i. *segregation*
j. *sharecropping*

11. *Write the date of founding for each colony or settlement.*

1733   a. *Georgia*   1607
1607   b. *Jamestown*   1620
1681   c. *Pennsylvania*   1681
1620   d. *Plymouth*   1733

B. Completion

Write the correct name for each description.

Andrew Johnson   12. *President who was impeached in 1868.*

Ulysses S. Grant   13. *Former Civil War general who became president.*

Rutherford B. Hayes   14. *President appointed after a disputed election and the Compromise of 1877.*

Booker T. Washington   15. *Black leader who founded Tuskegee Institute.*

Lord Baltimore   16. *Founder of Maryland.*

Jonathan Edwards, George Whitefield   17. *Two leaders of the colonial religious revival.*

William Penn   18. *Quaker who received a land grant as payment for a debt.*

John Smith   19. *Leader of Jamestown who established a policy of "no work, no food."*

Roger Williams   20. *Founder of Rhode Island who insisted on freedom of conscience.*

Great Awakening	21. *Religious revival of the 1700s.*
Alexander Hamilton	22. *Federalist leader and first secretary of the treasury.*
Meriwether Lewis, William Clark	23. *Two men who explored the Louisiana Purchase from 1804 to 1806.*
Daniel Boone	24. *Man who opened the Wilderness Road into Kentucky.*
John Marshall	25. *Chief justice who strengthened the Supreme Court.*

C. Multiple Choice

Write the letter of the correct answer.

26. *Those who wanted to purify the Church of England from within were*
    a. *Pilgrims.*   c. *Quakers.*
    b. Puritans.   d. *Scotch-Irish.*

27. *A group that withdrew from the Church of England and settled in New England was the*
    a. Pilgrims.   c. *Quakers.*
    b. *Puritans.*   d. *Scotch-Irish.*

28. *A legal document granting the right to settle an area and establish a government there was*
    a. *the Mayflower Compact.*   c. *a legislature.*
    b. a charter.   d. *a constitution.*

29. *An agreement signed by Pilgrims and Strangers to make "just and equal laws" was*
    a. the Mayflower Compact.   c. *the Act of Toleration.*
    b. *a charter.*   d. *a constitution.*

30. *A Maryland law that granted religious freedom was*
    a. *the Mayflower Compact.*   **c. the Act of Toleration.**
    b. *a charter.*   d. *a constitution.*

31. *The owner of an English colony was called*
    a. *an indentured servant.*   c. *a duke.*
    b. *a charter.*   **d. a proprietor.**

32. *The political party in favor of limited government and strict interpretation of the Constitution was*
    a. *the Federalists.*   **c. the Democratic-Republicans.**
    b. *the Whigs.*   d. *the Nationalists.*

33. *The treaty that ended the War of 1812 was*
    a. the Treaty of Ghent.   c. *the Adams-Onís Treaty.*
    b. *the Jay Treaty.*   d. *the Pinckney Treaty.*

34. *The agreement that gained Florida in 1819 was*
    a. *the Treaty of Ghent.*   **c. the Adams-Onís Treaty.**
    b. *the Jay Treaty.*   d. *the Pinckney Treaty.*

35. *The idea that states are supreme over the federal government is called*
    a. *sectionalism.*   c. *judicial review.*
    b. *the spoils system.*   **d. states' rights.**

36. *A declaration about involvement of European and American nations in each other's affairs was the*
    a. Monroe Doctrine.   c. *Era of Good Feelings.*
    b. *Missouri Compromise.*   d. *Emancipation Proclamation.*

37. *Practice in which the winner of an election rewards his supporters with government positions is called*
    a. *sectionalism.*   c. *judicial review.*
    b. the spoils system.   d. *states' rights.*

20 The Industrial Age

1. CHANGE IN INDUSTRY AND AGRICULTURE

New Technology

New Business Methods

New Developments in Labor

New Developments in Farming

2. CHANGE IN SOCIETY

The Golden Door

The Rise of the City

Intellectual and Religious Change

Changes in the Mennonite Church

3. CHANGE IN POLITICS

The Political Issues

The Presidents

1850

Drake drills the first successful oil well 1859

1860

Transatlantic cable laid 1866

1870 Standard Oil founded 1870

Great Chicago Fire 1871

Alexander Graham Bell patents
the telephone 1876

Rutherford B. Hayes becomes president 1877

Thomas Edison patents the light bulb 1879

1880 James A. Garfield elected president 1880

Garfield assassinated; Chester A. Arthur
becomes president 1881

Grover Cleveland elected president 1884

Statue of Liberty dedicated 1886

Benjamin Harrison elected president 1888

1890

Grover Cleveland elected to second term 1892

Panic of 1893

Coxey's Army marches on Washington 1894

William McKinley elected
president 1896

1900

"Labour not for the meat which perisheth, but for that meat which endureth unto everlasting life, which the Son of man shall give unto you: for him hath God the Father sealed."

John 6:27

Chapter 20 (pages 432–457)

THE INDUSTRIAL AGE

Chapter Objectives

- To understand the elements of the Industrial Revolution in the period from the Civil War to 1900, including inventions, new business organizations, and new methods of manufacturing and marketing.
- To learn about changes that affected farmers, especially in the realm of new machinery, better farming methods, and the founding of farm organizations.
- To learn about immigration and its effects on society.
- To understand the reasons for the rapid growth of cities, and the problems resulting from it.
- To learn about religious changes during this period, especially revivalism and the social gospel.
- To grasp the main political issues of 1877 to 1896 and to study the presidents of this era.

To the Teacher

The period 1865–1900 was a momentous era of United States history. The people living in this period could hardly have been aware of the sweeping changes that were taking place; but as we look back, we can discern the seeds that brought forth their fruit in the 1900s, and yet today. For example, Darwinism and the rejection of the Bible laid the groundwork for the evolutionary bias that continues today. Darwinism also provided the basis for naturalism, environmental determinism, and social Darwinism—and these in turn led to even worse philosophies and their harmful results in the 1900s (such as Hitler's mass destruction). Though students will hardly perceive all the ramifications of these things, try to give them a picture of what happens when man sets aside God's truth.

Be sure to highlight the points of human interest. Immigration lends itself well to this purpose, especially in relation to the Statue of Liberty and Ellis Island. Students should learn to appreciate the contribution of immigrants, and realize that most of us are descendants of immigrants. Interesting information that pertains to the presidents' personal lives can add appeal to the last section.

Some historians give the impression that the great changes in the Mennonite Church during this period were all beneficial, and that previously the church had been almost completely dead and formal. This is an unbalanced view. Although we appreciate such things as prayer meetings, evening services, and evangelistic meetings, innovations also have potential for problems. In particular, revivalism strongly emphasized the conversion experience while de-emphasizing the aspects of discipleship, obedience, and humility. Mission work represented a return to earlier Anabaptist practice, but working with other church groups on the mission fields (as in India) did have its detrimental effects. The teacher can point out how these great changes have affected the church over the years.

Note on chapter test: Chapter 20 has its own test.

Christian Perspectives

- The Bible sanctions the idea of private property and free enterprise (Exodus 20:15, 17; Matthew 25:14–30; Luke 19:12–27). The Christian should seek to earn money to provide for himself and his family as well as for people in need (Acts 20:35; Ephesians 4:28). On the other hand, the Bible condemns the ambitious pursuit of wealth (James 2:6, 7; 5:1–5).
- Man may develop his talents to a great degree in commerce and invention, but God has given him those abilities (Deuteronomy 8:18).
- One way that Christians serve the Lord is by serving others. Therefore, Christian businessmen should treat their workers fairly (Ephesians 6:9; Colossians 4:1), and Christian workers should do their work well (Ephesians 6:5–8; Colossians 3:22–25). Christians cannot take part in labor unions (2 Corinthians 6:14; Romans 12:17–21; Ephesians 6:5–8; Colossians 3:22–25).
- We should respect people of other nationalities and races because God is "no respecter of persons," and He "loveth the stranger." The Christian should "honour all men." We should also appreciate their contributions (Acts 10:34; Deuteronomy 10:18, 19; 1 Peter 2:17; Hebrews 13:2).
- Social reform and the social gospel cannot truly change men for the better, because these endeavors do not change man's basic heart condition or meet his primary needs, which are spiritual (Romans 3:23; 5:1).
- Man's philosophies and ideas constantly change according to human reasoning. Many of these have disastrous consequences for man because they take man farther away from the truth of God's Word. Darwinism falls into this category, along with theories such as naturalism and pragmatism ("if it works, it must be right"). In contrast, God's Word stands forever and is eternally fixed as absolute truth (Psalm 119:89; Romans 3:4).

Further Study

- Inventors and leading businessmen of the 1800s: Cyrus Field, Alexander Graham Bell, Thomas Alva Edison, John D. Rockefeller, Edwin L. Drake, and Andrew Carnegie.
- Changes in farming and agricultural technology during the 1800s.
- The Statue of Liberty and Ellis Island, along with experiences of immigrants.
- Skyscrapers and other great structures, such as the Brooklyn Bridge.
- Problems in cities of the 1800s.
- Changes in the Mennonite Church during the 1800s.
- The presidents discussed in this chapter.

Chapter 20 Quiz

Presidents

1. In office at the time of the "Billion Dollar Congress."

2. Supported the gold standard and conducted a "front-porch" campaign.

3. Came into office through a disputed election and served from 1877 to 1881.

4. In office for only a few months before being assassinated.

5. Only president who served two nonconsecutive terms.

6. Became president in 1881, after the previous president was assassinated.

Other Men

7. Famous evangelist in the latter half of the 1800s.

8. Man who brought revival meetings to the Mennonite Church.

9. Inventor of the telephone.

10. Inventor of the electric light bulb and many other electrical devices.

Terms

11. System for making large numbers of products by using interchangeable parts and assembly lines.

12. Scarce product + high demand = high price; abundant product + low demand = low price.

13. People from southern and eastern Europe who moved to the United States in the years 1890 to 1920.

14. Religious movement designed to improve present social conditions.

15. Movement to limit immigration.

Quiz Answers

1. Benjamin Harrison
2. William McKinley
3. Rutherford B. Hayes
4. James Garfield
5. Grover Cleveland
6. Chester A. Arthur
7. Dwight L. Moody
8. John S. Coffman
9. Alexander Graham Bell
10. Thomas Edison
11. mass production
12. supply and demand
13. new immigration
14. social gospel
15. nativism

Answer Key

Focus for Thought (pages 441, 442)

1. *Give at least two inventions or developments that promoted industrial growth in relation to communications.*
   the telegraph; the underwater telegraph cable across the Atlantic Ocean; the telephone

2. *How did Thomas Edison help people to benefit from the many electrical devices that he invented?*
   Edison designed a central power station to provide a steady source of electricity.

3. *How did Andrew Carnegie and John D. Rockefeller contribute to industrial growth in the United States?*
   Carnegie formed U.S. Steel, the first billion-dollar company in the United States. Rockefeller built up a huge organization of oil companies, which became the first trust and provided a pattern for other trusts.

4. *Describe three new methods that developed for selling the abundance of merchandise produced by factories.*
   Companies began advertising their products, putting them in appealing packages, and using brand names and slogans to promote them. Department stores and chain stores moved the merchandise. Some businesses began selling goods by mail.

5. *Give three details indicating that many laborers worked in unfavorable conditions.*
   (Any three.) Factories were poorly lighted and inadequately ventilated. Workers toiled as long as twelve hours a day. There were many industrial accidents. Children worked long hours at dangerous jobs.

6. a. *What four things were demanded by labor unions?*

higher pay; better working conditions; an eight-hour workday; the end of child labor

b. *What Scriptural principles are violated by membership in a labor union?*

Membership violates the principle of nonresistance, since labor unions use force in dealing with employers. It involves working against an employer rather than being obedient to him. It involves trying to do as little as possible for as much money as one can get. (It also involves being unequally yoked together with unbelievers.)

7. a. *Describe several ways in which machines helped to make farmers more productive.*

Machines made it easier to work the soil and to plant and harvest crops. Farmers could cultivate much more land in much less time. Tractors replaced horses as a source of power.

b. *How did the farmers' success cause hardships for them?*

Farmers sent so many products to market that prices declined steadily.

Focus for Thought (page 451)

8. a. *What things in the United States attracted a flood of immigrants?*

Immigrants were attracted by the many job opportunities in America. They were also drawn by the prospects of education, land ownership, freedom of worship, and a democratic society.

b. *In what ways did the United States benefit from immigrants?*

Immigrants brought in a great diversity of culture. They contributed their labor by taking jobs in factories, by working in mines, and by farming. Some immigrants became noted leaders in politics, business, science, and education.

9. *Give three reasons for the rapid population growth of American cities.*

(Any three.) Many immigrants settled in the cities. Many factories were located in cities, and provided work for people from far and near. Good transportation, especially railroads, promoted growth. Skyscrapers enabled cities to expand upward as well as outward.

10. *What improvements did reformers try to make in large cities?*

Reformers tried to help poor people by building settlement houses. They attacked liquor and alcoholism. They tried to reduce political corruption. Women campaigned for more rights.

11. *What were two new ideas that brought changes to the thinking of American people in the late 1800s?*

One was Darwinism, which taught that all living things had a natural

origin and that they gradually evolved into species existing today. Another was socialism, which promoted a classless society in which the government owned and controlled business production and the distribution of wealth.

12. *Describe the revivalism and the social gospel of the latter 1800s.*
Revivalism placed more emphasis on conversion than on discipleship. Its songs focused on religious experiences and feelings rather than on obedience and cross-bearing.

The social gospel was an effort to improve present social conditions instead of urging people to prepare for future bliss in heaven. Its adherents attacked evils such as saloons, poverty, and corrupt government.

13. *Give at least three changes that took place in the Mennonite Church during this period.*
The Mennonite Church accepted Sunday schools. Revivalism came into the church through the work of John S. Coffman. The Mennonite Church began mission work. New organizations were formed, including a mission board, the Mennonite General Conference, and the Elkhart Institute (later called Goshen College). The Old Order divisions took place. Preaching in the English language became accepted.

Focus for Thought (page 455)

14. a. *What problems resulted from the spoils system that had long been used in government?*
The spoils system involved much corruption. Many government offices were filled by men poorly qualified for them.

b. *What is meant by a civil service merit system?*
It means that government employees are appointed on the basis of what they can do rather than on whom they support.

15. a. *Why did some people favor high tariffs?*
Supporters of high tariffs said they encouraged new industries and helped to make America self-sufficient.

b. *Why did others want to reduce tariffs?*
Opponents argued that tariffs raise prices and protect inefficient businesses, thus hurting American consumers.

16. *Why did some people think that railroads and other giant businesses should be regulated by the federal government?*
They were afraid the giant businesses would become monopolies that would control the markets and raise prices while cheating workers and giving poor service.

17. *What things did the Populist Party promote?*

The Populist Party promoted an income tax; government ownership of railroad, telegraph, and telephone systems; new laws restricting immigration and setting shorter working hours; and a more democratic government with more control by the people.

18. *What things made President Cleveland's second term difficult?*

The Panic of 1893 struck soon after Cleveland took office. The president had to deal with Coxey's Army and with strikes. He wanted lower tariffs, but Congress would not reduce them as much as he wanted.

HISTORICAL HIGHLIGHTS (pages 455–457)

A. Matching: People

a. *Alexander Graham Bell*
b. *Andrew Carnegie*
c. *Charles Sheldon*
d. *Dwight L. Moody*
e. *George Washington Carver*
f. *Jane Addams*

g. *John D. Rockefeller*
h. *John S. Coffman*
i. *Luther Burbank*
j. *Thomas A. Edison*
k. *William Jennings Bryan*

c 1. *Man who wrote* In His Steps *to promote the social gospel.*
k 2. *Democrat who supported free silver in the 1896 presidential election.*
d 3. *Famous evangelist who preached in America and England.*
h 4. *Man who started revival meetings in the Mennonite Church.*
f 5. *Reformer who founded the Hull House in Chicago.*
b 6. *Man whose steel company made the United States a leading steel producer.*
j 7. *Inventor of the electric light bulb and many other electrical devices.*
g 8. *Man who founded Standard Oil as the first trust.*
e, i 9. *Men who introduced new uses or varieties of plants (two names).*
a 10. *Inventor of the telephone.*

B. Matching: Presidents

Each choice should be used twice.

a. *Rutherford B. Hayes*
b. *James A. Garfield*
c. *Chester A. Arthur*

d. *Grover Cleveland*
e. *Benjamin Harrison*
f. *William McKinley*

e 1. *In office when the Sherman Antitrust Act and the McKinley Tariff Act were passed.*

b 2. *In office for only a few months before being assassinated.*

a 3. *Came into office through a disputed election.*

d 4. *Only president who served two nonconsecutive terms.*

f 5. *Was opposed by William Jennings Bryan and the Populist Party in 1896.*

c 6. *Became president in 1881 when the previous president was assassinated.*

d 7. *In office during the Panic of 1893.*

a 8. *Removed the collector of the New York Custom House from office.*

b 9. *Had Chester A. Arthur for his vice-president.*

e 10. *In office at the time of the "Billion Dollar Congress."*

c 11. *In office when the Civil Service Commission was established.*

f 12. *Supported the gold standard and conducted a "front-porch" campaign.*

C. Matching: Terms 1

a. *collective bargaining*   h. *monopoly*

b. *cooperative*   i. *patent*

c. *corporation*   j. *share of stock*

d. *dividends*   k. *strike*

e. *free enterprise*   l. *supply and demand*

f. *labor union*   m. *trust*

g. *mass production*

i 1. *Exclusive right to make and sell an invention.*

f 2. *Organization of workers agreeing to require certain things of employers.*

c 3. *Large business owned by many people.*

m 4. *Related businesses combined into one large organization.*

h 5. *Company that has no competition because it controls a certain market.*

l 6. *Scarce product + high demand = high price; abundant product + low demand = low price.*

k 7. *Refusal to work until labor demands are met.*

a 8. *Negotiation of union leaders with employers for wages and working hours.*

e 9. *System that includes private ownership of property, free markets, and a minimum of government regulation.*

d 10. *Profits that corporations pay to stockholders.*

j 11. *One portion of a corporation, which is purchased by an investor.*

g 12. *System for making large numbers of products by using interchangeable parts and assembly lines.*

b 13. *Group of people who purchase things in large quantities to obtain lower prices.*

D. Matching: Terms 2

a. *Civil Service Commission*

b. *Darwinism*

c. *Interstate Commerce Act*

d. *McKinley Tariff Act*

e. *melting pot*

f. *nativism*

g. *"new immigration"*

h. *political machine*

i. *Populist Party*

j. *revivalism*

k. *Sherman Antitrust Act*

l. *social gospel*

m. *socialism*

h   1. *Organized group controlled by a powerful "boss."*

b   2. *Theory that living things had a natural origin and that they gradually evolved into the species existing today.*

g   3. *People from eastern and southern Europe who moved to the United States in the years 1890 to 1920.*

e   4. *Place where people of many different nationalities mingle together.*

f   5. *Movement to limit immigration.*

m 6. *Karl Marx's theory proposing a classless society and government ownership of businesses.*

j   7. *Religious movement emphasizing conversion more than discipleship.*

d   8. *Measure that raised taxes on imports and became unpopular for raising prices.*

i   9. *Group that developed from Farmers' Alliances and promoted radical changes.*

l 10. *Religious movement designed to improve present social conditions.*

c 11. *Measure that established the Interstate Commerce Commission to regulate railroads.*

a 12. *Group that checked the qualifications of prospective government employees.*

k 13. *Measure allowing the government to attack businesses that it considered monopolies.*

E. Deeper Discussion

1. *Why were new ways of selling necessary during the Industrial Revolution of the late 1800s?*

    Factories produced so many manufactured goods that new ways of selling had to be developed. Also, people became more dependent on business for their daily needs, since they no longer made so many of their own things. So it was necessary to have places where they could buy the things they needed.

2. *Read Ephesians 6:5–9 and Colossians 3:22–4:1, and answer the following questions.*

a. *How is the worker ("servant") to serve his employer ("master")? Be specific, and give both negative and positive ways.*

Negative ways: Do not serve "with eyeservice, as menpleasers," working only to make a good impression or only when the boss is around. Do not serve "unto men," working just to please the boss, but rather to please God.

Positive ways: Serve "in singleness of heart," with purpose, dedication, and loyalty. Serve "as the servants of Christ"—as if the master were Christ. Serve "with good will" rather than grudgingly. Recognize that the greatest reward comes from God; this is more than just the pay.

b. *How is the employer to treat his workers? Why?*

The employer is to pay his workers what is fair and just; he is to treat them as he would want to be treated; he is not to threaten them. The employer must recognize that Christ is his Master, and that God will not excuse him for wrongdoing simply because the employer is the boss.

3. *Discuss the economic problems caused by labor unions.*

In essence, labor unions hinder competition among workers for available jobs. They try to keep companies from hiring nonunion employees, thus restricting the available labor pool and preventing those who would work for less from taking their jobs. They also work against factory owners to demand their rights; this conflict keeps the business from being as productive as it could be. Instead of doing as much as possible, unions try to limit the hours and type of work their members may do. They inflate costs by keeping wages higher than market wages, especially in government contracts. Unions often resort to destructive violence in strikes and in attempts to sabotage nonunion contracts. All these things cause productivity to suffer.

4. *How did the law of supply and demand affect farmers?*

Farmers sent so many farm products to market that the prices for those products fell. However, tariffs protected manufacturers even though their production was also increasing, and this helped to keep the law of supply and demand from hurting them. So the price of manufactured products stayed high while the prices for farm products fell.

5. *Does immigration hinder the nation, as nativists say, or does it benefit the nation?*

For the most part, immigration has been a benefit to the United States, and immigrants have helped to build the nation. Nativists should remember that they or their ancestors were also immigrants at one time. On the other hand, immigration can be a hindrance if the immigrants become dependent on government aid. Immigrants should make themselves responsible to learn the language of the new country and to become contributing citizens.

6. a. *How does the social gospel fall short of true Christianity?*

The social gospel is for this world, not the next, whereas the Christian lives in this world to prepare for the next. The social gospel addresses physical and social needs of people, whereas their true need is spiritual. It looks to man rather than to God and His Word for the answers to man's needs. It fails to recognize that the main reason for man's social problems is his sinful nature.

b. *How should Christians respond to the social gospel?*

Christians should reject the methods of the social gospel even though it has noble aims. Christians do need to meet the physical and social needs of people, but they must always remember that the spiritual need is most important.

F. Chronology and Geography

From memory, list the presidents from Washington through McKinley, along with the dates of their terms in office. Remember that an elected president's term begins in the year after the election.

(Optional exercise.)

1. George Washington—1789–1797
2. John Adams—1797–1801
3. Thomas Jefferson—1801–1809
4. James Madison—1809–1817
5. James Monroe—1817–1825
6. John Quincy Adams—1825–1829
7. Andrew Jackson—1829–1837
8. Martin Van Buren—1837–1841
9. William Henry Harrison—1841
10. John Tyler—1841–1845
11. James Polk—1845–1849
12. Zachary Taylor—1849–1850
13. Millard Fillmore—1850–1853
14. Franklin Pierce—1853–1857
15. James Buchanan—1857–1861
16. Abraham Lincoln—1861–1865
17. Andrew Johnson—1865–1869
18. Ulysses S. Grant—1869–1877
19. Rutherford B. Hayes—1877–1881
20. James A. Garfield—1881
21. Chester A. Arthur—1881–1885
22. Grover Cleveland—1885–1889
23. Benjamin Harrison—1889–1893
24. Grover Cleveland—1893–1897
25. William McKinley—1897–1901

21 World Power

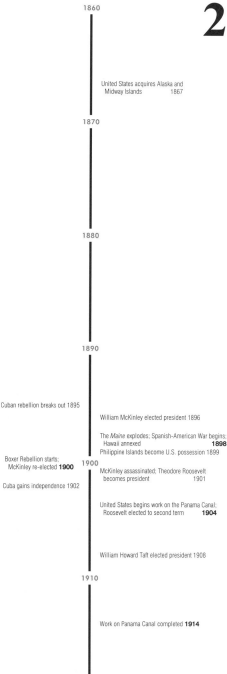

1860

United States acquires Alaska and
Midway Islands   1867

1870

1880

1890

Cuban rebellion breaks out 1895

William McKinley elected president 1896

The *Maine* explodes; Spanish-American War begins;
Hawaii annexed   **1898**
Philippine Islands become U.S. possession 1899

Boxer Rebellion starts;
McKinley re-elected **1900**   **1900**

Cuba gains independence 1902

McKinley assassinated; Theodore Roosevelt
becomes president   1901

United States begins work on the Panama Canal;
Roosevelt elected to second term   **1904**

William Howard Taft elected president 1908

1910

Work on Panama Canal completed **1914**

1920

*"The LORD maketh poor, and maketh rich: he
bringeth low, and lifteth up."*

1 Samuel 2:7

WORLD POWER

Chapter Objectives

- To understand that Americans turned to imperialism and expansionism in the 1890s.
- To learn how Hawaii became a part of the United States.
- To summarize the events of the Spanish-American War and learn the geographic locations of the events.
- To learn about the Open Door Policy as a basis for United States relations with the Far East.
- To understand the problems the United States needed to deal with after the Spanish-American War, particularly in Cuba and Puerto Rico.
- To learn about the building of the Panama Canal and about United States relations with Latin American countries.

To the Teacher

This chapter deals primarily with foreign affairs during the McKinley, Roosevelt, and Taft administrations (1897–1913). The next chapter covers domestic affairs from the time of Theodore Roosevelt's presidency through Woodrow Wilson's presidency. That is why Theodore Roosevelt and William Howard Taft are introduced in this chapter; however, the next chapter discusses the most significant happenings in their presidencies.

The events in this chapter are pivotal in that the United States was beginning to assume a major role on the world scene. Americans believed that their world influence should correspond to their size, economy, and power. But in some ways, the nation was unready to shoulder the responsibilities of world power. For example, John Hay tried to bluff his way through in China, without using military force to accomplish the ends desired by the United States. Another example is the use of "dollar diplomacy" (financial investment) to influence Latin American nations.

It is noteworthy that expansionist fervor was brief, basically just a six-month period in 1898 during which the United States fought the Spanish-American War and gained an assortment of new territories. Managing those territories was a problem! The United States did grant independence of sorts to Cuba and to the Philippines, and United States intervention did some good in the countries involved. But much of the harvest has been bitter, such as in Cuba.

The text is brief on the war itself; outside study will provide the teacher with additional information to enliven the class. The teacher should be careful not to endorse imperialism and conquest, and particularly not to glory in the swift defeat of Spain. The Christian viewpoint must be different from that of the worldly man.

On the Panama Canal, enough facts have been included to spark students' interest, but much information is available from other sources.

Note on chapter test: There is a single test for Chapters 21 and 22.

Christian Perspectives

- War is not a solution to problems, but often a cause of problems (James 4:1, 2).
- God holds sovereign power over the rulers of the earth, as shown in the assassination of President McKinley (Daniel 4:25, 32, 35; Proverbs 21:1).
- God allows man to accomplish astounding feats such as the Panama Canal, but let us remember that God deserves the glory and credit (Revelation 4:11).

Further Study

- Hawaii, the Philippines, and Cuba.
- The Panama Canal.
- The Spanish-American War.
- The Boxer Rebellion. (For the experience of one Christian man, see "The Promises of God" in Rod and Staff's Seventh Reader.)
- The life and presidency of William McKinley. (The presidencies of Roosevelt and Taft are covered in Chapter 22.)

Chapter 21 Quiz

1. Which president used the "big stick" in foreign relations?
   a. William McKinley   c. William Howard Taft
   b. Theodore Roosevelt

2. Which president served during the Spanish-American War and was assassinated in 1901?
   a. William McKinley   c. William Howard Taft
   b. Theodore Roosevelt

3. Which president used "dollar diplomacy" in Latin America?
   a. William McKinley   c. William Howard Taft
   b. Theodore Roosevelt

4. Which term refers to a policy of having little to do with foreign nations?
   a. isolationism   c. Open Door Policy
   b. imperialism   d. expansionism

5. Which term refers to the foreign policy that was the basis for American relations with countries in the Far East?
   a. Roosevelt Corollary   c. Open Door Policy
   b. Monroe Doctrine   d. sphere of influence

6. Which term refers to the uprising in China in 1900?
   a. Open Door Policy   c. Roosevelt Corollary
   b. imperialism   d. Boxer Rebellion

7. Which term is associated with a desire to gain control of foreign territories?
   a. imperialism   c. Monroe Doctrine
   b. isolationism   d. sphere of influence

8. What islands in the Far East were conquered in the Spanish-American War and purchased for $20 million?
   a. Hawaii   c. Philippines
   b. Guam   d. Jamaica

9. What Spanish island in the Caribbean was ceded to the United States in 1898?
   a. Puerto Rico   c. Guam
   b. Cuba   d. Jamaica

10. What group of Pacific islands was annexed in 1898 and later became a state?
    a. Philippines   c. Guam
    b. Hawaii   d. Samoa

Quiz Answers

| 1. **b** | 3. **c** | 5. **c** | 7. **a** | 9. **a** |
| 2. **a** | 4. **a** | 6. **d** | 8. **c** | 10. **b** |

Answer Key

Focus for Thought (page 465)

1. *What was the difference between isolationists and imperialists in America?*
Isolationists believed that the United States should not expand to any territory beyond its own continent. But imperialists clamored for possessions overseas, for greater military might, for world power, and even for war.

2. *What two things caused the growth of American interest in Hawaii?*
Ships began stopping at Hawaii for water and supplies in trading with China. A number of Americans settled in Hawaii by the 1820s, and their descendants began operating sugar plantations.

3. *For each date, tell what happened to move Hawaii toward becoming a state of the United States.*
   a. *1875* **A treaty permitted Hawaiian sugar to be sold to the United States without a tariff.**
   b. *1898* **Hawaii was annexed to the United States.**
   c. *1900* **Hawaii was organized as a territory of the United States.**
   d. *1959* **Hawaii became the fiftieth state of the Union.**

4. a. *In the Spanish-American War, why did the United States attack the Philippines when the main issues involved Cuba?*
   Commodore George Dewey had been ordered to attack the Spanish base in the Philippines if war started. (Spain governed the Philippines, and the United States was at war with Spain.)
   b. *In what two other places were battles fought?*
   in Cuba and Puerto Rico

5. *Answer these questions about the results of the Spanish-American War.*
   a. *What was to be the status of Cuba?*
   Cuba would be independent.
   b. *What two territories did the United States gain outright?*
   Guam and Puerto Rico
   c. *For which territory did the United States pay $20 million?*
   the Philippines

6. *What things did Americans do to help the Filipinos?*
They established a health bureau, sanitation programs, and schools. They taught the Filipinos new farming methods, and they built roads, bridges, and irrigation systems. They tried to prepare the Filipinos for independence.

7. *What were some major effects that the Spanish-American War had on the United States?*
The United States became a world power with colonial possessions. It reigned supreme in the Caribbean and also wielded power in the Far East. It could maintain the Monroe Doctrine on its own. The United States became more involved in world affairs and leadership.

Focus for Thought (page 468)

8. *Why could European nations take advantage of China in the 1800s?*
China was a backward country. It had not experienced an industrial revolution as European nations had.

9. *What was the main purpose of the Open Door Policy?*
to keep China open to trade with all nations equally

10. *Why did the Boxer Rebellion break out?*
The Chinese resented the Western influences coming into their country.

11. *Why was the Open Door Policy an important development in United States history?*
It marked a bold advance in United States involvement in world affairs.

12. *Why were Americans concerned over Japan's success in the Russo-Japanese War?*
Americans were afraid Japan might become so powerful in the Far East that it would threaten American interests there.

13. *For what two reasons did relations cool between the United States and Japan?*
The treaty that ended the Russo-Japanese War seemed unfair to the Japanese. Americans passed laws to restrict Asian immigration.

Focus for Thought (page 475)

14. a. *In what ways did the United States help to improve Cuba?*
Americans helped the sick, the poor, and the homeless; and they built schools, roads, and hospitals. They established better sanitation and helped eliminate yellow fever.

b. *Why did Cubans become resentful toward the United States?*
They resented American involvement in their affairs.

15. *What were the three steps by which Puerto Rico became a self-governing commonwealth of the United States?*
The United States set up a civil government in 1900. Puerto Ricans became American citizens in 1917. Puerto Rico adopted its own constitution and became a self-governing commonwealth in 1952.

16. a. *Why did the United States need the Panama Canal?*
A canal was needed because the United States had gained territories

in the Pacific Ocean and the Far East. A canal would save thousands of miles as well as much time and money.

b. *What were two problems that had to be overcome in building the Panama Canal?*

(Any two.) The problems included obtaining land for the canal, eliminating the threat of yellow fever, making a great cut through the continental divide, damming the Chagres River, and building huge locks in the canal.

17. *What was the reasoning behind the Roosevelt Corollary?*

Since European nations were to stay out of the Western Hemisphere, President Roosevelt thought the United States should keep order in Latin America so that Europeans would have no reason to move in.

18. *What did President Taft hope to accomplish through "dollar diplomacy"?*

President Taft hoped that American investment would stabilize Latin American countries and keep out the Europeans. He hoped to influence the countries without actually controlling them. He also hoped to prevent violence and to bring economic improvement.

19. *On what two occasions were United States troops sent to Mexico between 1910 and 1920?*

A United States army occupied Veracruz in 1914 during a period of violence and revolution. After Pancho Villa killed eighteen Americans in 1916, General Pershing went to Mexico to capture him.

HISTORICAL HIGHLIGHTS (pages 475–477)

A. Matching: People

You will use some letters twice.

a. *George Dewey*

b. *George Washington Goethals*

c. *John Hay*

d. *Theodore Roosevelt*

e. *William Gorgas*

f. *William Howard Taft*

g. *William McKinley*

f   1. *President who used "dollar diplomacy" in Latin America.*

b   2. *Man chiefly responsible for digging the Panama Canal.*

g   3. *President during the Spanish-American War.*

e   4. *Overcame yellow fever and malaria by controlling mosquitoes in Cuba and Panama.*

c   5. *Man who promoted the Open Door Policy.*

a 6. *Defeated the Spanish fleet in the Philippines during the Spanish-American War.*

d 7. *President who used the "big stick."*

g 8. *President assassinated in 1901.*

c 9. *Man who negotiated with Colombia for land to build the Panama Canal.*

B. Matching: Terms

a. *Boxer Rebellion*   e. *reparations*

b. *imperialism*   f. *Roosevelt Corollary*

c. *isolationism*   g. *sphere of influence*

d. *Open Door Policy*

c 1. *Policy of having little to do with foreign nations.*

f 2. *United States policy of intervening in the affairs of Latin America.*

b 3. *Desire to gain control of foreign territories.*

d 4. *Basis for American relations with countries in the Far East.*

g 5. *Area in China in which a foreign nation controlled the trade and port cities.*

a 6. *Uprising in China in 1900.*

e 7. *Money demanded from a defeated nation for war damages that it caused.*

C. Matching: Places

Match the following territories acquired by the United States to their descriptions.

a. *Cuba*   e. *Philippines*

b. *Guam*   f. *Puerto Rico*

c. *Hawaii*   g. *Samoa*

d. *Midway Islands*

c 1. *Group of Pacific islands about 2,000 miles (3,219 km) west of the United States; annexed in 1898.*

d 2. *Pacific islands acquired in 1867.*

b 3. *Spanish island in the Pacific that was ceded to the United States in 1898.*

g 4. *Pacific islands shared with Britain and Germany; American part annexed in 1900.*

e 5. *Far East islands conquered in the Spanish-American War and purchased for $20 million.*

f 6. *Spanish island in the Caribbean that was ceded to the United States in 1898.*

a 7. *Caribbean island that the United States conquered and gave independence in 1902.*

D. Multiple Choice

Write the letter of the correct answer.

1. *By becoming imperialistic, the United States was breaking what tradition?*
   a. *capitalism*
   c. *federalism*
   b. *socialism*
   d. isolationism

2. *Which one of these was* not *part of American empire building in the late 1800s and early 1900s?*
   a. Canada
   c. *Cuba*
   b. *Hawaii*
   d. *Panama Canal*

3. *Which one of these island possessions was acquired before the Spanish-American War?*
   a. *Guam*
   c. Midway Islands
   b. *American Samoa*
   d. *Puerto Rico*

4. *Which one of these was* not *a reason that some Americans began favoring imperialism?*
   a. *A new generation came into power that had not experienced the Civil War.*
   b. The United States was busy developing the land it already had.
   c. *Foreign trade could boost business production and provide markets for American goods.*
   d. *The United States had the ability to become a world power by building a strong merchant fleet and navy.*

5. *Which of these tell why the United States went to war with Spain in 1898?*
   a. *Americans had long wanted to possess Cuba.*
   b. *The revolution in Cuba threatened American business investments.*
   c. *American citizens in Cuba were endangered and mistreated.*
   d. *Americans remembered their own revolution a century before and sympathized with the Cubans.*
   e. All the reasons above.

6. *Which one of these was not a* new *challenge that arose when the United States became a world power?*
   a. *Cuban political chaos*
   d. *Open Door Policy in China*
   b. *building the Panama Canal*
   e. *Dominican Republic not paying its debts*
   c. corruption in politics

E. Deeper Discussion

1. *What effects did the change from isolationism to imperialism have on the United States?*
   Imperialism brought war—the Spanish-American War—and led to later wars, such as World War I. It brought conquest of foreign

territories and problems of relating to those territories, as in Cuba, Puerto Rico, and the Philippines. It brought the United States into a position of world power, which drew it into conflicts in many parts of the world (such as China and Japan). It produced a need for the Panama Canal. It led to intervention in Latin America affairs, which brought strained relationships between the United States and its southern neighbors.

2. *How might the war with Spain have been prevented?*

The war might have been prevented if Americans had kept their emotions under control instead of reacting so strongly to the Cuban oppression and the sinking of the *Maine*. Spain did give in to most of the conditions set by the United States, and it may have granted Cuban independence if a way had been found to save face. On the other hand, the Spanish did face a difficult choice: give up Cuba without a fight and lose political power, or go to war and at least retain domestic pride and support. Since they chose the latter, the United States and Spain went to war.

3. *Even though the United States did much good in the Philippines, Cuba, and Panama, why did their people still want to be independent?*

Like most other people, the Filipinos, Cubans, and Panamanians wanted freedom to govern themselves. They did not want to be controlled by the United States any more than by Spain or Colombia. They also resented the attitude that American civilization was superior and that they should be glad to give up their own culture for the American culture.

4. *How did the Open Door Policy mark a turning point in United States foreign policy?*

It marked a bold advance in United States intervention in the affairs of other nations. It marked an increase in world power, especially in the Far East. It also showed that the United States was satisfied to pursue its objectives without military control of colonies in lands such as China.

5. *Deuteronomy 10:18, 19 says that God "loveth the stranger, in giving him food and raiment. Love ye therefore the stranger: for ye were strangers in the land of Egypt."*

   a. *How were immigrants in America like the strangers to which this passage refers?*

They had left their native land and were strangers in America.

b. *This direction was given to the children of Israel, who had lived in the land of Egypt. How does it apply to many people in America?*

Most Americans are either immigrants or the descendants of immigrants. So they too were once strangers in the land.

c. *How should Christians relate to strangers, such as immigrants and other foreigners?*

The Christian should honor all men, as 1 Peter 2:17 says. We should respect them and appreciate them as persons. We should take an interest in them and help them as we have opportunity. "Be not forgetful to entertain strangers: for thereby some have entertained angels unawares" (Hebrews 13:2).

6. *Why did Latin Americans resent United States policy under the Roosevelt Corollary and the "dollar diplomacy"?*

They resented what they viewed as the United States bullying them, whether by military force or by financial power. They resented the fact that American armed forces might take over their nations whenever the United States considered it necessary.

F. Chronology and Geography

1. *Give the following dates.*
   a. *The Spanish-American War, from the United States declaration of war to the signing of the peace treaty.* **April 25, 1898, through December 10, 1898**
   b. *The Boxer Rebellion.* **1900**
   c. *The work on the Panama Canal by the United States, from start to finish.* **1904–1914**
2. *Answer with names listed in Part C.*
   a. *Which places are located in the Pacific Ocean?*

   Guam, Hawaii, Midway Islands, Philippines, Samoa

   b. *Which places are located on the Atlantic side of the Americas?*

   Cuba, Puerto Rico

   c. *Which places are United States territories today? Which one has become a state?*

   Guam, Midway Islands, Puerto Rico, Samoa (the American part); Hawaii

   d. *Find all these places on a world map. Be prepared to show their locations in class.*

   (Individual work. Have students show locations on a world map in class.)

So Far This Year (pages 478, 479)

A. Matching: People and Terms

h　1. *Inventor of the telegraph.*

i　2. *Man who brought textile manufacturing to America.*

f　3. *Publisher of the "blue-backed speller."*

g　4. *Man who built the first successful steamboat.*

d　5. *Inventor of the cotton gin.*

a　6. *Elimination of slavery.*

e　7. *Change from producing handmade goods at home to producing machine-made goods in factories.*

j　8. *Effort to stop the use of strong drink.*

c　9. *Region dependent on cotton.*

b　10. *Traveling preacher in the West.*

a. *abolition*
b. *circuit rider*
c. *Cotton Kingdom*
d. *Eli Whitney*
e. *Industrial Revolution*
f. *Noah Webster*
g. *Robert Fulton*
h. *Samuel F. B. Morse*
i. *Samuel Slater*
j. *temperance movement*

B. Matching: Presidents

b　11. *First president, 1789–1797.*

j　12. *First president to die in office.*

f　13. *Son of a former president.*

h　14. *Vice president under Andrew Jackson.*

c　15. *President during War of 1812; served from 1809 to 1817.*

g　16. *First vice president to fill the position of a president who died in office.*

d　17. *President during the Era of Good Feelings.*

a　18. *President who represented the common man.*

e　19. *Second president; Federalist; 1797–1801.*

i　20. *Leader of Democratic-Republicans; third president, 1801–1809.*

a. *Andrew Jackson*
b. *George Washington*
c. *James Madison*
d. *James Monroe*
e. *John Adams*
f. *John Q. Adams*
g. *John Tyler*
h. *Martin Van Buren*
i. *Thomas Jefferson*
j. *William H. Harrison*

C. Completion

Write the correct name or term for each description.

Terms

mass production　　21. *System for making large numbers of products by using interchangeable parts and assembly lines.*

supply and demand	22. *Scarce product + high demand = high price; abundant product + low demand = low price.*
"new immigration"	23. *People from eastern and southern Europe who moved to the United States in the years 1890 to 1920.*
social gospel	24. *Religious movement designed to improve present social conditions.*
nativism	25. *Movement to limit immigration.*
revivalism	26. *Religious movement emphasizing conversion more than discipleship.*
free enterprise	27. *Economic system that includes private ownership of property, free markets, and a minimum of government regulation.*
socialism	28. *Karl Marx's theory proposing a classless society and government ownership of business.*
Darwinism	29. *Belief that living things had a natural origin and that they gradually evolved into the species existing today.*

Presidents

Benjamin Harrison	30. *Served from 1889 to 1893; was in office when the Sherman Antitrust Act was passed.*
William McKinley	31. *Was opposed by William Jennings Bryan in 1896; supported the gold standard and conducted a "front-porch" campaign.*
Rutherford B. Hayes	32. *Came into office through a disputed election; served from 1877 to 1881.*
James Garfield	33. *Was assassinated only a few months after becoming president in 1881.*
Grover Cleveland	34. *Was the only president to serve two nonconsecutive terms.*
Chester A. Arthur	35. *Became president in 1881 when the previous president was assassinated.*

Other Persons

Dwight L. Moody	36. *Famous evangelist of the latter 1800s who preached in America and England.*
John S. Coffman	37. *Evangelist who started revival meetings in the Mennonite Church.*

Alexander Graham Bell	38. *Inventor of the telephone.*
Thomas Edison	39. *Inventor of the electric light bulb.*
John D. Rockefeller	40. *Founder of Standard Oil Company, the first trust.*
Andrew Carnegie	41. *Man whose company helped make the United States a leading steel producer.*

D. True or False

Write whether each statement is true *(T)* or false *(F)*.

T 42. *The Homestead Act allowed settlers to claim 160 acres (65 ha) of land for farming.*

T 43. *Charles Goodnight was one of the first Texas cattle ranchers.*

F 44. *The Dawes Act authorized a transcontinental railroad.*

F 45. *Joseph McCoy invented barbed wire in 1874.*

F 46. *Joseph Glidden built stockyards at Abilene, Kansas.*

T 47. *The transcontinental railroad was joined at Promontory, Utah, in 1869.*

F 48. *Sitting Bull was an Indian chief killed in the Sand Creek massacre.*

T 49. *The colonel defeated at the Battle of the Little Bighorn was George Custer.*

F 50. *In the "long drive," cowboys moved cattle north by railroad to Kansas.*

F 51. *Chief Joseph was an Apache leader who surrendered in 1886.*

T 52. *Wounded Knee was the site where one of the last Indian battles took place.*

22 Progressive Reform

1. THE PROGRESSIVE MOVEMENT

   Progressive Goals

   Advance of Progressive Reform

2. PROGRESSIVES IN POWER: THEODORE ROOSEVELT AND WILLIAM HOWARD TAFT

   The "Square Deal"

   The Taft Presidency

3. ANOTHER PROGRESSIVE IN POWER: WOODROW WILSON

   The "New Freedom"

1900

Theodore Roosevelt becomes president 1901

William McKinley assassinated 1901

Roosevelt elected to second term 1904

1905

Earthquake shatters San Francisco; Pure Food and Drug Act passed 1906

William Howard Taft elected president 1908

1910

Roosevelt Dam dedicated 1911

Woodrow Wilson elected president 1912

Progressive Party begins; the *Titanic* sinks 1912

Federal Reserve Act passed 1913

Sixteenth and Seventeenth Amendments ratified; Underwood Tariff Act passed 1913

World War I begins **1914**

1915

Wilson re-elected 1916

Eighteenth Amendment ratified 1919

Nineteenth Amendment ratified 1920 **1920**

"The way of man is not in himself: it is not in man that walketh to direct his steps."

Jeremiah 10:23

Chapter 22 (pages 480–497)

PROGRESSIVE REFORM

Chapter Objectives

- To understand the goals of the progressive reformers, and their effects on American government, business, and society.
- To learn about Theodore Roosevelt's domestic policy and about his promotion of progressive reforms through the Square Deal.
- To learn about domestic affairs in the presidency of William Howard Taft.
- To learn about Woodrow Wilson's presidency and his New Freedom program of domestic reform.
- To understand how progressives contributed to a reshaping of American attitudes about government, and to significant modification of the Constitution.

To the Teacher

The Progressive Era is generally considered as lasting roughly from 1900 to 1920. Historians have advanced various ideas about who the progressives were; this text follows an eclectic approach, including a broad spectrum of progressives rather than any narrow group. Theodore Roosevelt had much to do with making progressive reform acceptable to the American people—he was from the wealthy class, was an educated easterner, and was eminently respectable. With the stature of the presidency and the support of the masses, he made numerous changes in line with ideals of progressivism.

Point out several things about the progressives. This period was a reforming era as opposed to the reactionary era after the Civil War. Although some of the reformers' goals and accomplishments were good, their basic motivation for progressive reform ignored the most basic truths about man's nature. Their clamor to use government power for reform led to big, intrusive government. Their efforts led to great changes in American society, some helpful and some detrimental.

Be careful in the impressions you give to your class. Be especially judicious in discussing income tax, the Federal Reserve System, and the Constitutional amendments of this era. The same drive that gave women the right to vote has resulted in many other changes detrimental to morals. Understanding the progressive movement is crucial to an understanding of the twentieth century.

Note on chapter test: There is a single test for Chapters 21 and 22. Review "Historical Highlights," Part C (Constitutional Amendments), for the test.

Christian Perspectives

- The answer to man's needs is not stronger government or social reform; man needs Jesus Christ in his heart to live righteously (Romans 8:1–14; 2 Corinthians 5:17–21; Ephesians 4:20–24).

- Christians should be good stewards of God's world, but for reasons different from those of natural-minded conservationists (Genesis 1:28–30; Deuteronomy 20:19, 20; Psalm 24:1, 2).
- God shows His power in natural disasters (Nahum 1:3–6; Psalm 33:10, 11).
- Christians may have misgivings about the programs and expanding power of government, but they are still responsible to obey the government unless that would involve disobedience to God's laws. They should also pray for rulers (Acts 5:29; Romans 13:1–5; 1 Timothy 2:1–4).
- Christians are responsible to pay taxes, not to tell the government how to use tax money (Luke 20:21–26; Romans 13:6, 7).
- Though even the United States Constitution may be changed, God's Word never changes (Psalm 119:89; Matthew 5:17, 18).

Further Study

- The lives and administrations of the three presidents discussed in this chapter.
- The national parks of America. (A descriptive essay could be written about a visit to one of these.)
- The San Francisco earthquake of 1906.
- The sinking of the *Titanic*.

Chapter 22 Quiz

Write the correct name or term for each description.

1. Woodrow Wilson's reform program.

    _____

2. Amendment that allowed an income tax.

    _____

3. Progressive president who served from 1901 to 1909.

    _____

4. Theodore Roosevelt's reform program to treat everyone equally.

    _____

5. Amendment that prohibited alcoholic beverages.

    _____

6. Amendment that allowed women to vote.

    _____

7. Democrat who served as president from 1913 to 1921.

    _____

8. Law of 1913 that reduced taxes on imports and provided for an income tax.

    _____

9. Crusade that promoted reform and change.

    _____

10. Amendment that provided for the direct election of senators.

    _____

11. Progressive president who served from 1909 to 1913 and later served on the Supreme Court.

    _____

12. Law that established a central banking system in 1913.

    _____

Quiz Answers

1. **New Freedom**
2. **Sixteenth Amendment**
3. **Theodore Roosevelt**
4. **Square Deal**
5. **Eighteenth Amendment**
6. **Nineteenth Amendment**
7. **Woodrow Wilson**
8. **Underwood Tariff Act**
9. **progressive movement**
10. **Seventeenth Amendment**
11. **William Howard Taft**
12. **Federal Reserve Act**

Answer Key

Focus for Thought (page 486)

1. *What people took part in the progressive movement?*

   The progressives were a diverse group of Democrats, Republicans, and others who wanted to use government power to improve American society.

2. *What three reforms did the progressive reformers promote*

   a. *in government?*

   They wanted to purge the government of corruption. They wanted the government to serve society as a whole rather than serving special-interest groups. They wanted a more democratic government, one that was more responsive to the will of the people. Other progressive changes included the initiative, the referendum, and the recall.

   b. *in business?*

   They wanted to give the government power to regulate businesses and to break up the ones that became too large. They campaigned for laws to limit the working hours of women, to ban child labor, and to improve working conditions. They promoted workers' compensation and established minimum-wage laws.

   c. *in society?*

   They promoted building codes, zoning laws, and other laws to regulate tenements. Some promoted conservation to protect natural resources. Some favored prohibition. Others promoted women's suffrage. They wanted an income tax to redistribute wealth.

3. *What changes did the reformers make in education?*

   They emphasized using the schools to reform society and promoted child-centered teaching. They abandoned the teaching methods and strict discipline of the old schools. They taught more subjects such as sewing and cooking instead of the "three R's." They emphasized thinking skills rather than learning by memorization.

4. *Write* federal, state, *or* local *for each blank.*
   Progressives usually began reforming at the ___ *level of government. From there they went to the* ___ *level and finally to the* ___ *level.*
   local, state, federal

5. *Name at least three state reforms that progressives accomplished.*
   (Any three.) States began having direct primary elections. They passed laws for conservation, higher taxes on corporations, and state income taxes. They adopted the initiative and the referendum. They passed laws that limited working hours, set minimum wages, and provided workers' compensation. They prohibited alcoholic beverages and passed compulsory school attendance laws.

Focus for Thought (page 491)

6. a. *Why did Theodore Roosevelt label his program the Square Deal?*
   The goal of Roosevelt's program was to give everyone fair treatment, regardless of class.
   b. *What pattern did this establish?*
   a pattern for presidents to have a legislative program and give it a name

7. *What is significant about Roosevelt's handling of the coal strike in 1902?*
   It was the first time a president had personally intervened in employer–employee affairs. (It greatly expanded the power of the president and the federal government to intervene in private business matters.)

8. a. *How did Roosevelt deal with a number of trusts?*
   He broke up many trusts by using the Sherman Antitrust Act.
   b. *What three acts of 1906 increased the power of federal government to regulate trade between states?*
   the Hepburn Act, the Meat Inspection Act, and the Pure Food and Drug Act

9. *What did President Roosevelt do to promote conservation of natural resources and to make conservation a national issue?*
   A law was passed that provided funds to build dams for waterpower and irrigation projects. He created several new national parks and game preserves, as well as numerous national monuments and bird refuges. He called a conference on conservation that led to the National Conservation Commission and many state conservation commissions.

10. *Why did President Taft hesitate to act as aggressively as Roosevelt had?*
Taft believed that he should have a Constitutional basis for his actions.

11. *What progressive reforms did President Taft accomplish?*
Taft broke up more trusts than Roosevelt had. He signed the Mann-Elkins Act, which gave greater authority to the Interstate Commerce Commission. The Sixteenth and Seventeenth Amendments were passed by Congress during his term.

Focus for Thought (page 494)

12. *What three main areas did President Wilson want to reform?*
Wilson wanted to lower tariffs, reform the banking system, and attack business trusts.

13. a. *What changes did the Underwood Tariff Act make in tariffs?*
This act reduced tariffs from an average of 41 percent to about 26 percent. It placed some products, such as iron, steel, and sugar, on the free list.
b. *What did this act provide for new revenue?*
an income tax

14. *How did the Federal Reserve Act give the federal government power to control the economy?*
This act created the Federal Reserve System, which regulates the money supply and controls the growth of the economy. The Federal Reserve Board can control interest rates by raising or lowering the rates on money lent to member banks.

15. *What did the federal government do in 1914 to regulate the trusts?*
Congress established the Federal Trade Commission to stop unfair methods of competition. The Clayton Antitrust Act was passed to strengthen the Sherman Antitrust Act and exempt unions from antitrust laws.

16. *Which amendment to the Constitution provided for*
a. *women's suffrage?* **Nineteenth Amendment**
b. *direct election of senators?* **Seventeenth Amendment**
c. *prohibition of alcoholic beverages?* **Eighteenth Amendment**
d. *an income tax?* **Sixteenth Amendment**

HISTORICAL HIGHLIGHTS (pages 495, 496)

A. Matching: Presidents

Each choice will be used more than once.

a. *Theodore Roosevelt*   b. *William Howard Taft*   c. *Woodrow Wilson*

c   1. *President from 1913 to 1921.*
b   2. *The largest president.*
a   3. *President from 1901 to 1909.*
b   4. *Only president to become a justice of the Supreme Court.*
b   5. *President from 1909 to 1913.*
a   6. *President who promoted the Square Deal.*
c   7. *President who promoted the New Freedom.*
c   8. *A Democrat.*

B. Matching: Terms

Not all the choices will be used.

a. *Clayton Antitrust Act*
b. *Department of Commerce and Labor*
c. *Federal Reserve Act*
d. *Federal Trade Commission*
e. *initiative, referendum, recall*
f. *Meat Inspection Act*
g. *muckraker*

h. *New Freedom*
i. *progressive movement*
j. *Progressive Party*
k. *Pure Food and Drug Act*
l. *Square Deal*
m. *Underwood Tariff Act*

h   1. *Woodrow Wilson's reform program.*
l   2. *Theodore Roosevelt's reform program to treat everyone equally.*
m   3. *Law of 1913 that reduced taxes on imports and provided for an income tax.*
f, k   4. *First laws regulating the quality of goods shipped between states (two answers).*
d   5. *Agency set up to enforce fair trade practices.*
i   6. *Crusade promoting reform and change.*
j   7. *Group that nominated Theodore Roosevelt for president in 1912.*
a   8. *Law of 1914 that aimed to strengthen the Sherman Antitrust Act against big business.*
c   9. *Established a central banking system in 1913.*
b   10. *New department of the Cabinet set up in 1903 to regulate big business.*
e   11. *Measures for democratic reforms promoted by progressives.*
g   12. *Author of books or articles pointing out evils in society.*

C. Matching: Constitutional Amendments

One choice will be used more than once.
a. *Sixteenth Amendment*   c. *Eighteenth Amendment*
b. *Seventeenth Amendment*   d. *Nineteenth Amendment*

d 1. *Amendment that allowed women to vote.*
c 2. *Amendment that was later repealed.*
a 3. *Amendment that allowed an income tax.*
b 4. *Amendment that provided for the direct election of senators.*
c 5. *Amendment that prohibited alcoholic beverages.*

D. Deeper Discussion

1. a. *How did progressive reformers think they could solve problems in society?*
Reformers thought they could solve social problems by improving the government and increasing its power to reform society. They thought this because they believed that social problems resulted from flawed institutions and that man had the power to improve his own condition. They overlooked the fundamental problem of man's evil nature. External reform will never really improve man; rather, man will continue to grow worse and worse. The decades since 1900 have made that clear.

   b. *How did progressive educators depart from a Biblical premise?*
They departed from the Biblical teaching that parents are to "bring up" their children, and replaced it with a child-centered approach. They made the state responsible for educating children, instead of assigning that responsibility to parents as the Bible teaches. They moved away from the traditional, tried approach of "precept upon precept; line upon line" taught in the Bible. Progressive educators did not recognize the Biblical fact of the child's fallen nature and his need for discipline and moral training.

2. a. *Why was a third political party formed in 1912?*
Progressive Republicans wanted more change, while the conservatives did not want to change as fast. When the conservative President Taft was nominated for a second term, the others formed the Progressive Party and nominated Theodore Roosevelt as their candidate. To be fair, one should note that a National Progressive Republican League had been formed in 1911; so the split had been developing for a long time. Third parties have often formed when a major party did not represent what many of its members wanted.

b. *What were the effects of this party?*

It served to divide Republican votes between progressives and regular Republicans, thus allowing the more united Democrats to win the election. In some ways the new party was unsuccessful—its candidate lost the election. Yet many progressives were probably more willing to see Wilson in office than to have another four years under Taft. Ideas of a third party are often taken up by the major parties.

3. a. *Why did the progressives make so many amendments to the Constitution?*

This was an outworking of their idea that improving and strengthening the government could eliminate social problems. By making amendments to the Constitution, the progressives hoped to make their changes permanent.

b. *What were the effects?*

The effects were profound. Income tax had to be paid by almost every worker and businessman. The direct election of senators changed the balance of power between the federal government and the states. Prohibition led to much violence and later was repealed. Women's suffrage led to moral changes in society and in families that are still being felt today.

4. a. *What should be the Christian's attitude toward conservation? Give Bible verses to support your thinking.*

The Christian recognizes God's command that man subdue the earth and have dominion over it (Genesis 1:28, 29). He practices conservation because "the earth is the LORD's" (Psalm 24:1), and he must therefore be a good steward of it.

b. *How is this approach different from that of the progressives?*

Christians seek to avoid wasting natural resources or polluting the earth because of their accountability to God, not just for the sake of themselves and future generations. Also, Christians practice conservation voluntarily whereas the progressives promoted laws to mandate conservation.

5. *What should be the Christian's attitude toward taxation? Again, give Bible verses to support your thinking.*

The Christian is to pay taxes willingly and obediently. Jesus' command is to "render therefore unto Caesar" what belongs to him (Luke 20:24, 25). Paul gave instructions to pay tribute to the authorities because they are God's ministers (Romans 13:6, 7).

E. Chronology and Geography

Make a time line of the Progressive Era (1900–1920). On your time line, list the presidents by their year of election, the five laws (acts) listed in Part B, and the Constitutional amendments. Be sure to scale your time line correctly. Title it "The Progressive Era, 1900–1920."

(Sample time line.)

The Progressive Era, 1900–1920

1901   **President McKinley assassinated; Theodore Roosevelt becomes president**

1904   **Theodore Roosevelt elected to second term**

1906   **Meat Inspection Act and Pure Food and Drug Act passed**

1908   **William Howard Taft elected president**

1912   **Woodrow Wilson elected president**

1913   **Sixteenth and Seventeenth Amendments ratified; Underwood Tariff Act and Federal Reserve Act passed**

1914   **Clayton Antitrust Act passed**

1916   **Woodrow Wilson re-elected**

1919   **Eighteenth Amendment ratified**

1920   **Nineteenth Amendment ratified**

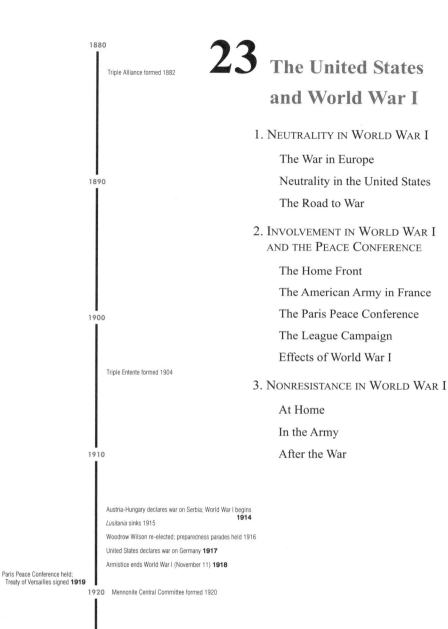

23 The United States and World War I

1. NEUTRALITY IN WORLD WAR I

    The War in Europe

    Neutrality in the United States

    The Road to War

2. INVOLVEMENT IN WORLD WAR I AND THE PEACE CONFERENCE

    The Home Front

    The American Army in France

    The Paris Peace Conference

    The League Campaign

    Effects of World War I

3. NONRESISTANCE IN WORLD WAR I

    At Home

    In the Army

    After the War

"For thus saith the LORD; We have heard a voice of trembling, of fear, and not of peace."

Jeremiah 30:5

Chapter 23 (pages 498–522)

The United States and World War I

Chapter Objectives

- To study the causes and the course of World War I in Europe.
- To learn how the United States was drawn into World War I, and how this helped to bring victory for the Allies.
- To learn about the Treaty of Versailles and the League of Nations, and to see why they were rejected in the United States.
- To grasp the significance of World War I historically.
- To learn about the experiences of conscientious objectors in World War I.
- To understand how World War I affected the Mennonites of that time and in the years since.

To the Teacher

World War I is a landmark event in history. It marked the dawning of the modern age as the ancient empires crumbled into dust and new European nations arose. One misconception about this conflict is that the United States was neutral at first, when actually it favored the Allies almost from the start. Even the sinking of the *Lusitania* had its other side: Americans had been warned not to travel on British ships, but they did anyway. Another questionable idea is that if the United States had joined the League of Nations, World War II could have been prevented. But the League agreement was too weak, and the nations were not really united—the oneness was merely external. So the League had little chance of succeeding whether or not the United States joined.

This chapter is deliberately designed to avoid a patriotic view of World War I. Yet God did allow the United States to make a difference in the outcome, and we need not apologize for that fact. Also, the United States did not agree to the Treaty of Versailles and thus had no part in the treaty's harshness.

Wartime experiences encouraged Mennonites to engage in relief services (though that had its pitfalls) and to produce a great amount of literature pertaining to nonresistance, from which we benefit today. The harrowing experiences of the conscientious objectors sharply highlighted their inner qualities of true nonresistance and noble courage to suffer valiantly for Christ. Encourage your students to do some outside reading on the experiences of COs during World War I, and challenge them with the faithfulness of many young nonresistant Christians who faced hard trials and sufferings for Christ.

Note on chapter test: Chapter 23 has its own test.

Christian Perspectives

- The conduct of earthly nations is beastly in the sight of God (Daniel 2, 7). Yet God overrules in the affairs of men and nations to accomplish His purposes (Daniel 4:34, 35).
- Man's efforts at bringing peace to the world will always fail, since his heart is evil. Uniting nations will not bring about peace and harmony. Likewise, no war will ever "make the world safe" and "end all wars" (Mark 13:7, 8). Only Christ can bring about true peace in men's hearts (Jeremiah 6:14; 8:11; Ezekiel 7:25; 13:10; John 16:33).
- There is always a line of tension and conflict between the Christian and the world, especially in times of war (James 4:4).
- Christians must obey God rather than men (Acts 5:29).
- Christians are called to suffer willingly for the cause of Christ, following His example (1 Peter 2:21).

Further Study

- World War I in Europe, before and after American involvement.
- The sinking of the *Lusitania*.
- The peace conference after the war.
- The League of Nations.
- Nonresistance in World War I.

Chapter 23 Quiz

Write the correct word or phrase for each blank.

1. World War I began in the year _____ and ended in ___.

   _____

2. _____ was president of the United States during World War I.

   _____

3. In World War I, the union of Germany, Austria-Hungary, Bulgaria, and Turkey was called the _____.

   _____

4. The union of Russia, France, Great Britain, and Italy in World War I was called the _____.

   _____

5. The United States entered World War I in the year _____.

   _____

6. The United States army sent to France was called the _____.

   _____

7. The United States general in France was _____.

   _____

8. The Treaty of _____ punished Germany harshly and proposed an alliance of nations.

   _____

9. The American president's ideas for world peace were known as the _____.

   _____

10. The international organization that the president proposed to maintain world peace was called the _____.

   _____

Quiz Answers

1. **1914, 1918**
2. **Woodrow Wilson**
3. **Central Powers**
4. **Allies**

5. **1917**
6. **American Expeditionary Force**
7. **John J. Pershing**

8. **Versailles**
9. **Fourteen Points**
10. **League of Nations**

Answer Key

Focus for Thought (page 505)

1. a. *What were four main causes of the war in Europe?*
   (1) competition among nations to build empires, (2) harsh rule in the empires, (3) militarism and buildup of armed forces, (4) formation of military alliances
   b. *What incident led to the outbreak of fighting?*
   the assassination of Francis Ferdinand, archduke of Austria-Hungary
   c. *Name the nations that made up the Central Powers, and those that made up the Allies.*
   Central Powers: Germany, Austria-Hungary, Bulgaria, Turkey
   Allies: Great Britain, France, Russia, Italy, and some others.
2. *Summarize what happened along the Western Front for over three years.*
   The two sides made repeated assaults against each other, which resulted in thousands of casualties but no real progress for either side.
3. *How did the following things influence the United States in favor of the Allies?*
   a. *economic involvements*
   Because the British blockaded the ports of the Central Powers, Americans had to trade with the Allies. Americans also lent money to the Allies, which naturally increased their interest in Allied success.
   b. *German submarine warfare*
   Americans became upset because the Germans sank many ships of neutral countries. This was a threat to the freedom of the seas. When the *Lusitania* was sunk with Americans on board, many people clamored for war against Germany.
   c. *preparedness*
   Preparedness parades and Wilson's re-election campaign influenced people to think they should prepare to fight Germany if necessary.
4. *What two main issues finally brought the United States into the war?*
   One was the Germans' declaration that they would resume unrestricted submarine warfare. The other was the Zimmermann telegram.
5. *What were the two stated reasons for the United States to enter World War I?*
   The reasons were to "make the world safe for democracy" and to "end all wars."

Focus for Thought (page 512)

6. *How was the American Expeditionary Force in Europe a "first" for America?*
   It was the first time American troops were sent to fight in Europe.

7. *Briefly describe what happened at the four main places where Americans helped the Allies in 1918.*
   The Americans helped to keep the Germans from crossing the Marne River. They helped to push the Germans back in the Battle of Belleau Wood. They helped to stop the Germans in the Second Battle of the Marne. They helped to drive the Germans back to the Hindenburg Line, their last line of defense.

8. *How and when did World War I come to an end?*
   An armistice ended World War I on November 11, 1918.

9. *How were the Fourteen Points to bring peace to the world?*
   They were to bring peace by means such as open agreements between nations, complete freedom of the seas, removal of trade barriers, and reduction of military forces.

10. *How did the Treaty of Versailles meet the goals*
    a. *of President Wilson?*
    It provided for a general association of nations, later called the League of Nations.
    b. *of the other members of the Big Four?*
    It laid severe penalties on the Germans, requiring them to pay reparations of over $30 billion, to distribute their colonies among the Allies, and to greatly reduce the size of their army, navy, and merchant fleet.

11. a. *How did President Wilson try to get the American public to support his ideas?*
    He went on a speaking tour to promote the League.
    b. *What became of his efforts?*
    He became ill, had to return to Washington, and suffered a stroke soon afterward. Later the Senate voted against the Treaty of Versailles. The United States never joined the League of Nations, and it made separate peace treaties with the Central Powers.

12. *In what way was World War I a turning point in history?*
    World War I marked the end of the old empires and the beginning of modern nations. Also, World War I helped to bring on World War II, and both wars have affected the world ever since.

Focus for Thought (pages 517, 518)

13. a. *What was the first provision that the government made for conscientious objectors?*

The government proposed to give noncombatant duties to conscientious objectors.

b. *Why was this provision unacceptable to nonresistant people?*

Performing any duty in the army was still part of the military effort.

14. *Give at least three specific reasons why Mennonites suffered at the hands of patriotic people around them.*

(Any three.) People resented the Mennonites because their young men did not face the risk of being killed in battle overseas. Some Mennonites suffered because they used the German language. The Mennonite teaching on Biblical nonresistance was viewed with suspicion. Mennonites suffered for refusing to buy Liberty Bonds. They suffered for refusing to display or salute the flag.

15. *Why did Mennonites generally refuse to buy Liberty Bonds?*

A person who bought war bonds was helping to finance the war of his own free will.

16. *What three main areas of testing did conscientious objectors face in the army camps?*

They were the tests of wearing the uniform, working in noncombatant service, and drilling for war.

17. *What happened when a conscientious objector refused to compromise?*

He was mocked and sometimes beaten or mistreated in other ways. He might receive a court-martial and be sentenced to a long term in a military prison, where treatment was often brutal.

18. *What legal provision was made for conscientious objectors in June 1918?*

The Furlough Act allowed COs to work at civilian jobs such as farming.

19. *What were two important effects of World War I on Mennonites?*

(Any two.) Mennonites were stirred to a greater interest in service and in relief work. World War I helped the nonresistant people to prepare for future conflicts (because it opened the way for voluntary service and because more literature was produced to give teaching on nonresistance). Many Christians were strengthened by the testimonies of the conscientious objectors.

HISTORICAL HIGHLIGHTS (pages 518–520)

A. Matching: Terms 1

a. *armistice*

b. *contraband of war*

c. *freedom of the seas*

d. *noncombatant*

e. *preparedness*

f. *Selective Service Act*

g. *Triple Alliance*

h. *Triple Entente*

i. *Western Front*

j. *Zimmermann telegram*

i   1. *Battle line extending through Switzerland, France, and Belgium.*

a   2. *Agreement to stop fighting.*

f   3. *Law providing for a military draft.*

h   4. *Union of Russia, France, and Great Britain.*

d   5. *Fulfilling military duties but not actually fighting.*

b   6. *Goods headed toward an enemy nation to support its war effort.*

c   7. *Right of any merchant ship to sail the ocean in peace or war.*

j   8. *Item proposing an alliance of Germany with Mexico and Japan.*

e   9. *The state of being prepared to fight if necessary.*

g 10. *Union of Germany, Austria-Hungary, and Italy.*

B. Matching: Terms 2

a. *Allies*

b. *Central Powers*

c. *Fourteen Points*

d. *Furlough Act*

e. *League of Nations*

f. *Liberty Bonds*

g. *American Expeditionary Force*

h. *Mennonite Central Committee*

i. *Treaty of Versailles*

j. *War Problems Committee*

f   1. *Items sold to help pay for the war.*

b   2. *Union of Germany, Austria-Hungary, Bulgaria, and Turkey.*

g   3. *United States army sent to France.*

c   4. *Woodrow Wilson's ideas for world peace.*

i   5. *Agreement that punished Germany harshly and proposed a League of Nations.*

d   6. *Law that allowed drafted men to work in civilian jobs.*

h   7. *Mennonite organization set up for relief work in Russia.*

e   8. *Organization designed to maintain world peace.*

j   9. *Group that appealed for government recognition of the Mennonite's stand on nonresistance.*

a 10. *Union of Russia, France, Great Britain, and Italy.*

C. People, Places, Dates

a. *April 6, 1917*

b. *Francis Ferdinand*

c. *John J. Pershing*

d. *July 28, 1914*

e. *Kaiser Wilhelm II*

f. *Newton D. Baker*

g. *November 11, 1918*

h. *Versailles*

i. *Woodrow Wilson*

d 1. *Date when World War I began.*

a 2. *Date when United States entered World War I.*

g 3. *Date when World War I ended.*

i 4. *President during World War I.*

f 5. *Secretary of war.*

c 6. *General of the American Expeditionary Force in France.*

b 7. *Archduke of Austria-Hungary.*

h 8. *Place where the peace treaty with Germany was signed.*

e 9. *Leader of Germany during World War I.*

D. Deeper Discussion

1. *Could the United States have remained genuinely neutral in World War I? Why or why not?*

   Probably not. To trade equally with both sides would have been ideal, but the realities of war made this almost impossible. It was also hard not to take sides in the conflict, especially since the Germans were the aggressors and Americans had closer ties to the British. With sympathies growing ever stronger in favor of the Allies, and with German submarines continuing to sink American ships, it became increasingly difficult to remain genuinely neutral.

2. a. *What was the main idea behind the League of Nations?*

   If all nations would unite, they could prevent war by peaceable negotiation when conflicts arise.

   b. *Why does this idea not work?*

   It does not work because war is a product of man's evil nature; until hearts are changed, war will continue. Before World War I, some people believed that a time of universal peace had come; they were disillusioned when the war broke out. Some tried to outlaw war before World War II, but they could not. World leaders did establish the United Nations since then, but it too has not prevented war. So the truth of the Bible is abundantly borne out in human experience.

3. *A military officer once made a statement to this effect: "The man behind a*

typewriter is in the war just as surely as the man behind a machine gun."
Why is this true?

All the people in the military are working together to defeat the enemy by force. Each one is directly involved in that effort, whether he actually fights or simply does paperwork. Therefore, no position in the army is better than any other for someone who professes to be nonresistant.

4. *Read 1 Peter 2:19–25; 4:12–19.*

   a. *How did these verses apply to nonresistant people in World War I?*

   Nonresistant people endured suffering because of their stand for truth, even as Jesus endured suffering. They suffered wrongfully (unjustly) in that they had committed no crime (2:19). They suffered willingly for Christ, giving glory to Him (2:19, 20; 4:13, 14).

   b. *How did nonresistant people put these principles to practice?*

   They forgave their enemies, as Jesus forgave His. The suffering was a purging experience and brought them closer to God; they committed their souls to Him (2:23; 4:17–19). They "reviled not" and "threatened not" (2:23). They showed a loving, Christlike spirit toward the ones who opposed them.

5. *How did World War I lead to World War II?*

   The League of Nations, established after World War I, failed to maintain peace because it was too weak. The Treaty of Versailles embittered the Germans and humiliated them by taking some of their land away. War reparations brought economic hardship that led many Germans to support Adolf Hitler, who set out to bring all Europe into one mighty German empire.

E. Chronology and Geography

The Treaty of Versailles dealt with Germany, but other treaties related to the other Central Powers. These treaties divided parts of the old empires of Russia, Germany, and Austria-Hungary into nine new nations, which are listed below.

    1. *Match the numbers on the map to the following countries.*

    7 a. *Austria*
    6 b. *Czechoslovakia*
    2 c. *Estonia*
    1 d. *Finland*
    8 e. *Hungary*
    3 f. *Latvia*
    4 g. *Lithuania*
    5 h. *Poland*
    9 i. *Yugoslavia*

Map legend:
- Russia in 1914
- Germany in 1914
- Austria-Hungary in 1914
- Boundaries after World War I
- Former boundaries

    2. *Compare this map with a modern map of eastern Europe since the fall of communism. Be prepared to discuss how these nine countries have changed since the early 1920s.*

    (Discuss in class. Some changes are as follows: The boundary between Finland and Russia has been moved west in some places. Poland lost some territory in the east and gained some in the west. Czechoslovakia is now the Czech Republic and Slovakia. Moldova is now located in what had been eastern Romania. The former Yugoslavia is now divided into Slovenia, Croatia, Bosnia and Herzegovina, Macedonia, and Yugoslavia [Serbia and Montenegro].)

So Far This Year (pages 521, 522)

A. Matching: Terms

Write the correct term for each description. Not all the choices will be used.

Boxer Rebellion
Eighteenth Amendment
Federal Reserve Act
Federal Trade Commission
imperialism
Isolationism
New Freedom
Nineteenth Amendment

Open Door Policy
progressive movement
Pure Food and Drug Act
Seventeenth Amendment
Sixteenth Amendment
Square Deal
Underwood Tariff Act

isolationism

1. *Policy of having little to do with foreign nations.*

Boxer Rebellion

2. *Uprising in China in 1900.*

Square Deal

3. *Theodore Roosevelt's reform program to treat everyone equally.*

Eighteenth Amendment

4. *Constitutional amendment that prohibited alcoholic beverages.*

progressive movement

5. *Crusade promoting reform and change.*

Underwood Tariff Act

6. *Law of 1913 that reduced import taxes and provided for an income tax.*

Sixteenth Amendment

7. *Constitutional amendment that allowed an income tax.*

New Freedom

8. *Woodrow Wilson's plans for reform.*

imperialism

9. *Desire to gain control of foreign territories.*

Open Door Policy

10. *Basis for American relations with countries in the Far East.*

Federal Reserve Act

11. *Measure that established a central banking system in 1913.*

Seventeenth Amendment

12. *Constitutional amendment that provided for the direct election of senators.*

Nineteenth Amendment

13. *Constitutional amendment that allowed women to vote.*

B. Matching: People, Places, and Dates

Write the correct answer for each description. Not all the choices will be used.

Guam   William Howard Taft
Hawaii   William McKinley
Philippines   Woodrow Wilson
Puerto Rico   1898
Theodore Roosevelt   1900

William McKinley   14. *President during the Spanish-American War.*

Theodore Roosevelt   15. *President of the Square Deal and the "big stick"; served from 1901 to 1909.*

Philippines   16. *Spanish islands in the Far East conquered by the United States and purchased for $20 million.*

1898   17. *Year the Spanish-American War was fought.*

Puerto Rico   18. *Spanish island in the Caribbean ceded to the United States after the Spanish-American War.*

William Howard Taft   19. *President who served from 1909 to 1913 and later became a Supreme Court justice.*

Hawaii   20. *Pacific islands lying about 2,000 miles (3,219) west of the United States; annexed in 1898.*

Woodrow Wilson   21. *Democratic president elected after a split in the opposing party; served from 1913 to 1921.*

Guam   22. *Spanish island in the Pacific ceded to the United States in 1898.*

C. True or False

Write whether each statement is true *(T)* or false *(F)*. If it is false, write the word or phrase that should replace the underlined part.

T   23. *Manifest destiny refers to the idea that the United States should spread over the whole North American continent.*

F; James Polk   24. *Zachary Taylor was the expansionist president from 1845 to 1849.*

F; Mexican Cession   25. *Land that the United States gained by the Mexican War was called the Gadsden Purchase.*

F; Stephen Austin   26. *Marcus Whitman was the man who began colonizing Texas.*

T	27. *The treaty that ended the Mexican War was the Treaty of <u>Guadalupe Hidalgo</u>.*
F; pony express	28. *The <u>Oregon Trail</u> was a mail system to connect California with the East.*
T	29. *The general who conquered Mexico City in the Mexican War was <u>Winfield Scott</u>.*
F; John Sutter	30. *<u>John Fremont</u> owned a fort in California near which gold was discovered in 1848.*
F; mountain men	31. *The <u>forty-niners</u> were hardy fur traders and explorers of the West.*
F; Rio Grande	32. *The <u>Colorado River</u> formed the disputed boundary between Texas and Mexico.*
T	33. *<u>Popular sovereignty</u> was the idea that people living in a territory should decide for themselves about slavery.*
F; Thirteenth Amendment	34. *The <u>Fourteenth Amendment</u> to the Constitution permanently outlawed slavery.*
T	35. *<u>Jefferson Davis</u> served as president of the Confederate States of America.*
T	36. *<u>Abraham Lincoln</u> was the Union president during the Civil War.*
F; Robert E. Lee	37. *<u>Ulysses S. Grant</u> was the chief general of the Confederate armies.*
T	38. *<u>Missouri</u> was a border state.*
T	39. Uncle Tom's Cabin, *written by <u>Harriet Beecher Stowe</u>, contributed to the Civil War.*
T	40. *The Civil War lasted from <u>1861 to 1865</u>.*
T	41. *<u>Fort Sumter</u> was the place where the Civil War began.*
F; Dred Scott	42. *<u>John Brown</u> was a black man whose appeal for freedom was rejected by the Supreme Court.*
F; Gettysburg	43. *The town of <u>Antietam</u> was known as the "high-water mark of the Confederacy."*
T	44. *<u>West Virginia</u> was a new state formed from a Confederate state during the Civil War.*
T	45. *The Emancipation Proclamation declared that, beginning in <u>1863</u>, slaves in the states of the Confederacy would be free.*
T	46. *The <u>Underground Railroad</u> aided slaves in escaping from the South.*

D. Dates

Write the correct years for these descriptions.

1754–1763   47. *Years when the French and Indian War began and ended.*

1775–1783   48. *Years when the Revolutionary War began and ended.*

1683   49. *Year when Mennonites first came to America.*

1787   50. *Year of the Constitutional Convention.*

1789   51. *Year when the government under the Constitution began operating.*

1791   52. *Year when the Bill of Rights was added to the Constitution.*

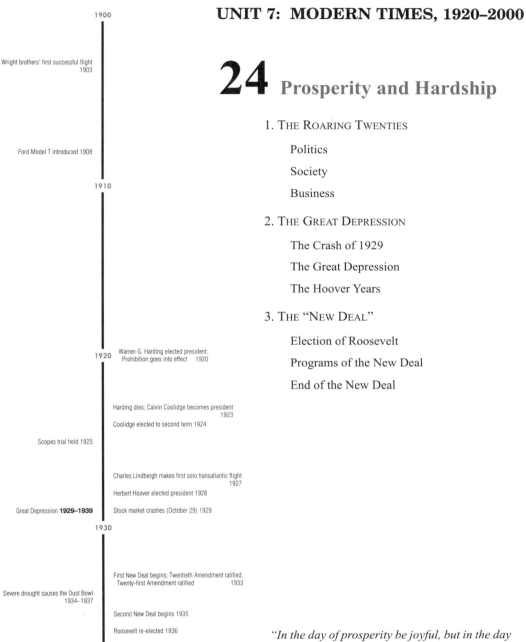

24 Prosperity and Hardship

1. THE ROARING TWENTIES

    Politics

    Society

    Business

2. THE GREAT DEPRESSION

    The Crash of 1929

    The Great Depression

    The Hoover Years

3. THE "NEW DEAL"

    Election of Roosevelt

    Programs of the New Deal

    End of the New Deal

Timeline:

- 1900
- Wright brothers' first successful flight 1903
- Ford Model T introduced 1908
- 1910
- 1920 — Warren G. Harding elected president; Prohibition goes into effect 1920
- Harding dies; Calvin Coolidge becomes president 1923
- Coolidge elected to second term 1924
- Scopes trial held 1925
- Charles Lindbergh makes first solo transatlantic flight 1927
- Herbert Hoover elected president 1928
- Great Depression **1929–1939** — Stock market crashes (October 29) 1929
- 1930
- First New Deal begins; Twentieth Amendment ratified; Twenty-first Amendment ratified 1933
- Severe drought causes the Dust Bowl 1934–1937
- Second New Deal begins 1935
- Roosevelt re-elected 1936
- 1940

"In the day of prosperity be joyful, but in the day of adversity consider: God also hath set the one over against the other, to the end that man should find nothing after him."

Ecclesiastes 7:14

Unit 7: Modern Times, 1920–2000

Chapter 24 (pages 524–547)

Prosperity And Hardship

Chapter Objectives

- To study the presidents of 1921 through 1945.
- To understand the technological changes of the 1920s, and the resulting social changes.
- To learn about Prohibition and its effects on the United States.
- To understand the clash between modernism and fundamentalism, and how this clash affected the Mennonites.
- To learn about the stock market crash of 1929 and the Great Depression that followed.
- To learn about Franklin D. Roosevelt and his New Deal, and how it has changed American government.

To the Teacher

The 1920s and 1930s are momentous decades in American history. They were crucial in shaping the attitudes of society toward business, religion, science, education, the economy, and the government. Rightly interpreting the events of these years, then, will be crucial to understanding history and to understanding where we are today.

Many historians misinterpret the events and misapply the lessons. For example, they blame businessmen for the "excesses" of the 1920s, attack the Republican presidents for their "do-nothing" policies, and magnify the scandals of the Harding Administration. They blame Hoover for not doing enough to end the Depression, and they laud Roosevelt for mitigating the Depression through government action. In reality, it was the government's own policy of credit expansion that led to some of the excesses. Smaller government and lack of intervention probably stimulated the economy. Thus Hoover's actions, rather than not being enough, might have been *too much* and may have extended the Depression by interfering with the normal operation of the business cycle. Neither did the New Deal alleviate the Depression, in spite of all the billions spent. It may rather have prolonged the Depression by the burdens it placed on industry.

The question of who should aid the helpless may be raised. People who are good citizens—and especially who are Christians—should voluntarily reach out and help others. Families and local communities should also provide for their own. When people become selfish and lose sight of their responsibility to others, the government will fill the gap. This does not mean that New Deal programs helped nobody, but that they encouraged an unhealthy dependence on the government.

The government's role should be that of protector, not provider.

Several moral principles must be remembered. One is that any money accepted from the government had to be taken from someone else (through taxation), and that the one receiving the money has not earned it. A second is that involvement in government programs constitutes an unequal yoke for the Christian—to participate, he must submit to rules dictated by the government. A third is that government programs encourage trust in an earthly kingdom rather than in God. Since these are all violations of Scriptural principles, Christians need to avoid entanglement in government programs.

Do not underestimate the impact of the Scopes trial on the intellectual climate of the nation. This trial had a tremendous impact on education and the views of society about science and the Bible. In relation to society and the great moral shift in the 1920s, make students aware of the changes that took place but avoid overemphasizing the details. This warning is given because many other books dwell at length on the changes, as if to help the reader enjoy the rowdy and immoral spirit. Such an approach only feeds the appetites of the carnal nature.

Try to understand the underlying causes of the stock market crash and the Great Depression, and convey them to your students. Emphasize the dangers of credit-based living. Show how the New Deal encouraged the growth of labor unions and government intervention. Also present the true nature of the social security program and the dangers it presents. Consider the profound impact of both the Depression and the New Deal on American society. Finally, point out that in the midst of social and economic upheavals, the Christian can always find security in his unchanging God and among God's people.

Note on chapter test: Chapter 24 has its own test.

Christian Perspectives

- The Bible stands, true and unchanged, even though the blows of skeptics rain upon it (Psalm 119:89; Matthew 5:18).
- In times of prosperity, man tends to forget God. In times of adversity, man may turn to stealing or other desperate behavior (Deuteronomy 8:10–18; Proverbs 30:8, 9).
- We must not set our heart upon riches or gain (Proverbs 23:4, 5; 1 Timothy 6:6–11). Wealth can disappear in a moment.
- The borrower is servant to the lender (Proverbs 22:7).
- God is our provider, not the government; hence, we must avoid entanglement in government programs. We should be thankful for what God gives us, and should share with the needy (James 1:17; Ephesians 4:28).
- Those who trust in God will not be unsettled by social and economic upheavals (Psalm 16:8; 112:5–7).

Further Study

The 1920s and 1930s are a fascinating time, although some subjects pertaining to that era are not appropriate for extensive study. Some of the suitable topics are listed below.

- The automobile. (Research could focus on a specific car such as the Model T, or on a company such as General Motors.)
- The Wright brothers and the airplane.
- The story of Henry Ford, Charles Lindbergh, or one of the presidents.
- The Scopes trial.
- Prohibition.
- J. Edgar Hoover and the FBI.
- George R. Brunk, Sr., or another Mennonite leader such as Daniel Kauffman or John Horsch. (Read some articles in a bound volume of the *Sword and Trumpet* if possible. See also the book *Faithfully, George R.*)
- The stock market crash.
- Hardships during the Great Depression, such as the experiences of hoboes.
- The New Deal. (Research could focus on a particular program, such as the TVA.)

Quiz Answers

1. **Franklin D. Roosevelt**
2. **Herbert Hoover**
3. **Warren Harding**
4. **Calvin Coolidge**
5. **modernism**
6. **business cycle**
7. **Prohibition**
8. **Great Depression**
9. **fundamentalism**
10. **Scopes trial**
11. **Dust Bowl**
12. **New Deal**

Chapter 24 Quiz

Write the correct name or term for each description.

1. President elected in 1932; introduced the New Deal.

   _____

2. President when the Great Depression began; served from 1929 to 1933.

   _____

3. President who served from 1921 to 1923 and died in office.

   _____

4. President who took office after the death of the previous president; served from 1923 to 1929.

   _____

5. Set of beliefs including the theory of evolution, rejection of the supernatural, and acceptance of science as the only source of truth.

   _____

6. Periodic swing between prosperity and decline in the economy.

   _____

7. Era when alcoholic drinks were outlawed.

   _____

8. Long economic downturn from 1929 to 1939.

   _____

9. Movement that asserted basic truths of the Bible and opposed modernism.

   _____

10. Event when modernists and fundamentalists clashed over evolution in 1925.

    _____

11. Region of severe drought in the 1930s.

    _____

12. Group of government programs designed to end the economic downturn in the 1930s.

    _____

Answer Key

Focus for Thought (pages 533, 534)

1. *In the 1920s, how did the three Republican presidents think the government should deal with businesses?*

   They thought the government should place few limits on businesses so that they would make maximum profits.

2. *Describe some effects of the automobile on American life.*

   Sunday drives became popular, and people went on long vacations. Rural people could more freely enjoy city life. Many people began living in the country and working in the city. The middle class grew larger. New terms entered the nation's vocabulary. The automobile brought problems such as accidents and traffic jams.

3. *What were some evidences of declining morals in the 1920s?*

   More women began cutting their hair, using cosmetics, and wearing shorter dresses. They began using tobacco and alcohol more freely. The popular jazz music of the age emphasized freedom of expression and the breaking of traditions. Americans pursued sports and entertainment.

4. *What were some problems resulting from Prohibition?*

   People made liquor in secret, and bootleggers sold it illegally. The government did not have enough officers to stop the trade. Violence erupted as gangsters carried on the liquor trade.

5. a. *What is modernism?*

   Modernism is a set of beliefs including Darwin's theory of evolution, the rejection of anything supernatural, and the idea that science is the only source of truth.

   b. *What were the five points emphasized by fundamentalism?*

   It emphasized the infallibility and inerrancy of the Scriptures, the virgin birth of Christ, the miracle-working power of Christ, the redemptive sacrifice of Christ, and the bodily resurrection of Christ.

6. *What was the general effect of the Scopes trial?*

   Belief in Creation was made to seem ignorant, while evolution appeared to be modern, enlightened, and scientific. Later, evolution came to be taught as fact in public schools, and the teaching of Creation became illegal.

7. a. *How did the stock market contribute to the business boom of the 1920s?*

   Because stock prices increased rapidly in value, many people began making large profits by trading in stocks.

b. *What people did not share in the prosperity?*

farmers and people in coal mining, textile industries, and shoe and leather manufacturing

Focus for Thought (pages 538, 539)

8. a. *When did the stock market crash?*
on October 29, 1929

b. *What were some reasons for the crash and the Depression that followed?*
Reasons included overproduction and the unhealthy farm economy. The main reason was the overuse of credit (too much borrowing of money).

9. *Briefly explain how business cycles operate.*
When people are borrowing money and buying many things, demand is strong and prosperity abounds. But when people are paying their debts and buying fewer things, demand drops and hard times come.

10. *Why did many banks fail during the Depression?*
Many people could not repay their bank loans; and at the same time, many people were withdrawing their savings.

11. *What were two ways in which farmers suffered because of the Depression?*
(Any two.) Many farmers lost their properties when they could not pay for them. Prices of grain and other farm products fell drastically. Some parts of Kansas and nearby states had a severe drought from 1934 to 1937.

12. *How did President Hoover respond to the Depression?*
Hoover thought that people (and businesses) should help themselves rather than depending on the government. He encouraged businessmen not to lay off workers and not to reduce wages and prices. He asked Congress for money to finance public-works projects.

13. *Describe several effects that the Great Depression had on Americans.*
People lost confidence in businessmen and in themselves. Some developed an unhealthy concern for earthly security. They went to extremes in their ambition for money and possessions.

Focus for Thought (page 543)

14. *Describe the two Constitutional amendments that Congress passed in 1933.*
The Twentieth Amendment moved the date of the presidential inauguration to January 20. The Twenty-first Amendment repealed the Eighteenth Amendment and brought an end to Prohibition.

15. *Name the New Deal act or agency that matches each description.*

a. *Supervised the building of dams to control flooding and produce electricity.*

Tennessee Valley Authority

b. *Tried to improve the economy by regulating business practices and establishing the amount that each industry should produce.*

National Recovery Administration

c. *Employed people at projects such as the building of roads, dams, and bridges.*

Public Works Administration

d. *Gave workers the right to join unions and to bargain collectively.*

National Labor Relations Act

e. *Insured bank deposits.*

Federal Deposit Insurance Corporation

f. *Tried to raise prices of farm products by paying farmers to destroy crops and livestock.*

Agricultural Adjustment Administration

g. *Helped to bring electricity to many farms.*

Rural Electrification Administration

h. *Employed people in projects such as improving parks and painting murals.*

Works Progress Administration

i. *Authorized the government to examine banks and allow sound banks to continue operating.*

Banking Act

j. *Provided money for retired workers and for unemployment compensation, aid to children, and public health programs.*

Federal Insurance Contributions Act (social security)

k. *Gave money to states to distribute directly to needy people.*

Federal Emergency Relief Administration

16. *How did it become evident that the New Deal was not effective?*

The Depression continued in spite of the New Deal programs and the billions of dollars spent.

17. *List two important effects of the New Deal.*

(Any two.) The government became more powerful than ever before. It could freely intervene in the economy. It held control over industries, banks, and money. Many people began to depend on government support. The government began a policy of deficit spending. The national debt increased.

HISTORICAL HIGHLIGHTS (pages 544, 545)

A. Matching: People

a. *Calvin Coolidge*
b. *Charles Lindbergh*
c. *Franklin D. Roosevelt*
d. *George R. Brunk*
e. *Henry Ford*

f. *Herbert Hoover*
g. *J. Edgar Hoover*
h. *Warren G. Harding*
i. *Wilbur and Orville Wright*

d 1. *Published the* Sword and Trumpet *to oppose modernism.*
a 2. *Served as vice president under Harding and as president from 1923 to 1929.*
e 3. *Made cars available to most people by introducing the Model T.*
c 4. *Was elected president in 1932; introduced the New Deal.*
i 5. *Made the first successful flight with a heavier-than-air machine in 1903.*
b 6. *Made the first solo flight across the Atlantic Ocean in 1927.*
f 7. *Was president when the Great Depression began; served from 1929 to 1933.*
h 8. *Was president from 1921 to 1923; died in office.*
g 9. *Served as director of the Federal Bureau of Investigation.*

B. Matching: Terms

a. *business cycle*
b. *coalition*
c. *Dust Bowl*
d. *foreclose*
e. *fundamentalism*
f. *Great Depression*
g. *Hundred Days*
h. *lame duck*

i. *modernism*
j. *New Deal*
k. *normalcy*
l. *Prohibition*
m. *Scopes trial*
n. *secular humanism*
o. *Twentieth Amendment*
p. *Twenty-first Amendment*

j 1. *Group of government programs designed to end the Depression.*
n 2. *Man-centered philosophy in which the existence of God is denied.*
l 3. *Period when alcoholic beverages were outlawed in the United States.*
i 4. *Set of beliefs including the theory of evolution, rejection of the supernatural, and acceptance of science as the only source of truth.*
a 5. *Periodic swing between prosperity and decline in the economy.*
h 6. *Person finishing a term after another is elected to replace him.*
k 7. *Condition desired by Americans after World War I, which included a less troubled life and less involvement in European affairs.*
p 8. *Measure that repealed the Eighteenth Amendment and ended Prohibition.*

d   9. *To take property serving as security for a loan.*

b 10. *Temporary alliance of various groups to accomplish a certain thing.*

e 11. *Movement to assert basic truths of the Bible and oppose modernism.*

m 12. *Event in 1925 when fundamentalists and modernists clashed over evolution.*

o 13. *Measure that reduced the lame-duck period to less than three months.*

c 14. *Region of severe drought in the 1930s.*

g 15. *Special session of Congress in 1933 when many new programs were approved.*

f 16. *Long economic downturn from 1929 to 1939.*

C. Agencies and Programs

The following initials (acronyms) designate agencies and programs established in the 1920s and 1930s, which are still in existence today. Give the full name of each one, and briefly describe its function.

1. *FBI*—**Federal Bureau of Investigation; enforcing federal laws**
2. *FDIC*—**Federal Deposit Insurance Corporation; insuring bank deposits**
3. *FICA*—**Federal Insurance Contributions Act; providing support for retired people**
4. *REA*—**Rural Electrification Administration; providing electricity in rural areas**
5. *SEC*—**Securities and Exchange Commission; preventing illegal and unsound practices in the stock market**
6. *TVA*—**Tennessee Valley Authority; providing dams to control flooding and produce electricity**

D. Deeper Discussion

1. *Give similarities and differences between the beliefs of Mennonites and of fundamentalists.*

   Similarities: Mennonites and fundamentalists both believe in the Bible as the infallible Word of God. Mennonites accept the five basic doctrines asserted by fundamentalists.

   Differences: Mennonites believe in nonresistance and separation from the world, which most fundamentalists do not practice. Mennonites believe in the New Testament as the primary source of direction for the Christian, whereas fundamentalists look to the Old Testament for some principles (such as Christians participating in politics). Mennonites reject unconditional eternal security and stress assurance based on faith and obedience.

2. *What contributed to the rapid social changes and the rebellion against traditions in the 1920s?*

Technology was one major factor. Electrical devices gave people more leisure time, and electric lights allowed them to stay up later. Technology also brought motion pictures and the radio, which had a profound effect on American society. The automobile made an especially great impact. Young people used the car to escape parental authority, and this contributed to moral breakdown. Traditional standards for women were broken by new styles of clothing (with rising hemlines), use of cosmetics, and the cutting of their hair. New ideas, especially those spawned by Darwinism, led people to think and act as if man were merely an animal. The business boom gave people money to spend on luxuries and entertainment. Prohibition led to a shameless disregard for laws and the admiration of criminals. Above all, rejection of the Bible led people to disregard its precepts for living.

3. *How was the prosperity of the 1920s based on a shaky foundation?*

Much of that prosperity was an illusion, based on a great credit expansion by the policies of the Federal Reserve System. More money was in circulation, which gave the impression of prosperity but actually contributed to inflation. Multitudes were spending money they had not yet earned, which meant that eventually they had to repay the debt. When the total indebtedness reached a certain point, the economy had to slow down and readjust. The stock market was driven high by speculation during 1928 and 1929; and when this "balloon" was pricked, it shrank to more realistic levels. So while the credit expansion of the 1920s looked like prosperity, it was actually borrowing from the future. The crash of 1929 and the ensuing Depression were that future.

4. *Read Proverbs 23:4, 5 and 30:8, 9.*

   a. *How do these verses apply to the boom times of the 1920s, the stock market crash, and the Great Depression?*

Proverbs 23:4, 5—In the 1920s, people set their hearts on riches and dreamed of making fortunes in the stock market. When it crashed, their riches disappeared before their eyes. Some people even committed suicide because of the crash.

Proverbs 30:8, 9—When times were prosperous, people turned away from God and indulged in selfish luxuries. When times became hard, people resorted to stealing and other desperate measures.

b. *How might these Scriptures apply to us?*

We must not set our hearts on riches, which are temporal and fleeting. Rather, we need to lay up treasures in heaven. We should thank God for the blessings He gives, and willingly share with people who have less.

5. *Why did the Great Depression continue for a whole decade?*

The New Deal, with its higher taxes and wealth redistribution programs, attacked the very industries that could have turned the economy around. Minimum wage laws raised business costs and contributed to unemployment. Encouraging labor unions brought higher costs as well as an increase in strikes. The Smoot-Hawley Tariff and the unwieldy plan for repaying World War I debts helped to make the Depression worldwide. It took a long time for business to improve because most of the industrial world was in a slump.

6. *How should Christians relate to government programs?*

Several moral principles must be remembered. One is that any money accepted from the government had to be taken from someone else (through taxation), and that the one receiving the money has not earned it. A second is that involvement in government programs constitutes an unequal yoke for the Christian—to participate, he must submit to rules dictated by the government. A third is that government programs encourage trust in an earthly kingdom rather than in God. Since these are all violations of Scriptural principles, Christians need to avoid entanglement in government programs.

E. Chronology and Geography

1. *Tell what important events took place at the following times.*
   a. *1903* **The Wright brothers made the first successful airplane flight.**
   b. *1927* **Charles Lindbergh made the first solo flight across the Atlantic Ocean.**
   c. *October 1929* **The stock market crashed.**

2. *Name the three Republican presidents who served in the 1920s, and give the dates of the terms they served in office. Remember that an elected president's term begins in the year after the election.*

   Warren G. Harding, 1921–1923; Calvin Coolidge, 1923–1929; Herbert Hoover, 1929–1933

3. *How did the geography and climate of the Plains contribute to the Dust Bowl?*

   The region already had a dry climate. When the weather was unusually dry for several years, the soil became dust and winds carried it away. The flat plains allowed dust to blow far and wide.

SO FAR THIS YEAR (pages 546, 547)

A. Matching: Names and Dates

Not all the choices will be used.

k   1. *United States president during World War I.*

a   2. *Year when World War I began.*

j   3. *Agreement that punished Germany harshly and proposed a League of Nations.*

g   4. *American president's ideas for world peace after World War I.*

e   5. *Nations that fought on one side in World War I, including Russia, France, Great Britain, and Italy.*

f   6. *Nations that fought on the other side in World War I, including Germany, Austria-Hungary, Bulgaria, and Turkey.*

c   7. *Year when World War I ended.*

i   8. *International organization designed to maintain world peace.*

b   9. *Year when the United States entered World War I.*

a. *1914*
b. *1917*
c. *1918*
d. *1919*
e. *Allies*
f. *Central Powers*
g. *Fourteen Points*
h. *John J. Pershing*
i. *League of Nations*
j. *Treaty of Versailles*
k. *Woodrow Wilson*

B. Completion

Write the correct name or term that belongs on each blank.

10. *Northerners who went south to help in Reconstruction were called* **carpetbaggers**.

11. *Southern whites who took part in Reconstruction governments were known as* **scalawags**.

12. **Reconstruction** *describes the rebuilding and restoration of the South after the Civil War.*

13. *In a system called* **sharecropping**, *farm workers rent cropland and use a share of the crops to pay the rent.*

14. *Former slaves freed during and after the Civil War were called* **freedmen**.

15. *A term that describes social separation based on race is* **segregation**.

16. *Laws that restricted blacks after the Civil War were known as* **black codes** *or* **Jim Crow laws**.

17. *The constitutional amendment that granted blacks the right to vote was the* **Fifteenth** *Amendment.*

18. *The constitutional amendment that granted citizenship to blacks was the* **Fourteenth** *Amendment.*
19. **Alaska** *was a territory purchased in 1867 and known as "Seward's Folly."*
20. *The black leader who founded Tuskegee Institute was* **Booker T. Washington**.

C. Matching: Presidents

i 21. *President when the Compromise of 1850 passed; 1850–1853.*

e 22. *President when Japan opened ports to Americans; 1853–1857.*

g 23. *President when Southern states began to secede; 1857–1861.*

a 24. *President during the Civil War; 1861–1865.*

b 25. *President impeached in 1868; 1865–1869.*

k 26. *Former Civil War general who became president; 1869–1877.*

j 27. *President chosen after a disputed election in 1876; approved the Compromise of 1877; served from 1877 to 1881.*

h 28. *President assassinated a few months after taking office in 1881.*

d 29. *Took office in 1881 after the former president was assassinated; 1881–1885.*

f 30. *Only president to serve two nonconsecutive terms; 1885–1889 and 1893–1897.*

c 31. *President when the Sherman Antitrust Act and the McKinley Tariff Bill passed; 1889–1893.*

l 32. *President elected in 1896; opposed by William Jennings Bryan.*

a. *Abraham Lincoln*
b. *Andrew Johnson*
c. *Benjamin Harrison*
d. *Chester Arthur*
e. *Franklin Pierce*
f. *Grover Cleveland*
g. *James Buchanan*
h. *James Garfield*
i. *Millard Fillmore*
j. *Rutherford B. Hayes*
k. *Ulysses S. Grant*
l. *William McKinley*

D. Multiple Choice

Write the letter of the correct answer.

33. *A law that allowed settlers to claim 160 acres (65 ha) of land for farming was*
   a. *the Dawes Act.*　　　　c. *the Pacific Railroad Act.*
   b. the Homestead Act.

34. *A law that divided Indian reservations into family farms was*
   a. the Dawes Act.　　　　c. *the Pacific Railroad Act.*
   b. *the Homestead Act.*

35. *The man who invented barbed wire in 1874 was*
    a. *Joseph McCoy.*   c. *George Westinghouse.*
    b. *Charles Goodnight.*   **d. Joseph Glidden.**

36. *A colonel defeated at the Battle of the Little Bighorn was*
    a. George Custer.   c. *Crazy Horse.*
    b. *Sitting Bull.*   d. *Nelson Miles.*

37. *The first transcontinental railroad was joined at*
    a. *Wounded Knee, South Dakota.* **c. Promontory, Utah.**
    b. *Pikes Peak, Colorado.*

38. *The last great Apache leader, who surrendered in 1886, was*
    a. *Chief Joseph.*   **c. Geronimo.**
    b. *Black Kettle.*   d. *Sitting Bull.*

39. *One of the first cattle ranchers in Texas was*
    a. *Joseph McCoy.*   c. *Joseph Glidden.*
    b. Charles Goodnight.   d. *Charles Crocker.*

40. *A term that refers to cowboys taking cattle north to cattle towns is*
    a. "long drive."   c. *open range.*
    b. *Comstock Lode.*   d. *homesteading.*

25 The United States and World War II

Timeline:

- 1915
- Treaty of Versailles signed **1919**
- 1925
- 1935
- Spanish Civil War 1936–1939
- Rome-Berlin Axis made 1936
- World War II begins with German invasion of Poland (September 1) **1939**
- Battle of Britain 1940–1941
- Franklin D. Roosevelt elected to third term 1940
- United States declares war on Japan (December 8) **1941**
- Battle of Stalingrad; Americans land in North Africa 1942
- Allies invade Sicily and Italy 1943
- Roosevelt elected to fourth term 1944
- Allies invade France on D-day (June 6); Battle of the Bulge; Battle of the Philippine Sea; Battle of Leyte Gulf 1944
- Roosevelt dies; Harry S. Truman becomes president 1945
- Allies celebrate victory over Germany on V-E Day (May 8); Japan surrenders and World War II ends on V-J Day (September 2); United Nations founded **1945**
- Truman elected to second term 1948
- China becomes communist; NATO formed 1949
- Warsaw Pact formed 1955 — 1955

"Fear and a snare is come upon us, desolation and destruction."

Lamentations 3:47

Chapter 25 (pages 548–573)

The United States and World War II

Chapter Objectives

- To learn about events that led to World War II.
- To learn about the course of World War II before and after the United States entered the war.
- To learn about the defeat of Germany in World War II.
- To learn about the defeat of Japan in World War II, which included the first use of nuclear weapons.
- To understand the purposes and the organization of the United Nations.
- To understand the costs and consequences of World War II.
- To learn about the effects of the Cold War.
- To learn about Civilian Public Service during World War II.

To the Teacher

World War II holds a morbid fascination for those who study it. The colossal scale of the conflict, the magnitude of the suffering and destruction, and the horror of the Holocaust tend to grip the imagination and interest of people. Why did God permit such a destructive conflict? Finite mortals can never grasp God's high purposes, but we may be sure He had His reasons for allowing the war (Isaiah 55:8, 9). God knows the end from the beginning, and what He will yet bring out of World War II, we cannot know (Isaiah 46:9, 10). After more than half a century, we see developments unfolding that in earlier years would hardly have been imagined (such as the collapse of Communist governments in Eastern Europe). God uses the wrath of the nations to praise Him, and the remainder of wrath He restrains (Psalm 76:10).

Several points should be cleared up. Some people have blamed Roosevelt for the Pearl Harbor disaster, claiming that he knew the attack was coming and did nothing to stop it because he wanted an excuse for entering the war. Although it is true that Americans had broken the Japanese code and knew that an attack was planned, they did not know exactly where and when it would come. United States forces in the Pacific were alert, but they were not properly prepared. Although United States policies helped precipitate war, they did not cause the Japanese attack at Pearl Harbor.

Another idea is that World War II ended the Depression. In some ways, this is true—America became prosperous again during the war, and unemployment ended. But this was only through a flood of government spending, and it came with much restriction and rationing of goods. The real end of the Depression came after the war, when industries switched back to civilian production and turned out vast quantities of goods to meet the tremendous pent-up demand.

Most books and articles will likely be quite favorable to the United Nations. Caution your students on the fallacies of the ideas behind such an organization. The

United Nations has promoted internationalism (one-world government) as well as socialistic, New Age, and extreme environmental ideas. Yet we also recognize that God allowed the United Nations to be formed, and that it does provide an international forum which has probably prevented some disputes from escalating into war.

In relation to Civilian Public Service, this was an attempt to provide something better than what conscientious objectors faced in World War I. However, the Mennonite leaders in charge of the program were mostly liberal-minded men, and they worked much too closely with the government than conservative leaders were comfortable with. The latter participated in the program only because they felt dragged into it; and as they feared, many of their young men were lost to liberalism and worldliness.

This chapter lays a foundation for studying the decades after the 1940s. Be sure to give sufficient attention to the main points, for they are crucial to a proper understanding of more recent events.

Note on chapter test: Chapter 25 has its own test.

Christian Perspectives
- God is King over all, and He controls the affairs of nations for His purposes and His glory (Psalm 2).
- God has a purpose for what He does and allows, even though we may not understand His ways. God alone knows what the future holds and how the affairs of nations fit into His plans (Isaiah 46:9, 10; Isaiah 55:8, 9).
- God allows the nations to rage, but He also restrains their wrath (Psalm 76:10).
- The Holocaust shows how far man can fall when he rejects God. It also shows what happens when men such as Hitler have authority and encourage others to follow their evil nature (Jeremiah 17:9; Romans 3:10–18).
- Man's justice is not perfect, but God's judgment is always completely righteous and thorough—none will escape their dues unless they repent beforehand. God will give retribution for oppression (Proverbs 6:16–19; Ecclesiastes 4:1–3; 5:8; John 5:22, 27–29; Romans 12:19; Hebrews 10:31; Revelation 19:11–15).
- God makes a way for His people in trying times (1 Corinthians 10:13).

Further Study
- The attack on Pearl Harbor.
- The life of Adolf Hitler.
- The life of Franklin D. Roosevelt or Harry Truman.
- The D-day invasion of France.
- The fall of Germany.
- The development of the atomic bomb and the story of Hiroshima.
- Nonresistance in World War II.
- The development of the Cold War.

Chapter 25 Quiz

T F 1. Germany and the nations that helped it in World War II were called the Axis powers.

T F 2. Great Britain, the United States, and the nations that helped them in World War II were called the Allies.

T F 3. Nazism was the political system of nationalism and totalitarian control in Germany during World War II.

T F 4. The policy of maintaining peace by letting an aggressor have his way is called appeasement.

T F 5. The Holocaust was Hitler's destruction of millions of Jews and others in Europe.

T F 6. The United Nations is an international organization that has worked since World War I to maintain world peace.

T F 7. The North Atlantic Treaty Organization was formed by the communist nations of Eastern Europe after World War II.

T F 8. Civilian Public Service was the program of alternate service for conscientious objectors in World War II.

T F 9. Douglas MacArthur was the supreme commander of the Allied forces in Europe.

T F 10. Franklin D. Roosevelt was president of the United States during World War II.

T F 11. The "date of infamy," when the Japanese attacked Pearl Harbor, was December 7, 1940.

T F 12. Tokyo was the Japanese city destroyed by an atomic bomb in 1945.

T F 13. The D-day invasion of France took place on June 6, 1944.

T F 14. V-E Day was May 8, 1945.

T F 15. V-J Day was September 2, 1945.

Quiz Answers

1. **T**		9. **F**	
2. **T**		10. **T**	
3. **T**		11. **F**	
4. **T**		12. **F**	
5. **T**		13. **T**	
6. **F**		14. **T**	
7. **F**		15. **T**	
8. **T**			

Answer Key

Focus for Thought (page 556)

1. *Name the three major dictators who became involved in World War II, along with the country each one controlled, the date he came to power, and the kind of political party he represented.*
Benito Mussolini—Italy, 1922, Fascist
Joseph Stalin—Soviet Union, 1929, Communist
Adolf Hitler—Germany, 1933, Nazi

2. a. *Why was Hitler not punished for violating the Treaty of Versailles?*
A spirit of appeasement prevailed in Europe.
   b. *What nation did the Germans take over in 1938? in 1939?*
Hitler took over Austria in 1938 and Czechoslovakia in 1939.

3. *What surprise move did Hitler make in 1939, and why did he make it?*
Hitler made a nonaggression treaty in which the Nazis became allies with the Communists of Russia. He did this so that he would not need to fight the Soviet Union as well as Britain and France if war broke out over his invasion of Poland.

4. *What event marked the beginning of World War II, and when did it happen?*
Hitler's invasion of Poland on September 1, 1939

5. a. *List five countries that the Germans conquered in 1940, and three that they conquered in 1941.*
1940: Denmark, Norway, the Netherlands, Belgium, France; 1941: Yugoslavia, Greece, Crete
   b. *Which European nation resisted German air raids until Hitler gave up the idea of an invasion?*
Britain

6. a. *When and why did the Japanese attack Pearl Harbor?*
They attacked on December 7, 1941. They wanted to destroy the United States Pacific Fleet in Hawaii, which threatened their plans to expand the Japanese empire.
   b. *How did the United States respond to the attack on Pearl Harbor?*
On December 8, Congress declared war on Japan; and the United States entered World War II.

Focus for Thought (pages 563, 564)

7. a. *Describe some ways that World War II affected Americans in general.*
Factories were devoted to producing war materials, and operated day and night. Millions of new workers were hired. Many goods that civilians needed were rationed. Unnecessary travel was discouraged,

and a speed limit of 35 miles (56 km) per hour was enacted. Daylight-saving time was used. (Japanese internment could be mentioned.)

b. *How did it change the lives of women?*

Millions of women began working away from home.

8. *What two events in 1942 were turning points in the war against Germany?*

One was the Allied victory at Stalingrad in the Soviet Union. The other was the Allied victory in North Africa.

9. *Give the date and place of the invasion in which the Allies began to liberate France.*

on June 6, 1944 (D-day), at Normandy, France

10. a. *Which conflict was the largest European battle of World War II?*

the Battle of the Bulge

b. *What day did the Allies celebrate as the date of German surrender?*

May 8, 1945 (V-E Day)

11. *What was the Holocaust?*

It was Hitler's effort to exterminate the Jews and other races that he considered inferior. Over 10 million people were destroyed, of which about 6 million were Jews.

12. a. *How did the Allies force Japan to surrender?*

They dropped atomic bombs on Hiroshima and Nagasaki.

b. *Give the date of the surrender and the end of World War II.*

September 2, 1945

Focus for Thought (page 570)

13. *Describe some costs of World War II.*

World War II was the most destructive war in human history. About 55 million people perished as a result of the war. Weapons and war materials cost over one trillion dollars, and the cost of destruction to property was in the millions of dollars.

14. a. *Into what four zones was Germany divided after the war?*

Germany was divided into four zones occupied by the Soviet Union, the United States, Great Britain, and France.

b. *Why did Germany remain divided after 1955?*

The three Allies that occupied West Germany gave it full independence in 1955, but the Soviets refused to withdraw from their zone.

15. *Describe four important consequences of World War II.*

Large European empires dissolved, and new nations formed. The Cold War began. China and a number of European nations became communist. The Iron Curtain divided Europe. The world became

divided into the democratic nations (the free world), the communist nations, and the Third World. The North Atlantic Treaty Organization and the Warsaw Pact were formed. The nuclear age began.

16. *What is meant by the Cold War?*

The Cold War was a conflict in which the United States and the Soviet Union worked against one another without actually fighting.

17. a. *What services were performed by young men in CPS?*

The young men worked at soil conservation projects, building dams, digging ditches, planting trees, and fighting forest fires. Some worked in hospitals, and some volunteered to be "guinea pigs" in experiments to test new drugs.

b. *What were some difficulties that they faced?*

The men had to get along with each other in close quarters. Many grew bored with the work and with camp life. They did not receive pay, so they had to depend on money from their churches for support. It was hard to find enough ministers to visit the camps regularly. A camp often contained a mixture of different church groups, which made it hard for conservative COs to stand for their convictions.

HISTORICAL HIGHLIGHTS (pages 571–573)

A. Matching: People

a. *Adolf Hitler*

b. *Benito Mussolini*

c. *Chester Nimitz*

d. *Douglas MacArthur*

e. *Dwight D. Eisenhower*

f. *Franklin D. Roosevelt*

g. *Harry S. Truman*

h. *Joseph Stalin*

i. *Winston Churchill*

h   1. *Dictator of the Soviet Union.*

e   2. *Supreme commander of Allied forces in Europe.*

d   3. *American general in the Far East.*

f   4. *President during the Great Depression and most of World War II; first president to serve more than two terms.*

a   5. *Dictator of Germany.*

c   6. *American admiral in charge during the Battle of Midway.*

i   7. *Prime minister of Great Britain during World War II.*

b   8. *Dictator of Italy.*

g   9. *President who replaced Roosevelt and ordered use of the atomic bomb.*

B. Matching: Terms 1

a. *Allies*

b. *amphibious*

c. *appeasement*

d. *Axis*

e. *blitzkrieg*

f. *communism*

g. *D-day*

h. *demilitarized*

i. *fascism*

j. *historic peace churches*

k. *Holocaust*

l. *Nazism*

m. *totalitarian*

h 1. *Free of troops and weapons.*

l 2. *Political system of nationalism and totalitarian control in Germany.*

g 3. *Date when Allies invaded France in World War II.*

c 4. *Policy of maintaining peace by letting an aggressor have his way.*

e 5. *"Lightning war" in which German planes and tanks swiftly took control of a region.*

b 6. *Pertaining to a combination of naval and land forces.*

d 7. *Germany and the nations that helped it in World War II.*

m 8. *Having a single authority with absolute control of everything.*

k 9. *Hitler's destruction of millions of Jews and others in Europe.*

a 10. *Great Britain, the United States, and the nations that helped them.*

i 11. *Political system of totalitarian control in Italy.*

j 12. *Mennonites, Brethren, and Friends.*

f 13. *System based on the socialistic ideas of Karl Marx, in which the government owns most of a nation's land and resources.*

C. Matching: Terms 2

a. *Civilian Public Service*

b. *Cold War*

c. *free world*

d. *General Assembly*

e. *Iron Curtain*

f. *Manhattan Project*

g. *National Service Board
    for Religious Objectors*

h. *North Atlantic Treaty Organization*

i. *Security Council*

j. *Third World*

k. *United Nations*

l. *Warsaw Pact*

i 1. *Body of the United Nations responsible for keeping world peace.*

f 2. *Program to build the atomic bomb.*

j 3. *Nations not aligned with either the United States or the Soviet Union.*

a 4. *Program of alternate service for conscientious objectors.*

k 5. *International organization to maintain world peace and security.*

c   6. *General name for the United States and other democratic nations.*
h   7. *Military alliance formed by Western nations in 1949 to oppose communism.*
g   8. *Group that made plans for alternate service in work camps.*
l   9. *Military alliance formed by communist nations of Eastern Europe in 1955.*
d 10. *Body of the United Nations in which every member nation has a voice.*
b 11. *Conflict in which enemy nations worked against each other without actually fighting.*
e 12. *Term introduced by Churchill to describe the barrier between communist nations and free nations.*

D. Matching: Dates

a. *September 1, 1939*
b. *December 7, 1941*
c. *December 8, 1941*
d. *June 6, 1944*
e. *May 8, 1945*
f. *September 2, 1945*

d   1. *D-day—Allies invade France.*
f   2. *V-J Day—World War II ends.*
b   3. *"Date of infamy"—Japanese attack Pearl Harbor.*
e   4. *V-E Day—Allies celebrate Germany's surrender.*
a   5. *World War II begins.*
c   6. *United States declares war on Japan.*

E. Matching: Battles and Places

a. *Battle of Leyte Gulf*
b. *Battle of Midway*
c. *Battle of Stalingrad*
d. *Battle of the Atlantic*
e. *Battle of the Bulge*
f. *East Germany*
g. *Hiroshima*
h. *Nagasaki*
i. *Nuremberg*
j. *Pearl Harbor*
k. *West Germany*

g, h   1. *Japanese cities devastated by atomic bombs in 1945 (two answers).*
c   2. *Battle in Russia that marked a turning point in the war against Germany.*
f, k   3. *Parts into which Germany was divided (two answers).*
j   4. *Place of Japanese surprise attack that brought the United States into the war.*
i   5. *Place where Nazi leaders were tried for war crimes.*
a, b   6. *Naval battles in the Pacific that resulted in great losses for Japan (two answers).*
e   7. *Hitler's desperate attempt to divide the Allies and save Germany in 1944.*
d   8. *Struggle against German submarines that attacked Allied ships.*

F. Deeper Discussion

1. *Why could the United States not remain neutral in World War II?*

Though many Americans wanted to stay out of the war, they did not want to see a Nazi victory. German conquests in Europe in 1940 and the threat against Britain made it seem that the United States must support Britain. People viewed the conflict as one of freedom against tyranny, and they began to perceive a Nazi threat to the United States. (Hitler did have plans to eventually attack the United States.) With the unofficial involvement in the Atlantic war, the United States was already at war in all but name.

Also, Japanese aggression in the Pacific could not be reconciled with the previously agreed-upon Open Door Policy concerning China, nor with the security of the Philippines, which still belonged to the United States. War with the Japanese was almost inevitable in light of their attack on Pearl Harbor and their invasion of the Philippines.

2. *How was the attack on Pearl Harbor actually the downfall of Japan?*

The attack on Pearl Harbor seemed like a great success for the Japanese. But it drew the United States into the war; and in light of that nation's great productive capacity, Japan had little hope of winning. So in the long run, Japan was doomed to defeat by the attack on Pearl Harbor.

3. *How could human beings treat their fellow men as the Jews and others were treated during the Holocaust? (See Ecclesiastes 4:1; Jeremiah 17:9; and Romans 3:10–18.)*

It is because the heart of man is desperately wicked; every person has the capacity for great wickedness if his evil nature is unrestrained. Man is perverted and has "gone out of the way" (Romans 3:12). When such evil men come to power, their power corrupts them and they oppress the people—who can do little to resist their oppressors. Such treatment results when men forget God and "there is no fear of God before their eyes" (Romans 3:18).

4. *How were the results of World War II as bad as the problems that caused it?*

(a) Tyranny—World War II was fought to end the Nazi tyranny. But the war produced a Communist tyranny over large parts of Eastern Europe and in China. (b) Peace—World War II was fought to bring peace to the world, but the Cold War and numerous other wars broke out in its wake, such as the ones in Korea and Vietnam. (c) Security—The Germans, Italians, and Japanese threatened the world. But after World War II, the United States and soon the Soviet Union possessed nuclear weapons that threatened the world with mass destruction. Truly the nations "are like the troubled sea, when it cannot rest, whose waters cast up mire and dirt. There is no peace, saith my God, to the wicked" (Isaiah 57:20, 21).

5. *Contrast God's justice with man's justice as demonstrated at Nuremberg, Germany. (See Ecclesiastes 5:8; Romans 12:19; and Revelation 20:11–13.)*

Man's justice is incomplete. Despite the trials at Nuremberg, many war criminals were never brought to trial, and some completely escaped justice by hiding in other lands. But God's justice is complete—no man will ever escape it. All the wicked will stand before the throne of God and be judged according to their works.

Man's justice is not always equitable. Some men accused of war crimes were executed, some were imprisoned, and some were acquitted. Were they really not guilty? Man never knows for sure. But God's justice is always equitable, for He is omniscient. God knows exactly what every person has done, and He can mete out exactly the right penalty for every crime.

Man's standards of justice vary from one time and place to another. After the war, many of the downtrodden people rose up and committed atrocities on the Germans to avenge their sufferings. This kind of revenge is not true justice. But God's justice never varies; it is always the same regardless of time and place. Also, God extends grace that allows wicked men to repent and change their ways. (A Nazi named Hans Frank is said to have repented.) God is faithful and just in granting forgiveness to the penitent.

6. *Why did the Cold War break out after World War II?*

The Cold War broke out because of Communist domination and expansion in Eastern Europe. With Soviet armies in control of that region, Stalin began to break his promises and consolidate his control. He had promised to allow free elections in conquered nations; but instead, Communist governments came to power by Soviet force. Stalin and the Communists then sought to extend their control, as in Berlin, France, Italy, and Greece. When the United States and the free world determined to stop this expansion, the Cold War resulted.

G. Chronology and Geography

1. *The following list gives some main events leading up to World War II. Arrange the list in the proper order, and supply the year for each event.*

Germany occupies Austria   *Japan attacks China*
Germany occupies Czechoslovakia   *Japan invades Manchuria*
Hitler comes to power in Germany   *Mussolini comes to power in Italy*
Hitler occupies the Rhineland   *Spanish Civil War*
Italy invades Ethiopia   *World War II begins with German invasion of Poland (September 1)*

1922—Mussolini comes to power in Italy

1931—Japan invades Manchuria

1933—Hitler comes to power in Germany

1935—Italy invades Ethiopia

1936–1939—Spanish Civil War

1936—Hitler occupies the Rhineland

1937—Japan attacks China

1938—Germany occupies Austria

1939—Germany occupies Czechoslovakia

1939—World War II begins with German invasion of Poland (September 1)

2. a. *List the four main Allied nations.*

Great Britain, the United States, the Soviet Union, China

b. *List the three main Axis nations.*

Germany, Italy, Japan

3. *Tell what geographic features hindered the Allies in each of these cases.*

a. *the fighting in North Africa*

North Africa has a hot desert terrain.

b. *the liberation of Italy*

A chain of mountains, the Apennines, runs lengthwise through Italy. The Allies had to arrive by water.

c. *the D-day invasion of France*

The Allies had to make an enormous amphibious landing against a fortified coast. They had to move all supplies and soldiers for the operation by boat to Normandy. A high bluff lay not far from the beach of Normandy, aiding the German defenders.

d. *the invasion of Germany itself*

The Rhine River was a barrier to crossing into the heart of Germany.

e. *the Pacific war*

There were many islands separated by vast expanses of open sea.

26 Tranquil Years: America in the 1950s

1. YEARS OF CONFRONTATION

 The "Fair Deal"

 The Korean War

 Anti-communism

2. YEARS OF PROSPERITY

 Eisenhower's Administration

 The Prosperous Years

 The Civil Rights Movement

3. YEARS OF PEACE

 Eisenhower's Foreign Policy

 The Cold War in the 1950s

Harry S. Truman becomes president; United Nations (UN) founded 1945 — **1945**

Truman elected to second term 1948

North Atlantic Treaty Organization (NATO) formed 1949

Korean War begins (June 25) **1950** — **1950**

Twenty-second Amendment ratified 1951

Dwight D. Eisenhower elected president 1952

Korean War ends (July 27) **1953**

Southeast Asia Treaty Organization (SEATO) formed 1954

1955 — Black boycott of buses in Montgomery 1955

Eisenhower re-elected; conflict over the Suez Canal 1956

Sputnik 1 launched by Soviets 1957

Explorer 1 launched by Americans 1958

Alaska and Hawaii become states 1959

John F. Kennedy elected president 1960 — **1960**

"We looked for peace, but no good came; and for a time of health, and behold trouble!"

Jeremiah 8:15

Chapter 26 (pages 574–593)
TRANQUIL YEARS: AMERICA IN THE 1950S
Chapter Objectives

- To review important developments in the Cold War.
- To learn about domestic affairs during the Truman administration (1945–1953).
- To understand the cause, course, and effects of the Korean War.
- To understand communism, along with the anti-communist fervor in the United States during the 1950s.
- To learn about the domestic and foreign policies of the Eisenhower administration (1953–1961).
- To learn about important social changes in the 1950s that affected present American society.

To the Teacher

Fifties nostalgia has made the fifties seem like wonderful times to have lived in. But the reality is that life then had problems as well as blessings. This chapter actually covers the time period from 1945 to 1961, since Chapter 25 says little about domestic affairs from 1945 to 1950. One also needs to link foreign events with the effects of World War II to gain a clear picture. So be sure to include enough review of Chapter 25 to provide a good foundation for this chapter.

Note that Harry S. Truman wanted to extend the New Deal, but many Americans were not interested. They often did not appreciate Truman, even though he exhibited great courage in many aspects of the Cold War. Historians today take a much more favorable view of Truman. President Eisenhower did not want to end the New Deal social programs, but neither did he expand them significantly. He wanted to shift power from the federal government to the state and local levels. Eisenhower could be termed a moderate. Though some scholars criticize his policies, he did handle many issues successfully in the 1950s, especially issues concerning the Cold War.

Conflict with communism was a defining theme of the era. The Korean War was a UN action, and American soldiers went to war under the UN flag. This "world army" concept represented a clear departure from the isolationism of earlier years. As regards the MacArthur controversy, Truman simply wanted to contain communism, but General MacArthur wanted to drive it back—even at the risk of war with China and the Soviet Union. Truman wanted a limited war, but MacArthur wanted to use all the force necessary to defeat the Communists. General MacArthur was dismissed because of his outspoken opposition—though he did not actually disobey the president. Truman's action had two important effects: (1) it showed that the civilian president is commander-in-chief with power over the military forces; and (2) it introduced the concept of limited war, which continued in the Vietnam War.

Nonresistance during the Korean War is covered in Chapter 27, along with the I-W system used during the Vietnam War.

Note on chapter test: There is a single test for Chapters 26 and 27.

Christian Perspectives

- Once again, the affairs of nations demonstrate their beastly character—in the Cold War, the Korean War, and the arms race (Daniel 7, 8).
- Christians do not depend on military strength for their security. National security is more dependent on God's overruling hand than on military power (Psalm 20:7; 118:8, 9; 127:1).
- Communism is a godless system that seeks to control the hearts and minds of men. This is what makes the system totalitarian. Communists also oppose the spread of the Gospel, which makes it difficult to reach people under that system. On the other hand, saving people from communism is not as important as saving them from sin and its eternal consequences.
- Satan has used television to distract and deceive multitudes of people.
- God may allow man to discover many new medical techniques, but human life is still in God's hands (Psalm 90:10).
- The culture of this world, such as rock music, expresses the evil imaginations of man's heart and is part of the "lust of the flesh" (Proverbs 6:16–19; 1 John 2:16).
- The Christian must respect all men, regardless of race. The Christian does not use nonviolent protest or other methods of the civil rights movement to fight social injustices. True nonresistance is the Bible way (Matthew 5:38–48).

Further Study

- The lives of Harry S. Truman and Dwight D. Eisenhower. (Eisenhower had Old Order River Brethren background.)
- The Korean War.
- The early years of Richard M. Nixon's life.
- Stories of companies such as Holiday Inn and McDonald's.
- The civil rights movement and the life of Martin Luther King, Jr.
- The Cold War.
- The space race.
- The U-2 incident.

Chapter 26 Quiz

Not all the choices will be used.

a. Alaska and Hawaii
b. *Brown v. Board of Education of Topeka*
c. civil rights movement
d. desegregation
e. Douglas MacArthur
f. Dwight D. Eisenhower

g. Fair Deal
h. Harry S. Truman
i. Interstate Highway Act
j. Martin Luther King, Jr.
k. 1950–1953
l. 1945–1953

____ 1. President through most of the 1950s (1953–1961).

____ 2. Years of the Korean War.

____ 3. Measure passed in 1956 to build a network of interstate highways.

____ 4. General in the Korean War who was dismissed by President Truman.

____ 5. Joined the Union in 1959.

____ 6. Drive to give blacks equal status with whites.

____ 7. Case in which separate but equal facilities for blacks were declared unconstitutional.

____ 8. Black minister who led the civil rights movement and promoted non-violent resistance.

____ 9. President who served from 1945 to 1953, after Franklin D. Roosevelt.

____ 10. Ending of separation by race.

____ 11. President Truman's program of social reforms.

Quiz Answers

1. **f**
2. **k**
3. **i**
4. **e**
5. **a**
6. **c**
7. **b**
8. **j**
9. **h**
10. **d**
11. **g**

Answer Key

Focus for Thought (pages 581, 582)

1. *How did President Truman try to help black people?*
Truman set up a committee on civil rights that proposed stronger civil rights laws. He gained Congressional approval of laws against lynching and poll taxes. He ordered the desegregation of the military forces.

2. *What did the Twenty-second Amendment provide for?*
It stated that a president could serve no more than two terms.

3. *Why were Americans distressed at China's fall to communism?*
The United States had a long history of friendship with China. (Also, if a large nation like China could fall to communism, people were afraid the United States could fall too.)

4. *How and when did the Korean War begin?*
It began when North Korean forces invaded South Korea on June 25, 1950.

5. a. *Why did President Truman want to fight only a limited war in Korea?*
Truman was afraid that if he fought an all-out war involving China, the Soviet Union would come to China's aid, and then World War III might begin.

   b. *What happened when General MacArthur disagreed with the president?*
General MacArthur voiced his disagreement so strongly that the president dismissed him as commander.

6. *Describe two effects of the Korean War.*
(Any two.) Millions of people were killed. Thousands of homes and factories were destroyed. The border between the two Koreas remained about where it had been before the war. The war showed that the United States intended to oppose communism anywhere in the world.

7. *Why were Americans afraid that Communists might take over America?*
China had become communist, and the Korean War made it clear that the Communists intended to expand their domain. Several spy cases seemed to show that Communists were working to overthrow the United States government.

Focus for Thought (page 585)

8. *Give some details about the following developments of the 1950s.*
   a. *the growing middle class*
Rising wages and productivity pushed more and more families into

the middle class. Families could afford bigger houses, better appliances, and new furniture.

b. *improved technology*

Better and cheaper products became available. Synthetic fabrics, such as nylon, began replacing natural fibers; and plastics replaced wood and metal. The first electronic computer was built.

c. *television*

The number of television sets increased until 90 percent of American families had one by 1960. Television brought commercial advertisements, political candidates, and professional sports right into American homes. Television began to "distract, delude, amuse, and insulate" millions of people.

d. *medical advances*

Dr. Jonas Salk introduced a vaccine for polio. Development of antibiotics helped control disease. The life expectancy of Americans approached seventy years.

e. *greater mobility*

Large numbers of Americans moved to housing developments in the suburbs. People bought more and bigger automobiles. Hundreds of miles of better highways were built. Chains of motels and fast-food restaurants sprang up.

9. *Describe the social conformity of the 1950s.*

In the suburbs, houses looked very similar and people followed similar lifestyles. Wives stayed at home and took care of the children while husbands worked for large companies.

10. *How did the Supreme Court change after Earl Warren became chief justice?*

The Warren Court became an activist court by making rulings that were the equivalent of new laws passed by Congress.

11. a. *What was the main idea of the Brown Decision?*

Segregation of black and white children in public schools was unconstitutional. "Separate educational facilities are inherently unequal."

b. *What effect did it have on schools?*

Many states that had segregated facilities for education took action to integrate their schools.

12. a. *What was the approach of Martin Luther King, Jr., in seeking rights for blacks?*

King promoted the use of nonviolent resistance, which included boycotts, protest marches, and civil disobedience.

b. *How is this different from Biblical nonresistance?*
Nonviolent resistance is still resistance. Biblical nonresistance avoids using force of any kind to gain one's ends.

Focus for Thought (page 588)

13. *How was Eisenhower's foreign policy different from the containment of communism that President Truman had promoted?*
Instead of merely keeping communism from spreading, Eisenhower wanted to liberate countries already under Communist rule.

14. a. *Why did American leaders work so hard against communism in Southeast Asia?*
The leaders feared that if one nation fell to communism, nearby nations would also fall (the domino theory).
b. *What actions were taken to oppose communism?*
The United States gave millions of dollars to help South Vietnam and Laos against the Communist guerrillas. The Southeast Asia Treaty Organization was formed in 1954.

15. a. *Why did Israel, Britain, and France go to war against Egypt in 1956?*
Egypt had seized the Suez Canal, which was a vital link for European oil supplies.
b. *What was stated in the Eisenhower Doctrine?*
It gave the president authority to send armed forces to any nation in the Middle East that requested military aid against Communist attack.

16. *How did Cuba become a communist nation?*
Fidel Castro took control of the government in 1959. He declared himself a Communist, became a Soviet ally, and accepted Soviet aid.

17. a. *Describe the arms race.*
In the arms race, the United States and the Soviet Union each tried to build more nuclear weapons than the other.
b. *Tell about the first successful satellite that the Soviets launched, and the first one that the Americans launched.*
The first Soviet satellite was *Sputnik 1*, launched in October 1957. The first American satellite was *Explorer 1*, launched in January 1958.

18. a. *How did Cold War tensions ease somewhat in the 1950s?*
Eisenhower and Khrushchev held several meetings in which tensions were eased.
b. *What spoiled the apparent progress?*
The Soviets shot down a U-2 plane that was spying on the Soviet Union.

HISTORICAL HIGHLIGHTS (pages 589–591)

A. People

a. *Alger Hiss*
b. *Douglas MacArthur*
c. *Dwight D. Eisenhower*
d. *Earl Warren*
e. *Fidel Castro*

f. *Harry S. Truman*
g. *Martin Luther King, Jr.*
h. *Nikita Khrushchev*
i. *Richard M. Nixon*
j. *Rosa Parks*

b 1. *General in the Korean War who was dismissed by President Truman.*
i 2. *Vice president under Dwight D. Eisenhower who met with Khrushchev.*
e 3. *Dictator who took over Cuba in 1959 and made it a Communist nation.*
g 4. *Black minister who led the civil rights movement and promoted nonviolent resistance.*
f 5. *President who served from 1945 to 1953, after Franklin D. Roosevelt.*
j 6. *Black person arrested for not yielding a bus seat to a white person.*
c 7. *President during most of the 1950s; served from 1953 to 1961.*
h 8. *Leader of the Soviet Union who succeeded Joseph Stalin.*
d 9. *Chief justice when the Supreme Court became more activist in the 1950s.*
a 10. *Former state department official accused of Communist activities and imprisoned for perjury.*

B. Terms 1

a. *arms race*
b. *Central Intelligence Agency*
c. *containment*
d. *demilitarized zone*
e. *domino theory*

f. *Eisenhower Doctrine*
g. *Korean War*
h. *massive retaliation*
i. *space race*
j. *summit meeting*

j 1. *Conference between heads of state.*
f 2. *Policy by which the president could send armed forces to countries of the Middle East that requested help against communism.*
e 3. *Idea that if one nation in a region falls to communism, nearby nations will also fall.*
b 4. *United States spy organization.*
d 5. *Place where no military activity is allowed.*
a 6. *Competition between the United States and the Soviet Union in building up a supply of weapons.*
h 7. *Threat of responding with nuclear weapons in case of attack on an American ally.*

c 8. *Policy of trying to keep communism from spreading.*

i 9. *Competition in which the United States and the Soviet Union tried to outdo each other in achievements in outer space.*

g 10. *Conflict in which UN forces opposed Communist aggression.*

C. Terms 2

a. *activist court*
b. *civil rights movement*
c. *desegregation*
d. *Fair Deal*
e. Brown v. Board of Education of Topeka
f. *Department of Health, Education, and Welfare*
g. *Interstate Highway Act*
h. *National Aeronautics and Space Administration*
i. *Twenty-second Amendment*

b 1. *Drive to give blacks equal status with whites.*

g 2. *Measure passed in 1956 to build a network of interstate highways.*

h 3. *Agency established in 1958 to direct the American space program.*

c 4. *Ending of separation by race.*

f 5. *Department of the Cabinet established to oversee federal aid.*

d 6. *President Truman's program of social reforms.*

i 7. *Measure limiting a president's administration to two terms.*

a 8. *Inclined to make decisions that are the equivalent of new laws.*

e 9. *Case in which separate but equal facilities for blacks were declared unconstitutional.*

D. Places and Dates

Not all the choices will be used.

a. *Alaska*
b. *Cuba*
c. *Hawaii*
d. *North Korea*
e. *South Korea*
f. *Vietnam*
g. *June 25, 1950*
h. *1945–1953*
i. *1953–1961*
j. *July 27, 1953*
k. *1956*
l. *1959*

d 1. *Communist nation that invaded its neighbor in 1950.*

a, c 2. *States added to the Union during Eisenhower's administration (two answers).*

h 3. *Years of the Truman administration.*

e 4. *Nation that was invaded by its Communist neighbor in 1950.*

i 5. *Years of the Eisenhower administration.*

f 6. *Nation aided by the United States in opposing Communist guerrillas.*

g, j 7. *Beginning and ending dates of the Korean War (two answers).*

l 8. *Year when two new states were admitted to the Union.*

E. Deeper Discussion

1. *Why did the United States consider it important to oppose communism everywhere in the world, even in faraway places such as Southeast Asia?*

   According to the domino theory, the fall of one nation to communism meant that its neighbors would also fall one by one, like a row of dominoes. So the United States thought it had to oppose communism wherever it existed. Another reason is that losing a country to communism was damaging to a president's political reputation. Republicans blamed Truman for losing China, so other presidents tried hard not to lose more nations to communism.

2. *Why did the United States and the Soviet Union engage in an arms race?*

   Each side was fearful and suspicious of the other. So each side had to make itself stronger than the other, or at least so strong that the other would not dare to attack. U-2 flights and other spy operations were considered necessary to gauge the strength of the opposite side.

3. *How might an activist Supreme Court upset the delicate balance of powers in the American system of federal government?*

   This might happen in two ways. First, an activist Supreme Court could infringe upon the division of powers between the states and the federal government. For example, the Court issued orders that forced states to desegregate their schools whether they wanted to or not. This tended to make the federal government stronger at the expense of state governments. Calling out federal soldiers to enforce Court rulings, as occurred in Arkansas, illustrates this basic conflict. When the states did not want to cooperate, they were compelled by force.

   Second, an activist Court could upset the balance of powers among the three branches of federal government. By issuing orders instead of restricting itself to deciding cases about laws, the Supreme Court usurped powers that belonged to the legislative branch. If the Court can make laws, then it is an oligarchy (rule by a few men), since the justices are not elected but appointed. An activist Court made rulings that eliminated Bible reading and prayer from public schools, made it harder to punish criminals, and made abortions legal. (Some of these matters are discussed in the next chapter.)

4. *Evaluate the goals and methods of the civil rights movement.*

   The civil rights movement aimed to end segregation, especially the legally sanctioned segregation in the South. Supporters wanted to make society more equal so that blacks and whites would be treated alike. These goals are worthy, since all people should be

treated with respect regardless of race or color. To segregate people suggests that one group has less value than the other. "God is no respecter of persons."

The methods of the civil rights movement involved court challenges, boycotts, nonviolent protests, and civil disobedience. These methods are inconsistent with New Testament nonresistance, since they are designed to bring changes by force rather than by appeal or by working through the legislative process. Civil rights leaders used the argument that they had waited for one hundred years after the Civil War and had still not received fair treatment, which was true. However, their methods resulted in clashes and violence with whites, as the conflict in Arkansas demonstrated. In contrast, the Christian must not hold racial prejudice but must love all men, just as Christ loves all men.

F. Chronology and Geography

1. *The United States became a global power after World War II.*

   a. *What defense alliance did the United States form in Europe? in Southeast Asia?*

   The United States formed the North Atlantic Treaty Organization (NATO) in Europe. It formed the Southeast Asia Treaty Organization (SEATO) in Southeast Asia.

   b. *List six nations in whose affairs the United States became directly involved.*

   The United States became involved in the affairs of Korea, Iran, Guatemala, Vietnam, Laos, and Cuba.

2. *Review all the presidents and their terms from George Washington through Dwight D. Eisenhower by writing from memory their names and the dates they were in office.*

   (Remember that an elected president's term begins in the year after the election. Also note that presidents before Franklin D. Roosevelt were inaugurated on March 4, and those after him on January 20.)

   (Optional exercise.)

   1. George Washington—1789–1797

   2. John Adams—1797–1801

   3. Thomas Jefferson—1801–1809

   4. James Madison—1809–1817

   5. James Monroe—1817–1825

   6. John Quincy Adams—1825–1829

7. Andrew Jackson—1829–1837
8. Martin Van Buren—1837–1841
9. William Henry Harrison—1841
10. John Tyler—1841–1845
11. James Polk—1845–1849
12. Zachary Taylor—1849–1850
13. Millard Fillmore—1850–1853
14. Franklin Pierce—1853–1857
15. James Buchanan—1857–1861
16. Abraham Lincoln—1861–1865
17. Andrew Johnson—1865–1869
18. Ulysses S. Grant—1869–1877
19. Rutherford B. Hayes—1877–1881
20. James A. Garfield—1881
21. Chester A. Arthur—1881–1885
22. Grover Cleveland—1885–1889
23. Benjamin Harrison—1889–1893
24. Grover Cleveland—1893–1897
25. William McKinley—1897–1901
26. Theodore Roosevelt—1901–1909
27. William Howard Taft—1909–1913
28. Woodrow Wilson—1913–1921
29. Warren G. Harding—1921–1923
30. Calvin Coolidge—1923–1929
31. Herbert Hoover—1929–1933
32. Franklin D. Roosevelt—1933–1945
33. Harry S. Truman—1945–1953
34. Dwight D. Eisenhower—1953–1961

3. *Label Alaska and Hawaii (and their dates of admission) on your map entitled "The States of the United States." Color them the same color as the other states admitted in the 1900s. Be sure you know the names and locations of all the states.*

(Check completed maps for accuracy and neatness. Sometime before the end of the course, make copies of Map A and have students fill in the states by memory.)

SO FAR THIS YEAR (pages 592, 593)

A. Matching: Terms

a. *appeasement*

b. *Allies*

c. *Axis*

d. *business cycle*

e. *Civilian Public Service*

f. *Cold War*

g. *Great Depression*

h. *Holocaust*

i. *Iron Curtain*

j. *modernism*

k. *Nazism*

l. *New Deal*

m. *North Atlantic Treaty Organization*

n. *Prohibition*

· o. *Third World*

p. *Twentieth Amendment*

q. *Twenty-first Amendment*

r. *United Nations*

j   1. *Set of beliefs including the theory of evolution, rejection of the supernatural, and acceptance of science as the only source of truth.*

l   2. *Government programs designed to end the Depression.*

n   3. *Period when alcoholic drinks were outlawed.*

g   4. *Long economic downturn from 1929 to 1939.*

d   5. *Periodic swing between prosperity and decline in the economy.*

q   6. *Measure that ended the ban on alcoholic drinks.*

p   7. *Measure that shortened the lame-duck period after presidential elections.*

c   8. *Germany and the nations that helped it in World War II.*

k   9. *Political system of nationalism and totalitarian control in Germany.*

r   10. *International organization to maintain world peace.*

h   11. *Hitler's destruction of millions of Jews and others in Europe.*

f   12. *Conflict in which enemy nations opposed each other without fighting.*

a   13. *Policy of maintaining peace by letting an aggressor have his way.*

m   14. *Military alliance formed by Western nations in 1949 to oppose communism.*

b   15. *Great Britain, the United States, and the nations helping them in World War II.*

e   16. *Program of alternate service for conscientious objectors in World War II.*

o   17. *Nations not aligned with either the United States or the Soviet Union.*

i   18. *Barrier to communication and travel between communist nations and free nations.*

B. Completion

Write the correct name or date for each description.

Wilbur and Orville Wright   19. *Made the first successful flight with a heavier-than-air machine in 1903.*

Henry Ford	20. *Made cars available to the masses by introducing the Model T.*
Warren G. Harding	21. *President from 1921 to 1923; died in office.*
Calvin Coolidge	22. *Took office after the death of the previous president; served from 1923 to 1929.*
Herbert Hoover	23. *President when the Great Depression began; served from 1929 to 1933.*
Franklin D. Roosevelt	24. *President during the Great Depression and most of World War II; first president to serve more than two terms.*
Dwight D. Eisenhower	25. *Supreme commander of the Allied forces in Europe in World War II.*
Douglas MacArthur	26. *American general in the Far East who helped to liberate the Philippines.*
Harry S. Truman	27. *President who replaced Roosevelt and ordered use of the atomic bomb.*
September 1, 1939	28. *Date when World War II began.*
December 7, 1941	29. *Date when Pearl Harbor was attacked.*
June 6, 1944	30. *Date of the D-day invasion of France.*
September 2, 1945	31. *Date when World War II ended (V-J Day).*

C. Filling the Blanks: American Government

Not all the choices will be used.

Articles of Confederation	*James Madison*
Bill of Rights	*judicial*
checks and balances	*monarchy*
constitution	*legislative*
executive	*republic*
Electoral College	*separation of powers*
federal	*Thomas Jefferson*
impeach	*veto*

32. *As a limit to the power of Congress, the president may* **veto** *a law that Congress has passed.*

33. *A written plan of government is called a* **constitution**.

34. *The "father of the Constitution" and fourth president of the United States was* **James Madison**.

35. *A* **republic** *is a nation with a government by elected representatives and without a king or queen.*

36. *The first ten amendments to the Constitution, added in 1791, are called the* **Bill of Rights**.

37. *The limits that the different government branches place on each other are called* **checks and balances**.
38. *The branch of government that decides cases about laws is the* **judicial** *branch.*
39. *The term* **separation of powers** *describes the division of government into three branches.*
40. *The branch of government that proposes new laws is the* **legislative** *branch.*
41. *The* **Electoral College** *is the group of men who actually elect the president.*
42. *In a* **federal** *system of government, powers are divided between the states and the national government.*
43. *The branch of government that enacts and enforces laws is the* **executive** *branch.*
44. *Congress may* **impeach** *a president, or bring him to trial for misconduct in office.*

D. True or False

Write whether each statement is true *(T)* or false *(F)*. If it is false, write the word or phrase that should replace the underlined part.

F; Democratic-Republicans 45. *The* <u>Federalists</u> *were a political party that favored strict interpretation and limited government.*

T 46. *The* <u>Monroe Doctrine</u> *was a declaration about involvement of European and American nations in each other's affairs.*

T 47. *The* <u>Treaty of Ghent</u> *ended the War of 1812.*

F; Pinckney Treaty 48. *The* <u>Adams-Onís Treaty</u> *settled differences with Spain in 1795.*

F; states' rights 49. <u>Sectionalism</u> *is the idea that states are supreme over the federal government.*

T 50. *The* <u>spoils system</u> *refers to the practice in which the winner of an election rewards his supporters with government positions.*

T 51. *The term* <u>judicial review</u> *describes the Supreme Court's power to declare a law unconstitutional.*

F; 1820 52. *The Missouri Compromise settled the issue of slavery in* <u>1850</u>.

T 53. <u>Alexander Hamilton</u>, *a Federalist leader, was the first secretary of the treasury.*

F; Daniel Boone 54. <u>Meriwether Lewis and William Clark</u> *opened the Wilderness Road to Kentucky.*

T 55. <u>John Marshall</u> *was an important chief justice who strengthened the Supreme Court in the early 1800s.*

27 Turbulent Years: America in the 1960s

1. Crisis and Tragedy

   Kennedy and the Cold War

   Kennedy and the "New Frontier"

   Assassination of President Kennedy

2. Change and Upheaval

   Johnson and the "Great Society"

   Social Changes in the 1960s

3. Discord, War, and Nonresistance

   Johnson and the Vietnam War

   Nixon and the Vietnam War

   Nonresistance

1950

I-W program begins 1952

1955

1960 John F. Kennedy elected president 1960

Berlin crisis; Twenty-third Amendment
ratified   1961

Supreme Court decisions end prayer
and Bible reading in public schools
1962

John Glenn becomes first American to orbit
the earth; Cuban missile crisis   1962

Kennedy assassinated;
Lyndon B. Johnson becomes
president   1963

Johnson re-elected; Twenty-fourth Amendment ratified;
Tonkin Gulf Resolution   1964

1965 Medicare and Medicaid established;
bombing of North Vietnam begins 1965

Miranda ruling on criminal's rights 1966

Twenty-fifth Amendment ratified 1967

(June) Tet Offensive in Vietnam 1968

Martin Luther King, Jr., assassinated (April); Robert Kennedy
assassinated; Richard M. Nixon elected president   1968

1970 Invasion of Cambodia; protests at Kent State
and other universities   1970

Twenty-sixth Amendment ratified 1971

Nixon re-elected 1972

United States withdraws from Vietnam;
military draft ends   **1973**

South Vietnam, Laos, and Cambodia
fall to the Communists   1975   1975

*"Their feet run to evil; . . . wasting and destruction
are in their paths. The way of peace they know not;
and there is no judgment in their goings."*

Isaiah 59:7, 8

Chapter 27 (pages 594–612)

TURBULENT YEARS: AMERICA IN THE 1960s

Chapter Objectives

- To grasp the turmoil and changes of the 1960s.
- To learn about domestic and foreign affairs during the Kennedy administration, and about Kennedy's assassination.
- To learn about Johnson's Great Society programs.
- To learn about the Vietnam War during the Johnson and Nixon administrations, and the bitter effects of the war.
- To study and appreciate nonresistance during the Korean and Vietnam wars.
- To learn about the apostasy and the conservative revival in the Mennonite Church during the 1950s and 1960s.

To the Teacher

The sixties *were* turbulent times. Before that, society at least had basic standards of right and wrong, of what was acceptable and what was not. But during the sixties, that gave way to a "do your own thing" mentality—which continues to be evident in areas such as dress and morals. Much of the change resulted from the introduction of humanistic, evolutionary ideas that denied God a place in human affairs and denied absolute truth. Sadly, the Mennonite Church as a denomination was unable to stand against these changes, and it apostatized except for a conservative remnant. Although the scene appeared very bleak, be sure to emphasize that many people still embraced traditional values and were aghast at the radical changes.

Confrontation with communism was another hallmark of the sixties. The Democratic presidents, Kennedy and Johnson, did not want to be charged by Republicans with losing ground to the Communists. So they staunchly stood up against the Communists in Berlin, Cuba, and Vietnam. The Cuban missile crisis may have been as close as the world ever came to a nuclear holocaust.

Be aware that the issues concerning Kennedy's assassination are by no means settled in the minds of many people. Some writers are sure that Oswald alone did the shooting, and others are just as sure that a conspiracy was involved in the assassination. The controversy is such that student research on the subject is not likely to be profitable.

In Vietnam, the United States tried again to maintain a limited war, as in Korea. The Vietnam War became a focal point for unrest and rebellion, especially among youth. As it dragged on, the cost in inflation, higher taxes, military supplies, and casualties rose to a point where the American people no longer considered the war worth the cost. Nixon's tough approach to Vietnam did seem to bring the North Vietnamese to the bargaining table, so he had in a measure achieved peace with honor. Yet subsequent events showed that there was little real peace and even less honor as South Vietnam collapsed. Especially emphasize the divisive bitterness that resulted from the Vietnam War.

Concerning I-W service, do not dwell only on the negative side, for it also had its good points. As church standards declined during the sixties, however, the dangers of I-W increased. Discussing I-W with those who went through it can be especially interesting and enlightening. Perhaps you could have someone come in to give a talk on his experiences. Likewise, it can be revealing to hear about the Mennonite apostasy from someone who lived through it. We should cherish the convictions that moved men of faith to leave apostate settings and re-establish a conservative church life. Be sensitive to different viewpoints as you discuss this section.

Note on chapter test: There is a single test for Chapters 26 and 27.

Christian Perspectives
- True peace is found only in Christ, the Prince of Peace. Man's search for peace is vain outside of Christ (Isaiah 57:20, 21).
- When a society rejects God and His absolute truth, it will decline as its morals decay (Proverbs 14:34).
- Rebellion against constituted authority results in chaos, violence, and tragedy, as in the violent riots of blacks during the civil rights movement and of college students during the Vietnam War.
- The church must be on guard against apostasy and against influences from the surrounding society.
- We should be thankful for God's blessing in enabling a conservative revival in this time.
- The need for nonresistance continues in everyday life, even though a draft may not be in effect.

Further Study
- The presidencies of Kennedy, Johnson, and Nixon.
- The assassination of Kennedy. (Beware of far-fetched and radical theories, since much controversy surrounds this subject.)
- The Vietnam War.
- The Cold War, including Berlin and Cuba, and especially the Cuban missile crisis.
- Domestic issues such as Supreme Court rulings, the Great Society, social changes, and the civil rights movement.
- I-W service. (If possible, talk to someone who experienced this personally.)
- The Mennonite-school movement and the expansion of Mennonite missions.
- The beginning of the conservative Mennonite movements. (Someone may be able to give information about this from personal experience.)

Chapter 27 Quiz

Write the correct name or term for each description.

1. President Johnson's social programs.

2. Incident in which Soviet weapons threatened United States security in 1962.

3. Young people who rebelled against established values and social customs in the 1960s.

4. President elected in 1960 and assassinated in 1963.

5. President in office when United States troops withdrew from Vietnam in 1973.

6. Measure that gave President Johnson power to use military force in Vietnam.

7. Program for conscientious objectors from the 1950s to the 1970s.

8. Communist guerrilla fighters in South Vietnam.

Quiz Answers

1. **Great Society**
2. **Cuban missile crisis**
3. **counterculture**
4. **John F. Kennedy**
5. **Richard M. Nixon**
6. **Tonkin Gulf Resolution**
7. **I-W service**
8. **Viet Cong**

Answer Key

Focus for Thought (page 600)

1. *What was President Kennedy's goal in establishing the Peace Corps?*
   He wanted to improve living conditions in poor countries so that they would be strengthened against communism.

2. *Why did the Communists build the Berlin Wall?*
   They wanted to keep the people in East Germany from escaping communism by going to East Berlin and then crossing to West Berlin.

3. *Who was the first American to orbit the earth, and when did he accomplish this?*
   John Glenn; in February 1962

4. *Explain what caused the Cuban missile crisis, and how it was resolved.*
   The crisis arose when the Soviet Union placed missiles in Cuba that could launch a nuclear attack on the United States. It was resolved when Kennedy and Khrushchev reached an agreement in which Kennedy promised that the United States would not invade Cuba if the Soviets withdrew the missiles. (Kennedy also agreed secretly to remove American missiles stationed in Turkey.)

5. *How did white people oppose the blacks' campaign for equal rights in the early 1960s?*
   White people used violence to oppose the blacks' campaign. In Alabama, a bus was burned at Anniston and freedom riders were assaulted in Birmingham. When blacks took part in marches to end segregation in Birmingham, the local police attacked them with high-pressure fire hoses, electric cattle prods, and fierce dogs.

6. *How was John Kennedy's presidency cut short?*
   He was assassinated on November 22, 1963.

Focus for Thought (pages 604, 605)

7. *Which part of Johnson's Great Society*
   a. *provided health care for poor people?*
   Medicaid
   b. *provided health care for the elderly?*
   Medicare
   c. *provided money to improve cities?*
   Model Cities Act

8. *What were some concerns about the Great Society programs?*
   Government spending increased greatly. Federal revenues were diverted from other purposes into welfare programs. Welfare

encouraged people to depend on government handouts when they could have been working to support themselves.

9. *What was the outcome of the Supreme Court cases involving*

   a. *separation of church and state?*

   Public schools were no longer allowed to hold sessions of Bible reading and prayer.

   b. *civil rights in relation to schools?*

   Children were bused from one community to another so that schools would have a mix of white and black students.

   c. *criminals' rights?*

   Before being questioned about a crime, a suspect must be informed of his right to remain silent and to have a lawyer present. (This decision seemed to give criminals so many rights that it actually encouraged crime.)

10. *How were the methods used in the riots of the late 1960s different from the methods promoted by Martin Luther King, Jr.?*

    The riots included much violence, whereas King had promoted the use of nonviolent methods.

11. *What were some expressions of rebellion among youth of the 1960s? of women?*

    Youth rebelled against traditional values and authority. Many became "hippies," who adopted long hair for men, wore faded blue jeans, and used mind-altering drugs such as marijuana, LSD, and heroin. Some lived in communes where they emphasized personal freedom, listened to rock music, and promoted their own version of "love" and "peace."

    Women protested because they rarely held positions of leadership and because they received less pay for doing the same work as men. They campaigned for a Constitutional amendment to guarantee women the same rights as men.

Focus for Thought (page 610)

12. *How did President Johnson gain authority to take military action in Vietnam?*

    Congress approved the Tonkin Gulf Resolution, which authorized the president to use military force in Vietnam.

13. *Why did Americans begin opposing the Vietnam War after the Tet Offensive?*

    People realized that the Communists were much stronger than they had thought, and that Johnson had been concealing the extent of American involvement. They were upset because of all the killing and destruction in the war.

14. a. *What was President Nixon's goal regarding the Vietnam War?*

Nixon's goal was to achieve "peace with honor" in Vietnam rather than withdrawing in defeat. (In his election campaign, Nixon had promised to end the war in Vietnam.)

b. *How did he expand the war in 1970 and 1971?*

Americans invaded Cambodia in 1970 and Laos in 1971.

15. a. *What were three results of the Vietnam War?*

(Any three.) Thousands of people were wounded or killed. Vietnam was devastated, and one-third of the surviving people were refugees. The war brought bitterness and division to the United States. It damaged the American people's image of their country.

b. *How was the outcome of the war a victory for the Communists?*

South Vietnam, Cambodia, and Laos all fell to the Communists in 1975.

16. a. *Describe three types of I-W service that were available to conscientious objectors.*

One type was Pax Service, in which single men went overseas to do relief work in nations devastated by war or natural disaster. Another type was voluntary service, in which the men usually worked in VS units at places such as children's homes or old people's homes. A third type was service at an approved public or private agency such as a hospital or an experimental farm.

b. *What were some spiritual dangers to young men in the I-W program?*

Young men were often placed in strange settings far away from home, where they faced many temptations. Men of different religious groups were mixed together, which tended to weaken convictions.

c. *What was one immediate effect and one long-term effect of the VS units?*

VS units helped the COs to remain faithful. They started the practice of young people going into voluntary service even when there was no military draft.

HISTORICAL HIGHLIGHTS (pages 610–612)

A. Matching: People

a. *Earl Warren*
b. *Hubert H. Humphrey*
c. *John F. Kennedy*
d. *John Glenn*
e. *Lyndon B. Johnson*
f. *Richard M. Nixon*

b 1. *Johnson's vice president who lost the 1968 election.*

f 2. *President when United States troops were withdrawn from Vietnam.*

e 3. *Vice president who succeeded John Kennedy as president in 1963 and was re-elected in 1964.*

a 4. *Chief justice who wrote that criminal suspects must be informed of their rights.*

d 5. *First American astronaut to orbit the earth.*

c 6. *President elected in 1960 and assassinated in 1963.*

B. Matching: Terms 1

a. *affirmative action*   f. *I-W service*
b. *counterculture*   g. *New Frontier*
c. *Cuban missile crisis*   h. *Tet Offensive*
d. *flexible response*   i. *Tonkin Gulf Resolution*
e. *Great Society*   j. *Viet Cong*

h 1. *Communist attack on South Vietnam in 1968.*

e 2. *Title of President Johnson's social programs.*

i 3. *Measure that gave President Johnson power to use military force in Vietnam.*

b 4. *Youth who rebelled against established values and violated social customs.*

g 5. *Name of Kennedy's domestic program.*

a 6. *Policy requiring companies to hire a certain percentage of people considered the victims of discrimination, such as women and blacks.*

c 7. *Incident in which Soviet weapons threatened United States security.*

j 8. *Communist guerrilla fighters in South Vietnam.*

f 9. *Program for conscientious objectors from the 1950s to the 1970s.*

d 10. *Policy of having both conventional and nuclear weapons for dealing with military threats.*

C. Matching: Terms 2

a. *Civil Rights Act of 1964*   f. *Voting Rights Act*
b. *Department of Housing and*   g. *Twenty-third Amendment*
     Urban Development   h. *Twenty-fourth Amendment*
c. *Department of Transportation*   i. *Twenty-fifth Amendment*
d. *Medicaid*   j. *Twenty-sixth Amendment*
e. *Medicare*

c 1. *Agency in the Cabinet responsible for things such as highway and waterway programs.*

i 2. *Measure that defined presidential disability and stated when a vice president should take over the presidency.*

g   3. *Measure that allowed people of Washington, D.C. to vote in presidential elections.*

f   4. *Measure that eliminated reading tests as a requirement for voting.*

e   5. *Program that funded health care for elderly people.*

h   6. *Measure that ended the poll tax in federal elections.*

b   7. *Agency established in 1965 to provide shelter and improve cities.*

a   8. *Measure that outlawed racial discrimination in public places.*

j   9. *Measure that lowered the voting age to eighteen.*

d 10. *Program that funded health care for poor people under age sixty-five.*

D. Matching: Places and Dates

a. *Berlin Wall*	e. *1963*
b. *Cuba*	f. *1964*
c. *North Vietnam*	g. *1968*
d. *South Vietnam*	h. *1973*

c   1. *Small communist land supported by China and the Soviet Union.*

e   2. *Year when John F. Kennedy was assassinated and Lyndon B. Johnson succeeded him.*

d   3. *Non-communist land in which the United States fought a long war.*

f   4. *Year when President Johnson won re-election and the Tonkin Gulf Resolution was passed.*

a   5. *Barrier between communist and democratic areas.*

h   6. *Year when the United States withdrew from Vietnam.*

b   7. *Island where Soviet missiles threatened the United States.*

g   8. *Year when Richard Nixon was elected president.*

E. Deeper Discussion

1. *Why was the United States so concerned about saving West Berlin and South Vietnam from communism?*

   This was partly a political concern, for the presidents of the United States did not want to appear soft on communism. It was also a humanitarian concern, based on a desire to spare people from the oppression of totalitarian Communist regimes. American prestige was at stake; for if the United States could not protect Berlin and South Vietnam, how could it help other nations? Further, if the United States allowed the Communists to gain ground at one place, they would try to gain elsewhere. Finally, the United States wanted to maintain its record of winning every war it fought.

2. *Why did society change so drastically in the 1960s?*

The Supreme Court decisions as well as the expanding government programs contributed to change. Blacks felt frustrated, as they thought they were not gaining fast enough. Women increasingly saw themselves as oppressed by men. Communists also tried to stir up dissatisfaction to weaken the United States; for example, Communists have been clearly linked with some aspects of the civil rights movement. Young people felt, perhaps justifiably, that their parents were hypocritical in promoting standards for youth that the adults themselves did not uphold.

Student revolts, rock music, drugs, and the counterculture were symptoms of an underlying "disease"—the humanistic mentality of a materialistic, militaristic, urban society. Atheistic evolution, lack of moral values, failure of churches to uphold Biblical standards, and a selfish outlook on life were other causes of social change. The Bible does tell us that in the last days, "evil men and seducers shall wax worse and worse" (2 Timothy 3:13). Man without Christ is headed for ruin, not for some utopian society.

3. *Why did blacks use violent methods to gain their ends in the middle and late 1960s?*

One reason was that the slower, nonviolent approach did not bring progress fast enough. Another was that many blacks in northern cities lived in poverty. Even though civil rights laws had been passed, they applied mainly in the South and gained few benefits for blacks in northern cities. These blacks felt frustrated and angry because of a system that kept them in a state of inferiority.

Black groups like the Congress of Racial Equality, and radical leaders such as Malcolm X, appealed to blacks' frustration because they appeared able to accomplish something. They emphasized "black power" (pride in being black), which many found attractive. The writings of blacks became increasingly violent—in *The Fire Next Time* (1963), James Baldwin said that blacks would fight back if they did not achieve "total liberation." In such an atmosphere of tension, relatively small incidents triggered massive rioting. An example is the rioting that followed the assassination of Martin Luther King, Jr.

4. *Why was the Vietnam War so divisive?*

The Vietnam War polarized Americans as nothing had since the Civil War era. One possible reason is that other conflicts in society came to a head over the war (such as the general spirit of rebellion, and the fact of being old enough to fight but not old enough to vote). Another reason was the deceptiveness of the presidents—especially Johnson—about the war. Further, liberals and radicals sympathized with communist ideas and opposed the United States "establishment." This was anathema to those who espoused conservative and traditional values. Finally, television made a strong impact as it beamed a steady stream of violence into American homes. Many people became so tired of the dragged-out conflict and mounting casualties that they turned completely against the war.

5. *According to the domino theory, if one nation falls to communism, neighboring nations will also fall. (See Chapter 26.) Did the domino theory prove true in Southeast Asia after American forces withdrew from Vietnam? Explain.*
   It proved true in that after South Vietnam fell to communism, Cambodia and Laos also fell. It proved untrue in that Asian countries near these three did not fall to communism. In fact, the communist nations put more effort into fighting each other than in spreading communism to other nations. In the 1990s, other nations of Southeast Asia were becoming more open to Western influences.

6. *During the Vietnam War, some Mennonites promoted being a "witness to the state" by urging the government to follow principles of right and wrong. Why is such an approach a departure from New Testament nonresistance?*
   New Testament nonresistance sees the state as a separate kingdom from the church. God overrules in the affairs of government, but the leaders are sinful, carnal, and worldly. Telling the government what it should do violates the principle of noninvolvement in government affairs and the spirit of nonresistance. Instead of two kingdoms, the church and the state are mixed together.

F. Chronology and Geography

1. *Give the years for the following events.*
   a. *election of John F. Kennedy*   **1960**
   b. *Kennedy administration*   **1961–1963**
   c. *Tonkin Gulf Resolution*   **1964**
   d. *Johnson administration*   **1963–1969**
   e. *beginning of the Nixon administration*   **1969**
   f. *United States withdrawal from Vietnam*   **1973**
   g. *end of the military draft*   **1973**

2. *Match the numbers on the map to the names below. (Countries are marked with larger numbers and cities with smaller numbers.)*

 5 a. *Cambodia*
 3 b. *China*
 7 c. *Laos*
 4 d. *North Vietnam*
 6 e. *South Vietnam*
 1 f. *Hanoi*
 2 g. *Saigon*

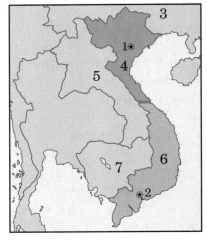

28 Recent Years: America From 1970 Into the 2000s

1960

Richard M. Nixon inaugurated; first man to walk on the moon 1969

1970

Watergate offices burglarized; Nixon re-elected 1972

Vice president Spiro Agnew resigns; Gerald R. Ford becomes vice president 1973

Nixon resigns; Ford becomes president 1974

Vietnam falls to Communists 1975

United States observes bicentennial (July 4);1976

James E. (Jimmy) Carter elected president **1976**

United States opens diplomatic relations with Communist China 1979

Ronald Reagan elected president 1980

1980

Sandra Day O'Connor appointed to Supreme Court 1981

Reagan wins re-election 1984

Space shuttle *Challenger* explodes 1986

George H. W. Bush elected president 1988

1990 Communist governments of Eastern Europe overthrown 1989–1990

Persian Gulf War; Soviet Union dissolves and Cold War ends **1991**

Twenty-seventh Amendment ratified; William J. "Bill" Clinton elected president 1992

Clinton wins re-election 1996

Clinton impeached and acquitted 1998

2000 George W. Bush elected president 2000

Terrorists attack the World Trade Center and the Pentagon 2001

2010

"Righteousness exalteth a nation: but sin is a reproach to any people."

Proverbs 14:34

Chapter 28 (pages 614–642)

RECENT YEARS: AMERICA FROM 1970 INTO THE 2000S

Chapter Objectives

- To learn about economic developments in the decades 1970 to 2000, especially the recession of the 1970s to early 1980s, the energy crisis, and the economic rebound in the 1980s and 1990s.
- To learn about foreign affairs in the decades 1970 to 2000, with emphasis on the Cold War and its end, and on the Middle East.
- To understand how the Watergate scandal led to the resignation of President Nixon.
- To understand how a more conservative approach to government under President Reagan helped restore confidence in America.
- To learn about the conservative direction in politics in the mid-1990s.
- To understand the changes and decline of society in the final decades of the twentieth century.

To the Teacher

Teaching recent history presents some challenges. Forming a broad perspective is more difficult, since we are closer to the events, and their long-term effects are yet unseen. However, teaching recent history is beneficial. What may seem like recent history to an adult may seem like ancient history to an eighth grader. Students may not even remember much about recent events unless they are unusually perceptive. So teachers need to increase their awareness of recent decades. An understanding of these events also helps to put their own experiences and those of their parents into perspective.

Use wisdom in discussing the Watergate scandal. The text presents only a summary of the main events, so you may want to study the subject further. Be careful in research, however, for many authors are as strongly partisan today as they were during the actual affair.

The 1970s were difficult times economically and politically. The nation seemed to be groping for direction after the traumas of Vietnam and Watergate. Nixon's resignation weakened the presidency, and Carter's informal approach did not improve matters. Ronald Reagan brought a much more conservative political philosophy to the presidency. He steered away from big government and government regulation, and he also restored confidence in the government and its leaders. These things helped to turn the nation around in the 1980s, both at home and in relation to other countries.

Though personally conservative, Reagan was not able to reverse the liberal tide, because Congress was largely controlled by Democrats. Another legacy of the Reagan years was a huge budget deficit that resulted from the arms buildup and the refusal of Congress to cut spending as Reagan wanted. In the Iran-Contra affair, Reagan was hoping that by selling arms to the Iranians, he could get them to influence the Lebanese to release the American hostages they held. Zealous aides then used the profits to help the Contras, which was against the law at that time. But it is not certain that Congress's prohibition of aid to the Contras was even legitimate.

The Bush years represented a continuation of Reagan's policies, though Bush was more moderate politically. The Persian Gulf War and the subsequent humanitarian interventions represented attempts to create and enforce the "new world order" that Bush envisioned after the Cold War. In the "new world order," nations would cooperate through the United Nations to maintain world harmony. The United States, as the world's remaining superpower, would be a sort of world policeman, settling disputes, opposing brutal dictators, and using its military strength to help the suffering. This has not worked especially well in actual practice.

Clinton was clearly a more liberal president, whereas the political mood of the country was more conservative—as shown by the Congressional swing to Republican control beginning in 1994. That swing tempered some of the more liberal programs that Clinton wanted to pass, such as medical insurance. Because the events surrounding the 1998 impeachment are so sordid, they should be passed over; however, the impeachment is a historical fact. It would merit reviewing the Constitutional process of impeachment, as well as the concept of checks and balances.

Pertaining to society, the text paints a gloomy picture because the times *were* dark and sinful. For reasons of propriety, only some of the issues are mentioned; the abortion debate is omitted entirely, as well as the issue of alternate lifestyles. The teacher should know that the Supreme Court decision *Roe v. Wade* (1973) declared that state laws banning abortions are unconstitutional, and that since then, millions of unborn babies have been slaughtered. Nevertheless, we as Christians cannot be pessimistic, for we know that God holds the future and that He will fulfill His will. So stress two things: (1) our trust in God to "guide the future as He has the past" and (2) our responsibility to be a light to the world as long as we have opportunity.

Note on chapter test: Chapter 28 has its own test, and there is also a final test on the whole book. The final test is based largely on the "So Far This Year" reviews, so be sure that the students study *all* of these. (The last "So Far This Year" contains some items that will not receive year-end review otherwise.) True-false items on the final test are taken from the chapter tests.

Christian Perspectives

- Man will get worse and worse, rather than better and better (2 Timothy 3:1–5, 13).
- When a society rejects God and His Word, it will reap a bitter harvest of immorality and violence.
- In spite of social decay, God has made provisions for Christians to live righteous, holy, and godly lives (John 14:27; John 16:7–15, 33; 1 Corinthians 10:13; 2 Corinthians 6:14–7:1; Ephesians 6:10–18).
- The Christian is called to be a light to the world (Ephesians 5:11–13; Philippians 2:15).
- God holds the future, and His purposes will be accomplished; so we should trust in Him.
- Jesus is coming quickly; therefore, we need to be ready when He comes (John 14:3; Revelation 22:20, 21).

Further Study

- The lives of the presidents from Nixon through Clinton.
- The Watergate scandal. (Be aware that many writers are openly biased against Nixon.)
- The Apollo space program and the moon landing.
- The explosion of the space shuttle *Challenger*.
- The end of the Cold War.
- The Persian Gulf War.
- The North American Free Trade Agreement.

Chapter 28 Quiz

Write the correct name or term for each description.

1. First man to walk on the moon.

_____

2. First unelected president; took office when previous president resigned; served from 1974 to 1977.

_____

3. President when the Cold War ended; served from 1989 to 1993.

_____

4. First president to resign from office; served from 1969 to 1974.

_____

5. President born after World War II; served from 1993 to 2001.

_____

6. President who brought economic recovery; served from 1981 to 1989.

_____

7. President who faced economic troubles and the Iran hostage crisis; served from 1977 to 1981.

_____

8. First woman appointed to the Supreme Court.

_____

9. Scandal in 1972 that led to the resignation of a president.

_____

10. Relaxing of tension between rivals.

_____

Quiz Answers

1. **Neil Armstrong**
2. **Gerald Ford**
3. **George H. W. Bush**
4. **Richard Nixon**
5. **William (Bill) Clinton**
6. **Ronald Reagan**
7. **James (Jimmy) Carter**
8. **Sandra Day O'Connor**
9. **Watergate**
10. **détente**

Answer Key

Focus for Thought (pages 621, 622)

1. *What was President Nixon able to accomplish*
   a. *with China?*
   Nixon visited China in 1972. He and Chinese leaders agreed to increase trade and cultural interchange between their nations.
   b. *with the Soviet Union?*
   Nixon signed a treaty for arms reduction (the SALT I treaty) in 1972. He used an approach called détente to reduce tensions with the Soviets.

2. *What resulted after Nixon supported Israel in the 1973 Yom Kippur War?*
   OPEC nations retaliated by banning oil exports to the United States, which brought fuel shortages and caused oil prices to rise nearly fourfold.

3. a. *Why did President Nixon resign from office in 1974?*
   It was proved that the president had lied about his involvement in the Watergate scandal.
   b. *Why did President Ford pardon Nixon soon afterward?*
   He wanted to heal the wounds caused by the Watergate affair and the Vietnam War.

4. *What date of special historical significance did Americans celebrate during Ford's presidency?*
   Americans celebrated July 4, 1976, as the bicentennial (two hundredth birthday) of the United States.

5. *What were two serious problems in American business during Carter's presidency?*
   the energy supply and a stagnant economy

6. *What were some of Carter's accomplishments in foreign affairs?*
   Carter held a conference in which the leaders of Egypt and Israel signed a peace plan. The United States established diplomatic relations with Communist China. Carter and the Soviet leader signed the SALT II treaty, which limited nuclear missiles. (But this treaty was never officially ratified.)

7. *In what two places did Carter's foreign policy fail to work?*
   One place was Afghanistan, which the Soviets invaded in December 1979. Another place was Iran, where a number of Americans were taken hostage in November 1979.

Focus for Thought (page 625)

8. a. *What things did Reagan do to improve the economy?*

He promoted tax cuts, reduced government spending, expanded the deregulation of business, and ended the breakup of companies that were considered monopolies.

b. *How well did this approach work?*

The recession became worse at first, but later inflation and unemployment fell, interest rates declined, business improved, and investment increased.

9. *What were Reagan's goals in his foreign policy?*

Reagan wanted to increase military spending so that the United States could take a stronger stand against enemies. He believed in peace through strength. He began a policy of more firmly resisting the Soviet Union.

10. *Name two countries where Reagan intervened, and tell why he intervened.*

(Any two.) Reagan helped the Contras in Nicaragua to oppose the Sandinistas, who were Communists. He sent armed forces to Grenada to oppose a Communist takeover there. He sent troops to Lebanon as part of an international peacekeeping force.

11. *What was the effect of Reagan's appointments to the Supreme Court?*

They made the Supreme Court more conservative and less activist.

12. *In what ways did American relations with the Soviet Union improve in Reagan's second term?*

Mikhail Gorbachev, the new Soviet president, took a more moderate approach in dealing with the United States. Reagan and Gorbachev held several summit meetings in which they discussed ways to reduce arms. In 1987, they signed an agreement to remove all intermediate-range nuclear missiles in Europe.

13. *Briefly explain what happened in the Iran-Contra affair.*

Arms were sold to Iran, and profits from the sale were used illegally to help the Contras in Nicaragua.

Focus for Thought (page 636)

14. *What events brought the Cold War to an end?*

Nations in Eastern Europe revolted against their Communist rulers in 1989. The people of East Germany overthrew their Communist government, and Germany was reunited in 1990. The Soviet Union broke apart in 1991.

15. *Why did President Bush send soldiers to Panama? to Iraq?*

He sent soldiers to Panama in 1989 to overthrow dictator Manuel Noriega and bring him to the United States for trial. He sent soldiers to free Kuwait after Iraq invaded it in 1990.

16. a. *After the Cold War, what was the general reason that the United States intervened in the affairs of other nations?*

for humanitarian reasons

b. *Describe one case in which the United States intervened for this purpose.*

(Any one.) In 1992, President Bush sent troops to Somalia to restore order so that food might be sent to starving people there. In 1999, President Clinton ordered the bombing of Kosovo in Yugoslavia because of its oppression of ethnic Albanians.

17. *On what charges was President Clinton impeached in 1998?*

on charges of perjury and obstruction of justice

18. *How did concerned Americans respond to the decline of public schools in the 1990s?*

Citizens demanded that public schools get "back to the basics." The number of private schools increased, especially Christian schools. Many parents began teaching their own children in home schools.

19. *How did technology affect society by the end of the 1900s?*

Many people were using personal computers. The Internet made it easier than ever before to obtain materials portraying violence and indecency. Ninety-eight percent of American homes had television, and many had devices to record and play videotapes.

HISTORICAL HIGHLIGHTS (pages 636–639)

A. Matching: People

a. *George H. W. Bush*

b. *Geraldine Ferraro*

c. *Gerald R. Ford*

d. *Henry Kissinger*

e. *James E. Carter*

f. *Neil Armstrong*

g. *Richard M. Nixon*

h. *Ronald Reagan*

i. *Sandra Day O'Connor*

j. *Spiro Agnew*

k. *William J. Clinton*

b   1. *Vice-presidential candidate in 1984 who was the first woman to run for that office.*

i   2. *First woman appointed to the Supreme Court.*

c   3. *First unelected president; took office when President Nixon resigned; served from 1974 to 1977.*

d   4. *Foreign policy adviser to Richard Nixon.*

j   5. *Nixon's vice president who resigned in 1973.*

g   6. *First president to resign from office; served from 1969 to 1974.*

f   7. *First man to walk on the moon.*

e   8. *President who faced economic troubles and the Iran hostage crisis; served from 1977 to 1981.*

h   9. *President who brought economic recovery in the 1980s; served from 1981 to 1989.*

a 10. *President when the Cold War ended and the Persian Gulf War was fought; served from 1989 to 1993.*

k 11. *Post-World War II president; served from 1993 to 2001.*

B. Matching: Terms

a. *bicentennial*
b. *Contras*
c. *deregulation*
d. *détente*
e. *Environmental Protection Agency*
f. *Iran-Contra affair*
g. *Iran hostage crisis*
h. *New Federalism*
i. *North American Free Trade Agreement*
j. *Organization of Petroleum Exporting Countries*

k. *Persian Gulf War*
l. *"Reaganomics"*
m. *SALT I*
n. *SALT II*
o. *stagflation*
p. *Strategic Defense Initiative*
q. *terrorist*
r. *Twenty-seventh Amendment*
s. *Watergate*

s   1. *Scandal in 1972 that led to the resignation of President Nixon.*

o   2. *Rising prices along with business stagnation in the 1970s.*

l   3. *Reagan's program for restoring the economy.*

c   4. *Removal of government controls.*

d   5. *Relaxing of tension between rivals.*

j   6. *Group of nations that banned oil exports to the United States in 1973.*

k   7. *Effort in which Iraqis were driven out of Kuwait in 1991.*

h   8. *Nixon's plan to give more authority to state and local governments.*

n   9. *Arms reduction agreement signed with the Soviet Union in 1979.*

a 10. *Two hundredth anniversary of the United States.*

q 11. *One who uses violence and threats to intimidate people, especially for political purposes.*

i 12. *Proposal approved by the Senate in 1993, involving Canada, Mexico, and the United States.*

p 13. *Proposed system of weapons orbiting in space to destroy missiles attacking the United States.*

m 14. *Arms reduction agreement made with the Soviet Union in 1972.*

e 15. *Government agency established in 1970 to limit pollution.*

b 16. *Group that opposed the Sandinistas in Nicaragua.*

g 17. *Incident when Americans were held captive in Tehran in 1979.*

r 18. *Measure stating that Congress could not raise its pay until after an election; ratified in 1992.*

f 19. *Incident when profits from weapons sold to Iran were used to help Contras in Nicaragua.*

C. Matching: Dates

a. *1972*   i. *1988*

b. *1974*   j. *1989*

c. *1976*   k. *1990*

d. *1979*   l. *1991*

e. *1980*   m. *1992*

f. *1983*   n. *1996*

g. *1984*   o. *1998*

h. *1986*

i 1. *Election of George H. W. Bush, the first vice president since 1836 to be elected as the next president.*

a 2. *Year of the Watergate break-in, Nixon's visit to China, and his re-election.*

l 3. *Persian Gulf War; Soviet Union collapses and the Cold War ends.*

c 4. *United States bicentennial year; Jimmy Carter wins election as president.*

e 5. *President Reagan elected for his first term.*

b 6. *Richard Nixon resigns and Gerald Ford becomes president.*

o 7. *President Clinton impeached.*

m 8. *President Clinton elected for his first term.*

g 9. *President Reagan re-elected.*

h 10. *Space shuttle Challenger explodes.*

d 11. *Three Mile Island nuclear accident and Iran hostage crisis.*

n 12. *President Clinton re-elected.*

f 13. *United States invasion of Grenada.*

k 14. *Germany reunited.*

j 15. *United States invasion of Panama.*

D. Matching: Places

a. *Afghanistan*
b. *China*
c. *Czechoslovakia, Hungary, Poland*
d. *Egypt*
e. *Germany*
f. *Grenada*
g. *Iran*

h. *Iraq*
i. *Israel*
j. *Lebanon*
k. *Nicaragua*
l. *Panama*
m. *Soviet Union*
n. *Three Mile Island*

i   1. *Country aided by the United States in the 1973 Yom Kippur War.*

a   2. *Country invaded by the Soviet Union in 1979, which caused American–Soviet relations to deteriorate.*

b   3. *Nation visited in 1972 by Richard Nixon, the first United States president to do so; diplomatic relations with the United States restored in 1979.*

j   4. *Country where President Reagan sent troops in 1983 to keep peace; bomb killed 241 soldiers; American troops recalled in 1984.*

n   5. *Place where a nuclear accident occurred in 1979, causing a fear of nuclear power.*

c   6. *Some nations whose Communist governments were overthrown in 1989.*

k   7. *Country in Central America where Contras fought the Sandinista government.*

g   8. *Country in which militants took American hostages in 1979.*

f   9. *Caribbean island invaded by American troops in 1983 to keep it from becoming Communist.*

e 10. *Nation divided since World War II but reunited in 1990 after its eastern part overthrew its Communist rulers.*

l 11. *Nation in Central America that was invaded by United States troops in 1989 to overthrow a dictator accused of dealing in illegal drugs.*

h 12. *Nation that invaded Kuwait in 1990 and triggered the Persian Gulf War in 1991, which it lost.*

m 13. *Nation that collapsed in 1991.*

d 14. *Nation that made peace with Israel in 1979, with encouragement from President Carter.*

E. Deeper Discussion

1. a. *Why did the United States experience such severe problems in the economy and with energy in the 1970s?*

   Inflation and unemployment were mere symptoms of deeper problems in the economy. Government spending on the Vietnam War and on social programs increased inflation until it was out of control.

Rising energy costs also contributed to inflation. Motorists paid more for gasoline, and businesses paid more for fuel to run their factories; so the manufactured items cost more. Of course, the Arab oil embargo was one reason for the energy crisis, but another major cause was price controls established by the government. Refineries were not about to put more money into producing gasoline than they could get out of it.

b. *Why did the economy turn around in the 1980s?*

When price controls were removed, the economy turned around and fuel became plentiful. That is the lesson of the 1970s and the 1980s—that a free, unfettered economy is far more productive than an economy regulated by the government.

2. *Trace the developments of the Cold War by answering the following questions.*

a. *How did the United States improve relations with China and the Soviet Union in the early 1970s?*

President Nixon made friends with China in the early 1970s, thus putting pressure on the Soviet Union to also be less hostile. (The Russians and the Chinese were at odds.) He also hoped this approach would help to end the Vietnam War, and it did help to do that. Thus Nixon improved relations with China while also pursuing détente with the Soviet Union. The SALT I agreement contributed to a relaxing of the arms race, and thereby of tension.

b. *What contributed to deepening Cold War tensions in the late 1970s and early 1980s?*

The Soviet invasion of Afghanistan soured relations with the United States. It revealed the expansionist spirit of the Soviets, and it also convinced American leaders that the Soviets were taking advantage of détente for their own benefit. Continued Soviet intervention in Eastern Europe, especially Poland, and the shooting down of a Korean passenger plane in 1983 further cooled relations. The arms buildup was renewed under Reagan, and he embarked on a campaign of fighting world communism, particularly in the Western Hemisphere. Reagan believed that a strong response was the only thing the Communists respected.

c. *Why did the Cold War thaw somewhat in the late 1980s?*

Reagan's approach of peace through strength began paying off. Unable to keep up with the United States military buildup, the Soviets wanted to slow down the arms race; and this led to the summits and arms reduction agreements. Another reason was new leadership in the Kremlin; Gorbachev recognized that the Soviet Union was deteriorating (because of the failure of communism) and needed to be rebuilt. So he introduced his policies of glasnost and perestroika, which led to a further moderating of Soviet policies. Finally, the Soviets withdrew from Afghanistan, a major sticking point in their relations with the United States.

d. *How did the Cold War end?*

Signs of the end began appearing in 1989. When Soviet satellites in Eastern Europe saw that Gorbachev would not intervene to prevent them from overthrowing their Communist governments, they did just that. In 1990, Germany was reunited, and this focal point of the Cold War passed into history. The Warsaw Pact dissolved in 1991, and Soviet troops later withdrew from Eastern Europe. Finally, the Soviet Union itself collapsed and the Communists were removed from power. This terminated the confrontation between Soviet and non-Soviet worlds, though several countries including China and Cuba remained communist. Thus the Cold War ended in 1991.

3. *What are the underlying causes for the deteriorating conditions in modern society?*

The condition of humanity throughout history has been a result of the Fall, man's sinful nature, and his rejection of God and His Word. In modern times, this rejection has so permeated society that many people are wholly given over to wickedness. As man gives expression to his sinful desires through movies, television, videos, computers, and other means, wickedness is compounded.

The violence and crime in modern society have much to do with the breakdown of families and moral standards. Churches have contributed by failing to uphold the truth in areas such as divorce and remarriage. Evolution has taught people that they are animals, the products of blind chance, and that they have nothing more to live for than the physical realm. Consequently, people freely indulge their lusts—"Let us eat and drink; for to morrow we die" (1 Corinthians 15:32). Ultimately, people worship themselves and reject God—though He, of course, will have the last word.

4. a. *What is the Christian's responsibility to the people in surrounding society? See Ephesians 5:11–13 and Philippians 2:15.*

The Christian should have no fellowship with the "unfruitful works of darkness" or take any pleasure in them. Rather, to be a consistent Christian witness, he should reprove them by words as well as conduct. **Christians should let their light shine in the darkness of society so that others may also come to the light of Jesus.**

b. *What gives the Christian hope in spite of the decay in society? See John 14:3 and Revelation 22:20, 21.*

Jesus promised that He would return and take His people to be with Him. So the Christian looks into eternity with a hope that transcends the things of this life.

F. Chronology and Geography

1. *Why was the Middle East of such importance to the United States in the latter decades of the twentieth century?*

   One primary reason was oil; the United States relied heavily on oil imported from Middle Eastern nations such as Saudi Arabia and Kuwait. To keep its automobiles, trucks, and factories running, the United States had to stay closely involved with the nations in the Middle East. The Persian Gulf War illustrates this.

   Another reason was global politics, especially during the Cold War, when the United States competed with the Soviet Union for influence and allies.

   Moreover, the volatile mix of religion and culture in the region resulted in numerous terrorist activities that affected the security of the United States. This is illustrated by the hostage crises in Iran and Lebanon, the dealings with Libya, and the bombing of Pan American Flight 103 in Scotland. (Not all these incidents are mentioned in the text.) Ever since World War II, and especially since Israel was re-established as a nation in 1948, the Middle East has been a sore trial for United States leaders. The United States has usually supported Israel against its Arab and Muslim enemies.

2. *On a world map, find the following countries discussed in Chapter 28. Be prepared to show their locations in class.*

   a. *Nations of the Middle East: Egypt, Iran, Iraq, Kuwait, Israel, Lebanon, Saudi Arabia, Syria*

   b. *Asian nations: Afghanistan, China, Russia (which is partly in Europe)*

   c. *European nations: Albania, Bulgaria, the Czech Republic and Slovakia (Czechoslovakia is now divided into these two nations), Germany, Hungary, Poland, Romania, Yugoslavia*

   d. *Nations of Central America and the Caribbean: Grenada, Nicaragua, Panama*

   (Individual work. In class, have students show locations on a world map.)

3. *List all the American presidents in order with the dates of their terms in office. Remember that an elected president's term begins in the year after the election.*

   1. **George Washington—1789–1797**
   2. **John Adams—1797–1801**
   3. **Thomas Jefferson—1801–1809**
   4. **James Madison—1809–1817**
   5. **James Monroe—1817–1825**
   6. **John Quincy Adams—1825–1829**
   7. **Andrew Jackson—1829–1837**
   8. **Martin Van Buren—1837–1841**
   9. **William Henry Harrison—1841**
10. **John Tyler—1841–1845**
11. **James Polk—1845–1849**
12. **Zachary Taylor—1849–1850**
13. **Millard Fillmore—1850–1853**
14. **Franklin Pierce—1853–1857**
15. **James Buchanan—1857–1861**
16. **Abraham Lincoln—1861–1865**
17. **Andrew Johnson—1865–1869**
18. **Ulysses S. Grant—1869–1877**
19. **Rutherford B. Hayes—1877–1881**
20. **James A. Garfield—1881**
21. **Chester A. Arthur—1881–1885**
22. **Grover Cleveland—1885–1889**
23. **Benjamin Harrison—1889–1893**
24. **Grover Cleveland—1893–1897**
25. **William McKinley—1897–1901**
26. **Theodore Roosevelt—1901–1909**
27. **William Howard Taft—1909–1913**
28. **Woodrow Wilson—1913–1921**
29. **Warren G. Harding—1921–1923**
30. **Calvin Coolidge—1923–1929**
31. **Herbert Hoover—1929–1933**
32. **Franklin D. Roosevelt—1933–1945**
33. **Harry S. Truman—1945–1953**
34. **Dwight D. Eisenhower—1953–1961**
35. **John F. Kennedy—1961–1963**
36. **Lyndon B. Johnson—1963–1969**
37. **Richard M. Nixon—1969–1974**

38. **Gerald R. Ford—1974–1977**
39. **James E. Carter, Jr.—1977–1981**
40. **Ronald Reagan—1981–1989**
41. **George H. W. Bush—1989–1993**
42. **William J. Clinton—1993–2001**
43. **George W. Bush—2001–**

SO FAR THIS YEAR (pages 640–642)

A. Completion

Write the correct name, term, or date for each description.

Brown v. Board of Education of Topeka
1. *Case in which separate but equal facilities for blacks were declared unconstitutional.*

counterculture
2. *Youth who rebelled against established values and violated social customs.*

civil rights movement
3. *Drive to give blacks equal status with whites.*

Cuban missile crisis
4. *Incident in which Soviet weapons threatened United States security in 1962.*

desegregation
5. *Ending of separation by race.*

domino theory
6. *Idea that if one nation in a region falls to communism, nearby nations will also fall.*

Fair Deal
7. *President Truman's program of social reforms.*

Great Society
8. *Title of President Johnson's social programs.*

I-W service
9. *Program for conscientious objectors from the 1950s to the 1970s.*

New Frontier
10. *Name of President Kennedy's domestic program.*

Tonkin Gulf Resolution
11. *Measure that gave President Johnson power to use military force in Vietnam.*

Twenty-second Amendment
12. *Constitutional amendment that limited a president's administration to two terms.*

Twenty-sixth Amendment
13. *Constitutional amendment that lowered the voting age to eighteen.*

Twenty-fifth Amendment
14. *Constitutional amendment that defined presidential disability and stated when a vice president should take over the presidency.*

Douglas MacArthur
15. *General in the Korean War who was dismissed by President Truman.*

John Glenn
16. *First American astronaut to orbit the earth.*

Martin Luther King, Jr.
17. *Black minister who led the civil rights movement and promoted nonviolent resistance.*

Alaska, Hawaii
18. *Two states added to the Union in 1959.*

1950–1953
19. *Years of the Korean War.*

1973
20. *Year when the United States withdrew from Vietnam.*

Interstate Highway Act
21. *Measure passed in 1956 to build a network of interstate highways.*

B. Matching: Presidents

a. *Dwight D. Eisenhower*   f. *John F. Kennedy*
b. *George H. W. Bush*   g. *Lyndon B. Johnson*
c. *Gerald Ford*   h. *Richard M. Nixon*
d. *Harry S. Truman*   i. *Ronald Reagan*
e. *James E. (Jimmy) Carter*   j. *William (Bill) Clinton*

d 22. *President who served from 1945 to 1953, after Franklin D. Roosevelt.*

a 23. *President during most of the 1950s; served from 1953 to 1961.*

f 24. *President elected in 1960 and assassinated in 1963.*

g 25. *Vice president who became president in 1963 and was elected in 1964; served from 1963 to 1969.*

h 26. *President when United States troops were withdrawn from Vietnam; first president to resign; served from 1969 to 1974.*

c 27. *First unelected president; in office during the American bicentennial; served from 1974 to 1977.*

e 28. *President who faced economic troubles and the Iran hostage crisis; served from 1977 to 1981.*

i 29. *President who brought economic recovery in the 1980s; served from 1981 to 1989.*

b 30. *President when the Cold War ended and the Persian Gulf War was fought; served from 1989 to 1993.*

j 31. *First president born since World War II; served from 1993 to 2001.*

C. Multiple Choice

Write the letter of the correct answer.

32. *Policy of having little to do with foreign nations.*
    a. *imperialism*   c. *Roosevelt Corollary*
    b. isolationism   d. *Open Door Policy*

33. *Basis for American relations with countries in the Far East.*
    a. *Monroe Doctrine*   **c. Open Door Policy**
    b. *Roosevelt Corollary*   d. *New Deal*

34. *Campaign promoting reform and change around the beginning of the 1900s.*
    a. progressive movement c. *New Freedom*
    b. *Square Deal*   d. *New Frontier*

35. *President Roosevelt's reform program to treat everyone equally.*
    a. *Roosevelt Corollary*   **c. Square Deal**
    b. *Great Society*   d. *New Freedom*

36. *Constitutional amendment that provided for the direct election of senators.*
    a. *Sixteenth Amendment*   c. *Eighteenth Amendment*
    b. Seventeenth Amendment   d. *Nineteenth Amendment*
37. *Constitutional amendment that prohibited alcoholic beverages.*
    a. *Sixteenth Amendment*   **c. Eighteenth Amendment**
    b. *Seventeenth Amendment*   d. *Nineteenth Amendment*
38. *Constitutional amendment that allowed an income tax.*
    a. Sixteenth Amendment   c. *Eighteenth Amendment*
    b. *Seventeenth Amendment*   d. *Nineteenth Amendment*
39. *Constitutional amendment that allowed women to vote.*
    a. *Sixteenth Amendment*   c. *Eighteenth Amendment*
    b. *Seventeenth Amendment*   **d. Nineteenth Amendment**
40. *Law that established a central banking system in 1913.*
    a. Federal Reserve Act   c. *Federal Trade Commission*
    b. *Underwood Tariff Act*   d. *Pure Food and Drug Act*
41. *President during the Spanish-American War; served from 1897 to 1901.*
    a. *Theodore Roosevelt*   **c. William McKinley**
    b. *Woodrow Wilson*   d. *William Howard Taft*
42. *Democratic president who promoted the New Freedom program; served from 1913 to 1921.*
    a. *Theodore Roosevelt*   c. *William McKinley*
    b. Woodrow Wilson   d. *William Howard Taft*
43. *President who served from 1909 to 1913 and later became a Supreme Court justice.*
    a. *Theodore Roosevelt*   c. *William McKinley*
    b. *Woodrow Wilson*   **d. William Howard Taft**
44. *President with the "big stick"; served from 1901 to 1909.*
    a. Theodore Roosevelt   c. *William McKinley*
    b. *Woodrow Wilson*   d. *William Howard Taft*
45. *Spanish islands in the Far East conquered by the United States in the Spanish-American War and purchased for $20 million in 1898.*
    a. *Guam*   c. *Puerto Rico*
    b. *Hawaii*   **d. Philippines**
46. *Spanish island in the Caribbean ceded to the United States after the Spanish-American War.*
    a. *Guam*   **c. Puerto Rico**
    b. *Cuba*   d. *Philippines*

Understanding North American History

Chapter 1 Test   Score _____

Name _____   Date _____

A. Matching: Terms

Not all the choices will be used.

<u>n</u> 1. Of the city.

<u>a</u> 2. Low bowl-shaped area surrounded by higher land.

<u>c</u> 3. High ridge that separates water flowing into the Pacific from water flowing into the Gulf of Mexico.

<u>g</u> 4. Break in the earth's surface, where earthquakes occur.

<u>i</u> 5. Permanently frozen soil.

<u>m</u> 6. River that flows into a larger river.

<u>j</u> 7. High, fairly level stretch of land.

<u>f</u> 8. Place where water descends from the Piedmont to the lower Coastal Plain.

<u>d</u> 9. Land formed by soil deposited at the mouth of a river.

<u>e</u> 10. Broad bay at the mouth of a river.

<u>h</u> 11. Long, narrow bay extending inland in a steep-sided valley.

<u>b</u> 12. In contact; adjoining.

<u>l</u> 13. Surface features of a region.

a. basin

b. contiguous

c. Continental Divide

d. delta

e. estuary

f. Fall Line

g. fault

h. fiord

i. permafrost

j. plateau

k. rural

l. topography

m. tributary

n. urban

(13 points)

B. Matching: Climates

<u>c</u> 14. Sunny and mild; good for oranges and olives.

<u>b</u> 15. Very warm and moist.

<u>e</u> 16. Wet and mild; found in the Pacific valleys.

<u>d</u> 17. Cold climate in Canada and Alaska.

<u>a</u> 18. Climate of four seasons.

a. humid continental

b. humid subtropical

c. Mediterranean

d. subarctic

e. west coast marine

(5 points)

C. Matching: Features of the United States

Not all the choices will be used.

_c_ 19. Broad, flat region bordering the Atlantic Ocean and the Gulf of Mexico.

_e,n,o_ 20. Main features of the Pacific Coast region (3 answers).

_a,b,p_ 21. Main features of the Appalachian region (3 answers).

_g_ 22. Dry, low-lying area in the Rocky Mountain region.

_m_ 23. Highest mountain in the contiguous United States.

_l_ 24. Highest mountain in North America.

_j_ 25. River draining about 40 percent of the United States.

_k_ 26. Major tributary of the river in number 25.

_i_ 27. Volcanic islands in the Pacific Ocean.

_d_ 28. Long, wide mouth of the Susquehanna River.

_h_ 29. Salty body of water in the Great Basin region.

_r_ 30. Alaskan river flowing into the Pacific Ocean.

a. Allegheny and Cumberland Plateaus
b. Appalachian Mountains
c. Atlantic Coastal Plain
d. Chesapeake Bay
e. Coast Ranges
f. Columbia
g. Great Basin
h. Great Salt Lake
i. Hawaii
j. Mississippi
k. Missouri
l. Mt. McKinley
m. Mt. Whitney
n. Pacific ranges
o. Pacific valleys
p. Piedmont
q. St. Lawrence
r. Yukon

(16 points)

D. Matching: Features of Canada

Not all the choices will be used.

_i_ 31. River flowing from the Great Lakes to the Atlantic Ocean.

_b_ 32. Rocky region curving like a horseshoe around Hudson Bay.

_f_ 33. Vast stretch of level land in the central area.

_e_ 34. Heartland of Canada in Ontario and Quebec.

_g_ 35. Longest river in Canada.

_a_ 36. Region of the provinces along the Atlantic Ocean.

_h_ 37. Highest of the Canadian Rockies.

_d_ 38. Region including Rocky Mountains and Coast Ranges.

a. Appalachian region
b. Canadian Shield
c. Columbia
d. Cordillera region
e. Great Lakes-St. Lawrence Lowlands
f. Interior Plains
g. Mackenzie
h. Robson
i. St. Lawrence

(8 points)

E. Essay Questions

39. How are history and geography related?

   The things that happened (history) took place somewhere (geography). Understanding what happened involves understanding where it happened. The geography of a place provides the setting for its history, and it even affects its history.

40. How has the climate of Canada affected the settlement of the nation?

   Because of the cold winters and short summers, farming is impossible in much of northern Canada. Most of the people live within 200 miles (322 km) of the United States, and much of Canada is sparsely populated.

(2 points)
Total points: 44

Teacher: **Suggested point values are given for the answers on the tests. You may use a different scoring system if you prefer.**

Understanding North American History

Chapters 2 and 3 Test

Score _____

Name _____   Date _____

A. Matching: Terms—Chapter 2

Not all the choices will be used.

_h_ 1. Rebirth of learning.

_e_ 2. The East.

_b_ 3. Boundary drawn by the pope to give Spain rights to the New World.

_k_ 4. Viking settlement in North America.

_a_ 5. Person who invests money to make a profit.

_c_ 6. System in which a lord owned land, and serfs farmed it for him.

_d_ 7. People who were neither lords nor serfs.

_i_ 8. Island on which Columbus landed.

_j_ 9. Country for which Columbus sailed.

_g_ 10. Major change in the religious system of Europe.

a. capitalist

b. Line of Demarcation

c. manorialism

d. middle class

e. Orient

f. Portugal

g. Reformation

h. Renaissance

i. San Salvador

j. Spain

k. Vinland

(10 points)

B. Matching: Terms—Chapter 3

Not all the choices will be used.

_c_ 11. A particular way of life.

_g_ 12. Indian village of multilevel apartment houses made of stone or adobe.

_f_ 13. Crumbled meat mixed with buffalo tallow.

_e_ 14. Dwelling made of poles bent in a U shape and covered with bark.

_a_ 15. Bricks made of sun-dried clay.

_h_ 16. One of the old men who governed the Iroquois.

_d_ 17. Region where tribes lived similarly.

_b_ 18. Manmade object, such as a tool or weapon, that is of interest in archaeology.

_i_ 19. Pair of poles drawn by a dog or horse, used by Plains Indians to carry their belongings.

a. adobe

b. artifact

c. culture

d. culture area

e. longhouse

f. pemmican

g. pueblo

h. sachem

i. travois

j. wigwam

(9 points)

C. Completion: People—Chapter 2

Write the correct name for each description.

__Christopher Columbus__ 20. "Admiral of the Ocean Sea" who discovered the New World in 1492.

__Giovanni da Verrazano__ 21. Explorer of the North American coast for France in 1524.

__Amerigo Vespucci__ 22. Italian for whom the lands of the New World were named.

__Leif Ericson__ 23. Scandinavian explorer who reached the northeastern coast of North America around A.D. 1000.

__John Cabot__ 24. Explorer of the northeastern coast of North America for England in 1497.

__Ferdinand Magellan__ 25. Captain of five ships, one of which became the first to sail around the world.

__Henry Hudson__ 26. Explorer who claimed part of America for the Netherlands in 1609.

__Vikings__ 27. Scandinavian people who settled Iceland, Greenland, and Vinland around A.D. 1000.

__Jacques Cartier__ 28. Explorer of the St. Lawrence River area for France in 1534.

__Vasco de Balboa__ 29. Explorer who discovered in 1513 that a great ocean lay west of America.

__Vasco da Gama__ 30. Explorer who reached the Orient by sailing around Africa.

__Isabella__ 31. Queen of Spain who financed Columbus's voyage of discovery.

(12 points)

D. Matching: Areas and Tribes—Chapter 3

_b_ 32. Area from North Carolina to the Gulf of Mexico and from the Atlantic Ocean to the Mississippi River.

_c_ 33. Area from the Mississippi River to the Rocky Mountains.

_e_ 34. Area in California, the Great Basin, and the Columbia Plateau.

_d_ 35. Area in present-day Arizona, New Mexico, and parts of Texas.

_a_ 36. Area between the Great Lakes and North Carolina.

a. Northeast
b. Southeast
c. Plains
d. Southwest
e. Far West

In the set below, choices may be used more than once or not at all.

_k_ 37. Culture that made heaps of earth for ceremonies and burial.

_h_ 38. Tribe that lived in pueblos.

_j_ 39. Tribe that lived in longhouses.

_h_ 40. Tribe that used kivas.

_i_ 41. Another name for Eskimos.

_j_ 42. Tribes called the Five Nations.

_h, l_ 43. Indians that lived in dry Southwest (two tribes).

f. California Indians
g. Great Basin Indians
h. Hopi
i. Inuit
j. Iroquois
k. Mound Builders
l. Navajo
m. Plateau Indians

(12 points)

E. True or False—Chapter 2

Circle T *for* True *or* F *for* False.

(T) F   44. Before the Crusades, the average European knew little about sugar, spices, and other goods from the Far East.

T (F)   45. The Portuguese were the first Europeans to control the trade routes to the East.

(T) F   46. Columbus thought he could reach the East by sailing west.

(T) F   47. The Anabaptists promoted the idea that church and state should be separate.

(T) F   48. European countries had a practice that the first country to claim land in the New World could possess it.   (5 points)

F. Essay Questions—Chapters 2 and 3

49. Why does Columbus receive credit for discovering America when the Vikings had been there five hundred years earlier?

     The Viking settlements were not permanent, but Columbus's discovery led to a continuing

     exploration and settlement by Europeans. Viking settlements held little importance to later

     people. Europe in the eleventh century was not ready to settle America.

50. What were three changes other than the Reformation, which increased European interest in exploration? Along with each change, explain how it contributed to further exploration.

     (Any three.) trade with the Orient—introduced Europeans to new luxuries, which led them

     to search for new trade routes

     the Crusades—promoted trade to obtain Oriental goods

     nationalism—caused nations to compete with each other for trade routes

     spirit of adventure—aroused interest in Asia and desire to travel there   *(Answer continues on next page.)*

51. What are two contributions

    a. of the Europeans to the Indians?

     (Any two.) livestock (sheep and horses); the Bible and Christianity; crops (wheat, sugar cane,

     bananas); tools (kettles, traps, guns); liquor; diseases

    b. of the Indians to the Europeans?

     (Any two.) teaching on how to hunt and fish, and how to grow new crops (tomatoes, corn,

     potatoes, peanuts, pumpkins); inventions (canoe, hammock, snowshoes); words (including

     many place names)

52. What was one main cause of conflict between the Europeans and the Indians?

   (Either answer.) One cause of the conflict was the economic difference, because the Indians
   had no concept of private land ownership as the Europeans did. The Indians also believed
   that the earth was sacred because of their nature gods, but the Europeans believed in God's
   command to subdue the earth.   _(Answer continues below.)_

(12 points)
Total points (complete test): 60
(Chapter 2 portion): 34

(Answer Key continued):

50. **advances in scientific thought—moved men to experiment and explore**
    improvements in navigation—explorers were able to go on long voyages

52. **Another cause of conflict was religious. The white men saw the Indians as savages to be con-**
    verted, and they fought the Indians who refused to accept Christian beliefs.

Understanding North American History

Chapters 4 and 5 Test   Score _____

Name _____   Date _____

A. Matching: Terms

Not all the choices will be used.

_f_   1. Tribe who sided with the English.

_b_   2. "Forest runners" who gathered furs from the Indians and brought them to trading centers.

_e_   3. Tribes of Indians who were baptized in large numbers; sided with the French.

_h_   4. Spanish outposts intended to convert and civilize Indians.

_d_   5. French Protestants.

_i_   6. Form of manorialism, transplanted to New France.

_a_   7. Policy in which all power is held by one person or group at the head.

_j_   8. French landholders.

_c_   9. Settlers who worked a seigneur's land in New France.

a. absolutism

b. coureurs de bois

c. habitants

d. Huguenots

e. Huron, Algonquin

f. Iroquois

g. Jesuits

h. missions

i. seigneurial system

j. seigneurs

(9 points)

B. Matching: Places and Dates

Not all the choices will be used.

_h_   10. River along the Quebec and Montreal settlements.

_e_   11. Location of Pueblo land settled by Oñate and Spanish colonists.

_g_   12. Town founded by Champlain in 1608.

_d_   13. Name derived from Indian word for *village*.

_j_   14. Date when Florida was discovered.

_a_   15. French name for the area around the Bay of Fundy.

_f_   16. Poutrincourt's beloved settlement, destroyed by the English.

_l_   17. Date when the Spanish Armada was defeated.

_k_   18. Date when the oldest European town in the United States was founded.

_b_   19. Present-day state where Eusebio Kino set up missions.

_c_   20. Present-day state that was settled in the 1700s to prevent English and Russian claims.

a. Acadia

b. Arizona

c. California

d. Canada

e. New Mexico

f. Port Royal

g. Quebec

h. St. Lawrence

i. Texas

j. 1513

k. 1565

l. 1588

(11 points)

C. Completion: People

Write the correct name for each description.

<u>Samuel de Champlain</u>　21. "Father of New France."

<u>Jacques Marquette</u>　22. Jesuits who explored part of the Mississippi (two men).

<u>Louis Jolliet</u>

<u>Robert de La Salle</u>　23. Claimed for France the area drained by the Mississippi.

<u>Jacques Cartier</u>　24. Early explorer who made three trips to the St. Lawrence region.

<u>Francisco Coronado</u>　25. Explorer who sought the Seven Cities of Cíbola.

<u>Giovanni da Verrazano</u>　26. First explorer sent by France.

<u>Ponce de León</u>　27. Man who discovered Florida while seeking the Fountain of Youth.

<u>Hernando de Soto</u>　28. Explorer who discovered the Mississippi River.

(9 points)

D. True or False

Circle T *for* True *or* F *for* False.

T (F)　29. The Spanish respected the Indians and treated them fairly and kindly.

(T) F　30. The early Spanish explorers in North America were so eager to find gold that they tended to take little interest in other discoveries.

(T) F　31. One reason that the Spanish built missions was to protect their frontier against foreign nations.

T (F)　32. The Spanish operated their missions on the basis of democracy and freedom.

T (F)　33. Settlers in New France had freedom to own their own land, choose their own church, and set up their own government.

(T) F　34. The economic prosperity of New France depended on the fur trade.

(T) F　35. New France failed to develop rapidly.

T (F)　36. The French expanded into the Mississippi River valley because they wanted to farm the land.

(8 points)

E. Essay Questions

37. How was the defeat of the Spanish Armada a turning point in history?

After this defeat, Spain's power declined while England's power increased. The result was that North America was not settled by Catholics from Spain but by Protestants from England.

38. What were two effects that the Spanish had on southwestern North America?

(Any two.) The Spanish increased geographical knowledge about the area. They brought new animals and crops, and a new religion. Their names and customs survive in the Southwest. The Spanish influenced architecture.

39. What were the duties of seigneurs in New France? of habitants?

(Sample answers.) A seigneur was to get settlers established on his land to clear it. He was to build a manor house for himself and provide a winepress and buildings such as a mill and a bakery. He was to find a priest for the community.

An habitant was to work his own fields, work for the seigneur several days a year, and make annual rent payments of money, grain, and poultry to his seigneur.

40. What were two effects that the French colonies had on North America?

(Any two.) French is one official language of Canada. Quebec has many French people who are Catholics. The French Canadians follow French customs and laws. Louisiana is divided into parishes instead of counties, and many people in its southern part are Catholic. Many places have French names.

(7 points)
Total points: 44

Understanding North American History

Chapters 6 and 7 Test   Score _____

Name _____   Date _____

A. Matching: Terms

Not all the choices will be used.

_b_   1. Aristocracy; upper-class people.

_f_   2. Person working to repay the cost of his voyage to America.

_o_   3. Colony governed by the king.

_m_   4. Colony owners hoping to rent land to people of lower rank.

_l_   5. Colony governed by a proprietor.

_j_   6. Small farmers and craftsmen.

_e_   7. Colony operating on the basis of its charter.

_d_   8. Legal document granting the right to settle and govern a certain region.

_k_   9. People who withdrew from the Church of England and moved to America.

_n_   10. People who wanted to purify the Church of England from within.

_a_   11. Maryland law granting religious freedom.

_i_   12. Unskilled laborers who did not own land.

_h_   13. Agreement signed by Pilgrims and Strangers to make "just and equal laws."

_g_   14. Group of people appointed to make laws.

a. Act of Toleration

b. better class

c. buffer

d. charter

e. charter colony

f. indentured servant

g. legislature

h. Mayflower Compact

i. meaner sort

j. middling class

k. Pilgrims

l. proprietary colony

m. proprietors

n. Puritans

o. royal colony

(14 points)

B. Completion: Names

Write the correct name for each description.

__Great Awakening__   15. Religious revival in the 1700s.

__Christopher Dock__   16. Noted schoolteacher in colonial Pennsylvania.

__William Penn__   17. Quaker who received a land grant as payment for a debt.

__Anglican Church__   18. Church of England; official church in the South.

__Roger Williams__   19. Founder of Rhode Island, who insisted on freedom of conscience.

__Congregational Church__ 20. Puritan church, dominant in New England.

__George Whitefield__   21. Leaders of the colonial religious revival (two men).

__Jonathan Edwards__

**Enlightenment**   22. Age of Reason.

**James Oglethorpe**   23. Trustee leader in the founding of Georgia.

**John Smith**   24. Jamestown leader who established a rule of "no work, no food."

**Lord Baltimore**   25. Founder of Maryland.   (12 points)

C. Matching: Places and Dates

Not all the choices will be used.

_c_ 26. Colony intended as a haven for debtors.

_e_ 27. Dutch territory in America.

_g_ 28. Pilgrim settlement.

_f_ 29. City of Brotherly Love.

_a_ 30. Name taken from the Latin form of *Charles*.

_h_ 31. Roger Williams's settlement.

_b_ 32. Thomas Hooker's settlement.

_d_ 33. Puritan settlement.

_i_ 34. Jamestown is founded.

_j_ 35. Plymouth is founded.

a. Carolina
b. Connecticut
c. Georgia
d. Massachusetts Bay Colony
e. New Netherland
f. Philadelphia
g. Plymouth
h. Providence
i. 1607
j. 1620
k. 1664

(10 points)

D. True or False

Circle T *for* True *or* F *for* False.

T (F) 36. Maryland was founded as a haven for Quakers.

T (F) 37. Jamestown was settled primarily for religious freedom.

(T) F 38. The Carolinas were to be modeled on the feudal system.

T (F) 39. Pennsylvania was founded as a place of freedom for Catholics.

(T) F 40. The Puritans, who came for religious freedom, refused to grant full religious freedom to others.

(T) F 41. The Southern Colonies used the headright system.

T (F) 42. A triangular trade route helped to promote trade among three different American colonies.

(T) F 43. Colonial charters granted colonists the same privileges as Englishmen.

T (F) 44. The Bible had little effect on the people of early colonial days.

T (F) 45. Shipping and manufacturing were important in the South because of the many good harbors.

(10 points)

E. Essay Questions

46. What are two reasons that English settlers came to America?

    (Any two.) for economic opportunity, to find gold and easy wealth, for political freedom, for religious freedom

47. Describe the founding of any two English colonies by answering two of the following questions about each. Who founded it? What were the goals? What did the colony experience as those goals were pursued?

    Connecticut *was founded by Thomas Hooker as a place to have more land and freedom. The colony prospered.*

    Delaware *was granted by the Duke of York to William Penn, who later made it a separate colony.*

    Georgia *was founded by James Oglethorpe and other trustees as a haven for debtors and as a buffer between English and Spanish lands. When few debtors came, it became a royal colony and developed in much the same way as South Carolina.*   *(Answer continues below.)*

48. What were two effects of the colonial religious revival in the 1700s?

    It helped to unite the colonies. It divided several churches, including the Congregationalists and the Presbyterians (and the Mennonites).   *(Answer continues on next page.)*

(8 points)
Total points: 54

(Answer Key continued):

47. **Maryland** *was founded by Lord Baltimore as a haven for Roman Catholics. People of other faiths also moved in, and the colony prospered.*

    Massachusetts *was founded by the Pilgrims and Puritans, who came to find religious freedom. They planned to have a colony where nothing evil was tolerated, but they found it impossible to reach this ideal.*

    New Hampshire *was granted to John Mason, but settlers from Massachusetts gradually moved in. It became part of Massachusetts, and later it was made a separate colony.*

    New Jersey *was founded by Lord John Berkeley and Sir George Carteret. Later it was sold to the Quakers, who made it a haven for persecuted members of their group.*

    New York *was a colony captured from the Dutch and renamed in honor of its new owner, the*

Duke of York. The colony prospered.

North and South Carolina *were founded by eight proprietors who wanted to set up a feudal system like that in Europe. Their plan failed, and the Carolinas developed in much the same way as other colonies.*

Pennsylvania *was founded by William Penn as a haven for Quakers and other persecuted people. The colony was to be a "Holy Experiment" in which godly people lived by New Testament principles, but this ideal could not be achieved. The colony was prosperous otherwise.*

Rhode Island *was founded by Roger Williams as a place of religious freedom for people of all faiths. The colony prospered.*

Virginia *was founded by the London Company for the purpose of making a profit. The settlers experienced great hardship until they stopped looking for gold and began working to support themselves.*

48. *It favored the common people and the popular churches over the established churches (thus bringing about greater separation of church and state). It led to more outreach work, including missionary endeavors to the Indians and the founding of numerous colleges. It set a pattern for later revival movements. It produced only a limited degree of spiritual improvement.*

Understanding North American History

Chapters 8 and 9 Test   Score _____

Name _____   Date _____

A. Matching: Terms and Dates

Not all the choices will be used.

__b__ 1. Dutch organization to help Mennonite emigrants.

__n__ 2. Date when first Mennonites came to America.

__q__ 3. Time of the Revolutionary War.

__p__ 4. Date when the French and Indian War began.

__o__ 5. Date when the French and Indian War ended.

__c__ 6. Pamphlet promoting independence.

__g__ 7. Promise to support the patriot government.

__j__ 8. Law that closed lands west of the Appalachians to settlement.

__d__ 9. Document approved on July 4, 1776.

__i__ 10. Persons favoring independence.

__f__ 11. Supporters of Great Britain.

__a__ 12. Parliamentary action for punishing the colonies.

__l__ 13. Parliamentary action for raising revenue.

__k__ 14. Assembly that declared independence.

__e__ 15. Assembly where leaders reasoned that Parliament had no authority over them.

__m__ 16. Agreement that ended the Revolution.

a. Coercive Acts

b. Commission for Foreign Needs

c. *Common Sense*

d. Declaration of Independence

e. First Continental Congress

f. Loyalists

g. Oath of Allegiance

h. Olive Branch Petition

i. patriots

j. Proclamation of 1763

k. Second Continental Congress

l. Stamp Act

m. Treaty of Paris

n. 1683

o. 1763

p. 1754

q. 1775–1783

(16 points)

B. Matching: People and Places

Not all the choices will be used.

_j_ 17. Prime minister of Great Britain during French and Indian War.

_f_ 18. French general in the French and Indian War.

_a_ 19. British general defeated at Fort Duquesne.

_e_ 20. British general who won the battle of Quebec.

_i_ 21. Site of the decisive battle in the French and Indian War.

_c_ 22. Town in Pennsylvania where Mennonites first settled.

_g_ 23. Place where conflicting claims led to the French and Indian War.

_d_ 24. Northern feature around which the British developed fur trade.

_b_ 25. French fortification built where Pittsburgh now stands.

a. Braddock
b. Fort Duquesne
c. Germantown
d. Hudson Bay
e. James Wolfe
f. Montcalm
g. Ohio River valley
h. Prince Rupert
i. Quebec
j. William Pitt

(9 points)

C. Completion: People and Places

Write the correct name for each description.

George Washington 26. Patriot general in command of the entire American army.

Cornwallis 27. British general whose defeat ended the Revolution.

Thomas Paine 28. Writer of *Common Sense*.

Saratoga 29. Location of the battle that was the turning point in the Revolution.

Thomas Jefferson 30. Writer of the Declaration of Independence.

Philadelphia 31. Meeting place of the First and Second Continental Congress.

George III 32. King of Great Britain during the Revolution.

Lexington or Concord 33. Location of the beginning battle of the Revolution (either one of two towns).

Yorktown 34. Location of the last major battle of the Revolution.

Valley Forge 35. Place where the American army endured great hardship during the winter of 1777–1778.

(10 points)

D. True or False

Circle T for True or F for False.

(T) F 36. The French and Indian War is important in the history of North America because the French were removed as a North American power.

T (F) 37. Mennonites came to America to establish an ideal government.

(T) F 38. The Quakers refused to protect the Scotch-Irish against the Indians.

(T) F 39. The Americans and British disagreed about Parliament's authority over the colonies.

T (F) 40. The British had no right to tax the American colonies.

(T) F 41. The Americans believed that "taxation without representation is tyranny."

T (F) 42. The nonresistant groups were Tories.

(7 points)

E. Essay Questions

43. What were two issues that led to fighting between the British and the French in North America?

 (Any two.) conflicting claims, the fur trade, alliances with the Indians, and religious and
 political differences

44. What did the British gain by the treaty that ended the French and Indian War?

 all the land from the Hudson Bay south to Florida and west to the Mississippi (except New
 Orleans)

45. a. What did the British acknowledge in the Treaty of Paris after the American Revolution?

 that the former thirteen colonies were now "free, sovereign, and independent states"

 b. What territory did the United States include at that time?

 all the land south of Canada (except Florida) and east of the Mississippi River

46. a. What things did the Mennonites do to maintain nonresistance before and during the French and Indian War?

 Before the war, the Mennonites had the Ausbund *published and the* Martyrs Mirror *translated*
 and published in German. During the war, they suffered rather than killing the Indians, and
 they did not take part in the fighting. They helped refugees who had suffered from Indian raids.

 b. What were two main issues of nonresistance during the American Revolution?

 (Any two.) fines, war taxes, and the Oath of Allegiance

(9 points)
Total points: 51

Understanding North American History

Chapter 10 Test

Score _____

Name _____ Date _____

A. Matching: Terms

Not all the choices will be used.

_j_ 1. To bring to trial for misconduct in office.

_a_ 2. People who opposed the Constitution.

_f_ 3. Written plan of government.

_p_ 4. To reject a proposed law.

_b_ 5. Having a legislature with two houses.

_m_ 6. The act of giving formal agreement to.

_e_ 7. Legislative body of the United States.

_h_ 8. Plan with government powers divided between the states and the national government.

_q_ 9. Proposal calling for states to have proportionate representation.

_l_ 10. Law that provided a plan of government and statehood for new territories.

_k_ 11. Proposal calling for all states to have equal representation.

_d_ 12. Weak union in which states have more power than the national government.

_g_ 13. People who supported the Constitution.

_o_ 14. Dividing of government into three branches.

_c_ 15. Limits that government branches place on each other's powers.

_i_ 16. Proposal that settled the issue of representation.

a. Anti-Federalists

b. bicameral

c. checks and balances

d. confederation

e. Congress

f. constitution

g. Federalists

h. federal system

i. Great Compromise

j. impeach

k. New Jersey Plan

l. Northwest Ordinance of 1787

m. ratification

n. republic

o. separation of powers

p. veto

q. Virginia Plan

(16 points)

B. Completion: Names and Terms

Write the correct name or term for each description.

____*legislative*____ 17. Branch of government that makes laws.

____*Preamble*____ 18. Introduction to the Constitution.

____*executive*____ 19. Branch of government that enacts laws.

____*James Madison*____ 20. "Father of the Constitution."

_____judicial_____   21. Branch of government that decides cases about laws.

___Federalist Papers___   22. Series of articles defending the Constitution.

___George Washington___   23. Chairman of the Constitutional Convention.

_House (of Representatives)_24. Part of legislative branch with states represented proportionately.

_____Senate_____   25. Part of legislative branch with states represented equally.

___Electoral College___   26. Group of men who elect the president.

(10 points)

C. Dates

Give the years when the following events took place.

_____1781_____   27. The Articles of Confederation were ratified.

_____1787_____   28. The year of the Constitutional Convention.

_____1789_____   29. The year when government under the Constitution began.

_____1791_____   30. The year when the Bill of Rights was added to the Constitution.

(4 points)

D. True or False

Circle T *for* True *or* F *for* False.

Ⓣ F   31. In the United States, the highest level of government is the national, or federal, government.

T Ⓕ   32. A republic has no king and is a pure democracy.

Ⓣ F   33. The Constitution prevents power from being concentrated in the hands of any one man or group of men.

T Ⓕ   34. The Constitution, like the laws of the Medes and Persians, may never be changed.

Ⓣ F   35. The purpose of the Bill of Rights is to guarantee freedoms to citizens of the United States.

(5 points)

E. Essay Questions

36. a. What was the main reason that government under the Articles of Confederation did not work?

**The Articles made the national government too weak to govern the nation effectively.**

b. What were two problems that showed the ineffectiveness of the government under the Confederation?

(Sample answers.) The states taxed each other on interstate commerce. They considered fighting each other when disputes arose. The United States received little respect from other nations. The central government had no power to levy taxes and no money to pay debts. It had no power to deal with rebellions.

37. How were the following matters settled at the Constitutional Convention?

a. The issue of representation.

It was agreed that there would be a House of Representatives in which representation was according to population, and a Senate in which representation was according to states.

b. The issue of slavery.

(Either one.) For purposes of Congressional representation, only three-fifths of the slaves would be counted. It was agreed that Congress could not end the slave trade before 1808.

38. What are two examples of checks and balances in the Constitutional government?

(Any two.) The president can veto laws passed by Congress. The president can appoint judges. The Senate must approve judges appointed by the president. Congress can override vetoes. Congress can impeach the president. The Supreme Court can declare laws unconstitutional.

(7 points)
Total points: 42

Understanding North American History

Chapters 11 and 12 Test   Score _____

Name _____   Date _____

A. Matching: Terms

Not all the choices will be used.

_c_ 1. Favored strict interpretation and limited government.

_l_ 2. Boldly promoted the War of 1812.

_k_ 3. Ended the War of 1812.

_g_ 4. Settled differences with Britain.

_i_ 5. Pride in belonging to one's country.

_b_ 6. Head judge of the Supreme Court.

_h_ 7. Power of the Supreme Court to declare a law unconstitutional.

_a_ 8. Laws that restricted criticism of the government.

_j_ 9. Settled differences with Spain.

_e_ 10. Favored loose interpretation and strong government.

_d_ 11. Law that stopped all exports.

_m_ 12. Resistance to paying taxes in western Pennsylvania.

a. Alien and Sedition Acts
b. chief justice
c. Democratic-Republicans
d. Embargo Act
e. Federalists
f. impress
g. Jay Treaty
h. judicial review
i. nationalism
j. Pinckney Treaty
k. Treaty of Ghent
l. war hawks
m. Whiskey Rebellion

(12 points)

B. Matching: Terms

Not all the choices will be used.

_j_ 13. Idea that states are supreme over the federal government.

_g_ 14. To withdraw formally from an organization.

_d_ 15. Agreement that settled a slavery problem.

_c_ 16. Time of national unity and harmony.

_k_ 17. Political party that opposed Andrew Jackson.

_i_ 18. Practice in which the winner of an election rewards his supporters with government positions.

_e_ 19. Declaration about involvement of European and American nations in each other's affairs.

_b_ 20. Plan for a protective tariff, internal improvements, and a national bank.

_a_ 21. Agreement that gained Florida in 1819.

_h_ 22. Strong devotion to the interests of a local region.

a. Adams-Onís Treaty
b. American System
c. Era of Good Feelings
d. Missouri Compromise
e. Monroe Doctrine
f. nullify
g. secede
h. sectionalism
i. spoils system
j. states' rights
k. Whigs

(10 points)

C. Matching: Presidents

_b_ 23. First president; served from 1789 to 1797.

_j_ 24. First president to die in office.

_f_ 25. Son of a former president.

_h_ 26. Vice president under Andrew Jackson.

_c_ 27. President during War of 1812; served from 1809 to 1817.

_g_ 28. First vice president to fill the position of a president who died in office.

_d_ 29. President during the Era of Good Feelings.

_a_ 30. Represented the common man.

_e_ 31. Second president; Federalist; served from 1797 to 1801.

_i_ 32. Leader of Democratic-Republicans; third president; served from 1801 to 1809.

a. Andrew Jackson

b. George Washington

c. James Madison

d. James Monroe

e. John Adams

f. John Quincy Adams

g. John Tyler

h. Martin Van Buren

i. Thomas Jefferson

j. William H. Harrison

(10 points)

D. Completion: People

Write the correct name for each description.

John Marshall   33. Chief justice who strengthened the Supreme Court.

Henry Clay   34. War hawks (two men).

John C. Calhoun

Tecumseh   35. Tried to create an Indian confederacy.

Zebulon Pike   36. Explorer for whom a mountain in Colorado is named.

Daniel Boone   37. Opened the Wilderness Road to Kentucky.

Alexander Hamilton   38. Federalist leader and first secretary of the treasury.

Meriwether Lewis   39. Explorers of the Louisiana Purchase from 1804 to 1806 (two men).

William Clark

(9 points)

E. True or False

Circle T for True or F for False.

(T) F   40. Hamilton's financial plans increased the power of the government.

T (F)   41. President Jefferson increased the size of the government.

T (F)   42. The Whig party was more like the Democratic-Republicans than like the Federalists.

T (F)   43. Andrew Jackson was a dignified president from an aristocratic family.

T (F) 44. State nullification of federal laws would have led to chaos and breakup of national unity.

T (F) 45. The Panic of 1837 occurred during Martin Van Buren's term as president.

T (F) 46. Indian removal was done to open new lands for tobacco growing.

T (F) 47. Andrew Jackson opposed the Bank of the United States because he believed it favored the wealthy and was unconstitutional.

T (F) 48. The Whigs used speeches, parades, and songs to help William Henry Harrison win election as president.

T (F) 49. John Tyler was a highly successful Whig president.

(10 points)

F. Essay Questions

50. a. What were two causes of the War of 1812?

   (Any two.) (1) Trade: The British and French had been seizing American merchant ships and restricting United States trade. (2) Problems with the Indians: Settlers west of

   (Answer continues below.)

   b. What were two effects of that war?

   (Any two.) Canadians were embittered, but European nations gained respect for the United States. Relations with Britain slowly improved. Nationalism increased, manufacturing grew, and westward expansion increased.

51. What are two of the main points in the Monroe Doctrine?

   (Any two.) European nations were not to establish any new colonies in America. European nations were to stay out of the affairs of the independent American nations. Americans would stay out of the affairs of European nations.

(6 points)
Total points: 57

(Answer Key continued):

50. a. *the Appalachians blamed Britain for the conflict, believing that the British had stirred up the Indians and provided them with weapons. They believed that their troubles with the Indians would cease if the British were driven out. (3) War hawks: The war hawks strongly promoted war with Britain. They also believed that by going to war, the United States could take Canada from the British and Florida from Spain.*

Understanding North American History

Chapters 13 and 14 Test   Score _____

Name _____   Date _____

A. Matching: Terms

Not all the choices will be used.

_c_   1. Traveling preacher in the West.

_f_   2. Waterway joining Lake Erie to the Hudson River.

_d_   3. Machine for removing seeds from cotton.

_m_ 4. Route extending from Cumberland to Vandalia.

_i_   5. Change from producing handmade goods at home to producing machine-made goods in factories.

_e_   6. Region dependent on cotton.

_n_   7. Large farm that produced one main crop by slave labor.

_a_   8. Elimination of slavery.

_h_   9. Strip of land obtained from Mexico to build a railroad.

_b_ 10. Independent California.

_o_ 11. Meeting place for fur traders to sell furs and buy supplies.

_k_ 12. Land gained by the Mexican War.

_j_ 13. Independent Texas.

_g_ 14. People who rushed to find gold in 1849.

_l_ 15. Hardy fur traders and explorers of the West.

a. abolition
b. Bear Flag Republic
c. circuit rider
d. cotton gin
e. Cotton Kingdom
f. Erie Canal
g. forty-niners
h. Gadsden Purchase
i. Industrial Revolution
j. Lone Star Republic
k. Mexican Cession
l. mountain men
m. National Road
n. plantation
o. rendezvous
p. slave code

(15 points)

B. Completion: People

Write the correct name for each description.

Horace Mann   16. Promoter of educational reform.

Samuel F. B. Morse   17. Inventor of the telegraph.

Eli Whitney   18. Inventor of the cotton gin.

Samuel Slater   19. Brought textile manufacturing to America.

John Deere   20. Designed an improved plow made of steel.

Robert Fulton   21. Built the first successful steamboat, the *Clermont*.

Cyrus McCormick   22. Invented the mechanical reaper.

Adoniram Judson   23. "Father of American missions."

___*Noah Webster*___   24. Published the "blue-backed speller."

___*Charles Finney*___   25. Evangelist who used new methods to win converts.

(10 points)

C. Matching: People and Places

Not all the choices will be used.

_h_ 26. First president of the Lone Star Republic.

_m_ 27. General in the Mexican War who became president in 1848.

_j_ 28. Man who began colonizing Texas.

_a_ 29. Expansionist president who served from 1845 to 1849.

_e_ 30. Area of modern Oregon, Washington, and Idaho.

_k_ 31. Conqueror of New Mexico and California in the Mexican War.

_d_ 32. Missionary in Oregon who promoted settlement there.

_c_ 33. Fort owner on whose land gold was discovered.

_i_ 34. Harsh ruler and military leader of Mexico.

_g_ 35. Disputed boundary between Texas and Mexico.

_l_ 36. Conqueror of Mexico City in the Mexican War.

_f_ 37. Was followed by Oregon-bound travelers for hundreds of miles.

a. James K. Polk
b. James Watt
c. John Sutter
d. Marcus Whitman
e. Oregon Territory
f. Platte River
g. Rio Grande
h. Sam Houston
i. Santa Anna
j. Stephen Austin
k. Stephen Kearny
l. Winfield Scott
m. Zachary Taylor

(12 points)

D. True or False

Circle T for True or F for False.

(T) F   38. Industry grew rapidly in the North because of energy, natural resources, and transportation.

(T) F   39. The Erie Canal served to divert much trade away from New Orleans to New York City.

T (F)   40. Man's inventions and technology make people better.

(T) F   41. The cotton gin helped to firmly establish slavery in the South.

T (F)   42. Slavery helped to make the South a rich, prosperous region.

T (F)   43. The Bible directly condemns slavery.

T (F)   44. Large numbers of Americans moved to the Pacific Coast for religious reasons.

T (F)   45. The United States gained Texas as part of the Mexican Cession.

(T) F   46. Oregon was formerly shared with the British.

(T) F   47. The Mexican War contributed to the Civil War.

(10 points)

E. Essay Questions

48. What are two changes that the Industrial Revolution brought to America?

   (Any two; other answers possible.) People began working in factories. Workers made only part of a finished product instead of the entire product. Manufactured goods became cheaper. Cities grew as immigrants and others moved in to work in factories. Large slum areas developed.

49. What are two lasting effects that the Second Great Awakening had on the United States?

   (Any two.) Foreign mission work increased. The American Tract Society and the American Bible Society were founded. The Sunday school movement began. Several false religions began.

50. What was manifest destiny, and how was it expressed?

   It was the idea that the United States was clearly destined by God to spread over all of North America. The United States expanded significantly by gaining various new territories such as Texas, the Mexican Cession, and the Gadsden Purchase.

51. What was one cause and one effect of the Mexican War?

   Causes: The Mexican government had never recognized the treaty signed by Santa Anna (or the independence of Texas). Mexico and the United States disputed over the boundary of Texas. Mexico had not paid the debt owed to some citizens of the United States.   *(Answer continues below.)*

52. Choose one of the following things, and write some specific details about it.

   the pony express

   traveling on the Oregon Trail

   the life of the miner during the California gold rush

   Pony express: *Riders galloped from one station to another, changing horses at each station and passing the mail from one rider to the next. They could carry mail between Missouri and California in about ten days. They faced many dangers, such as storms and*   *(Answer continues on next page.)*

   (10 points)
   Total points: 57

(Answer Key continued):

51. *John Slidell had not been able to negotiate with the Mexicans. General Taylor advanced to the Rio Grande, which Mexicans believed was their territory.*

   Effects: The Americans gained a vast stretch of land. They gained the ill feelings of the Mexicans.

The question of slavery in new territories was reopened. The Mexican War contributed to the Civil War.

52. *attacks by bandits or wild animals. The pony express lasted about eighteen months before the telegraph put it out of business.*

Oregon Trail: *Many pioneers traveled together in wagon trains. They worked together to overcome the many difficulties of the trail. They had to cross hot deserts, deep rivers, and steep mountains. At night, they formed a tight circle with their wagons to defend themselves against Indians and wild animals, and to corral their livestock. They needed to keep moving in order to cross the high western mountains before winter.*

Miners' life: *The miners had to work very hard to obtain gold. They used panning, cradles, Long Toms, or sluices to obtain gold. Fighting, robbery, and murder increased. Many miners spent their gold on strong drink and riotous living. Prices rose exorbitantly.*

Understanding North American History

Chapters 15 and 16 Test   Score _____

Name _____   Date _____

A. Matching: Terms

Not all the choices will be used.

_d_ 1. Statement declaring that slaves in the Confederacy were free.

_h_ 2. Confederate soldiers.

_c_ 3. Agreement that let California become a free state.

_i_ 4. Measure that permanently outlawed slavery.

_g_ 5. Idea that people living in an area should decide for themselves about slavery.

_a_ 6. Delaware, Maryland, Kentucky, and Missouri.

_k_ 7. Northern soldiers.

_b_ 8. Payment to avoid military service.

_j_ 9. Secret system that aided slaves in escaping.

_f_ 10. Ship that changed naval warfare.

a. border states
b. commutation fee
c. Compromise of 1850
d. Emancipation Proclamation
e. Fugitive Slave Law
f. ironclad
g. popular sovereignty
h. "Rebels"
i. Thirteenth Amendment
j. Underground Railroad
k. "Yankees"

(10 points)

B. Completion: People

Write the correct name for each description.

Jefferson Davis   11. President of the Confederate States of America.

Levi Coffin   12. "President of the Underground Railroad."

Abraham Lincoln   13. Union president during the Civil War.

Dred Scott   14. Black man who was denied freedom by the Supreme Court.

James Buchanan   15. Union president who did little about Southern secession.

Stephen Douglas   16. Man who promoted popular sovereignty and debated with Lincoln.

Harriet Beecher Stowe 17. Author of *Uncle Tom's Cabin.*

John Brown   18. Man who tried to free the slaves through an armed uprising.

Ulysses S. Grant   19. Chief Union general at the end of the Civil War.

Philip Sheridan   20. Union general who devastated the Shenandoah Valley.

William T. Sherman   21. Union general who led the destructive March to the Sea.

_____Robert E. Lee_____ 22. Chief general of the Confederate armies.

Stonewall Jackson 23. Confederate general shot by his own men at Chancellorsville.

David Farragut 24. Union naval commander who took New Orleans and Mobile.

(14 points)

C. Matching: Places

Not all the choices will be used.

_e_ 25. Town where the Confederacy reached its "high-water mark."

_d_ 26. Place where the Civil War began.

_f_ 27. Confederate capital.

_g_ 28. Stronghold whose fall allowed Union control of the Mississippi.

_a_ 29. Battle that gave Lincoln an occasion to issue the Emancipation Proclamation.

_h_ 30. New state formed during the Civil War.

_b_ 31. Early battle that showed the war would be long and hard.

a. Antietam
b. First Battle of Bull Run
c. Chancellorsville
d. Fort Sumter
e. Gettysburg
f. Richmond
g. Vicksburg
h. West Virginia

(7 points)

D. True or False

Circle T *for* True *or* F *for* False.

(T) F   32. Southern states began to secede from the Union after Lincoln was elected in 1860.

T (F)   33. The Civil War began as a war to free the slaves.

T (F)   34. The South hoped to win the war by crushing the North.

(T) F   35. The Civil War lasted from 1861 to 1865.

(T) F   36. Lincoln's assassination was a great loss to both the North and the South.

(5 points)

E. Essay Questions

37. a. How did slavery relate to states' rights?

   Southerners thought the federal government had no authority to forbid slavery in new territories, but Northerners believed the federal government did have this authority.

   b. How did slavery relate to control of the federal government?

   Southerners had to maintain control of the federal government in order to maintain slavery.

38. How did each side hope to win the Civil War?

   The South hoped to win enough battles so that the North would grow weary of fighting and

   give up. The South also hoped to gain assistance from foreign nations.

   The North planned to blockade Southern ports so that cotton could not be shipped

   (Answer continues below.)

39. What were two important results of the Civil War?

   (Any two.) The war led to the end of slavery. It ended the idea that states were supreme over

   the federal government. It caused the need for reconstruction in the South.

40. What was one difficulty that nonresistant people faced in the North? in the South?

   North: (Any of these.) Men had to decide how to respond to the draft: pay a commutation fee,

   hire a substitute, go into hiding, or flee to Canada. People near Gettysburg suffered the plun-

   dering of their goods when Lee's army invaded. A few suffered threats to their lives. *(Answer*
   continues below.)

   (8 points)

   Total points: 44

(Answer Key continued):

38. *out or supplies brought in, to divide the South by taking control of the Mississippi River, and to capture the Confederate capital of Richmond.*

49. *South: (Any of these.) Men had to decide how to respond to the draft: pay a commutation fee, hire a substitute, go into hiding, or flee to West Virginia or Pennsylvania. People in the Shenandoah Valley suffered much plundering and destruction in Sheridan's raid. An epidemic of diphtheria broke out.*

Understanding North American History

Chapter 17 Test   Score _____

Name _____   Date _____

A. Matching: Terms

Not all the choices will be used.

<u>g</u> 1. Government agency that aided the South after the Civil War.

<u>q</u> 2. President Lincoln's plan for Reconstruction.

<u>c</u> 3. Northerners who went south to help in Reconstruction.

<u>o</u> 4. System in which farm workers rent cropland and use a share of the crops to pay the rent.

<u>e</u> 5. Measure that granted citizenship to blacks.

<u>j</u> 6. Rebuilding and restoration of the South after the Civil War.

<u>f</u> 7. Former slaves.

<u>h</u> 8. Secret society that terrorized blacks.

<u>n</u> 9. Social separation based on race.

<u>m</u> 10. Southern whites who took part in Reconstruction governments.

<u>i</u> 11. Group that wanted to punish and reform the South.

<u>p</u> 12. Dependable Southern support of the Democratic Party.

<u>l</u> 13. To restore government control by whites to a Southern state.

<u>d</u> 14. Measure granting all citizens the right to vote.

<u>k</u> 15. Measure that provided military control to enforce Reconstruction.

<u>b</u> 16. Laws that restricted blacks.

a. Amnesty Act
b. black codes
c. carpetbaggers
d. Fifteenth Amendment
e. Fourteenth Amendment
f. freedmen
g. Freedmen's Bureau
h. Ku Klux Klan
i. Radical Republicans
j. Reconstruction
k. Reconstruction Act
l. redeem
m. scalawags
n. segregation
o. sharecropping
p. solid South
q. ten percent plan

(16 points)

B. Completion: People and Places

Write the correct name for each description.

__*Andrew Johnson*__ 17. President who was impeached in 1868.

__*Ulysses S. Grant*__ 18. Former Civil War general who became president.

__*Alaska*__ 19. "Seward's Folly."

__*Rutherford B. Hayes*__ 20. President appointed after disputed election and the Compromise of 1877.

__*Booker T. Washington*__ 21. Black leader who founded the Tuskegee Institute.

__*William Seward*__ 22. Johnson's secretary of state who purchased a new territory.

__*George Washington Carver*__ 23. Black scientist who encouraged raising peanuts in the South.

(7 points)

C. True or False

Circle T *for* True *or* F *for* False.

Ⓣ F   24. The Radicals wanted to make blacks and whites equal by law.

T Ⓕ   25. Southern states established black codes to aid the blacks' adjustment to freedom.

T Ⓕ   26. President Johnson was impeached because he had done something unconstitutional.

Ⓣ F   27. Redeemed governments tried to undo the accomplishments of the Reconstruction governments.

(4 points)

D. Essay Questions

28. What are two reasons that Reconstruction was necessary?

   (Any two.) The South had suffered much destruction in the war. The freedmen needed help to become responsible citizens. The Southern states needed to be restored to the Union.

29. a. What was one accomplishment of the Reconstruction governments?

   (Any one.) They improved local governments, allowed more people to vote, provided more schools, repaired war damages, and encouraged the building of hospitals and factories.

   b. What was one of their problems?

   (Any one.) Taxes were raised, which angered many whites. The states went deeply into debt. Some money was wasted through corruption.

30. What were two difficulties that blacks faced during and after Reconstruction?

   (Sample answers.) Blacks were insulted, whipped, and even killed by whites, for such things as not removing a hat or for using disrespectful language. They faced legal discrimination through the black codes. They found it hard to support themselves, and many were trapped in sharecropping. The Ku Klux Klan used violence to terrorize them. Various means were used to keep blacks from voting. Jim Crow laws enforced segregation.

(6 points)
Total points: 33

Understanding North American History

Chapter 18 Test   Score _____

Name _____   Date _____

A. Matching: Terms

Not all the choices will be used.

_c_   1. Union of provinces under a single government.

_o_   2. Strong French-Canadian canoe paddlers.

_l_   3. Métis uprising that led to the establishment of Manitoba.

_h_   4. Rule by a small group of people.

_d_   5. Nobleman's proposal for changes in Canadian government.

_a_   6. Law that joined two provinces into the Province of Canada.

_i_   7. Meeting where the Confederation was planned.

_g_   8. Men sent to stop the whiskey trade and to deal with the Indians.

_n_   9. Left the United States to remain under British rule.

_k_   10. Trade agreement with the United States.

_b_   11. Law that created the Dominion of Canada.

_m_   12. Government controlled by the people rather than by aristocrats.

_e_   13. Small group of wealthy men who controlled Canadian government.

_f_   14. Program that included tariffs, railroad construction, and settlement of the Northwest.

a. Act of Union

b. British North America Act

c. confederation

d. Durham Report

e. Family Compact

f. National Policy

g. North West Mounted Police

h. oligarchy

i. Quebec Conference

j. Rebellion of 1837

k. Reciprocity Treaty

l. Red River Rebellion

m. responsible government

n. United Empire Loyalists

o. voyageurs

(14 points)

B. Completion: Names

Write the correct name for each description.

__John A. Macdonald__   15. First prime minister of Canada.

__Louis Riel__   16. Métis leader of rebellions.

__Alexander Mackenzie__   17. Reached the Pacific by land in trying to find the Northwest Passage.

__James Douglas__   18. Governor of British Columbia who built the Cariboo Road.

__David Thompson__   19. Famous surveyor who explored the Columbia River.

_____Parliament_____ 20. Legislature of the Dominion, including Senate and House of Commons.

_____Lord Durham_____ 21. Produced a report that led to changes in Canadian government.

_____Isaac Brock_____ 22. Canadian colonel in the War of 1812.

(8 points)

C. True or False

Circle T *for* True *or* F *for* False.

(T) F   23. The oligarchy of Upper Canada opposed responsible government.

T (F)   24. The French people were eager to modernize Lower Canada by adopting English ways.

(T) F   25. The Fraser River gold rush had more law and order than the California gold rush did.

T (F)   26. The Canadian Parliament created the Dominion of Canada.

(T) F   27. The Dominion of Canada became a nation on July 1, 1867.

(T) F   28. The first prime minister of the Dominion of Canada promoted a transcontinental railroad to link the provinces together.

T (F)   29. The four provinces that formed the Dominion of Canada were Ontario, Quebec, New Brunswick, and Newfoundland.

(7 points)

D. Essay Questions

30. What are two ways that the War of 1812 affected Canada?

(Any two.) It brought greater prosperity because of increased British military spending. It gave Canadians a stronger sense of nationalism. Many Canadians became bitter because of invasions by United States armies.

31. What were two factors that moved the Canadian provinces toward uniting as a nation?

(Any two.) The factors were commerce, relations with the United States, and political problems.

32. How was British Columbia persuaded to join the Dominion of Canada rather than to join the United States?

The Canadian government promised to build a railroad that would link British Columbia to the eastern provinces.

(5 points)
Total points: 34

Understanding North American History

Chapter 19 Test   Score _____

Name _____   Date _____

A. Matching: People and Places

Not all the choices will be used.

__j__   1. Invented barbed wire in 1874.

__g__   2. Lost the Battle of the Little Bighorn.

__k__   3. Built stockyards at Abilene, Kansas.

__i__   4. Last great Apache leader, who surrendered in 1886.

__a__   5. Indian leader whose people were massacred at Sand Creek.

__e__   6. Rich gold and silver strike in Nevada.

__h__   7. Man who invented the air brake for trains in 1869.

__c__   8. Nez Perce leader who went on a long flight with his people before capture.

__f, n__   9. Indian chiefs at the Battle of the Little Bighorn (two answers).

__d__   10. Route of cattle herds moving north to Kansas.

__m__   11. Place where the transcontinental railroad was joined.

__b__   12. One of the first cattle ranchers in Texas.

__o__   13. Place where last Indian war took place.

a. Black Kettle
b. Charles Goodnight
c. Chief Joseph
d. Chisholm Trail
e. Comstock Lode
f. Crazy Horse
g. George Custer
h. George Westinghouse
i. Geronimo
j. Joseph Glidden
k. Joseph McCoy
l. Pikes Peak
m. Promontory
n. Sitting Bull
o. Wounded Knee

(14 points)

B. Matching: Terms

Not all the choices will be used.

__h__   14. Built railroad west from Nebraska.

__c__   15. Belief in return of Indians and buffalo.

__b__   16. Law that divided reservations into family farms.

__a__   17. Built railroad east from California.

__f__   18. Taking of cattle over a trail to cattle towns.

__g__   19. Law that authorized a transcontinental railroad.

__d__   20. Law that allowed settlers to claim 160 acres (65 ha) of land for farming.

a. Central Pacific
b. Dawes Act
c. Ghost Dance religion
d. Homestead Act
e. Indian Reorganization Act
f. "long drive"
g. Pacific Railroad Act
h. Union Pacific

(7 points)

C. Completion: Terms

Write the correct term for each description.

<u>   *mother lode*   </u>   21. Main vein of ore.

<u>   *homesteader*   </u>   22. Person who claimed land and settled on it for five years.

<u>   *public domain*   </u>   23. Land owned by the government.

<u>*vigilance committee*</u>   24. Group that meted out swift and stern justice.

<u>   *open range*   </u>   25. Unfenced grazing land.

(5 points)

D. True or False

Circle T *for* True *or* F *for* False.

T (F)   26. When prospectors found gold, they often used their wealth to establish a gold mining corporation.

(T) F   27. The miners exemplified the American tendency to govern themselves in the absence of established government.

(T) F   28. Greed was a chief cause of the Indian wars.

T (F)   29. The cattle kingdom had little to do with transportation.

(T) F   30. The Homestead Act encouraged settlement of the West by providing cheap or free land.

(5 points)

E. Essay Questions

31. Both miners and railroads contributed to settling the West.

    a. How did miners help?

       When miners rushed to an area to seek gold or silver, other people also flocked there. The result was often a permanent town or city in that area.

    b. How did railroads help?

       Railroads promoted settlement by providing good transportation for the remote sections of the West. The railroad companies advertised for immigrants to settle on their land grants.

32. What were two main causes of the Indian wars?

       (Any two.) The government placed the Indians on reservations, and greedy whites often settled on the land that had been promised to the Indians. Settlement of the West and destruction of the buffalo threatened the Indian way of life. Misunderstandings and bad

(Answer continues on next page.)

33. Give two answers to each question.

    a. What were some major difficulties that homesteaders experienced?

    A homesteader had to build a dwelling with scarce materials. He had to dig a well by hand if no water was near. He had to break the sod and plant crops. Money was scarce. He faced natural calamities like fires, storms, and grasshopper plagues.

    b. How did they overcome those difficulties?

    The homesteaders overcame by perseverance, hard work, and their God-given mental abilities. Other things that helped were new crops and technology, such as hard wheat, improved plows, windmills, and barbed wire.

(8 points)
Total points: 39

(Answer Key continued):

32. _attitudes brought war. Cultural differences played a large part in the struggle. A general reason was the greed of white men._

Understanding North American History

Chapter 20 Test   Score _____

Name _____   Date _____

A. Matching: People and Terms

Not all the choices will be used.

_i_ 1. Evangelist who introduced revival meetings into the
        Mennonite Church.

_g_ 2. Reformer who founded the Hull House in Chicago.

_a_ 3. Inventor of the telephone.

_n_ 4. Inventor of the electric light bulb.

_b_ 5. Man whose company helped make the United States a
        leading steel producer.

_e_ 6. Famous evangelist in the latter half of the 1800s.

_o_ 7. Presidential candidate in 1896 who supported free silver.

_j_ 8. Scientist who developed new varieties of plants.

_c_ 9. Group that checked the qualifications of prospective
        government employees.

_h_ 10. Man who developed the Standard Oil corporation.

_f_ 11. Measure that established an agency to regulate railroads.

_k_ 12. Group that developed from Farmers' Alliances and promoted
        radical changes.

_m_ 13. Measure allowing the government to attack businesses
        that it considered monopolies.

_d_ 14. Theory that living things had a natural origin and that
        they gradually evolved into the species existing today.

a. Alexander Graham Bell

b. Andrew Carnegie

c. Civil Service Commission

d. Darwinism

e. Dwight L. Moody

f. Interstate Commerce Act

g. Jane Addams

h. John D. Rockefeller

i. John S. Coffman

j. Luther Burbank

k. Populist Party

l. Republican Party

m. Sherman Antitrust Act

n. Thomas Alva Edison

o. William Jennings Bryan

(14 points)

B. Matching: Presidents

_d_ 15. Served two nonconsecutive terms.

_c_ 16. Took office in 1881 when the previous president was assassinated.

_e_ 17. Served at the time of the "Billion Dollar Congress."

_a_ 18. Came into office through a disputed election.

_f_ 19. Supported the gold standard and conducted a "front-porch" campaign.

_b_ 20. Served only a few months before being assassinated.

a. Rutherford B. Hayes

b. James A. Garfield

c. Chester A. Arthur

d. Grover Cleveland

e. Benjamin Harrison

f. William McKinley

(6 points)

C. Completion: Terms

Write the correct term for each description.

free enterprise 21. System including free markets and private ownership of property.

corporation 22. Large business owned by many people.

supply and demand 23. Scarce product + great demand = high price; abundant product + low demand = low price.

mass production 24. System for making large numbers of products by using interchangeable parts and assembly lines.

political machine 25. Organized group controlled by a powerful "boss."

nativism 26. Movement to limit immigration.

social gospel 27. Religious movement designed to improve social conditions.

melting pot 28. Place where people of many different nationalities mingle together.

socialism 29. Karl Marx's theory proposing a classless society and government ownership of businesses.

revivalism 30. Religious movement emphasizing conversion more than discipleship.

(10 points)

D. True or False

Circle T for True or F for False.

(T) F 31. Labor unions are inconsistent with the Bible doctrine of nonresistance and a Scriptural approach to working.

(T) F 32. Darwin's theory of evolution had wide influence.

T (F) 33. A cooperative is a company that has no competition because it controls a certain market.

T (F) 34. Immigrants made only a few contributions to the United States.

(T) F   35. American farmers suffered hardships because they were so successful.

T (F)   36. Regulation of big business corporations decreased in the 1890s.

(6 points)

E. Essay Questions

37. What is one way that the United States benefited from the many immigrants who came?

 (Any one.) Immigrants brought in a great diversity of culture. They contributed their labor by taking jobs in factories, by working in mines, and by farming. Some immigrants became noted leaders in politics, business, science, and education.

38. What was one reason that cities grew so rapidly in the latter 1800s?

 (Any one.) Many immigrants settled in the cities. Factories drew many workers to the cities. Good transportation, especially railroads, promoted city growth. Skyscrapers enabled cities to expand upward as well as outward.

39. How did promoters of the social gospel try to make reforms?

 These reformers tried to improve people by changing social conditions rather than by emphasizing spiritual regeneration. They worked against saloons, poverty, and corrupt government.

40. What was one change that the Mennonite Church experienced by 1900?

 (Any one.) The Mennonite Church accepted Sunday schools. Revivalism came into the church through the work of John S. Coffman. The Mennonite Church began mission work.   *(Answer continues below.)*

(4 points)
Total points: 40

(Answer Key continued):

40. *New organizations were formed, including a mission board, the Mennonite General Conference, and the Elkhart Institute (later called Goshen College). The Old Order divisions took place. Preaching in the English language became accepted.*

Understanding North American History

Chapters 21 and 22 Test   Score _____

Name _____   Date _____

A. Matching: Terms

Not all the choices will be used.

_h_ 1. Crusade that promoted reform and change.

_m_ 2. Law that reduced import taxes and provided for an income tax.

_g_ 3. Basis for American relations with countries in the Far East.

_k_ 4. Area in China in which a foreign nation controlled the trade and port cities.

_c_ 5. Policy of gaining control over foreign territory.

_b_ 6. Established a central banking system in 1913.

_l_ 7. Theodore Roosevelt's reform program to treat everyone equally.

_d_ 8. Policy of having little to do with foreign nations.

_j_ 9. Policy of United States intervention in Latin America.

_f_ 10. Woodrow Wilson's reform program to restore competition in business.

_a_ 11. Uprising in China in 1900.

_i_ 12. New political group that started in 1912.

a. Boxer Rebellion
b. Federal Reserve Act
c. imperialism
d. isolationism
e. muckraker
f. New Freedom
g. Open Door Policy
h. progressive movement
i. Progressive Party
j. Roosevelt Corollary
k. sphere of influence
l. Square Deal
m. Underwood Tariff Act

(12 points)

B. Matching: Places and Dates

Not all the choices will be used.

_d_ 13. Spanish islands in the Far East conquered by the United States and purchased for $20 million.

_c_ 14. Pacific islands lying about 2,000 miles west of the United States; annexed in 1898.

_e_ 15. Spanish island in the Caribbean that was ceded to the United States in 1898.

_b_ 16. Spanish island in the Pacific that was ceded to the United States in 1898.

_a_ 17. Island in the Caribbean that the United States conquered and gave independence in 1902.

_h_ 18. Year the Boxer Rebellion broke out.

_g_ 19. Year the Spanish-American War was fought.

_j_ 20. Year when Hawaii became a state of the United States.

a. Cuba
b. Guam
c. Hawaii
d. Philippines
e. Puerto Rico
f. Samoa
g. 1898
h. 1900
i. 1934
j. 1959

(8 points)

C. Matching: People and Amendments

Choices may be used twice or not at all.

_k_ 21. Amendment that allowed women to vote.

_i_ 22. Amendment that provided for the direct election of senators.

_j_ 23. Amendment that prohibited alcoholic beverages.

_h_ 24. Amendment that allowed an income tax.

_f_ 25. President during the Spanish-American War.

_b_ 26. Secretary of state who dealt with China and Panama.

_e_ 27. President who used "dollar diplomacy" in Latin America.

_c_ 28. President of the Square Deal and the "big stick."

_g_ 29. Democrat who was elected president after a split in the
opposing party.

_e_ 30. President who later became a justice of the Supreme Court.

_g_ 31. President who promoted the New Freedom program.

a. John Dewey

b. John Hay

c. Theodore Roosevelt

d. William Gorgas

e. William Howard Taft

f. William McKinley

g. Woodrow Wilson

h. Sixteenth Amendment

i. Seventeenth Amendment

j. Eighteenth Amendment

k. Nineteenth Amendment

(11 points)

D. True or False

Circle T *for* True *or* F *for* False.

(T) F   32. The imperialism of the 1890s marked a major shift from the isolationism of the previous thirty years.

T (F)   33. The United States had no interest in foreign territories before the 1890s.

(T) F   34. The Open Door Policy marked a bold advance in United States involvement in world affairs.

T (F)   35. The Open Door Policy was designed to let various foreign nations divide China among themselves.

T (F)   36. Latin American countries welcomed United States intervention to solve their problems.

(T) F   37. The United States actively tried to help the territories it had conquered.

T (F)   38. Progressive reformers believed that social problems resulted from man's sinful condition.

T (F)   39. Progressive educators changed the schools to be more traditional.

T (F)   40. Progressive reform usually began at the federal level and then moved down to states and cities.

(T) F   41. Theodore Roosevelt promoted government involvement in conservation of natural resources.

(10 points)

E. Essay Questions

42. What were two effects of the Spanish-American War?

   (Any two.) The United States gained Guam, Puerto Rico, and the Philippines. Cuba became independent. The United States became a world power with colonial possessions.

43. Why did the United States need the Panama Canal?

   A canal was needed because the United States had gained territories in the Pacific Ocean and the Far East. A canal would save thousands of miles as well as much time and money.

44. a. Who were the progressive reformers?

   They were a diverse group of Democrats, Republicans, and others who wanted to use government power to improve American society.

   b. What two reforms did they want to make in the government?

   (Any two.) They wanted to purge the government of corruption. They wanted the government to serve society as a whole rather than serving special-interest groups. They wanted a more democratic government, one that was more responsive to the will of the people. Other progressive changes included the initiative, the referendum, and the recall.

   c. What two reforms did they want to make in society?

   (Any two.) They promoted building codes, zoning laws, and other laws to regulate tenements. Some promoted conservation to protect natural resources. Some favored prohibition. Others promoted women's suffrage. They wanted an income tax to redistribute wealth.   *(Answer continues below.)*

(8 points)
Total points: 49

(Answer Key continued):

44. c. *(The following may also be considered correct.) They urged the passing of laws to limit working hours for women, to ban child labor, and to improve working conditions. They promoted workers' compensation and minimum wage laws.*

Understanding North American History

Chapter 23 Test   Score _____

Name _____   Date _____

A. Matching: Terms

Not all the choices will be used.

b   1. United States army sent to France.

d   2. Woodrow Wilson's ideas for peace.

f   3. Organization to maintain world peace.

a   4. Russia, France, Great Britain, and Italy.

e   5. Right of any merchant ship to sail the ocean in peace
        or war.

j   6. Agreement that punished Germany harshly and
        proposed an international organization for world peace.

g   7. Items sold to help pay for the war.

c   8. Germany, Austria-Hungary, Bulgaria, and Turkey.

i   9. Law providing for a military draft.

a. Allies
b. American Expeditionary Force
c. Central Powers
d. Fourteen Points
e. freedom of the seas
f. League of Nations
g. Liberty Bonds
h. noncombatant
i. Selective Service Act
j. Treaty of Versailles

(9 points)

B. Completion: People, Places, Dates

Write the correct name or date for each description.

_____*1914*_____   10. Year when World War I began.

_____*1917*_____   11. Year when the United States entered World War I.

_____*1918*_____   12. Year when World War I ended.

*Woodrow Wilson*   13. United States president during World War I.

*John J. Pershing*   14. General of the American army in France.

_____*Versailles*_____   15. Place where Germany signed the peace treaty.

(6 points)

C. True or False

Circle T for True or F for False.

(T) F   16. World War I was the first war in which American soldiers fought in Europe.

T (F)   17. At the peace conference in Paris, Woodrow Wilson wanted to harshly punish Germany while
           the other Allied leaders wanted to be more lenient.

T (F)   18. If all nations would unite, there would be no more war.

(T) F   19. World War I led to World War II.

(T) F   20. World War I prompted Mennonites to become more active in relief work, to provide a better alternative for conscientious objectors in future wars, and to produce more literature to give clear teaching on nonresistance.

(5 points)

D. Essay Questions

21. a. What was the spark that ignited the Great War in Europe?

the assassination of Francis Ferdinand, the archduke of Austria-Hungary

   b. What happened along the Western Front for over three years?

The two sides made repeated assaults against each other, which resulted in thousands of casualties but no real progress for either side.

22. a. What was one reason that the United States began favoring the Allies in the Great War?

Americans traded with Allies. They loaned money to the Allies. German submarines sank many ships of neutral nations, including the United States.

   b. What was one specific issue that brought the United States into the war?

One issue was the declaration that the Germans would resume unrestricted submarine warfare. Another was the Zimmermann telegram.

23. How did the Treaty of Versailles meet the goals of both the American president and the leaders of the Allied nations in Europe?

It provided for a general association of nations, later called the League of Nations, as proposed by the American president. It laid severe penalties on the Germans according to the wishes of the European Allies.

24. What are two ways in which World War I brought suffering to nonresistant people?

(Sample answers.) Conscientious objectors had to go to army camps when they were drafted, and there they faced persecution for their beliefs. Some were sentenced to long terms in military prisons, where treatment was often brutal. Mennonites suffered persecution for refusing to salute the flag, for using the German language, and for refusing to buy Liberty Bonds.

(8 points)
Total points: 28

Understanding North American History

Chapter 24 Test   Score _____

Name _____   Date _____

A. Matching: People

Not all the choices will be used.

_c_ 1. Was elected president in 1932; introduced the New Deal.

_a_ 2. Took office after the death of the previous president; served from 1923 to 1929.

_f_ 3. Was president when the Great Depression began; served from 1929 to 1933.

_h_ 4. Was president from 1921 to 1923; died in office.

_b_ 5. Made the first solo flight across the Atlantic Ocean in 1927.

_e_ 6. Made cars available to the masses by introducing the Model T.

_i_ 7. Made the first successful flight with a heavier-than-air machine in 1903.

_g_ 8. Served as director of the Federal Bureau of Investigation.

a. Calvin Coolidge

b. Charles Lindbergh

c. Franklin D. Roosevelt

d. George R. Brunk

e. Henry Ford

f. Herbert Hoover

g. J. Edgar Hoover

h. Warren G. Harding

i. Wright brothers

(8 points)

B. Matching: Agencies and Programs

Not all the choices will be used.

a. Federal Bureau of Investigation

b. Federal Deposit Insurance Corporation

c. Federal Emergency Relief Administration

d. Federal Insurance Contributions Act

e. National Recovery Administration

f. Rural Electrification Administration

g. Securities and Exchange Commission

h. Tennessee Valley Authority

_d_ 9. Provided money for retired workers and for unemployment compensation, aid to children, and public health programs.

_a_ 10. Enforced federal laws.

_h_ 11. Provided dams to control flooding and produce electricity.

_g_ 12. Prevented illegal and unsound practices in the stock market.

_f_ 13. Brought electricity to farms and homes in the country.

_b_ 14. Insured bank deposits.

(6 points)

C. Completion: Terms

Write the correct term for each description.

modernism	15. Set of beliefs including the theory of evolution, rejection of the super-natural, and acceptance of science as the only source of truth.
Dust Bowl	16. Region of severe drought in the 1930s.
business cycle	17. Periodic swing between prosperity and decline in the economy.
Scopes trial	18. Event in 1925 when fundamentalists and modernists clashed over evolution.
lame duck	19. Person finishing a term after another is elected to replace him.
New Deal	20. Group of government programs designed to end the economic downturn in the 1930s.
Prohibition	21. Period when alcoholic drinks were outlawed.
fundamentalism	22. Movement to assert basic truths of the Bible and oppose modernism.
Great Depression	23. Long economic downturn from 1929 to 1939.

(9 points)

D. True or False

Circle T *for* True *or* F *for* False.

T (F) 24. The Republican presidents of the 1920s increased government regulation of business.

T (F) 25. Most farmers prospered in the 1920s.

(T) F 26. Prohibition failed because laws and social pressure cannot reform man's sinful nature.

T (F) 27. The only thing President Hoover did about the Depression was to encourage people to help themselves.

T (F) 28. The New Deal helped to shorten the Depression.

(5 points)

E. Essay Questions

29. What are two ways in which the automobile changed American life?

(Any two.) Sunday drives became popular. People went on long vacations. Rural people could more freely enjoy city life. Many people began living in the country and working in the city. The middle class grew larger. New terms entered the nation's vocabulary. The automobile brought problems such as accidents and traffic jams.

30. What were two basic points that fundamentalism emphasized?

   (Any two points.) It emphasized the infallibility and inerrancy of the Scriptures, the virgin

   birth of Christ, the miracle-working power of Christ, the redemptive sacrifice of Christ, and

   the bodily resurrection of Christ.

31. What were two effects of the Great Depression?

   (Any two.) People lost confidence in businessmen and in themselves. Some developed an

   unhealthy concern for earthly security. They went to extremes in their ambition for money

   and possessions.

32. What were two long-term effects of the New Deal?

   (Any two.) The government became more powerful than ever before. It could freely intervene

   in the economy. It held control over businesses, banks, and money. Many people began to

   depend on government support. The government began a policy of deficit spending. The

   national debt increased.

(8 points)
Total points: 36

Understanding North American History

Chapter 25 Test   Score _____

Name _____   Date _____

A. Matching: Terms 1

Not all the choices will be used.

_c_ 1. Germany and the nations that helped it in World War II.

_h_ 2. Political system of nationalism and totalitarian control in Germany.

_g_ 3. Barrier to communication and travel between communist nations and free nations.

_f_ 4. Hitler's destruction of millions of Jews and others in Europe.

_i_ 5. Having a single authority with absolute control of everything.

_b_ 6. Policy of maintaining peace by letting an aggressor have his way.

_a_ 7. Great Britain, the United States, and the nations that helped them.

_e_ 8. Political system of totalitarian control in Italy.

a. Allies
b. appeasement
c. Axis
d. communism
e. fascism
f. Holocaust
g. Iron Curtain
h. Nazism
i. totalitarian

(8 points)

B. Matching: Terms 2

Not all the choices will be used.

_g_ 9. Nations not aligned with the United States or the Soviet Union.

_h_ 10. International organization to maintain world peace.

_d_ 11. Program to build the atomic bomb.

_a_ 12. Program of alternate service for conscientious objectors.

_e_ 13. Military alliance formed by Western nations in 1949 to oppose communism.

_b_ 14. Conflict in which enemy nations worked against each other without actually fighting.

_i_ 15. Military alliance formed by communist nations of Eastern Europe in 1955.

_f_ 16. Body of the United Nations responsible for keeping peace.

a. Civilian Public Service
b. Cold War
c. General Assembly
d. Manhattan Project
e. North Atlantic Treaty Organization
f. Security Council
g. Third World
h. United Nations
i. Warsaw Pact

(8 points)

C. Completion: People and Dates

Write the correct name or date for each description.

   Joseph Stalin   17. Dictator of the Soviet Union.

  Dwight Eisenhower   18. Supreme commander of Allied forces in Europe.

Franklin D. Roosevelt 19. United States president during most of World War II; first president to serve more than two terms.

  Harry S. Truman   20. President who replaced Roosevelt and ordered use of the atomic bomb.

   Adolf Hitler   21. Dictator of Germany.

  Benito Mussolini   22. Dictator of Italy.

  Winston Churchill   23. Prime minister of Great Britain during World War II.

 Douglas MacArthur 24. American general who helped to liberate the Philippines.

      1939   25. Year when World War II began.

      1941   26. Year when the United States entered World War II.

      1945   27. Year when World War II ended.

   Pearl Harbor   28. Place attacked by the Japanese on the "date of infamy."

Hiroshima or Nagasaki 29. Japanese city devastated by an atomic bomb in 1945.

   East Germany   30. Part of Germany with a Communist government after the war.

(14 points)

D. True or False

Circle T *for* True *or* F *for* False.

T F   31. Hitler believed that Germans were a superior race and that Jews were inferior.

T F   32. In World War II, the Soviet Union was first an ally and later an enemy of Germany.

T **F**   33. The Americans engaged in an island-hopping campaign against Germany.

T **F**   34. The Mennonite Church did little to make things easier for conscientious objectors in World War II.

(4 points)

E. Essay Questions

Give at least two answers for each question.

35. What were some ways that World War II affected the American people?

     Factories were devoted to producing war materials, and operated day and night. Millions of new workers were hired. Many goods that civilians needed were rationed.   *(Answer continues on next page.)*

36. a. What were some costs of World War II?

__World War II was the most destructive war in human history. About 55 million people per-__

__ished as a result of the war. Weapons and war materials cost over one trillion dollars, and__

__the cost of destruction to property was in the millions of dollars.__

  b. What were some major consequences of the war?

__Large European empires dissolved, and new nations formed. The Cold War began. China and__

__a number of European nations became communist. The Iron Curtain divided Europe.__   *(Answer*
continues below.)

37. a. What kinds of work did conscientious objectors do in Civilian Public Service?

__The young men worked at soil conservation projects, building dams, digging ditches, plant-__

__ing trees, and fighting forest fires. Some worked in hospitals, and some volunteered to be__

__"guinea pigs" in experiments to test new drugs.__

  b. What difficulties did they face?

__The men had to get along with each other in close quarters. Many grew bored with the work__

__and with camp life. They did not receive pay, so they had to depend on money__   *(Answer*
continues below.)
(10 points)
Total points: 44

(Answer Key continued):

35. *Unnecessary travel was discouraged, and a speed limit of 35 miles (56 km) per hour was enacted.*
Daylight-saving time was used. Millions of women began working away from home. (Japanese
internment could be mentioned.)

36. b. *The world became divided into the democratic nations (the free world), the communist*
nations, and the Third World. The North Atlantic Treaty Organization and the Warsaw Pact
were formed. The nuclear age began.

37. b. *from their churches for support. It was hard to find enough ministers to visit the camps reg-*
ularly. A camp often contained a mixture of different church groups, which made it hard
for conservative CO's to stand for their convictions.

Understanding North American History

Chapters 26 and 27 Test   Score _____

Name _____   Date _____

A. Matching: Terms and Dates

Not all the choices will be used.

_f_ 1. Idea that if one nation in a region falls to communism, nearby nations will also fall.

_b_ 2. Drive to give blacks equal status with whites.

_n_ 3. Measure that lowered the voting age to eighteen.

_k_ 4. Measure that gave President Johnson power to use military force in Vietnam.

_g_ 5. President Truman's program of social reforms.

_a_ 6. Case in which separate but equal facilities for blacks were declared unconstitutional.

_l_ 7. Measure limiting a president's administration to two terms.

_i_ 8. Program for conscientious objectors from the 1950s to the 1970s.

_h_ 9. Title of President Johnson's social programs.

_e_ 10. Ending of separation by race.

_d_ 11. Incident in which Soviet weapons threatened United States security.

_c_ 12. Youth who rebelled against established values and violated social customs.

_j_ 13. Name of Kennedy's domestic program.

_p_ 14. Years of the Korean War.

_s_ 15. Year when the United States withdrew from Vietnam.

a. *Brown v. Board of Education of Topeka*

b. civil rights movement

c. counterculture

d. Cuban missile crisis

e. desegregation

f. domino theory

g. Fair Deal

h. Great Society

i. I-W service

j. New Frontier

k. Tonkin Gulf Resolution

l. Twenty-second Amendment

m. Twenty-fifth Amendment

n. Twenty-sixth Amendment

o. Viet Cong

p. 1950–1953

q. 1964–1973

r. 1968

s. 1973

(15 points)

B. Completion: People and Places

Write the correct name for each description.

Douglas MacArthur   16. General in the Korean War who was dismissed by President Truman.

Martin Luther King, Jr. 17. Black minister who led the civil rights movement and promoted nonviolent resistance.

Harry S. Truman   18. President who served from 1945 to 1953, after Franklin D. Roosevelt.

Dwight D. Eisenhower 19. President during most of the 1950s; served from 1953 to 1961.

Lyndon B. Johnson   20. Vice president who succeeded John Kennedy as president in 1963 and was re-elected in 1964.

John F. Kennedy   21. President elected in 1960 and assassinated in 1963.

Richard M. Nixon   22. President when United States troops were withdrawn from Vietnam.

Alaska or Hawaii   23. One of two new states added to the Union in 1959.

South Korea   24. Nation that was invaded by its communist neighbor in 1950.

South Vietnam   25. Non-communist land supported by the United States in the Vietnam War.

John Glenn   26. First American astronaut to orbit the earth.

(11 points)

C. True or False

Circle T *for* True *or* F *for* False.

T F   27. The Supreme Court became more activist in the 1950s and 1960s.

T **F**   28. The first space satellite was *Explorer 1,* which the United States launched in 1957.

T F   29. President Truman limited the war in Korea for fear that World War III might break out.

T F   30. The Cold War eased somewhat in the middle 1950s.

T **F**   31. The Cuban missile crisis was resolved when the United States invaded Cuba and destroyed the missiles.

T F   32. The New Frontier was Kennedy's program for federal aid to education, medical care for the elderly, urban renewal, and help for the poor.

T F   33. The Great Society increased government spending on welfare programs and encouraged people to receive welfare instead of working.

T **F**   34. Supreme Court decisions in the 1960s allowed Bible reading and prayer in public schools.

(8 points)

D. Essay Questions

35. What were two effects of the Korean War?

   (Any two.) Millions of people were killed. Thousands of homes and factories were destroyed.

   The border between the two Koreas remained about where it had been before the war. The war

   showed that the United States intended to oppose communism anywhere in the world.

36. What were two results of the Vietnam War?

   (Any two.) Thousands of people were wounded or killed. Vietnam was devastated, and one-

   third of the surviving people were refugees. The war brought bitterness and division to the

   United States. It damaged the American people's image of their country.

   South Vietnam, Cambodia, and Laos later fell to communism.

37. What were some social changes among blacks in the 1960s? among youth? among women? Describe at least one for each group.

   Many blacks became radical and violent in their demand for equality with whites. Their

   demands led to riots in northern cities. New laws granted more rights to blacks.

   Youth rebelled against traditional values and authority. This was manifested in the (Answer
   continues below.)

38. a. What was one kind of work that young men did in the I-W program?

   (Any one.) One kind was Pax service, in which single men went overseas to do relief work in

   nations devastated by war or natural disaster. Another kind was Voluntary Service, (Answer
   continues below.)

   b. Name two spiritual dangers that they faced.

   Young men were often placed in strange settings far away from home, where they faced many

   temptations. Men of different religious groups were mixed together, which tended to weaken

   convictions.

   (10 points)
   Total points: 44

(Answer Key continued):

37. *riots at colleges and in the counterculture, rock music, and drugs.*
   Women protested because they rarely held positions of leadership and because they received less pay for doing the same jobs as men. Feminists established the National Organization for Women. They campaigned for a Constitutional amendment to guarantee women the same rights as men.

38. a. *in which men usually worked in VS units at places such as children's homes or old people's homes. A third kind was service at an approved public or private agency such as a hospital or an experimental farm.*

Understanding North American History

Chapter 28 Test   Score _____

Name _____   Date _____

A. Matching: Terms and Dates

Not all the choices will be used.

__p__ 1. Year of the Persian Gulf War.

__h__ 2. Program for restoring the economy in the 1980s.

__n__ 3. United States bicentennial year.

__j__ 4. Rising prices along with business decline in the 1970s.

__g__ 5. Effort in which Iraqis were driven out of Kuwait.

__i__ 6. Arms reduction agreement made with the Soviet Union in 1972.

__e__ 7. Incident when Americans were held captive in Tehran.

__b__ 8. Relaxing of tension between rivals.

__l__ 9. Measure stating that Congress could not raise its pay until after an election; ratified in 1992.

__c__ 10. Government agency established in 1970 to limit pollution.

__a__ 11. Removal of government controls.

__m__ 12. Scandal that led to the resignation of a president.

__k__ 13. One who uses violence and threats to intimidate people, especially for political purposes.

__d__ 14. Incident when profits from the sale of weapons were used to help fighters in Nicaragua.

a. deregulation

b. détente

c. Environmental Protection Agency

d. Iran-Contra affair

e. Iran hostage crisis

f. North American Free Trade Agreement

g. Persian Gulf War

h. "Reaganomics"

i. SALT I

j. stagflation

k. terrorist

l. Twenty-seventh Amendment

m. Watergate

n. 1976

o. 1979

p. 1991

(14 points)

B. Completion: People and Places

Write the correct name for each description.

__Sandra Day O'Connor__ 15. First woman appointed to the Supreme Court.

__Neil Armstrong__ 16. First man to walk on the moon.

__Gerald R. Ford__ 17. First unelected president; took office when the previous president resigned; served from 1974 to 1977.

__William (Bill) Clinton__ 18. First president to be born after World War II; served from 1993 to 2001; was impeached.

__Richard M. Nixon__ 19. First president to resign from office; served from 1969 to 1974.

__Ronald Reagan__ 20. President who brought economic recovery; served from 1981 to 1989.

<u>George H. W. Bush</u>   21. President when the Cold War ended and the Persian Gulf War was fought; served from 1989 to 1993.

<u>James (Jimmy) Carter</u>   22. President who faced economic troubles and the Iran hostage crisis; served from 1977 to 1981.

<u>Panama</u>   23. Nation of Central America that the United States invaded in 1989 to remove a corrupt dictator from office.

<u>Grenada</u>   24. Caribbean island invaded by American troops in 1983 to keep it from becoming communist.

<u>Soviet Union</u>   25. Large communist nation that dissolved in 1991.   (11 points)

C. True or False

Circle T *for* True *or* F *for* False.

(T) F   26. The United States was plagued with economic problems in the 1970s.

(T) F   27. An economic expansion began in the middle 1980s.

T (F)   28. The Cold War ended when Communist governments of Eastern Europe fell during 1979 and 1980.

(T) F   29. In the 1990s, the United States tended to intervene in the affairs of other nations for humanitarian reasons.

(T) F   30. One reason for social decay is the failure of many churches to uphold the truth.

T (F)   31. Ronald Reagan's appointments to the Supreme Court made it more liberal and activist.

(6 points)

D. Essay Questions

32. For what wrongdoing did President Nixon resign from office in 1974?

   He had lied about his involvement in the Watergate scandal.

33. What were two things that President Reagan did to improve the economy?

   (Any two.) He promoted tax cuts, reduced government spending, expanded the deregulation of business, and ended the breakup of companies that were considered monopolies.

34. What were two events that brought the Cold War to an end?

   Nations in Eastern Europe revolted against their Communist rulers in 1989. The people of East Germany overthrew their Communist government, and Germany was reunited in 1990. The Soviet Union broke apart in 1991.

(5 points)
Total points: 36

Understanding North American History

Final Test   Score _____

Name _____   Date _____

Each set of matching exercises has at least one choice that will not be used.

A. Matching: Terms
Part 1

_h_   1. Colony owners.

_g_   2. Persons who withdrew from the Church of England and moved to America.

_f_   3. Persons favoring independence from Britain in the Revolution.

_c_   4. Supporters of Great Britain in the Revolution.

_k_   5. Agreement that ended the American Revolution.

_j_   6. Modified form of manorialism, transplanted to New France.

_d_   7. System in which a lord owned land and serfs farmed it for him.

_b_   8. Religious revival in the 1700s.

_a_   9. Legal document granting rights to settle an area and to establish a government there.

_e_ 10. Agreement signed by Pilgrims and Strangers to make "just and equal laws."

a. charter
b. Great Awakening
c. Loyalists
d. manorialism
e. Mayflower Compact
f. patriots
g. Pilgrims
h. proprietors
i. Puritans
j. seigneurial system
k. Treaty of Paris

Part 2

_h_ 11. Branch of government that decides cases about laws.

_d_ 12. Political party that favored strict interpretation and limited government.

_a_ 13. First ten amendments to the Constitution, added in 1791.

_f_ 14. Political party that favored loose interpretation and strong government.

_b_ 15. Limits that government branches place on each other's powers.

_c_ 16. Written plan of government.

_e_ 17. Branch of government that enacts and enforces laws.

_k_ 18. Dividing of government into three branches.

_i_ 19. Branch of government that makes laws.

_g_ 20. Part of legislative branch with states represented proportionately.

a. Bill of Rights
b. checks and balances
c. constitution
d. Democratic-Republicans
e. executive
f. Federalists
g. House
h. judicial
i. legislative
j. Senate
k. separation of powers

Part 3

a. abolition	j. Monroe Doctrine
b. black codes	k. popular sovereignty
c. carpetbaggers	l. Reconstruction
d. Emancipation Proclamation	m. sectionalism
e. Era of Good Feelings	n. segregation
f. freedmen	o. sharecropping
g. Industrial Revolution	p. spoils system
h. manifest destiny	q. states' rights
i. Missouri Compromise	

_n_ 21. Social separation based on race.

_h_ 22. Idea that the United States was intended to spread over the whole North American continent.

_a_ 23. Elimination of slavery.

_g_ 24. Change from producing handmade goods at home to producing machine-made goods in factories.

_j_ 25. Declaration about involvement of European and American nations in each other's affairs.

_k_ 26. Idea that people living in an area should decide for themselves about slavery.

_d_ 27. Measure which declared that slaves in the Confederacy were free.

_c_ 28. Northerners who took part in Reconstruction governments.

_m_ 29. Strong devotion to the interests of a local region.

_e_ 30. Time of national unity and harmony with only one political party.

_q_ 31. Idea that states are supreme over the federal government.

_p_ 32. Practice of replacing former officeholders with supporters.

_i_ 33. Agreement that settled a slavery problem in 1820.

_b_ 34. Laws that restricted blacks after the Civil War.

_o_ 35. System in which farm workers rent cropland and use a share of the crops to pay the rent.

Part 4

a. Civilian Public Service

b. Darwinism

c. free enterprise

d. Great Depression

e. imperialism

f. isolationism

g. League of Nations

h. mass production

i. New Deal

j. "new immigration"

k. Open Door Policy

l. progressive movement

m. Prohibition

n. socialism

o. social gospel

p. Treaty of Versailles

_**n**_ 36. Karl Marx's theory proposing a classless society and government ownership of business.

_**m**_ 37. Period when alcoholic drinks were outlawed.

_**o**_ 38. Religious movement designed to improve present social conditions.

_**p**_ 39. Agreement that punished Germany harshly after World War I.

_**k**_ 40. Basis for American relations with countries in the Far East.

_**b**_ 41. Theory that living things had a natural origin and that they gradually evolved into the species existing today.

_**g**_ 42. International peace organization established after World War I.

_**h**_ 43. System for making large numbers of products by using interchangeable parts and assembly lines.

_**e**_ 44. Policy of gaining control over foreign territory.

_**i**_ 45. Government programs designed to end the Great Depression.

_**f**_ 46. Policy of having little to do with foreign nations.

_**j**_ 47. People who moved from eastern and southern Europe to the United States in the years 1890 to 1920.

_**a**_ 48. Program of alternate service for conscientious objectors in World War II.

_**l**_ 49. Campaign promoting reform and change.

_**d**_ 50. Long economic downturn from 1929 to 1939.

Part 5

_h_ 51. Military alliance formed by Western nations in 1949 to oppose communism.

_j_ 52. International organization to maintain world peace.

_c_ 53. Conflict without fighting between enemy nations.

_f_ 54. Barrier to communication and travel between communist nations and free nations.

_e_ 55. Measure passed in 1956 to build a network of interstate highways.

_a_ 56. Case in which separate but equal facilities for blacks were declared unconstitutional.

_i_ 57. Measure that gave President Johnson power to use military force in Vietnam.

_d_ 58. Title of President Johnson's social programs.

_b_ 59. Drive to give blacks equal status with whites.

_g_ 60. Program for conscientious objectors from the 1950s to the 1970s.

a. *Brown v. Board of Education of Topeka*
b. civil rights movement
c. Cold War
d. Great Society
e. Interstate Highway Act
f. Iron Curtain
g. I-W service
h. North Atlantic Treaty Organization
i. Tonkin Gulf Resolution
j. United Nations
k. Warsaw Pact

(60 points)

B. Matching: People

Part 6

a. Alexander Hamilton
b. Christopher Columbus
c. Cornwallis
d. Daniel Boone
e. Eli Whitney
f. Francisco de Coronado
g. George Whitefield
h. Henry Hudson
i. Hernando de Soto
j. Jacques Cartier
k. James Oglethorpe

l. John Cabot
m. John Marshall
n. John Smith
o. Meriwether Lewis
p. Ponce de León
q. Robert de La Salle
r. Robert Fulton
s. Roger Williams
t. Samuel de Champlain
u. William Penn

_b_ 61. "Admiral of the Ocean Sea" who discovered the New World.

_l_ 62. Explorer of the northeastern coast of North America for England in 1497.

_j_ 63. Explored the area of the St. Lawrence River for France in 1534.

_p_ 64. Spanish explorer who discovered Florida while seeking the Fountain of Youth.

_i_ 65. Spanish explorer who discovered the Mississippi River in 1541.

_f_ 66. Spanish explorer who sought the Seven Cities of Cíbola in the Southwest.

_t_ 67. The "father of New France."

_h_ 68. Explorer who claimed part of North America for the Netherlands in 1609.

_n_ 69. Leader of Jamestown who established a policy of "no work, no food."

_s_ 70. Founder of Rhode Island, who insisted on freedom of conscience.

_u_ 71. Quaker who received a land grant as payment for a debt.

_k_ 72. Trustee leader in the founding of Georgia.

_g_ 73. Leader of the colonial religious revival in the 1700s.

_c_ 74. British general who surrendered in the last major battle of the American Revolution.

_o_ 75. Man who explored the Louisiana Purchase from 1804 to 1806.

_d_ 76. Man who opened the Wilderness Road to Kentucky.

_r_ 77. Man who built the first successful steamboat, the *Clermont*.

_m_ 78. Chief justice who strengthened the Supreme Court in the early 1800s.

_e_ 79. Inventor of the cotton gin.

_a_ 80. Federalist leader and first secretary of the treasury.

Part 7

a. Alexander Graham Bell	j. Marcus Whitman
b. Andrew Carnegie	k. Martin Luther King, Jr.
c. Booker T. Washington	l. Noah Webster
d. Douglas MacArthur	m. Robert E. Lee
e. Dred Scott	n. Samuel F. B. Morse
f. Dwight L. Moody	o. Samuel Slater
g. George Custer	p. Stephen Austin
h. Jefferson Davis	q. Thomas Edison
i. John D. Rockefeller	r. Wright brothers

_n_ 81. Inventor of the telegraph.

_o_ 82. Brought textile manufacturing to America.

_p_ 83. Man who began colonizing Texas.

_j_ 84. Missionary who encouraged settlement of Oregon.

_h_ 85. President of the Confederate States of America.

_m_ 86. Chief general of the Confederate armies.

_e_ 87. Black man whose appeal for freedom was rejected by the Supreme Court.

_c_ 88. Black leader who founded Tuskegee Institute.

_g_ 89. Colonel defeated at the Battle of the Little Bighorn in 1876.

_q_ 90. Man who invented a practical electric light bulb.

_a_ 91. Man who invented the telephone.

_f_ 92. Famous evangelist in the latter half of the 1800s.

_i_ 93. Man who founded Standard Oil as the first trust.

_b_ 94. Man whose company helped to make the United States a leading steel producer.

_r_ 95. Made the first successful flight with a heavier-than-air machine in 1903.

_d_ 96. General who served in World War II and the Korean War, and was dismissed by President Truman.

_k_ 97. Black minister who led the civil rights movement and promoted nonviolent resistance.

Part 8 (Presidents of 1789–1849)

_b_ 98. First president; 1789–1797.

_d_ 99. President during War of 1812; 1809–1817.

_e_ 100. President during the Era of Good Feelings; 1817–1825.

_g_ 101. Son of a former president; 1825–1829.

_h_ 102. First vice president to fill the position of a president who died in office; 1841–1845.

_j_ 103. Leader of the Democratic-Republicans; third president; 1801–1809.

_f_ 104. Second president; Federalist; 1797–1801.

_k_ 105. First president to die in office; 1841.

_a_ 106. President who represented the common man; 1829–1837.

_i_ 107. Former vice president under Andrew Jackson; 1837–1841.

a. Andrew Jackson
b. George Washington
c. James K. Polk
d. James Madison
e. James Monroe
f. John Adams
g. John Quincy Adams
h. John Tyler
i. Martin Van Buren
j. Thomas Jefferson
k. William Henry Harrison

Part 9 (Presidents of 1849–1901)

_h_ 108. President when the Compromise of 1850 passed; 1850–1853.

_f_ 109. President when Southern states began to secede; 1857–1861.

_a_ 110. President during the Civil War; 1861–1865.

_b_ 111. President impeached in 1868; 1865–1869.

_j_ 112. Former Civil War general; 1869–1877.

_i_ 113. President appointed after a disputed election; 1877–1881.

_g_ 114. President assassinated after only a few months in office; 1881.

_d_ 115. Became president when the former president was assassinated; 1881–1885.

_e_ 116. Only president to serve two nonconsecutive terms; 1885–1889 and 1893–1897.

_k_ 117. President during the Spanish-American War; was assassinated; 1897–1901.

a. Abraham Lincoln
b. Andrew Johnson
c. Benjamin Harrison
d. Chester Arthur
e. Grover Cleveland
f. James Buchanan
g. James Garfield
h. Millard Fillmore
i. Rutherford B. Hayes
j. Ulysses S. Grant
k. William McKinley

Part 10 (Presidents of 1901–2000)

_k_ 118. President of the New Freedom program; served during World War I; 1913–1921.

_j_ 119. President of the Square Deal and the "big stick"; 1901–1909.

_h_ 120. President when United States troops withdrew from Vietnam; first president to resign; 1969–1974.

_f_ 121. President elected in 1960 and assassinated in 1963.

_c_ 122. President of the New Deal; served during World War II; only one to serve more than two terms; 1933–1945.

_i_ 123. President who brought economic recovery in the 1980s; 1981–1989.

_b_ 124. President during most of the 1950s; 1953–1961.

_g_ 125. Vice president who became president in 1963 and was re-elected in 1964; promoted the Great Society; 1963–1969.

_e_ 126. President who replaced Franklin Roosevelt; ordered use of the atomic bomb; promoted the Fair Deal; 1945–1953.

_d_ 127. President when the Cold War ended and the Persian Gulf War was fought; 1989–1993.

a. Calvin Coolidge

b. Dwight D. Eisenhower

c. Franklin D. Roosevelt

d. George H. W. Bush

e. Harry S. Truman

f. John F. Kennedy

g. Lyndon B. Johnson

h. Richard M. Nixon

i. Ronald Reagan

j. Theodore Roosevelt

k. Woodrow Wilson

(67 points)

C. Matching: Dates

a. 1588	f. July 4, 1776	j. 1861–1865	n. 1939–1945
b. 1607	g. 1775–1783	k. 1877	o. 1941
c. 1620	h. 1787	l. 1898	p. 1950–1953
d. 1733	i. 1789	m. 1914–1918	q. 1973
e. 1763			

_e_ 128. Treaty of Paris after the French and Indian War.

_n_ 129. World War II.

_f_ 130. Declaration of Independence signed.

_p_ 131. Korean War.

_m_ 132. World War I.

_b_ 133. Jamestown founded.

_d_ 134. Georgia founded.

_a_ 135. Spanish Armada defeated.

_c_ 136. Plymouth Colony founded.

_o_ 137. Pearl Harbor attacked.

_g_ 138. American Revolution.

_i_ 139. Beginning of government under the Constitution.

_q_ 140. United States withdrawal from Vietnam.

_h_ 141. Constitutional Convention.

_l_ 142. Spanish-American War.

_j_ 143. Civil War.

(16 points)

D. True or False

Circle T *for* True *or* F *for* False.

(T) F   144. Columbus thought he could reach the East by sailing west.

(T) F   145. One reason that the Spanish built missions was to protect their frontier against foreign nations.

T (F)   146. The Spanish operated their missions on the basis of democracy and freedom, and treated the Indians fairly and respectfully.

(T) F   147. The economic prosperity of New France depended on the fur trade.

T (F)   148. Pennsylvania was founded as a place of freedom for Catholics.

(T) F   149. The Carolinas were to be modeled on the feudal system.

(T) F   150. The Puritans came to America for religious freedom but would not grant full religious freedom to others.

T (F)   151. Jamestown was settled primarily for religious freedom.

(T) F   152. Colonial charters granted colonists the same privileges as Englishmen.

T (F)   153. Shipping and manufacturing were more important in the South than in New England.

T (F)   154. The Bible had little effect on people living in early colonial days.

(T) F   155. The French and Indian War is important in history because the French were removed as a power in North America.

(T) F   156. The Americans and British disagreed about Parliament's authority over the colonies.

T (F)   157. The Constitution, like the laws of the Medes and Persians, may never be changed.

(T) F   158. The purpose of the Bill of Rights is to guarantee freedoms to citizens of the United States.

T (F)   159. The American republic has no king and is a pure democracy.

T (F)   160. President Jefferson increased the size of the government.

(T) F   161. State nullification of federal laws would have led to chaos and breakup of national unity.

(T) F   162. Andrew Jackson opposed the Bank of the United States because he believed it favored the wealthy and was unconstitutional.

(T) F   163. The cotton gin helped to firmly establish slavery in the South.

(T) F   164. Industry grew rapidly in the North because of energy, natural resources, and transportation.

(T) F 165. The Erie Canal served to divert much trade away from New Orleans to New York City.

T (F) 166. The Civil War began as a war to free the slaves.

(T) F 167. Lincoln's assassination was a great loss to both the North and the South.

(T) F 168. The Radical Republicans wanted to make blacks and whites equal by law.

T (F) 169. Southern states passed black codes to aid the blacks' adjustment to freedom.

(T) F 170. The Homestead Act encouraged settlement of the West by providing cheap or free land.

T (F) 171. The cattle kingdom had little to do with transportation.

(T) F 172. Greed was a chief cause of the Indian wars.

(T) F 173. Labor unions are inconsistent with the Bible doctrine of nonresistance and with the Scriptural approach to working.

(T) F 174. Darwin's theory of evolution had wide influence.

T (F) 175. Progressive educators changed the schools to be more traditional.

T (F) 176. Immigrants made only a few contributions to the United States.

(T) F 177. The imperialism of the 1890s marked a significant shift from the isolationism of the previous thirty years.

(T) F 178. The United States actively tried to help the territories it had conquered.

T (F) 179. Progressive reformers believed that social problems resulted from man's sinful condition.

T (F) 180. At the peace conference at Paris after World War I, Woodrow Wilson wanted to harshly punish Germany while the other Allied leaders wanted to be more lenient.

T (F) 181. The Republican presidents of the 1920s increased government regulation of business.

T (F) 182. The New Deal helped to shorten the Great Depression.

T (F) 183. The Mennonite Church did little for the benefit of conscientious objectors in World War II.

T (F) 184. Supreme Court decisions in the 1960s allowed Bible reading and prayer in public schools.

(T) F 185. The United States faced economic problems in the 1970s.

(T) F 186. An economic expansion began in the middle 1980s.

(T) F 187. The Cold War ended when Communist governments of Eastern Europe fell during 1989 and 1990.

(44 points)
Total points: 187